Household Finance

Sumit Agarwal • Wenlan Qian • Ruth Tan

Household Finance

A Functional Approach

palgrave
macmillan

Sumit Agarwal
National University of Singapore
Singapore, Singapore

Wenlan Qian
National University of Singapore
Singapore, Singapore

Ruth Tan
National University of Singapore
Singapore, Singapore

ISBN 978-981-15-5525-1 ISBN 978-981-15-5526-8 (eBook)
https://doi.org/10.1007/978-981-15-5526-8

This Palgrave Macmillan imprint is published by the registered company Springer Nature Singapore Pte Ltd.
The registered company address is: 152 Beach Road, #21-01/04 Gateway East, Singapore 189721, Singapore

Acknowledgments

The authors thank Chun Weng Boey, Wai Leng Boey and Marshall Too for research assistance and Jolene Bay, Sue Chua, Kai Xiang Lim, Brandon Low, Jiaxin Song and Joel Yeo for editorial assistance. They also thank Daniel Aaronson, Andrew Abel, Facundo Abraham, Katharine Abraham, Darron Acemoglu, Pablo Acosta, Morse Adair, Dale Adams, Gerard Adams, William Adams, Manuel Adelino, Saman Adhami, Jeroen Aerts, Philippe Aghion, Shalu Agrawal, Mark Aguiar, Haseeb Ahmed, Javed Ahmed, George Akerlof, Stefania Albanesi, Rob Alessie, Horatio Alger, Anari Ali, Franklin Allen, Jason Allen, Johan Almenberg, Kumar Alok, Shashwat Alok, Adrian Alter, Fernando Alvarez, Brent Ambrose, Sandro Ambuehl, Gene Amromin, Gombavic Ana, Kanin Anantanasuwong, Steffen Andersen, Anders Anderson, Drew Anderson, Siwan Anderson, Albert Ando, Kazuya Ando, Brown Andres, Coleman Andrew, Marianne Andries, Marco Angrisani, Lunn Anna, Sophia Anong, Saniya Ansar, Masahiko Aoki, Lindsey Appleyard, Jean Arcand, Wayne Archer, Shirley Ardener, Hal Arkes, Luc Arrondel, Nava Ashraf, Ajita Atreya, Orazio Attanasio, Alan Auerbach, Siobhan Austen, Lawrence Ausubel, Robert Avery, Diana Ayala, Padmaja Ayyagari, Pierre Bachas, Cristian Badarinza, Martin Bailey, Michael Bailey, Malcolm Baker, Scott Baker, Jean-Marie Baland, Abhijit Banerjee, James Banks, Marcus Banks, Adolfo Barajas, Brad Barber, Nicholas Barberis, Solon Barocas, David Barros, Laura Bartiloro, Robert Bartlett, Debarati Basu, Hazel Bateman, Milford Bateman, Brian Baugh, Donald Baum, Duane Baumann, Marianne Baxter, Patrick Bayer, Marius Beckamp, Bo Becker, Jim Been, Lisa Bell, Shlomo Benartzi, Itzhak Ben-David, Daniel Benjamin, Marx Benjamin, Efraim

Benmelech, Paul Bennett, Tobias Berg, Sven Berger, Jeroen Bergh, Nittai Bergman, Daniel Bergstresser, Enrico Berkes, Douglas Bernheim, Carol Bertaut, Marianne Bertrand, John Beshears, Timothy Besley, Eric Bettinger, Sondra Beverly, Truman Bewley, Prashant Bharadwaj, Neil Bhutta, Ran Bi, Bruno Biais, Clement Biddle, Yannis Bilias, Christophe Bisiere, Daniel Bjorkegren, Phil Blackman, Alan Blinder, David Bloom, Dave Blumberg, Marshall Blume, Catherine Blumer, Richard Blundell, Angela Boatman, Ronald Bodkin, Claudie Bolduc, Wilko Bolt, Patrick Bolton, Michael Bordo, Winston Borgen, Bradley Borkan, Axel Börsch-Supran, Ron Borzekowski, Marieke Bos, Michael Boskin, John Bossons, Raphael Bostic, Barry Bosworth, Matthew Botsch, Wouter Botzen, Woutzer Botzen, Matthieu Bouvard, Lans Bovenberg, Cathy Bowen, Dina Bowman, Peter Brady, Glen Bramley, Maria Brancati, Joachim Braun, Emily Breza, Cesira Brancati, Joel Brockner, Samuel Brody, Sally Brooks, Jeffrey Brown, Richard Brown, Sebastian Brown, Mark Browne, Martin Browning, Carlin Bruce, Jan Brueckner, Richard Brumberg, Luigino Bruni, Finn Brunton, Joanna Bryson, Greg Buchak, Tabea Bucher-Koenen, Willem Buiter, David Bunting, Joy Buolomwini, Valentin Burg, Sandra Burman, Leonard Bursztyn, Andrea Butelmann, Brian Cadena, Gregorio Caetano, Phillip Cagan, Aylin Caliskan, John Campbell, Glenn Canner, David Canning, Andrew Caplin, Charles Capone, Carlo Caponecchia, Santiago Carbo-Valverde, Elena Carletti, Bruce Carlin, Ziv Carmon, Scott Carrell, Chris Carroll, Christopher Carroll, Catherine Casamatta, Christian Catalini, Rajashri Chakrabarti, Sujit Chakravorti, John Chalmers, Emily Chamlee-Wright, Marcos Chamon, Wing Chan, Arun Chandrasekhar, Regina Chang, Yan Chang, Song Changcheng, Kerwin Charles, Ben Charoenwong, David Chaum, Michael Cheang, Daphne Chen, Keith Chen, Lipeng Chen, Mark Chen, Tan Cheng, Catherine Cheung, Pierre-Andre Chiappori, Lydia Child, Andrew Ching, Peter Chinloy, Jonathan Chiu, Maria Chiuri, Soo Cho, Youngha Cho, Hyun-Soo Choi, James Choi, Souphala Chomsisengphet, Guan Chong, Hugh Chow, Dimitris Christelis, Clayton Christensen, David Chuen, Ching-Fan Chung, Young-Iob Chung, Liu Chunlin, Martin Čihák, Margaret Clancy, Noreen Clancy, Colin Clark, Robert Clark, Alison Clarke, Stephen Coate, Joao Cocco, Mark Cohen, Ethan Cohen-Cole, Shawn Cole, Andrew Coleman, Maria Collado, Francesco Columba, John Conroy, Francesco Contesso, Johnathan Conzelmann, James Copestake, Dean Corbae, Alejo Costa, Don Coursey, Benjamin Cowan, James Cox, Josue Cox, Ricardo Cristadoro, Thomas Crossley, Christopher Crowe,

Marianne Crowe, Robert Cull, Riccardo Curtale, Vilsa Curto, Amy Cutts, Francesco D'Acunto, Marek Dabrowski, Amy Dalton, Sreyoshi Das, Thomas Davidoff, Eduardo Davila, Philipe De Vreyer, Angus Deaton, Anamitra Deb, Daniel Defoe, Robert Dekle, Thomas DeLeire, Giovanni Dell'Ariccia, Stefano Della, Stefano DellaVigna, Asli Demirguc-Kunt, Carmen DeNavas-Walt, Yongheng Deng, Cevdet Denizer, Kalpesh Desai, Sharon Devaney, Jeffery Dew, Ravi Dhar, Upinder Dhillon, Peter Diamond, Alisa DiCaprio, Astrid Dick, Rik Dillingh, Stephen Dimmock, Ding Ding, Jie Ding, Georges Dionne, Lloyd Dixon, Will Dobbie, Christine Dobridge, Jeff Dominitz, Duddy Donna, Rudiger Dornbusch, Singer Dorothe, Zdenek Drabek, Patricia Drentea, John Driscoll, James Duesenberry, Esther Duflo, Lucia Dunn, Thomas Durkin, Irene Dushi, Maren Duvendack, Tomáš Dvorak, Anne Dyhrberg, Karen Dynan, Susan Dynarski, David Eastwood, Janice Eberly, Paul Edelstein, Florian Ederer, Sebastian Edwards, Gauti Eggertsson, Michael Ehrmann, Liran Einav, Gorham Elizabeth, Kiser Elizabeth, Gregory Elliehausen, Glenn Ellison, Ronel Elul, Gary Engelhardt, Fulya Ersoy, Francisco Eva, Douglas Evanoff, Brent Evans, Sheri Faircloth, Pablo Fajnzylber, Eugene Fama, Jessie Fan, George Fane, Hanming Fang, Michael Farrell, Scott Fay, Richard Feinberg, Martin Feldstein, Alan Feng, Niall Ferguson, Bruno Ferman, Elyas Fermand, Daniel Fernandes, Francisco Fernandez, Jesus Fernandez-Villaverde, Rosellina Ferraro, Susana Ferreira, Pirmin Fessler, Erik Feyen, Erica Field, Emel Filiz-Ozbay, Amy Finkelstein, Stefano Fiorin, Stanley Fischer, Patti Fisher, Peter Fishman, Delbert Fitchett, Marjorie Flavin, Bjorn Flesaker, Franz Flögel, Gabriele Foa, Stephen Foerster, Sean Foley, James Follain, Christopher Foote, Jake Ford, Elsa Fornero, Lorenzo Forni, Modigliani Franco, Allen Franklin, Benjamin Franklin, Donald Fraser, Michael Fratantoni, Charles Freeman, Xavier Freixas, Eric French, Kenneth French, Shaun French, Milton Friedman, Irwin Friend, Rene Frydman, Yuming Fu, George Furstenberg, Andreas Fuster, Xavier Gabaix, Daniela Gabor, Blaise Gadanecz, John Galbraith, William Gale, Steven Gallaher, Francisco Gallego, Leonardo Gambacorta, Karthik Ganesan, Peter Ganong, Joshua Gans, Feng Gao, Yuan Gao, Zhenyu Gao, Howard Garland, Sheldon Garon, John Gathergood, John Geanakoplos, Timnit Gebru, Michael Gelman, Amromin Gene, Dimitris Georgarakos, Loewenstein George, Kristopher Gerardi, Patrick Gerhard, Mark Gertler, Paul Gertler, Pulak Ghosh, Stefano Giglio, Xavier Gine, Ralph Ginsberg, Anders Giorgi, Giacomo Giorgi, Giancarlo Giudici, Edward Glaeser, Fabian Gleisner, Dennis Glennon, Andrew Glover,

Lorenz Goette, William Goetzmann, Keng Goh, Jagadeesh Gokhale, Avid Goldfarb, Christian Gollier, Ana Gombavic, Nathalie Gons, Peter Gordon, Elizabeth Gorham, Sergio Gorjon, Padma Gotur, Christian Gouriéroux, Pierre-Olivier Gourinchas, John Gourville, Gautam Gowrisankaran, Bryan Graham, John Graham, Stephen Graves, Marco Greco, Richard Green, Claire Greene, Alan Greenspan, Shane Greenstein, Terrance Grieb, John Griffin, Francesco Grigoli, Michele Grimaldi, Mark Grinblatt, Darrell Grissen, David Gross, Michael Grubb, Jonathan Gruber, Gustavo Grullon, Quanlin Gu, Alessandra Guariglia, Diane Guercio, Veronica Guerrieri, Mary Gugerty, Luigi Guiso, Bulent Gultekin, Sudip Gupta, Adam Guren, Umit Gurun, Thorvaldur Gylfason, Andreas Hackethal, Christian Haddad, Valentin Haddad, Marietta Haffner, Steffen Hagmayer, Steven Haider, Homa Hajibaba, Michael Haliassos, Robert Hall, Ella Halmari, Koichi Hamada, Bing Han, Felizia Hanemann, Katja Hanewald, Sherman Hanna, Arnold Harberger, Donna Haris, Campbell Harvey, Joel Hasbrouck, Michael Haselhuhn, Justin Hastings, Andrew Haughwout, Jerry Hausman, Fumiko Hayashi, Fumio Hayashi, Friedrich Hayek, Celia Hayhoe, Daifeng He, Dong He, Geoffrey Heal, John Heaton, James Heckman, Stuart Heckman, Charles Hegji, Franz Heidhues, Richard Hemming, Robin Henager-Greene, Patric Hendershott, Kyle Herkenhoff, Alexander Herman, John Hershey, Jake Hess, John Hicks, Sean Higgins, Wesley Highfield, Christian Hilber, Marianne Hilgert, Elizabeth Hirschman, David Hirshleifer, Stephen Hoch, Steve Hoch, Stefan Hochguertel, Jeanne Hogarth, Harrison Hong, Lee Hooper, Charles Horioka, Lars Hornuf, Frank Horst, Ali Hortacsu, Jean-Francois Houde, David Howard, Sabrina Howell, Eugene Howrey, Robert Hoyt, Albert Hu, Luojia Hu, Hai Huang, Jinbo Huang, Ming Huang, Xing Huang, Glenn Hubbard, Gur Huberman, Angela Hung, Robert Hunt, Michael Hurd, Erik Hurst, Sandra Huston, Wesley Hutchinson, Norman Hutchison, Soosung Hwang, Saul Hymans, Roger Ibbotson, Deniz Igan, Seppo Ikaheimo, Dan Immergluck, Joachim Inkmann, Jeffrey Inman, Zaida Isa, Tsuneo Ishikawa, Takatoshi Ito, Zoran Ivkovic, Sheena Iyengar, Rajkamal Iyer, Howell Jackson, Matthew Jackson, Song Jae, Julapa Jagtiani, Abhishek Jain, Lukasz Janikowski, Carrie Jankowski, Thomas Jansson, Tullio Jappelli, Kaushik Jayaram, Therese Jefferson, Mark Jenkins, Aalie Jensen, Tobacman Jeremy, Urban Jermann, He Jia, Ruo Jia, Zhang Jian, Li Jiang, Kim Jinhee, Hasbrouck Joel, Chalmers John, David Johnson, Eric Johnson, Zinman Jonathan, Emily Jones, Lawrence Jones, Steven Jones, Nicole Jonker, Srivastava Joydeen, Yu Jun, Moritz Jünger, Daniel

Kahneman, George Kanatas, Ron Kaniel, Martin Kanz, Greg Kaplan, Arie Kapteyn, Yigitcan Karabulut, Dynan Karen, Shachar Kariv, Heikki Karjaluoto, Dean Karlan, Jonathan Karlsen, Niklas Karlsson, Yosh Kasahara, George Katona, Norman Katz, Jeff Kauflin, Alex Kaufman, Matthias Keese, Morgan Kelly, Matti Keloharju, Jake Kendall, James Kennedy, Arthur Kennickell, Christopher Kent, Amir Kermani, Charles Kerwin, John Keynes, Benjamin Keys, Amir Khandani, Asim Khwaja, Thomas Kigabo, Lutz Kilian, Dongshin Kim, Hugh Kim, Hyungsoo Kim, Jinhee Kim, Youngmi Kim, Miles Kimball, Cynthia Kinnan, Wilbert Klaauw, Leora Klapper, Elizabeth Klee, Linda Klein, Henrik Kleven, Jeffrey Kling, Stefan Klonner, Chris Knittel, Samuli Knupfer, Alla Koblyakova, Thorsten Koeppl, Paul Kohler, Donald Kohn, James Kolari, Jane Kolodinsky, Piyabha Kongsamut, Kang Koo, Peter Kooreman, George Kopits, Sanket Korgaonkar, Anton Korinek, George Korniotis, Erkki Koskela, Botond Koszegi, Laurence Kotlikoff, Sergei Koulayev, Carolyn Kousky, Roy Kouwenberg, Irving Kravis, Daniel Kreisman, Dirk Krueger, Paul Krugman, Jeffrey Kubik, Mike Kubzansky, Theresa Kuchler, Peter Kuhn, Camelia Kuhnen, Alok Kumar, Raynil Kumar, Michael Kumhof, Edward Kung, Howard Kunreuther, Kenneth Kurihara, Sri Kusumastuti, Kenneth Kuttner, Simon Kuznets, Smith Kylie, Annette Kyobe, Austin Lacy, David Laibson, John Laitner, Sylvie Lambert, Lauren Lambie-Hanson, Timothy Lambie-Hanson, Tim Landvoigt, Shana Lavarreda, Paul Lavrakas, Rob Law, Edward Lawrence, Jeremy Lawson, Minh Le, Carvalho Leandro, Jesse Leary, David Lee, Donghoon Lee, Jae Min Lee, Kuan Lee, Leonard Lee, David Leece, Andreas Lehnert, Feng Lei, Catherine Lemieux, Richard Lemmon, Bursztyn Leonardo, Mark Lepper, Alec Levenson, Andrew Levin, Eric Levin, Jonathan Levin, Laurence Levin, Ross Levine, Helen Levy, Andrew Leyshon, Chu-Shiu Li, Feng Li, Geng Li, Hongbin Li, Huang Li, Yan Li, Yong Li, Jiang Liang, Andres Liberman, Jeffrey Liebman, Cheng Lim, Chong Lim, Minfeng Lin, William Lin, Zhenguo Lin, Michael Lindell, Peter Lindner, Alf Lindqvist, David Ling, Juhani Linnainmaa, Francesco Lippi, Jeremy Lise, Chunlin Liu, Chwen-Chi Liu, Ada Lo, Andrew Lo, Norman Loayza, Lance Lochner, Lee Lockwood, George Loewenstein, Lara Loewenstein, Dennis Logue, Roger Loh, Todor Lohwasser, Vernon Loke, Yoon Loke, Bridget Long, Paula Lopes, Humberto Lopez, Florencio Lopez-de-Silanes, Guido Lorenzoni, Glen Loury, Lerong Lu, Xiaomeng Lu, Deborah Lucas, Charles Luckett, Sydney Ludvigson, Melanie Luhrmann, Guiso Luigi, Mi Luo, Annamaria Lusardi, Erzo Luttmer, John Lynch,

Angela Lyons, Brigitte Madrian, Marco Maggio, Neale Mahoney, Kaveh Majlesi, Dean Maki, Burton Malkiel, Ulrike Malmendier, Lewis Mandell, Puri Manju, Rebecca Mann, Ronald Mann, Daniela Marconi, Eling Martin, Stefano Martinazzi, Nathan Marwell, Benjamin Marx, Lisa Mason, Massimo Massa, Giovanni Mastrobuoni, Thomas Matha, Rabin Matthew, Weinberg Matthew, Ester Matthijsen, Minna Mattila, Jerome Mattis, Gonzalo Maturana, Gregor Matvos, Teresa Mauldin, Jurgen Maurer, Raimond Maurer, Andrea Mauro, Christopher Mayer, Bhashkar Mazumder, Maurizio Mazzocco, Isaac Mbiti, James McAndrews, Gary McClelland, Rory McDonald, Gary McGill, Leslie McGranahan, Timothy McQuade, James Meade, Neil Meads, Paolina Medina, Costas Meghir, Andre Meier, Stephan Meier, Stephen Meier, Brian Melzer, Brock Mendel, Meichen Meng, Robert Merton, Jacqueline Meszaros, Lloyd Metzler, Robert Meyer, David Meza, Atif Mian, Haliassos Michael, Alexander Michaelides, Erwann Michel-Kerjan, Lawrence Mielnicki, Mark Mietzner, Klus Milan, Todd Milbourn, David Miles, Louis Miller, Sarah Miller, Camelia Minoiu, Eugenio Miravete, Ida Mirzaie, Arul Mishra, Himanshu Mishra, Paolo Mistrulli, James Mitchel, Olivia Mitchell, Kurt Mitman, Andrei Miu, Franco Modigliani, Alex Moler, Simon Mongey, Gordon Monsen, Alberto Montagnoli, Catherine Montalto, Aldo Montesano, Edward Montgomery, John Moon, Danna Moore, James Moore, Page Moreau, Yoko Moriizumi, Marlene Moris, Adair Morse, Fiona Morton, Tanmoy Mukherjee, Sendhil Mullainathan, Alicia Munnell, Papa N'Diaye, Stefan Nagel, Tahany Naggar, Prabhala Nagpuranand, Satoshi Nakamoto, Yunju Nam, Michio Naoi, Arvind Narayanan, Machiko Narita, Ashraf Nava, Dhananjay Nayakankuppam, Njuguna Ndung'u, Richard Netemeyer, Stephanie Newport, Serena Ng, Lam Nguyen, Jordan Nickerson, Sarah Nield, Kasper Nielsen, Marina Niessner, Stijn Nieuwerburgh, Theo Nijman, Pascal Noel, Jaromir Nosal, Tanya Nyamadzawo, Shaun O'Brien, Maurice Obstfeld, Terrance Odean, Noemi Oggero, Lee Ohanian, Arna Olafsson, Zoe Oldfield, Rachel Ong, Robert Order, Philip Oreopoulos, PIeter Orszag, Francois Ortalo-Magne, Daniel Osei, Juan Ospina, Akira Otani, Adrian Overton, Erkut Ozbay, Vance Packard, Marco Pagano, Michaela Pagel, Monica Paiella, Miguel Palacios, Amanda Pallais, Daniel Palmer, Richard Palmer-Jone, Jessica Pan, Stavros Panageas, Rohini Pande, Ugo Panizza, Bhuvanesh Pareek, Hoonsuk Park, Andre Parker, Jonathan Parker, Christine Parlour, Parag Pathak, Harry Patrinos, Sullivan Paul, Anna Paulson, Mark Pauly, John Payne, Richard Peach, Joe Peek, Kanin Peijnenberg, Kim Peijnenburg, Loriana Pelizzon,

Anthony Pellechio, Karen Pence, Anthony Pennington-Cross, Tapio Pento, Stavros Peristiani, Vanessa Perry, Sock Phang, Edmund Phelps, Thomas Philippon, Gordon Phillips, Monika Piazzesi, Tomasz Piskorski, Luigi Pistaferri, Jeremy Pizzala, Steven Plaut, Saul Pleeter, Matthew Plosser, Robert Pollak, Alejandro Ponce, Devin Pope, Jaren Pope, Rafael Porta, Richard Porter, Thomas Post, James Poterba, Michael Power, Alberto Pozzolo, Nagpurnanand Prabhala, Eswar Prasad, Henriette Prast, Andrea Prat, John Pratt, Drazen Prelec, Andrea Presbitero, Alessandro Previtero, Charles Prinsep, Bernadette Proctor, Marcel Prokopczuk, Stefano Puntoni, Talis Putnins, Jun Qian, Li Qiang, John Quigley, Pau Rabanal, Claudio Raddatz, Priya Raghubir, Rajan Raghuram, Jonathan Raiff, Maurer Raimond, Raghuram Rajan, Uday Rajan, Tarun Ramadorai, Esmeralda Ramalho, Rodney Ramcharan, Cristiana Rampazzi, Adriano Rampini, Dave Ramsey, Romain Rancière, Susan Ranney, Gautum Rao, Jyoti Rao, Kamalesh Rao, Nitya Rao, Max Raskin, Joshua Rauh, Enrichetta Ravina, Michael Raynor, Hendon Redzuan, Joppe Ree, Robert Reich, Ricardo Reis, Michael Reitter, Corry Renselaar, Andrea Repetto, Jonathan Reuter, Jong-Youn Rha, Byung-Kun Rhee, Changyong Rhee, Ghon Rhee, Wooheon Rhee, Rosen Richard, Harry Richardson, Timothy Riddiough, Alicia Robb, Cliff Robb, Sean Roberts, Adriana Robertson, David Robinson, Marguerite Robinson, Jean-Charles Rochet, Christian Rogg, Matthew Rognlie, Kenneth Rogof, Susann Rohwedder, Ehud Ronn, Maarten Rooij, Harvey Rosen, Richard Rosen, Eric Rosenblatt, Mark Rosenzweig, Alberto Rossi, Mariacristina Rossi, Benjamin Roth, Jerome Rothenberg, Calebe Roure, Nikolai Roussanov, Ioanna Roussou, Stuart Rutherford, Marc Rysman, Christian Saborowski, Emmanuel Saez, Phillip Sagi, Ratna Sahay, Kazuya Saito, Mustafa Saiyid, Bernard Salanie, Fahad Saleh, Katherine Samolyk, Paul Samuelson, Lisa Sanbonmatsu, Anthony Sanders, Paola Sapienza, Itay Saporta-Eksten, Igor Sarman, Steve Satchell, John Savage, Jenny Säve-Söderbergh, Frederique Savignac, John Say, Mark Scher, Carlo Scheresberg, Andrei Schleifer, Maximilian Schmeiser, Tobias Schmidt, Kalus Schmidt-Hebbel, Hendrik Schmitz, Sergio Schmukler, Philipp Schnabl, Martin Schneider, Antoinette Schoar, Barry Scholnick, John Scholz, Mark Schreiner, Gertrud Schrieder, Samuel Schueth, Scott Schuh, William Schulze, Daniel Schunk, Martin Schurz, Maurice Schweitzer, Armin Schwienbacher, Judith Scott-Clayton, Seth Seabury, Mark Seasholes, Satheeshkumar Seenivasan, Enrique Seira, Andrew Selbst, Lemma Senbet, Duane Seppi, Amit Seru, Luis Serven, Felipe Severino, Jesse Shapiro, Joel Shapiro, Matthew Shapiro, Eleanor

Sharman, Gauri Shastry, John Shea, Hersh Shefrin, Thomas Sheils, Shane Sherlund, Michael Sherraden, Ron Shevlin, Xinzheng Shi, Ahmed Shiaster, Hiroshi Shibuya, James Shilling, Ilhyock Shim, Miyohei Shinohara, Parker Shipton, Andrei Shleifer, Suzanne Shu, Kelly Shue, Haiyan Shui, Oz Shy, Clemens Sialm, Nachum Sicherman, Holger Sieg, Angelo Sifaleras, Andre Silva, Vania Silva, Jorge Silva-Russo, Dan Silverman, Rebecca Simms, Ester Simoes, Curtis Simon, John Simon, Andrei Simonov, John Sims, Alp Simsek, Todd Sinai, Dorothe Singer, Austen Siobhan, C. Sirmans, Paige Skiba, William Skimmyhorn, Jonathan Skinner, Jakob Skovgaard, Joel Slemrod, Samuel Smiles, Adam Smith, Geoff Smith, James Smith, Jessica Smith, Michael Sockin, Steven Soderlind, Susanne Soederberg, Adriann Soetevent, Adela Soliz, Dilip Soman, Tsuriel Somerville, Kamila Sommer, Changcheng Song, Cindy Soo, Nicholas Souleles, Stephen Spiller, Martin Spindler, Avia Spivak, Charles Sprenger, Frank Stafford, Victor Stango, Richard Stanton, Laura Starks, Joanna Stavins, Meyer Steffen, Jeremy Stein, Melvin Stephens, Arlie Sterling, Neil Stewart, Emmanouil Stiakakis, Joseph Stiglitz, Todd Stinebrickner, Christina Stoddard, Johannes Stroebel, Burkhard Strumpel, René Stulz, Peter Sturm, Amir Sufi, Catur Sugiyanto, Chakravorti Sujit, Utku Suleymanoglu, Paul Sullivan, Lawrence Summers, Tavneet Suri, Paolo Surico, Katsiaryna Svirydenka, Rick Swedloff, Teo Swee, Chad Syverson, Steven Tadelis, David Tan, Dragon Tang, Huan Tang, Sarah Tanner, Vito Tanzi, Alexi Tchistyi, Allan Teger, Joshua Teitelbaum, Paulina Teller, Ed Tellez, Irina Telyukova, Josephine Teo, Federica Teppa, Daniele Terlizzese, Jose Tessada, Anjan Thakor, Richard Thaler, Manoj Thomas, Beck Thorsten, Nigel Thrift, West Tim, Piyush Tiwari, Jeremy Tobacman, James Tobin, Trever Tompson, Desmond Toohey, Petia Topalova, Olivier Toubia, Robert Townsend, Joseph Tracy, Claire Tsai, Catherine Tucker, Peter Tufano, Giuseppe Tullio, Lesley Turner, Tracy Turner, Amos Tversky, Larry Tzeng, Christopher Udry, Kazuo Ueda, Harald Uhlig, Carly Urban, Stephen Utkus, Nico Valckx, Burg Valentin, Patricio Valenzuela, Boris Vallee, Charles Vanasse, Harold Vatter, Thorstein Veblen, Laura Veldkamp, Steven Venti, Philip Vermeulen, Roine Vestman, Luis Viceira, James Vickery, Carlos Vieira, Vikrant Vig, Pareto Vilfredo, Curto Vilsa, Yao Vincent, Giovanni Violante, Matti Viren, Robert Vishny, Annette Vissing-Jorgensen, Siva Viswanathan, Vish Viswanathan, Fos Vyacheslav, Susan Wachter, Johan Walden, Nancy Wallace, Jennifer Wang, Jialan Wang, Jun Wang, Susan Wang, Yao Wang, Yu Wang, Zhengwei Wang, John Warner, Mark Warshawsky, Wako Watanabe, David Watkins, Passmore Wayne,

Anthony Webb, David Webb, Guglielmo Weber, Joerg Weber, Michael Weber, Warren Weber, Ian Webster, Justin Weidner, David Weil, Stephan Weiler, Matthew Weinberg, Steven Weinberg, Scott Weisbenner, Li Wenli, Bas Werker, James Weston, Torsten Wezel, Michelle White, Henry Whorwood, Glen Whyte, Paul Willen, Jack William, Pablo Winant, Russell Winer, Joachim Winter, James Winters, David Wise, Holger Wolf, Brian Wolfe, Gavin Wood, Michael Woodfor, Ngaire Woods, Susan Woodward, Ann Woodyard, Sheri Worthy, Colin Wright, Robert Wright, Marian Wrobel, Binzhen Wu, Qinxi Wu, Shang Wu, Xiaoyong Wu, Yan Wu, Jeffrey Wurgler, Steve Wyatt, Tracey Xiang, Jing Xiao, Wei Xiong, Menachim Yaari, Rubayah Yakob, Takashi Yamashita, Baozhong Yang, Botao Yang, Haiyang Yang, Constantine Yannelis, Vincent Yao, Xinze Yao, Yi Yao, Ying Yao, Abdullah Yavas, Jia-Hsing Yeh, David Yermack, Bernard Yeung, Kam Yeung, Yildiray Yildirim, Wesley Yin, Yvonne Ying, Phang Yong, Woongsun Yoo, Joanne Yoong, Naoyuki Yoshino, Alwyn Young, Seyed Yousefi, Noah Yuchtman, Yoonkyung Yuh, Norifumi Yukutake, Basit Zafar, Sammy Zahran, Guillermo Zamarripa, Alberto Zanni, Tibor Zavadil, Howell Zee, Kathryn Zeiler, Robert Zeithammer, Stephen Zeldes, Manfred Zeller, Ofer Zellermayer, Yao Zeng, Florian Zettelmeyer, Jian Zhang, Man Zhang, He Zhiguo, Li-An Zhou, Christina Zhu, Haoxiang Zhu, Ning Zhu, Luigi Zingales, Jonathan Zinman, Alan Ziobrowski and Xin Zou whose outstanding work they have referenced.

All errors are those of the authors.

Contents

List of Figures

List of Tables

CHAPTER 1

Introduction

The study of Household Finance encompasses the topics of (1) how households make financial decisions relating to the functions of saving, consumption, investment, housing, payment, borrowing and risk management, (2) how organizations provide goods and services to satisfy these financial functions and (3) how interventions by firms, governments and other parties affect the provision of financial services. This functional definition shows that household finance is a substantial component of the financial sector.

This approach of reviewing the field of household finance, as opposed to a product or institutional approach, allows us to have a household-oriented focus. For example, households who want to save, consume, invest, pay, borrow and manage risk will likely look across a variety of products, various formal and informal institutions as well as the legal frameworks within which contractual relationships can be enforced.

The scope of household finance spans multidisciplines, embracing not just finance and economics but also industrial organization (e.g., automatic enrolment in workplace saving plan), law (e.g., regulation of retail financial transactions), psychology (e.g., decisions affected by framing and cognitive biases) and sociology (e.g., decisions shaped by social networks).

A better understanding of household finance can help to improve household decision making through better financial products, supervision and regulation and avoid problems such as inadequate retirement

S. Agarwal et al., *Household Finance*,
https://doi.org/10.1007/978-981-15-5526-8_1

planning, over-leveraging, uninformative sales tactics and poorly designed products.

This book is divided into nine chapters comprising (1) Introduction and the seven functions of (2) Saving, (3) Consumption, (4) Investment, (5) Housing, (6) Payment, (7) Borrowing and (8) Risk Management, as well as a concluding chapter on (9) Financial Inclusion and Financial Technology. Below is a short description of each of the chapters.

1 Saving

The saving function enables households to smooth their consumption so that they can have a reasonable standard of living during retirement, have funds to get through tough times and leave bequests if they so desire.

Under the inter-temporal substitution motive and life cycle motive, households smooth their consumption by borrowing when they have insufficient funds and saving when they have excess to sustain their consumption in their later years (Keynes 1936; Katona 1975; Sturm 1983; Fisher and Anong 2012; Lee and Hanna 2015).

In the presence of uncertainty regarding employment, healthcare expenses and liquidity constraints, the precautionary motive of saving kicks in (Deaton 1991; Hubbard et al. 1995; Browning and Lusardi 1996).

There is some overlap between the precautionary motive and the bequest motive. If money set aside for contingencies is not depleted, what is left naturally becomes bequests (Dynan et al. 2002). The evidence that the elderly do not dissave as quickly as expected is also consistent with the bequest motive (Kotlikoff 1988; Browning and Lusardi 1996; Coleman 1998; Chamon and Prasad 2010). In Japan, the high cost of housing gives rise to a phenomenon where the elderly move in with their children and are cared for by them in return for a bequest upon their demise (Horioka 1984; Ando and Kennickell 1987; Shibuya 1987).

The decision to save is affected by various factors. A change in the interest rate and a change in the inflation can affect household saving through the income effect and the substitution effect (Weber 1975; Friend and Hasbrouck 1983; Shibuya 1987; Wright 1969; Boskin 1978; Gylfason 1981; Tullio and Contesso 1986; Howard 1978; Shinohara 1982; Grigoli et al. 2018).

If markets are perfect, corporate saving can substitute for personal saving (Montgomery 1986; Grigoli et al. 2018; Feldstein 1973).

Demographic factors such as age (Hayhoe et al. 2012; Grigoli et al. 2018), ethnicity, household composition (Rha et al. 2006; Yuh and Hanna 2010; Browning and Lusardi 1996; Attanasio 1998; Denizer et al. 2002), employment (Yuh and Hanna 2010), education status (Yuh and Hanna 2010; Fisher and Montalto 2010) and health status (Yuh and Hanna 2010; Fisher and Montalto 2010; Heckman and Hanna 2015) also affect saving behavior.

In addition, socio-economic factors such as productivity growth (Kapteyn et al. 2005), income level (Avery and Kennickell 1991; Chang and Huston 1995; Rha et al. 2006; Yuh and Hanna 2010; Henager and Mauldin 2015; Grigoli et al. 2018), credit availability (Shinohara 1982) and financial literacy (Lusardi and Mitchell 2007; Agarwal et al. 2009a; Agarwal et al. 2011a; Lusardi and Mitchell 2014) also play a role in how households approach saving decisions.

Finally, the government can use incentives such as tax deferral, tax exemptions and long-term saving plans to encourage saving among the people so that there will be less need for social support later (Carroll and Summers 1987; Tanzi and Zee 2000; Duflo et al. 2006; Sommer and Sullivan 2018).

2 Consumption

The consumption function examines how consumption is affected by anticipated and unanticipated changes in income under the Keynesian model, permanent income model and life cycle model. The way that consumption responds to changes in income has important implications for macroeconomic stabilization policies, both fiscal and monetary.

Economists embrace the view that households save and borrow to smooth consumption over their life cycle. However, this notion of smoothing is challenged by imperfections such as liquidity constraints.

Studies have shown that the drop in consumption around retirement is larger for households with lower income replacement rate from social security and their pensions (Bernheim et al. 2001), that the consumption of food stamp beneficiaries rise on receipt of payment and decline until the next payment (Stephen Jr 2003; Mastrobuoni and Weinberg 2009), that households cut consumption when they reach the predictable end of their eligibility for unemployment benefits (Ganong and Noel 2019) and that the average caloric intake drops at retirement (Stephens Jr and Toohey 2018).

Access to better loan terms appears to stimulate consumption. Brady et al. (2000), Canner et al. (2002) and Greenspan and Kennedy (2008) find that homeowners who refinance their mortgages on more favorable terms spend more.

Income shocks can affect consumption spending. Agarwal and Qian (2014) study consumption response to a one-time cash payment to Singaporeans. They find that consumers with low liquid assets or with low credit card limit experienced stronger consumption responses. Di Maggio et al. (2017) examine unanticipated income changes using US home mortgages subject to a mortgage rate reset. They find that households who are more constrained tend to be more responsive to positive income shocks.

Studies find that predictable income streams can cause changes in spending behavior too. Stephens Jr (2008) examines consumption reaction following the final payment of a vehicle loan and observes that an increase in discretionary income leads to an increase in non-durable consumption. In an earlier paper, Stephens Jr (2006) finds that consumption is excessively sensitive to paycheck receipt.

Aside from liquidity constraints, standard consumption models have also been augmented to incorporate behavioral factors such as mental accounting (Sheffrin and Thaler 1988; Thaler 1990; Tversky and Kahneman 1981; Baker et al. 2007; Di Maggio et al. 2018), present bias (Meier and Sprenger 2010), hyperbolic preferences (Laibson 1997, 1998) and bounded rationality (Scholnick 2009).

In addition, market imperfections such as income uncertainty and lifetime uncertainty may lead to precautionary behavior (Ben-David et al. 2018), where individuals consume less and save more. Some may opt to annuitize to protect against longevity risk.

3 Investment

The investment function is embodied in products and services, such as mutual funds, annuities, bank products, stocks, housing and other durables, which vary in terms of time horizon, risk, tax treatment, liquidity and other factors.

Although generally households find adequate solutions to their investment problems, many make mistakes, for example, non-participation in risky asset markets, under-diversification of risky portfolios and investment in financial products with high fees.

They do not hold any stocks although equity premium is positive. The non-participation could be due to failure of one or more of the standard assumptions (Bertaut and Haliassos 2000; Heaton and Lucas 2000; Barberis et al. 2006). One possibility is that households are unaware of equity as an asset class (Guiso and Jappelli 2005). Another possibility is the high entry cost or ongoing participation costs (Vissing-Jorgensen 2003). Yet another possibility is the substitution of private business assets for public equity (Heaton and Lucas 2000).

Household characteristics that are associated with the willingness to take financial risks include trust (Hong et al. 2004; Guiso et al. 2008), personal experience (Malmendier and Nagel 2011), socio-economic status (Kuhnen and Miu 2017), education (Cole et al. 2014), intelligence quotient (Grinblatt et al. 2011), financial literacy (Van Rooij et al. 2011) and social interaction (Hong et al. 2004).

Many households own few individual stocks (Blume and Friend 1975; Kelly 1995; Barber and Odean 2000). Under-diversification could be due to information advantage in the stocks held (Van Nieuwerburgh and Veldkamp 2010) but it is not clear that the higher returns, if any, adequately compensate for the additional unsystematic risk. Goetzmann and Kumar (2008) find that under-diversification hurts most households.

The demographic predictors of under-diversification are similar to those of non-participation. Some households are aware of their limited investment skills and choose not to invest in risky assets or to invest cautiously (Graham et al. 2009; Goetzmann and Kumar 2008; Benjamin et al. 2013).

Many studies find that actively managed mutual funds underperform passive funds (French 2008; Fama and French 2010). It is therefore a puzzle why investors pick active funds. Some possible reasons include marketing efforts (Gallaher et al. 2015), broker incentives (Bergstresser et al. 2009) and investor overconfidence (Kim et al. 2019).

Another puzzle is the high fees paid to mutual funds. Some possible explanations include bundling with customer service and financial advice, high search costs (Hortacsu and Syverson 2004) and financial illiteracy (Grinblatt et al. 2016).

It is also confounding that there are so many financial products that reward sophisticated decision making and require continuous monitoring, leaving much room for costly mistakes. There are calls for financial instruments that are simpler or that automatically switch to lower cost options when available (Flesaker and Ronn 1993). However, there is inertia in financial innovation.

4 Housing

Housing serves the dual purpose of consumption and investment. For most homeowners, housing is the largest component of their net wealth and often also the most expensive item. Despite the high weightage of a house in the portfolio of a household, few papers incorporate houses as a component asset in portfolios.

Early in the life cycle of a household where the ratio of house value to net worth is high, less is invested in stocks. In the later part of the life cycle where the ratio of house value to net worth is lower, stocks become more attractive (Marjorie and Yamashita 2002).

House price volatility and house price growth incentivize homeownership (Banks et al. 2015; Agarwal et al. 2016a). Households tend to move between correlated housing markets (Sinai and Souleles 2013). People who perceive housing as risky investments are more likely to be renters than owners (Adelino et al. 2018) but homeowners amass more wealth than renters (Somerville et al. 2007).

In an imperfect world where there is information asymmetry, transaction costs (Hayashi et al. 1988), liquidity constraint (Chiuri and Jappelli 2003) and uncertainties (Naoi et al. 2013; Leece 2001; Piskorski and Tchistyi 2011; Bailey et al. 2019), mortgage demand is complex.

The choice of mortgage instrument, whether fixed rate (FRM) or adjustable rate (ARM), depends on income stability, risk aversion and the probability of moving (Koblyakova et al. 2014; Campbell and Cocco 2003).

Less informed, less educated and low-income consumers are more susceptible to manipulation and to be steered to expensive mortgages (Gurun et al. 2016; Agarwal et al. 2017a, 2016b).

Many borrowers fail to refinance because they are too busy (Agarwal et al. 2013) but they make smaller mistakes if the mortgage is important to them (Agarwal et al. 2016c). The error of commission and omission in refinancing is correlated with the borrowers' financial sophistication (Agarwal et al. 2016c).

Risk characteristics that play a role in explaining default rates include credit scores, loan to value ratios, prime versus subprime mortgages (Agarwal et al. 2012a), recourse versus non-recourse loans (Naoi et al.

2019), negative equity (Gerardi et al. 2018) and illiquidity (Elul et al. 2010).

The monetization of home equity can be facilitated through refinancing (Agarwal et al. 2016c; Hurst and Stafford 2004), home equity loans (Agarwal et al. 2006; Mian and Sufi 2012), home equity lines (Canner et al. 1998; Agarwal et al. 2006) and reverse mortgages (Jefferson et al. 2017; Fornero et al. 2016; Dillingh et al. 2017; Davidoff et al. 2017; Hanewald et al. 2019).

Some possible causes of the subprime crisis include financial innovation and deregulation (Mian and Sufi 2009, 2018), government-backed housing programs (Agarwal et al. 2012b), improper rating of mortgage-backed securities and house price expectations (Adelino et al. 2017). However, there are some who find that mortgage delinquencies are not due to the growth of subprime loans but prime loans (Albanesi et al. 2017).

In the post-crisis period, the US government implemented relief programs to help households cope with distressed mortgages and to forestall foreclosures (Agarwal et al. 2011b, 2017b; Piskorski et al. 2010; Piskorski and Seru 2019). Measures were put in place to increase oversight by requiring financial counseling for borrowers (Agarwal et al. 2020a). In addition, macro-prudential policies such as capital requirements, loan to value ratios and debt to income ratios were introduced to control credit supply (Crowe et al. 2013).

5 Payment

The payment function has to do with the transfer of money for the purchase of goods and services. The act of paying evokes positive and negative emotions. The pain of paying restrains consumption while mitigation through price bundling and other price incentives may result in overspending.

Theories on the psychology of payment include acquisition and transaction utility, buffering hypothesis, payment transparency hypothesis and sunk cost fallacy.

The pain of paying also depends on the payment mode, which can affect spending behavior through the consumer's recall and through the manner in which wealth is depleted (Soman 2001).

Popular payment modes include cash, debit card, check and credit card. The choice of payment mode depends on characteristics such as social status, reward program, credit limit, speed, convenience and security

(Stango and Zinman 2009; Bolt et al. 2010a, b; Schuh and Stavins 2010, 2013, 2015; Bursztyn et al. 2017).

The more transparent the payment outflow, the greater the aversion to spending and the pain of paying (Prelec and Loewenstein 1998; Hirschman 1979; Feinberg 1986; Raghubir and Srivastava 2008).

Some consumers incur high transaction fees. Stango and Zinman (2014) attribute overdraft fee to inattention. Agarwal et al. (2009a) observe that households learn to reduce late fee, over limit fee and cash advance fee as they gain experience but the fees increase when their cognitive ability declines with age. Agarwal et al. (2008) find that when memory fades, consumers forget to be vigilant. They backslide and commit the same costly mistakes again.

Given that consumer inattention and forgetfulness can result in costly mistakes, there are attempts to leverage on technology to provide timely reminders (Medina 2017; Carlin et al. 2018).

6 Borrowing

The borrowing function is facilitated through secured instruments such as mortgages and vehicle loans and unsecured instruments such as student loans and personal loans.

Households borrow for various reasons—to smooth out temporary fluctuations in income (Guerrieri and Lorenzoni 2017), to finance investments in closely held businesses (Robb and Robinson 2014), when they ran out of patience waiting for their savings to accumulate (Eggertsson and Krugman 2012) and when they invest in illiquid assets such as housing.

Household leverage has ballooned over the years. Reasons for the growth include technological change in loan production such as reduction in distribution costs (Dynan 2009), technology of persuasion such as uninformative sales tactics (Gabaix and Laibson 2006), teaser pricing (Stango and Zinman 2014), credit card introductory rates (Agarwal et al. 2015a), the rise in real house prices (Christelis et al. 2017), income inequality (Rajan 2010; Kumhof et al. 2015) and demographic shifts (Christelis et al. 2017).

There are various ways to measure whether households make good borrowing decisions. Studies have sought to examine whether the financial condition and subjective well-being of households improve after borrowing (Zinman 2015), whether borrowers default optimally (Agarwal et al. 2017b), whether they choose deals that minimize their costs (Stango and Zinman 2014; Campbell et al. 2011) and whether they refinance appropriately (Agarwal and Mazumder 2013; Agarwal et al. 2016c).

Household borrowing choices present several puzzles. The persistent high amount of debt which leaves money on the table is confounding.

In the wake of the financial crisis, interventions that seek to protect consumers' interests and prevent future recurrences have proliferated. They include mandating point-of-sale disclosure (Bertrand and Morse 2011), promoting financial literacy (Lusardi and Mitchell 2014) and controlling price, quantity and access to debt.

7 Risk Management

The risk management function can be achieved through products such as insurance (e.g., health, life, property and casualty) and through means such as precautionary saving, social safety nets and government assistance schemes.

In classical economics, households use insurance products to smooth consumption. However, empirical evidence shows that households do not make optimal insurance decisions. Low-income households are the most exposed to the risk of financially harmful events but they are also the most likely to lack insurance coverage (Rampini and Viswanathan 2016).

Life insurance policies take three basic forms, namely, term or temporary insurance, whole life or permanent insurance and endowment. They protect against the possible death (protect against dying too soon) of household members so that surviving members can continue to consume as before.

Annuities protect against longevity risk. Data shows that households spend too little on private market annuities (Warshawsky 1988, 1997). There are a few explanations for this puzzle. Adverse selection drives up the premiums and erodes the attractiveness of annuities (Mitchell et al. 1999; Finkelstein and Poterba 2002). Pre-existing public annuities reduce the need to further annuitize (Dushi and Webb 2004). Households who wish to bequest some wealth will annuitize less (Bernheim 1991). Married couples place lower value on annuities (Brown and Poterba 2000). Uncertainty surrounding medical payments and long-term nursing care increase the need for liquidity and reduce the amount set aside for annuities (Peijnenburg et al. 2017). The lack of cognitive ability, the lack of financial literacy and the way that annuity is framed whether as a consumption or an investment are other possible explanations (Inkmann et al. 2011; Brown et al. 2008).

Unlike life insurance policies which protect against events that will definitely happen, general insurance policies provide protection against events that may or may not happen.

The health insurance market is well developed. It increases with income and age (DeNavas-Walt et al. 2008). However, the same cannot be said for the long-term care insurance market for the elderly (Brown and Finkelstein 2009). Plausible explanations include the lack of understanding, the role of substitutes such as families providing care and the role of public insurance programs (Brown and Finkelstein 2009).

Households purchase too little property and casualty insurance against catastrophic events. Some underestimate the probability of a disaster (McClelland et al. 1993), some are myopic in focusing on the upfront costs (Meyer and Hutchinson 2001), some have separate mental accounts (Thaler 1999), some are affected by neighbors (Heal and Kunreuther 2005), while some find it costly to gather information on the probability and premiums (Kunreuther and Pauly 2004).

The take-up rate of flood insurance is positively related to variables such as prior year disaster losses (Browne and Hoyt 2000), the likelihood of coastal flooding (Dixon et al. 2006), proximity to floodplains (Kousky 2010), higher educational attainment and age (Kunreuther et al. 1978, Baumann and Sims 1978; Zahran et al. 2009; Atreya et al. 2015).

Evidence suggests that the expectation of disaster relief and government mitigation efforts does not reduce the demand for such insurance (Kunreuther 2006; Zahran et al. 2009; Botzen et al. 2009).

8 Financial Inclusion and Financial Technology

Financial technology holds promise of financial inclusion for the unbanked and underbanked. The reluctance of banks to respond to the needs of this neglected segment has created opportunities for new contenders to enter the fray.

Stulz (2019) ascribes the reluctance of banks to the stringent regulations which stifle their growth, the legacy IT systems that hinders the integration of FinTech innovation and the organizational friction inherent in diversified financial conglomerates that reduce their efficiency.

The disruptive nature of FinTech is aided by the proliferation of digital footprint harvested from mobile transactions, e-commerce and online payment systems (Berg et al. 2019; Agarwal et al. 2020b).

The general perception is that using technology and algorithm in the lending and robo-advising space can help to remove human discrimination and bias (Bartlett et al. 2019) but there are evidences to the contrary (Morse and Pence 2020; Caliskan et al. 2017; Barocas and Selbst 2016; Buolomwini and Gebru 2018).

The most active areas of FinTech innovations are blockchain, smart contracting, cryptocurrency, peer-to-peer lending and robo-advising. The growth of FinTech varies widely across countries depending on the network externality (Karlan et al. 2016; Demirguc-Kunt et al. 2017), the level of financial and technological education of the populace (Jünger and Mietzner 2019; Carlin et al. 2017), the dependability of the general infrastructure and mobile network (Yermack 2018), the presence of a stable financial infrastructure (Demirguc-Kunt et al. 2018) and the population density (Allen et al. 2012).

Digital revolution has accelerated financial inclusion in many countries including China, India, Kenya and Rwanda.

9 Impact of Interventions

Within each of the functions, the impact of interventions in the form of education, peer and social influence, product design, market design and fiscal stimulus are also addressed.

9.1 Education

Studies show that the efficacy of learning is complicated by changes in cognitive ability over the life cycle and by behavioral biases that differ from standard economic models, which may lead people to act in ways that are not in their own self-interests.

Behaviors that lead to poor financial outcomes are largely due to the lack of financial knowledge. Many households are ill prepared to achieve their financial goals (Agarwal et al. 2009b). Some take on payday loans at astronomical interest rates when cheaper forms of credit are available (Agarwal et al. 2009c). Others choose sub-optimal credit contracts (Agarwal et al. 2015a), fail to refinance mortgages when it is optimal to do so (Agarwal et al. 2012c) or fail to plan for retirement (Lusardi et al.

2014). Agarwal and Mazumder (2013) find that consumers with higher math scores are less likely to make financial mistakes.

Perhaps over time, households will acquire financial literacy and learn to overcome their behavioral biases. There is evidence of a U-shaped pattern to financial mistakes with cost minimizing performance at around age 53 (Agarwal et al. 2009a).

9.2 Peer and Social Influence

Hong et al. (2004) find that consumers who interact with neighbors and attend church are more likely to invest in stocks. Whether peer influence and social network will lead to better performance is debatable.

According to some, peer-to-peer communication on the quality of investments can improve decision making (Ambuehl et al. 2018).

Others, however, find that investors possess biases when promoting their personal investing strategies, focusing on wins rather than losses, which spurs people around them to adopt active investing strategies (Han et al. 2018).

9.3 Product Design

Certain financial products are complex because of the way they are structured by financial intermediaries.

In the area of credit cards, the complexity stems from the great variety of rates and fee structures to cater to diverse consumer risk profiles and preferences.

For mortgages, shopping for the "best" rates can be tedious because of all the information and forms that need to be submitted to get quotes. When interest rates fall, the mortgages do not automatically adjust. Instead, households have to actively seek to refinance. Evidences show that a large fraction of households fail to do so even when the saving can be substantial (Campbell et al. 2011).

Agarwal et al. (2016b) find evidence of loan steering where good credit quality customers take up high-margin mortgage products. However, the role of predatory lending in precipitating the subprime crisis is relatively limited (Agarwal et al. 2014).

9.4 *Market Design*

Apart from product design, the interaction between financial intermediaries and households can lead to sub-optimal outcomes.

Borrowers, who are financially constrained, have the incentive to influence the valuation process in order to borrow more or reduce the interest rate (Agarwal et al. 2015b). Mortgages with inflated valuations are more likely to default although lenders typically factor the valuation bias into their pricing.

Some lenders use direct mail or junk mail to influence consumer choices (Agarwal and Ambrose 2018). Evidences show that naïve borrowers are persuaded by these advertising efforts.

Gurun et al. (2016) find a strong positive relationship between the intensity of advertising and the cost of mortgages extended by lenders.

In addition, borrowers may be misled by teaser rates and complex pricing structures where lenders offer lower initial rates but shroud back-loaded pricing features to earn more revenue. There tend to be more shrouding when there are more naïve borrowers (Agarwal et al. 2017c).

9.5 *Fiscal Stimulus*

The effectiveness of fiscal policies such as tax rebates, wage laws and sales tax hinges on the responses of households.

In 2001, the Bush administration announced tax rebates for about two-thirds of US tax-filers. In response, households paid down their debt and the spending of those who were most likely to be constrained rose (Agarwal et al. 2007).

Sales tax holidays (STH) in the US induce households to spend, with no inter-temporal substitution either before or after the STH (Agarwal et al. 2017d).

Finally, paternalistic policies that encourage lower income households to become homeowners substantially increase their risk from a financial portfolio perspective. This can explain why lower income households are less willing to assume the risk of stock investment. The result is an undiversified portfolio with few other assets (Ambrose and Goetzmann 1998).

References

Adelino, Manuel, Antoinette Schoar, and Felipe Severino. 2017. Dynamics of Housing Debt in the Recent Boom and Great Recession. NBER Working Paper #23502

———. 2018. Perception of House Price Risk and Homeownership. NBER Working Paper #25090.

Agarwal, Sumit, and Brent W. Ambrose. 2018. The Effect of Advertising on Home Equity Credit Choices. In *Research Handbook on Behavioral Law and Economics*, ed. Joshua C. Teitelbaum and Kathryn Zeiler, 122–152. Elgar Publishing.

Agarwal, Sumit, and Bhashkar Mazumder. 2013. Cognitive Abilities and Household Financial Decision Making. *American Economic Journal: Applied Economics* 5 (1): 193–207.

Agarwal, Sumit, Chunlin Liu, Nicholas S. Souleles, (2007) The Reaction of Consumer Spending and Debt to Tax Rebates—Evidence from Consumer Credit Data. *Journal of Political Economy* 115 (6): 986–1019

Agarwal, Sumit, and Wenlan Qian. 2014. Consumption and Debt Response to Unanticipated Income Shocks: Evidence from a Natural Experiment in Singapore. *American Economic Review* 104: 4205–4230.

Agarwal, Sumit, Brent W. Ambrose, Souphala Chomsisengphet, and Chunlin Liu. 2006. An Empirical Analysis of Home Equity Loan and Line Performance. *Journal of Financial Intermediation* 15: 444–469.

Agarwal, Sumit, John C. Driscoll, Xavier Gabaix, and David Laibson. 2008. Learning in the Credit Card Market. NBER Working Paper #13822.

———. 2009a. The Age of Reason: Financial Decisions over the Life Cycle and Implications for Regulation. *Brookings Papers on Economic Activity* 2009 (Fall): 51–101.

Agarwal, Sumit, Gene Amromin, Itzhak Ben-David, Souphala Chomsisengphet, and Douglas D. Evanoff. 2009b. Do Financial Counseling Mandates Improve Mortgage Choice and Performance? Evidence for a Legislative Experiment. Working Paper. Federal Reserve Bank of Chicago.

Agarwal, Sumit, Paige Skiba, and Jeremy Tobacman. 2009c. Payday Loans and Credit Cards: New Liquidity and Credit Scoring Puzzles? *American Economic Review: Papers and Proceeding* 99 (2): 412–417.

Agarwal, Sumit, Gene Amromin, Itzhak Ben-David, Souphala Chomsisengphet, and Douglas D. Evanoff. 2011a. Financial Counseling, Financial Literacy, and Household Decision-Making. In *Financial Literacy: Implications for Retirement Security and the Financial Marketplace*, ed. Olivia S. Mitchell and Annamaria Lusardi, 181–205. Oxford and New York: Oxford University Press.

———. 2011b. The Role of Securitization in Mortgage Renegotiation. *Journal of Financial Economics* 102 (3): 559–578.

Agarwal, Sumit, Brent W. Ambrose, Souphala Chomsisengphet, and Anthony B. Sanders. 2012a. Thy Neighbor's Mortgage: Does Living in a Subprime Neighborhood Affect One's Probability of Default? *Real Estate Economics* 40 (1): 1–22.

Agarwal, Sumit, Efraim Benmelech, Nittai Bergman, and Amit Seru. 2012b. Did the Community Reinvestment Act Lead to Risky Lending? NBER Working Paper #18609

Agarwal, Sumit, Rosen Richard, and Yao Vincent. 2012c. Why Do Borrowers Make Mortgage Refinancing Mistakes? Working Paper. Federal Reserve Bank of Chicago.

Agarwal, Sumit, John C. Driscoll, and David Laibson. 2013. Optimal Mortgage Refinancing: A Closed Form Solution. *Journal of Money, Credit and Banking* 45 (4): 591–622.

Agarwal, Sumit, Gene Amromin, Itzhak Ben-David, Souphala Chomsisengphet, and Douglas D. Evanoff. 2014. Predatory Lending and the Subprime Crisis. *Journal of Financial Economics* 113 (1): 29–52.

Agarwal, Sumit, Souphala Chomsisengphet, Chunlin Liu, and Nicholas S. Souleles. 2015a. Do Consumers Choose the Right Credit Contracts? *The Review of Corporate Finance Studies* 4 (2): 239–247.

Agarwal, Sumit, Itzhak Ben-David, and Vincent Yao. 2015b. Collateral Valuation and Borrower Financial Constraints: Evidence from the Residential Real Estate Market. *Management Science* 61 (9): 2220–2240.

Agarwal, Sumit, Luojia Hu, and Xing Huang. 2016a. Rushing into the American Dream? House Prices Growth and the Timing of Homeownership. *Review of Finance* 20 (6): 2183–2218.

Agarwal, Sumit, Gene Amromin, Itzhak Ben-David, and Douglas D. Evanoff. 2016b. Loan Product Steering in Mortgage Market. NBER Working Paper #22696

Agarwal, Sumit, Richard J. Rosen, and Vincent Yao. 2016c. Why do Borrowers make Mortgage Refinancing Mistakes? *Management Science* 62 (12): 3494–3509.

Agarwal, Sumit, Changcheng Song, and Vincent W. Yao. 2017a. Banking Competition and Shrouded Attributes: Evidence from the US Mortgage market. *SSRN*. Accessed March 20, 2020. https://papers.ssrn.com/sol3/papers.cfm?abstract_id=2900287

Agarwal, Sumit, Gene Amromin, Itzhak Ben-David, Souphala Chomsisengphet, Tomasz Piskorski, and Amit Seru. 2017b. Policy Intervention in Debt Renegotiation: Evidence from the Home Affordable Modification Program. *Journal of Political Economy* 125 (3): 654–712.

Agarwal, Sumit, Changcheng Song, and Vincent W. Yao. 2017c. Banking Competition and Shrouded Attributes: Evidence from the US Mortgage

Market. Georgetown McDonough School of Business Research Paper No. 2900287.
Agarwal, Sumit, Nathan Marwell, and Leslie McGranahan. 2017d. Consumption Responses to Temporary Tax Incentives: Evidence from State Sales Tax Holidays. *American Economic Journal: Economic Policy* 9 (4): 1–27.
Agarwal, Sumit, Gene Amromin, Itzhak Ben-David, Souphala Chomsisengphet, and Douglas D. Evanoff. 2020a. Financial Education Versus Costly Counseling: How to Dissuade Borrowers from Choosing Risky Mortgages? *American Economic Journal: Economic Policy* 12 (1): 1–32.
Agarwal, Sumit, Shashwat Alok, Pulak Ghosh, and Sudip Gupta. 2020b. Financial Inclusion and Alternate Credit Scoring for the Millennials: Role of Big Data and Machine Learning in Fintech. *SSRN*. Accessed March 20, 2020. https://ssrn.com/abstract=3507827
Albanesi, Stefania, Giacomo De Giorgi, and Jaromir Nosal. 2017. Credit Growth and the Financial Crisis: A New Narrative. NBER Working Paper #23740.
Allen, Franklin, Elena Carletti, Robert Cull, Jun Qian, Lemma Senbet, and Patricio Valenzuela. 2012. Resolving the African Financial Development Gap: Cross-Country Comparisons and a Within-Country Study of Kenya. NBER Working Paper #18013.
Ambrose, Brent W., and William N. Goetzmann. 1998. Risks and Incentives in Underserved Mortgage Markets. *Journal of Housing Economics* 7 (3): 274–285.
Ambuehl, Sandro, Douglas Bernheim, Fulya Ersoy, and Donna Harris. 2018. Peer Advice on Financial Decisions: A Case of the Blind Leading the Blind? NBER Working Paper #25034
Ando, Albert, and Arthur Kennickell. 1987. How Much (or Little) Life Cycle Is There in Micro Data? The Cases of the United States and Japan. In *Macroeconomics and Finance, Essays in Honor of Franco Modigliani*, ed. Rudiger Dornbusch, Stanley Fischer, and John Bossons. Cambridge: MIT Press.
Atreya, Ajita, Susana Ferreira, and Erwann Michel-Kerjan. 2015. What Drives Households to Buy Flood Insurance? New Evidence from Georgia. *Ecological Economics* 117: 153–161.
Attanasio, Orazio P. 1998. Cohort Analysis of Saving Behavior by US Households. *The Journal of Human Resources* 33 (3): 575–609.
Avery, Robert B., and Arthur B. Kennickell. 1991. Household saving in the U.S. *Review of Income and Wealth* 37 (4): 409–430.
Bailey, Michael, Eduardo Davila, Theresa Kuchler, and Johannes Stroebel. 2019. House Price Beliefs and Mortgage Leverage Choice. *Review of Economic Studies* 86: 2403–2452.
Baker, Malcolm, Stefan Nagel, and Jeffrey Wurgler. 2007. The Effect of Dividends on Consumption. *Brookings Papers on Economic Activity* 2007 (1): 231–276.
Banks, James, Richard Blundell, Zoe Oldfield, and James P. Smith. 2015. House Price Volatility and the Housing Ladder. NBER Working Paper #21255

Barber, Brad M., and Terrance Odean. 2000. Trading is Hazardous to Your Wealth: The Common Stock Investment Performance of Individual Investors. *Journal of Finance* 55: 773–806.

Barberis, Nicholas, Ming Huang, and Richard H. Thaler. 2006. Individual Preferences, Monetary Gambles, and Stock Market Participation: A Case for Narrow Framing. *The American Economic Review* 96 (4): 1069–1090.

Barocas, Solon, and Andrew D. Selbst. 2016. Big Data's Disparate Impact. *California Law Review* 104 (3): 671–732.

Bartlett, Robert, Adair Morse, Richard Stanton, and Nancy Wallace. 2019. Consumer Lending Discrimination in the FinTech Era. NBER Working paper #25943.

Baumann, Duane D., and John H. Sims. 1978. Flood Insurance: Some Determinants of Adoption. *Economic Geography* 54 (3): 189–196.

Ben-David, Itzhak, Elyas Fermand, Camelia M. Kuhnen, and Geng Li. 2018. Expectations Uncertainty and Household Economic Behavior. NBER Working Paper #25336

Benjamin, Daniel J., Sebastian Andres Brown, and Jesse M. Shapiro. 2013. Who is 'Behavioral'? Cognitive Ability and Anomalous Preferences. *Journal of the European Economic Association* 11 (6): 1231–1255.

Berg, Tobias, Burg Valentin, Gombavic Ana, and Puri Manju. 2019. On the Rise of FinTechs: Credit Scoring Using Digital Footprints. *The Review of Financial Studies.* Accessed March 20, 2020. https://doi-org.libproxy1.nus.edu.sg/10.1093/rfs/hhz099.

Bergstresser, D., John M.R. Chalmers, and Peter Tufano. 2009. Assessing the Costs and Benefits of Brokers in the Mutual Fund Industry. *The Review of Financial Studies* 22 (10): 4129–4156.

Bernheim, Douglas B. 1991. How Strong Are the Bequest Motives? Evidence Based on Estimates of the Demand for Life Insurance and Annuities. *Journal of Political Economy* 99 (5): 899–927.

Bernheim, Douglas B., Jonathan Skinner, and Steven Weinberg. 2001. What Accounts for he Variation in Retirement Wealth among U.S. Households? *American Economic Review* 91: 832–857.

Bertaut, Carol C., and Michael Haliassos. 2000. Why Do So Few Hold Stocks? *The Economic Journal* 105 (432): 1110–1129.

Bertrand, Marianne, and Adair Morse. 2011. Information Disclosure, Cognitive Biases and Payday Borrowing. *The Journal of Finance* 66 (6): 1865–1893.

Blume, Marshall, and Irwin Friend. 1975. The Asset Structure of Individual Portfolios and Some Implications for Utility Functions. *Journal of Finance* 30: 585–603.

Bolt, Wilko, Nicole Jonker, and Corry van Renselaar. 2010a. Incentives at the Counter: An Empirical Analysis of Surcharging Card Payments and Payment

Behaviour in the Netherlands. *Journal of Banking and Finance* 34 (8): 1738–1744.

Bolt, Wilko, Santiago Carbo-Valverde, Sujit Chakravorti, Sergio Gorjon, and Francisco Roiguez Fernandez. 2010b. What is the Role of Public Authorities in Retail Payment Systems? *Chicago Fed Letter* 280a (280a): 1.

Boskin, Michael J. 1978. Taxation, Saving, and the Rate of Interest. *Journal of Political Economy* 86: S3–S27.

Botzen, Wouter J.W., Jeroen C.J.H. Aerts, and Jeroen Van den Bergh. 2009. Willingness of Homeowners to Mitigate Climate Risk through Insurance. *Ecological Economics* 68 (8): 2265–2277.

Brady, Peter J., Glenn B. Canner, and Dean M. Maki. 2000. The Effects of Recent Mortgage Refinancing. *Federal Reserve Bulletin* 86 (7): 441–450.

Brown, Jeffrey R., and Amy Finkelstein. 2009. The Private Market for Long-Term Care Insurance in the United States: A Review of the Evidence. *The Journal of Risk and Insurance* 76 (1): 5–29.

Brown, Jeffrey R., and James Poterba. 2000. Joint Life Annuities and Annuity Demand by Married Couples. *Journal of Risk and Insurance* 67 (4): 527–553.

Brown, Jeffrey R., Jeffrey R. Kling, Sendhil Mullainathan, and Marian V. Wrobel. 2008. Why Don't People Insure Late-Life Consumption? A Framing Explanation of the Under-Annuitization Puzzle. *The American Economic Review* 98 (2): 304–309.

Browne, Mark J., and Robert E. Hoyt. 2000. The Demand for Flood Insurance: Empirical Evidence. *Journal of Risk and Uncertainty* 20 (3): 291–306.

Browning, Martin, and Annamaria Lusardi. 1996. Household Saving: Micro Theories and Micro Facts. *Journal of Economic Literature* 34: 1797–1855.

Buolomwini, Joy, and Timnit Gebru. 2018. Gender Shades: Intersectional Accuracy Disparities in Commercial Gender Classification. *Proceedings of Machine Learning Research* 81: 1–15.

Bursztyn, Leonard, Bruno Ferman, Stefano Fiorin, Martin Kanz, and Gautum Rao. 2017. Status Goods: Experimental Evidence from Platinum Credit Cards. *The Quarterly Journal of Economics* 133 (3): 1561–1595.

Caliskan, Aylin, Joanna J. Bryson, and Arvind Narayanan. 2017. Semantics Derived Automatically from Language Corpora Contain Human-Like Biases. *Science.* 356 (6334): 183–186.

Campbell, John Y., and Joao F. Cocco. 2003. Household Risk Management and Optimal Mortgage Choice. *Quarterly Journal of Economics* 118: 1449–1494.

Campbell, John Y., Howell E. Jackson, Brigitte C. Madrian, and Peter Tufano. 2011. Consumer Financial Protection. *Journal of Economic Perspectives* 25 (1): 91–113.

Canner, Glenn B., Thomas A. Durkin, and Charles A. Luckett. 1998. Recent Developments in Home Equity Financing. *Federal Reserve Bulletin* 84: 241–251.

Canner, Glenn, Dynan Karen, and Passmore Wayne. 2002. Mortgage Refinancing in 2001 and early 2002. *Federal Reserve Bulletin* 88 (12): 469–481.

Carlin, Bruce, Arna Olafsson, and Michaela Pagel. 2017. FinTech Adoption Across Generations: Financial Fitness in the Information Age. NBER Working Paper #23798.

Carlin, Bruce I., Li Jiang, and Stephen A. Spiller. 2018. Millennial-Style Learning: Search Intensity, Decision Making, and Information Sharing. *Management Science* 64 (7): 3313–3330.

Carroll, Chris, and Lawrence H. Summers. 1987. Why Have Private Saving Rates in the United States and Canada Diverged? *Journal of Monetary Economics* 20: 249–279.

Chamon, Marcos, and Eswar S. Prasad. 2010. Why are Saving Rates of Urban Households in China Rising? *American Economic Journal: Macroeconomics* 2 (1): 93–130.

Chang, Y. Regina, and Sandra J. Huston. 1995. Patterns of Adequate Household Emergency Fund Holdings: A Comparison of Households in 1983 and 1986. *Journal of Financial Counseling and Planning* 6: 119.

Chiuri, Maria Concetta, and Tullio Jappelli. 2003. Financial Market Imperfections and Home Ownership: A Comparative Study. *European Economic Review* 47 (5): 857–875.

Christelis, Dimitris, Michael Ehrmann, and Dimitris Georgarakos. 2017. Exploring Differences in Household Debt across the United States and Euro Area Countries. Centre for Studies in Economics and Finance Working Papers 465, University of Naples, Italy.

Cole, Shawn, Anna Paulson, and Gauri Shastry. 2014. Smart Money? The Effect of Education on Financial Outcomes. *Review of Financial Studies* 27 (7): 2022–2051.

Coleman, Andrew. 1998. Household Savings: A Survey of Recent Microeconomic Theory and Evidence. New Zealand Treasury. Treasury Working Paper Series 98/08.

Crowe, Christopher, Giovanni Dell'Ariccia, Deniz Igan, and Pau Rabanal. 2013. How to Deal with Real Estate Booms: Lessons from Country Experiences. *Journal of Financial Stability* 9 (3): 300–319.

Davidoff, Thomas, Patrick Gerhard, and Thomas Post. 2017. Reverse Mortgages: What Homeowners (Don't) Know And How It Matters. *Journal of Economic Behavior & Organization* 133: 151–171.

Deaton, Angus. 1991. Saving and Liquidity Constraints. *Econometrica* 59 (4): 1221–1248.

Demirguc-Kunt, Asli, Klapper Leora, and Singer Dorothe. 2017. Financial Inclusion and Inclusive Growth: A Review of Recent Empirical Evidence. World Bank Policy Research Working Paper Series 8040.

Demirguc-Kunt, Asli, Leora Klapper, Dorothe Singer, Saniya Ansar, and Jake Hess. 2018. *Global Findex Database 2017 : Measuring Financial Inclusion and the Fintech Revolution*. Washington, DC: World Bank.
DeNavas-Walt, Carmen, Bernadette D. Proctor, and Jessica C. Smith. 2008. Income, Poverty and Health Insurance Coverage in the US: 2007. US Department of Commerce Economics and Statistics Administration.
Denizer, Cevdet, Holger C. Wolf, and Yvonne Ying. 2002. Household Savings in the Transition. *Journal of Comparative Economics* 30: 463–475.
Di Maggio, Marco, Amir Kermani, Benjamin J. Keys, Tomasz Piskorski, Rodney Ramcharan, Amit Seru, and Vincent Yao. 2017. Interest rate Pass-Through: Mortgage Rates, Household Consumption, and Voluntary Deleveraging. *American Economic Review* 107 (11): 3550–3588.
Di Maggio, Marco, Amir Kermani, and Kaveh Majlesi. 2018. Stock Market Returns and Consumption. NBER Working Paper #24262
Dillingh, Rik, Henriette Prast, Mariacristina Rossi, and Cesira Urzì Brancati. 2017. Who Wants To Have Their Home And Eat It Too? Interest In Reverse Mortgages in the Netherlands. *Journal of Housing Economics* 38: 25–37.
Dixon, Lloyd, Noreen Clancy, Seth A. Seabury, and Adrian Overton. 2006. The National Flood Insurance Program's Market Penetration Rate: Estimates and Policy Implications. Rand Corporation
Duflo, Esther, William Gale, Jeffrey Liebman, PIeter Orszag, and Emmanuel Saez. 2006. Saving Incentives for Low- and Middle-Income Families: Evidence from a Field Experiment with H&R Block. *The Quarterly Journal of Economics* 121 (4): 1311–1346.
Dushi, Irene, and Anthony Webb. 2004. Annuitization: Keeping Your Options Open. Boston College Center for Retirement Research Working Paper No. 2004-04.
Dynan, Karen E. 2009. Changing Household Financial Opportunities and Economic Security. *Journal of Economic Perspectives* 23 (4): 49–68.
Dynan, Karen E., Jonathan Skinner, and Stephen P. Zeldes. 2002. The Importance of Bequests and Life-Cycle Saving in Capital Accumulation: A New Answer. *American Economic Review* 92 (2): 274–278.
Eggertsson, Gauti B., and Paul Krugman. 2012. Debt, Deleveraging, and the Liquidity Trap: A Fisher-Minsky-Koo Approach. *The Quarterly Journal of Economics* 127 (3): 1469–1513.
Elul, Ronel, Nicholas S. Souleles, Souphala Chomsisengphet, Dennis Glennon, and Robert Hunt. 2010. What 'Triggers' mortgage default? *American Economic Review: Papers and Proceedings* 100 (2): 490–494.
Fama, Eugene F., and Kenneth R. French. 2010. Luck versus Skill in the Cross-Section of Mutual Fund Returns. *The Journal of Finance* 65 (5): 1915–1947.
Feinberg, Richard A. 1986. Credit Cards as Spending Facilitating Stimuli: A Conditioning Interpretation. *Journal of Consumer Research* 13 (3): 348–356.

Feldstein, Martin S. 1973. Tax Incentives, Corporate Saving, and Capital Accumulation in the United States. *Journal of Public Economics* 2 (2): 159–171.

Finkelstein, Amy, and James Poterba. 2002. Selection Effects in the United Kingdom Individual Annuities Market. *The Economic Journal* 112 (476): 28–50.

Fisher, Patti J., and Sophia Anong. 2012. Relationship of Saving Motives to Saving Habits. *Journal of Financial Counseling and Planning* 23 (1): 63–79.

Fisher, Patti J., and Catherine P. Montalto. 2010. Effect of Saving Motives and Horizon on Saving Behaviors. *Journal of Economic Psychology* 31: 92–105.

Flesaker, Bjorn, and Ehud I. Ronn. 1993. The Pricing of FIREARMs (Falling Interest Rate Adjustable-Rate Mortgages). *Journal of Real Estate Finance and Economics* 6: 251–275.

Fornero, Elsa, Mariacristina Rossi, and Maria Cesira Urzi Brancati. 2016. Explaining Why, Right or Wrong, (Italian) Households Do Not Like Reverse Mortgages. *Journal of Pension Economics & Finance* 15 (2): 180–202.

French, Kenneth R. 2008. Presidential Address: The Cost of Active Investing. *The Journal of Finance* 63 (4): 1537–1573.

Friend, Irwin, and Joel Hasbrouck. 1983. Saving and After-Tax Rates of Return. *The Review of Economics and Statistics* 65 (4): 537–543.

Gabaix, Xavier, and David Laibson. 2006. Shrouded Attributes, Consumer Myopia, and Information Suppression in Competitive Markets. *Quarterly Journal of Economics* 121 (2): 505–540.

Gallaher, Steven, Ron Kaniel, and Laura T. Starks. 2015. Advertising and Mutual Funds: From Families to Individual Funds. Centre for Economic Policy Research Discussion Paper No. DP10329.

Ganong, Peter, and Pascal J. Noel. 2019. Consumer Spending During Unemployment: Positive and Normative Implications. NBER Working Paper #25417.

Gerardi, Kristopher, Kyle F. Herkenhoff, Lee E. Ohanian, and Paul Willen. 2018. Can't Pay or Won't Pay? Unemployment, Negative Equity, and Strategic Default. *Review of Financial Studies* 31 (3): 1098–1131.

Goetzmann, William N., and Alok Kumar. 2008. Equity Portfolio Diversification. *Review of Finance* 12 (3): 433–463.

Graham, John R., Campbell R. Harvey, and Hai Huang. 2009. Investor Competence, Trading Frequency, and Home Bias. *Management Science* 55 (7): 1094–1106.

Greenspan, Alan, and James Kennedy. 2008. Sources and Uses of Equity Extracted from Homes. *Oxford Review of Economic Policy* 24 (1): 120–144.

Grigoli, Francesco, Alexander Herman, and Kalus Schmidt-Hebbel. 2018. Saving in the World. *World Development* 104: 257–270.

Grinblatt, Mark, Matti Keloharju, and Juhani Linnainmaa. 2011. IQ and Stock Market Participation. *Journal of Finance* 66 (6): 2121–2164.

Grinblatt, Mark, Seppo Ikaheimo, Matti Keloharju, and Samuli Knupfer. 2016. IQ and Mutual Fund Choice. *Management Science* 62 (4): 924–944.

Guerrieri, Veronica, and Guido Lorenzoni. 2017. Credit Crises, Precautionary Savings, and the Liquidity Trap. *Quarterly Journal of Economics* 132 (3): 1427–1467.

Guiso, Luigi, and Tullio Jappelli. 2005. Awareness and Stock Market Participation. *Review of Finance* 9 (4): 537–567.

Guiso, Luigi, Paola Sapienza, and Luigi Zingales. 2008. Trusting the Stock Market. *Journal of Finance* 63 (6): 2557–2600.

Gurun, Umit G., Gregor Matvos, and Amit Seru. 2016. Advertising Expensive Mortgages. *Journal of Finance* 71 (5): 2371–2416.

Gylfason, Thorvaldur. 1981. Interest Rates, Inflation, and the Aggregate Consumption Function. *Review of Economics and Statistics* 63: 233–245.

Han, Bing, Johan Walden, and David Hirshleifer. 2018. Social Transmission Bias and Investor Behavior. NBER Working Paper #24281

Hanewald, Katja, Hazel Bateman, Hanming Fang, and Shang Wu. 2019. Is there a Demand for Reverse Mortgages in China? Evidence from Two Online Surveys. NBER Working Paper #25491.

Hayashi, Fumio, Takatoshi Ito, and Joel Slemrod. 1988. Housing Finance Imperfections, Taxation and Private Saving: A Comparative Simulation Analysis of the United States and Japan. *Journal of the Japanese and International Economies* 2: 215–238.

Hayhoe, Celia R., Soo Hyun Cho, Sharon A. DeVaney, Sheri Lokken Worthy, Jinhee Kim, and Elizabeth Gorham. 2012. How Do Distrust and Anxiety Affect Saving Behavior? *Family and Consumer Sciences Research Journal* 41 (1): 69–85.

Heal, Geoffrey, and Howard Kunreuther. 2005. You Can Only Die Once: Interdependent Security in an Uncertain World. In *The Economic Impacts of Terrorist Attacks*, ed. Harry W. Richardson, Peter Gordon, and James E. Moore II. Cheltenham UK: Edward Elgar.

Heaton, John, and Deborah Lucas. 2000. Portfolio Choice and Asset Prices: The Importance of Entrepreneurial Risk. *Journal of Finance* 55: 1163–1198.

Heckman, Stuart J., and Sherman D. Hanna. 2015. Individual and Institutional Factors Related to Low-Income Household Saving Behavior. *Journal of Financial Counseling and Planning* 26 (2): 187–199.

Henager-Greene, Robin, and Teresa Mauldin. 2015. Financial Literacy: The Relationship to Saving Behavior in Low- to Moderate- income Households. *Family and Consumer Sciences Research Journal* 44 (1): 73-87.

Hirschman, Elizabeth. 1979. Differences in Consumer Purchase Behavior of Credit Card Payment System. *Journal of Consumer Research* 6: 58–66.

Hong, Harrison, Jeffrey D. Kubik, and Jeremy Stein. 2004. Social Interaction and Stock-market Participation. *Journal of Finance* 59: 137–163.

Horioka, Charles Yuji. 1984. The Applicability of the Life-cycle Hypothesis to Japan. *Kyoto University Economics Review* 54: 31–56.
Hortacsu, Ali, and Chad Syverson. 2004. Product Differentiation, Search Costs, and Competition in the Mutual Fund Industry: A Case Study of S&P 500 Index Funds. *Quarterly Journal of Economics* 119: 403–456.
Howard, David H. 1978. Personal Saving Behavior and the Rate of Inflation. *The Review of Economics and Statistics* 60 (4): 547–554.
Hubbard, Glenn R., Jonathan Skinner, and Stephen P. Zeldes. 1995. Precautionary Saving and Social Insurance. *Journal of Political Economy* 103 (2): 360–399.
Hurst, Erik, and Frank Stafford. 2004. Home is Where the Equity is: Mortgage Refinancing and Household Consumption. *Journal of Money, Credit and Banking* 36 (6): 985–1014.
Inkmann, Joachim, Paula Lopes, and Alexander Michaelides. 2011. How Deep is the Annuity Market Participation Puzzle? *Review of Financial Studies* 24 (1): 279–319.
Jefferson, Therese, Austen Siobhan, Rachel Ong, Marietta E.A. Haffner, and Gavin A. Wood. 2017. Housing Equity Withdrawal: Perceptions of Obstacles among Older Australian Home Owners and Associated Service Providers. *Journal of Social Policy* 46 (3): 623–642.
Jünger, Moritz, and Mark Mietzner. 2019. Banking Goes Digital: The Adoption of FinTech Services by German Households. *Finance Research Letters*. Accessed March 20, 2020. https://doi.org/10.1016/j.frl.2019.08.008
Kapteyn, Arie, Rob Alessie, and Annamaria Lusardi. 2005. Explaining the Wealth Holdings of Different Cohorts: Productivity Growth and Social Security. *European Economic Review* 49: 1361–1391.
Karlan, Dean, Jake Kendall, Rebecca Mann, Rohini Pande, Tavneet Suri, and Jonathan Zinman. 2016. Research and impacts of Digital Financial Services. NBER Working Paper #22633
Katona, George. 1975. *Psychological Economics*. Oxford, England: Elsevier.
Kelly, Morgan. 1995. All their Eggs in One Basket: Portfolio Diversification of U.S. Households. *Journal of Economic Behavior and Organization* 27: 87–96.
Keynes, John Maynard. 1936. *The General Theory of Employment, Interest and Money*. London: Macmillan.
Kim, Hugh Hoikwang, Olivia S. Mitchell, and Maurer Raimond. 2019. How Cognitive Ability and Financial Literacy Shape the Demand for Financial Advice at Older Ages. NBER Working Paper #25750
Koblyakova, Alla, Norman Hutchison, and Piyush Tiwari. 2014. Regional Differences in Mortgage Demand and Mortgage Instrument Choice in the UK. *Regional Studies* 48 (9): 1499–1513.
Kotlikoff, Laurence J. 1988. Intergenerational Transfers and Savings. *Journal of Economic Perspectives* 2 (2): 41–58.
Kousky, Carolyn. 2010. Understanding the Demand for Flood Insurance. *Natural Hazards Review* 12 (2): 96–110.

Kuhnen, Camelia M., and Andrei C. Miu. 2017. Socioeconomic Status and Learning from Financial Information. *Journal of Financial economics* 124 (2): 349–372.

Kumhof, Michael, Romain Rancière, and Pablo Winant. 2015. Inequality, Leverage, and Crises. *American Economic Review* 105 (3): 1217–1245.

Kunreuther, Howard. 2006. Disaster Mitigation and Insurance: Learning from Katrina. *The Annals of the American Academy of Political and Social Science* 604 (1): 208–227.

Kunreuther, Howard, and Mark Pauly. 2004. Neglecting Disaster: Why Don't People Insure Against Large Losses? *The Journal of Risk and Uncertainty* 28 (1): 5–21.

Kunreuther, Howard, Ralph Ginsberg, Louis Miller, Philip Sagi, Paul Slovic, Bradley Borkan, and Norman Katz. 1978. *Disaster Insurance Protection: Public Policy Lessons.* New York: John Wiley and Sons.

Laibson, David. 1997. Golden Eggs and Hyperbolic Discounting. *Quarterly Journal of Economics* 112 (2): 443–477.

———. 1998. Life-cycle Consumption and Hyperbolic Discount Functions. *European Economic Review* 42 (3–5): 861–871.

Lee, Jae Min, and Sherman D. Hanna. 2015. Savings Goals and Saving Behavior from a Perspective of Maslow's Hierarchy of Needs. *Journal of Financial Counseling and Planning* 26 (2): 129–147.

Leece, David. 2001. Regressive Interest Rates Expectations and Mortgage Instrument Choice in the United Kingdom Housing Market. *Real Estate Economics* 29: 589–614.

Lusardi, Annamaria, and Olivia S. Mitchell. 2007. Financial literacy and Retirement Preparedness: Evidence and Implications for Financial Education. *Business Economics* 42: 35–44.

Lusardi, Annamaria, and Olivia S. Mitchell. 2014. The Economic Importance of Financial Literacy: Theory and Evidence. *Journal of Economic Literature* 52 (1): 5–44.

Lusardi, Annamaria, Olivia S. Mitchell, and Vilsa Curto. 2014. Financial Literacy among the Young: Evidence and Implications for Consumer Policy. *Journal of Pension Economics and Finance* 13 (4): 347–366.

Malmendier, Ulrike, and Stefan Nagel. 2011. Depression Babies: Do Macroeconomic Experiences Affect Risk-Taking? *Quarterly Journal of Economics* 126 (1): 373–416.

Marjorie, Flavin, and Takashi Yamashita. 2002. Housing and Portfolio Composition. *The American Economic Review* 92 (1): 345–362.

Mastrobuoni, Giovanni, and Matthew Weinberg. 2009. Heterogeneity in Intra-monthly Consumption Patterns, Self-control, and Savings at Retirement. *American Economic Journal: Economic Policy* 1 (2): 163–189.

McClelland, Gary, William D. Schulze, and Don L. Coursey. 1993. Insurance for Low Probability Hazards: A Bimodal Response to Unlikely Events. *Journal of Risk and Uncertainty* 7: 95–116.
Medina, Paolina C. 2017. Selective Attention in Consumer Finance: Evidence from a Randomized Intervention in the Credit Card Market. Unpublished Paper, Northwestern University.
Meier, Stephan, and Charles Sprenger. 2010. Present-Biased Preferences and Credit Card Borrowing. *American Economic Journal: Applied Economics* 2 (1): 193–210.
Meyer, Robert J., and Wesley J. Hutchinson. 2001. Bumbling Geniuses: The Power of Everyday Reasoning in Multi-stage Decision Making. In *Wharton on Making Decisions*, ed. Steve Hoch and Howard Kunreuther, 37–61. New York: John Wiley and Sons.
Mian, Atif, and Amir Sufi. 2009. The Consequences of Mortgage Credit Expansion: Evidence from the US Mortgage Default Crisis. *Quarterly Journal of Economics* 124: 1449–1496.
———. 2012. House Prices, Home Equity-Based Borrowing, and the US Household Leverage Crisis. *American Economic Review* 89: 959–973.
———. 2018. Credit Supply and Housing Speculation. NBER Working Paper No. 24823.
Mitchell, Olivia S., James M. Poterba, Mark J. Warshawsky, and Jeffrey R. Brown. 1999. New Evidence on the Money's Worth of Individual Annuities. *The American Economic Review* 89 (5): 1299–1318.
Montgomery, Edward. 1986. Where Did All the Saving Go? A Look at the Recent Decline in the Personal Saving Rate. *Economic Inquiry* 24 (4): 681–697.
Morse, Adair, and Karen Pence. 2020. Technological Innovation and Discrimination in Household Finance. NBER Working Paper 26739.
Naoi, Michio, Yoko Moriizumi, and Norifumi Yukutake. 2013. Income Risk and Mortgage Choice among Japanese Households. *SSRN*. Accessed March 20, 2020. https://papers.ssrn.com/sol3/papers.cfm?abstract_id=2211396
Naoi, Michio, Piyush Tiwari, Yoko Moriizumi, Norifumi Yukutake, Norman Hutchison, Alla Koblyakova, and Jyoti Rao. 2019. Household Mortgage Demand: A Study of the UK, Australia and Japan. *International Journal of Housing Markets and Analysis* 12 (1): 110–130.
Peijnenburg, J.M.J., Theo Nijman, and Bas Werker. 2017. Health Cost Risk: A Potential Solution to the Annuity Puzzle. *The Economic Journal* 127: 1598–1625.
Piskorski, Tomasz, and Amit Seru. 2019. Debt Relief and Slow Recovery: A Decade after Lehman. NBER Working Paper #25403.
Piskorski, Tomasz, and Alexei Tchistyi. 2011. Stochastic House Appreciation and Optimal Mortgage Lending. *The Review of Financial Studies* 24 (5): 1407–1446.

Piskorski, Tomasz, Amit Seru, and Vikrant Vig. 2010. Securitization and Distressed Loan Renegotiation: Evidence from the Subprime Mortgage Crisis. *Journal of Financial Economics* 97 (3): 369–397.

Prelec, Drazen, and George Loewenstein. 1998. The Red and the Black: Mental Accounting of Savings and Debt. *Marketing Science* 17: 4–28.

Raghubir, Priya, and Joydeen Srivastava. 2008. Monopoly Money: The Effect of Payment Coupling and Form on Spending Behavior. *Journal of Experimental Psychology* 14 (3): 213–225.

Rajan, Raghuram G. 2010. *Fault Lines: How Hidden Fractures Still Threaten the World Economy*. Princeton, NJ: Princeton University Press.

Rampini, Adriano, and Vish S. Viswanathan. 2016. Household Risk Management. NBER Working Paper #22293.

Rha, Jong-Youn, Catherine P. Montalto, and Sherman D. Hanna. 2006. The Effect of Self-Control Mechanisms on Household Saving Behavior. *Journal of Financial Counseling and Planning* 17 (2): 3–16.

Robb, Alicia M., and David T. Robinson. 2014. The Capital Structure Decisions of New Firms. *The Review of Financial Studies* 27 (1): 153–179.

Scholnick, Barry. 2009. Credit Card Use After the Final Mortgage Payment: Does the Magnitude of Income Shocks Matter? European Central Bank Working Paper #1142.

Schuh, Scott, and Joanna Stavins. 2010. Why are (some) Consumers (Finally) Writing Fewer Checks? the Role of Payment Characteristics. *Journal of Banking and Finance* 34 (8): 1745–1758.

———. 2013. How Consumers Pay: Adoption and Use of Payments. *Accounting and Finance Research* 2 (2): 1–21.

———. 2015. How Do Speed and Security Influence Consumers' Payment Behavior? European Central Bank Working Paper Series No 1871: 1–40.

Sheffrin, Hersh M., and Richard H. Thaler. 1988. The Behavioral Life-Cycle Hypothesis. *Economic Inquiry* 26: 609–643.

Shibuya, Hiroshi. 1987. Japan's Household Saving Rate: An Application of the Life Cycle Hypothesis. International Monetary Fund Working Paper 87/15.

Shinohara, Miyohei. 1982. The Determinants of Post-War Savings Behavior in Japan. In *The Determinants of National Saving and Wealth*, ed. Modigliani Franco and Richard Hemming. London: Macmillan.

Sinai, Todd, and Nicholas S. Souleles. 2013. Can Owning a Home Hedge the Risk of Moving? *American Economic Journal: Economic Policy* 5 (2): 282–312.

Soman, Dilip. 2001. Effects of Payment Mechanism on Spending Behavior: The Role of Rehearsal and Immediacy of Payments. *Journal of Consumer Research* 27: 460–474.

Somerville, Tsuriel C., Paulina Teller, Michael Farrell, Yosh Kasahara, and Li Qiang. 2007. Do Renters Miss the boat? Homeownership, Renting, and

Wealth Accumulation. In *Household Credit Usage*, ed. Sumit Agarwal and Brent W. Ambrose, 203–217. Palgrave Macmillan.

Sommer, Kamila, and Paul Sullivan. 2018. Implications of US Tax Policy for House Prices, Rents and Home Ownership. *American Economic Review* 108 (2): 241–274.

Stango, Victor, and Jonathan Zinman. 2009. What Do Consumers Really Pay on Their Checking and Credit Card Accounts? Explicit, Implicit, and Avoidable Costs. *American Economic Review Papers and Proceedings* 99 (2): 424–429.

———. 2014. Limited and Varying Consumer Attention: Evidence from Shocks to the Salience of Bank Overdraft Fees. *The Review of Financial Studies* 27 (4): 990–1030.

Stephens, Melvin Jr. 2003. "3rd of the month": Do Social Security Recipients Smooth Consumption between Checks? *American Economic Review* 93 (1): 406–422.

———. 2006. Paycheck Receipt and the Timing of Consumption. *The Economic Journal* 116 (513): 680–701.

———. 2008. The Consumption Response to Predictable Changes in Discretionary Income: Evidence from the Repayment of Vehicle Loans. *Review of Economics and Statistics* 90: 241–252.

Stephens, Melvin Jr., and Desmond Toohey. 2018. Changes in Nutrient Intake at Retirement. NBER Working Paper #24621.

Stulz, Rene M. 2019. FinTech, BigTech and the Future of Banks. *Journal of Applied Corporate Finance* 31: 86–97.

Sturm, Peter H. 1983. Determinants of Saving: Theory and Evidence. *OECD Economic Studies* 1: 147–196.

Tanzi, Vito, and Howell H. Zee. 2000. Taxation and the Household Saving Rate: Evidence from OECD Countries. *Banca Nazionale Del Lavoro Quarterly Review* 53 (212): 31.

Thaler, Richard H. 1990. Anomalies: Saving, Fungibility and Mental Accounts. *Journal of Economic Perspectives* 4 (1): 193–205.

Thaler, Richard. 1999. Mental Accounting Matters. *Journal of Behavioral Decision Making* 12: 183–206.

Tullio, Giuseppe, and Francesco Contesso. 1986. Do After-Tax Interest Rates Affect Private Consumption and Savings? Empirical Evidence for 8 Industrial Countries: 1980–83. Economic Papers 51.

Tversky, Amos, and Daniel Kahneman. 1981. The Framing of Decisions and the Psychology of Choice. *Science* 211: 453–458.

Van Nieuwerburgh, Stijn, and Laura Veldkamp. 2010. Information Acquisition and Under-Diversification. *The Review of Economic Studies* 77 (2): 779–805.

Van Rooij, Maarten, Annamaria Lusardi, and Rob Alessie. 2011. Financial Literacy and Stock Market Participation. *Journal of Financial Economics* 101 (2): 449–472.

Vissing-Jorgensen, Annette. 2003. Perspectives on Behavioral Finance: Does "Irrationality" Disappear with Wealth? Evidence from Expectations and Actions. In *NBER Macroeconomics Annual 2003*, ed. Mark Gertler and Kenneth Rogoff. Cambridge, MA: MIT Press.

Warshawsky, Mark J. 1988. Private Annuity Markets in the United States: 1919–1984. *Journal of Risk and Insurance* 55 (3): 518–528.

———. 1997. The Market for Individual Annuities and the Reform of Social Security. *Benefits Quarterly* 13: 66–76.

Weber, Warren E. 1975. Interest Rates, Inflation and Consumer Expenditures. *American Economic Review* 65 (5): 843–858.

Wright, Colin. 1969. Saving and the Rate of Interest. In *The Taxation of Income from Capital*, ed. Arnold C. Harberger and Martin J. Bailey. Washington: The Brookings Institution.

Yermack, David. 2018. FinTech in Sub-Saharan Africa: What Has Worked Well, and What Hasn't. NBER Working Paper #25007.

Yuh, Yoonkyung, and Sherman D. Hanna. 2010. Which Households Think They Save? *The Journal of Consumer Affairs* 44 (1): 70–97.

Zahran, Sammy, Stephan Weiler, Samuel D. Brody, Michael K. Lindell, and Wesley E. Highfield. 2009. Modeling National Flood Insurance Policy Holding at the County Scale in Florida, 1999–2005. *Ecological Economics* 68 (10): 2627–2636.

Zinman, Jonathan. 2015. Household Debt: Facts, Puzzles, Theories and Policies. *Annual Review of Economics* 7: 251–276.

CHAPTER 2

Saving

1 Introduction

Saving and being prepared for times of want is wise. For centuries, people have been urged to live frugal lives. Thrift is a virtue widely encouraged. Pearls of wisdom include "A penny saved is a penny earned" and "Rather go to bed without dinner than to rise in debt" (Franklin 1963).

The spread of organized thrift, where social reformers and governments systematically champion the social virtues of prudence and self-reliance, started more recently in the eighteenth century when living standards of the masses and networks of communication have improved enabling people to learn from one another.

1.1 The Experience in Britain and Europe

The philosophy of thrift in Britain and Europe originated from a group of European philosophers who advocated for frugality in the early 1700s.

1.1.1 1700–1800s: Thrift and Individual Self-Reliance

Through his first book *An Essay Upon Projects* Daniel Defoe championed for a national insurance system in England where citizens would be assured of their basic amenities (Defoe 1999). His second book *The Complete English Tradesman* was one of the most influential books on thrift (Defoe 1726).

S. Agarwal et al., *Household Finance*,
https://doi.org/10.1007/978-981-15-5526-8_2

Another celebrated philosopher was Samuel Smiles who advocated for government intervention to encourage thrift through saving banks and school saving programs in Britain. He wrote *Self-Help* and the best seller *Thrift* (Smiles 1859, 1875).

The advent of the first post office saving bank (POSB) in Britain in 1861 (Great Britain Post Office 1911) and the school saving program in 1891 helped to cultivate the habit of saving among the rank and file (Garon 2012). The objective was to build the spirit of self-reliance.

1.1.2 1900–1940s: Thrift to Finance Infrastructure and War

In the 1900s, there arose a new motivation among European governments. The saving of the common people was used to finance national projects such as the military, urban infrastructure, education, health and welfare (Ferguson 1998).

The start of World War II saw an overheated British economy. In order to avoid hyperinflation, economists such as Keynes advocated for mandatory saving schemes. Although compulsory saving schemes did not succeed, the policy debate helped to further saving at workplaces, communities and schools to finance military efforts to expand the British Empire.

1.1.3 1940s–1960s: Restoration Through Thrift

After the war, many European economies emphasized saving among the people to fund reconstruction, generate more investments and more jobs.

Many rejected the Keynesian approach of stimulating demand through fiscal deficits.

1.1.4 From 1960s: Decline of Saving

The Europeans, mainly welfare states, were great savers. Instead of credit cards, debit cards were the norm. Homeownership was low because of the significant down payments required. Rather than real estate, Europeans invested in financial assets.

But from the 1960s, policies among the European economies began to diverge. Britain pivoted toward a consumption-driven economy. In 1986, the British finance industry underwent deregulation. Credit card debt, mortgages and home equity loans grew.

1.2 *The Experience in the US*

There was considerable exchange of ideas on thrift between Europe and US. Well-known books and guides to inculcate thrift include *Poor Richard's Almanac* by Benjamin Franklin, *Ragged Dick* by Alger and *The American Frugal Housewife* by Childs (Franklin 1963; Alger 1868; Child 1832).

1.2.1 1800s–1900s: Weak Commitment

In the early years, most commercial saving banks were in the North-eastern states of the US where commerce was vibrant. There was weak commitment to promote saving and a markedly lack of accessible saving banks.

The idea of a postal saving bank was shot down because of the fear of a drain of funds from rural communities. Finally, in 1910, postal saving offices were established to protect worried depositors after the financial panic of 1907. The deposits were left for use in the locales.

1.2.2 1930–1950: The Golden Age of Saving in the US

The golden age of saving in the US was attributed to key measures undertaken in the wake of major bank failures in 1933 and the outbreak of World War II in 1939.

One such measure was the Federal Deposit Insurance Corporation (FDIC) which was established in June 1933 to guarantee deposits in banks.

Another was the massive campaign to finance the war through payroll saving plans, school saving plans and door-to-door canvassing which very successfully revolutionized the saving behavior of the people (Garon 2012).

1.2.3 1950s: Consumption-Oriented Economics

At the end of World War II, US emerged a victorious military super power. The home front was intact with little reconstruction needed. There was no need for austerity campaigns. Saving at the workplace and at school reduced sharply.

The mean family income had shot up between 1941 and 1944. There was pent-up demand. The US economy pivoted to become more consumption oriented. Thrift was "Un-American" and old-fashioned.

1.2.4 1980s–2008: Further Collapse of Saving

The US golden age of saving ended in the 1980s. There were several contributing factors.

First, fiscal policies such as tax cuts and tax-deductibility of interest expense on home mortgages, personal loans and installment purchase promoted a consumption-driven economy. There was little incentive to save.

Although Keynes had challenged the conventional wisdom that saving was always good, he was never a champion of increased consumer spending per se. He advocated countercyclical policies in a deep recession where government should spend to stimulate production, employment and consumer demand. However, he also said that it was "quite right" for households to save more in boom times and especially during war times.

Similarly, John Kenneth Galbraith's The Affluent Society (1958) and Van Packard's The Hidden Persuaders (1957) were of the view that a consumption-driven economy is unsustainable.

Second, consumers had no qualms about buying big-ticket items on installment credit. However, some argued that installment credit had a disciplinary saving effect as households had to abide by some payment schemes and consumer durables might be considered as assets under the category of household saving.

Third, cheap financing encouraged households to build bigger homes. The incentive structure of affordable home mortgages and tax breaks encourage households to put the bulk of their wealth into houses instead of diversifying across asset classes.

Fourth, the structure of retirement saving plans induced the affluent to save but not so much the lower- and middle-income workers.

Fifth, financial deregulation in the early 1980s ended interest rate caps. Saving and Loan Associations (S&Ls) could pay market rates on deposits and make risky loans. Credit card companies expanded aggressively. The securitization of mortgage enabled lenders to offload risky loans and use the money to grant more loans.

Sixth, sweeping tax reforms were passed in 1986. Interest expense on home mortgages remained tax deductible (which promoted borrowing for purchase of homes). Deductibility of interest expense on installment purchases, credit cards, personal loans and student loans were removed (which discouraged borrowing). However, interest expense on home equity loans became tax deductible (which encouraged borrowing against home equity). Financial institutions started to offer loans secured by home equity at half the interest rates of credit cards. Homeowners tapped on home equity to pay for frivolous expenditures which quickly depleted their assets.

Seventh, the democratization of credit removed policies that denied credit to single and divorced women, expanded lending to lower-income class families (Community Reinvestment Act of 1977), removed discrimination against African Americans and minorities and promoted homeownership among lower-income residential districts. The spirit behind democratization of credit was to remove unfair bias and discrimination, but the lack of financial regulation resulted in over-extension of credit.

The final contributing factor to the collapse of saving was the decline in household income. From 1970, the growth in household income slowed and during the 1990s, jobless recovery (economy experienced growth but level of employment decreased) occurred.

From a respectable 7% in the 1990s, the saving rate fell to a record low of 2.2% in July 2005 (Garon 2012).

1.2.5 After 2008: Post Financial Crisis

Households struggled to rebuild their wealth in the post-crisis period. US leaders announced a new agenda which called for the people to go back to "saving their pennies to buy their dream house".

Keynes advocated that, in a sluggish economy, countercyclical measures should be used to stimulate production and employment. Was the message from the US leaders to save counter-intuitive?

No, it was not counter-intuitive because Keynes called upon the government to run a deficit to stimulate the economy, not the people on the streets. Financially embattled households should be encouraged to save and pay down their debts so that they do not become a burden to society. Once they manage to have adequate saving, they can do their part to increase consumer demand.

1.3 The Experience in Asia

Many of the European powers introduced the concept of postal saving to their colonies in Asia.

After independence from colonial rule, the POSB in various colonies evolved in different directions. Some became National Saving Banks (e.g., in Malaysia, Singapore and Sri Lanka), while others served as agencies of National Saving Organizations (e.g., in Bangladesh and India).

1.3.1 Indonesia

Indonesia was a colony of the Dutch. The postal saving service began with the establishment of the Postspaarbank (Dutch name for POSB) in 1897. Under Japanese occupation during World War II from 1942 to 1945, the renamed Saving Office was used to raise funds to support the Greater East Asia War.

After the Dutch's recognition of Indonesian sovereignty in 1949, the Saving Office was renamed Bank Tabungan Pos. In 1963, it became known as Bank Tabungan Negara (BTN) which meant "State Saving Bank". BTN was the first bank to provide mortgage financing to the lower- and middle-income households. In 2009, BTN was listed on the Indonesian Stock Exchange.

1.3.2 Philippines

The Philippines established postal saving in 1906 under the US-appointed Civil Governor William Howard Taft, who was later elected US president. The postal saving system was crippled during the Japanese occupation from 1942 to 1944 but resumed operations in 1946 and functioned until 1976, when fierce competition from private banks resulted in its demise.

In 1994, the Philippine Postal Bank was re-established on the condition that it did not "unduly compete with rural, commercial or universal banks" (Scher and Yoshino 2004). It was organized as a credit granting and deposit taking thrift bank with high reserve requirements. Its main products included credit facilities in the countryside and remittance services for Overseas Filipino Workers.

1.3.3 India

India was under British rule from 1757 to 1947. It was the British who introduced postal saving to India. The POSB opened its first branch in 1882. Its fundamental role was to encourage thrift and take in small deposits.

After India gained independence in 1947, the POSB came under the National Saving Organization (NSO). In 2003, the NSO was renamed National Saving Institute (NSI). All the mobilized saving were controlled by the Ministry of Finance, with some loaned to state governments for developmental purposes for up to 25 years (Scher and Yoshino 2004).

In order to maintain steady collections, the POSB marketed its products and services through diverse strategies.

In 1972, it introduced a Women's Local Area Saving Plan to educate housewives on thrift and subsequently recruited them as agents to secure deposits from small investors.

Cooperative societies, social service organizations, universities and local institutions were authorized to collect deposits on its behalf in return for commissions.

It also started a Pay Roll Saving Group Plan where a fixed amount was automatically deducted from the employee's paycheck every month.

Over the years, the POSB has become a provider of diversified financial services ranging from deposits, saving certificates, payroll saving, mutual funds, international money transfer, currency exchange, electronic funds transfer, electronic banking and insurance products.

The Indian postal saving network is one of the most extensive with close to 90% situated in rural areas. Although the ratio of rural to urban deposits is low, the POSB has an advantage in terms of branch network and reach.

1.3.4 Singapore

Singapore was a British colony from 1819 to 1942. During World War II, it was occupied by the Japanese Empire from 1942 to 1945. When the Japanese Empire surrendered to the Allies at the end of World War II, Singapore was returned to the British and became a Crown Colony from 1946 to 1963.

1870–1940: Building a POSB

The British introduced the POSB to Singapore in 1877. The impetus came from the lack of banking facilities during the pioneering years.

Despite being constrained to a single office, the POSB grew steadily from 1877 to 1890. The amount of deposits increased from S$19,862 to S$95,655 with the number of depositors increasing from 211 to 676 (Consulton Research Bureau 1977). The majority of depositors during this period were European residents and Eurasians.

In 1902, the Singapore POSB was combined with those in Penang and Malacca to become the Straits Settlement POSB. By 1940, the amount of deposits had increased to S$14.3 million and the number of accounts to 57,674 (Consulton Research Bureau 1977).

1940–1945: Japanese Model of Thrift

The Japanese occupied Singapore from 1942 to 1945. During this time, they implemented saving campaigns in schools and among the public. This led to further expansion of the postal saving system in Singapore. Although Allied Forces took back Singapore from the Japanese after World War II, the Japanese's model of mobilizing domestic saving to overcome resource limitation left a lasting impression.

After Japanese Occupation: Independence

In 1949, the POSB was re-established as a separate saving bank for Singapore only. In 1951, the Singapore POSB had 74,246 accounts with deposits totaling S$27.4 million. By 1955, there were 154,668 accounts with S$57.6 million in deposits (Consulton Research Bureau 1977).

However, the deposits began to decrease after 1957. By the end of 1966, total deposits stood at S$37.4 million. The decreasing trend caught the attention of the then Minister of Finance, Goh Keng Swee, who appointed a committee to review the issue. Several new saving campaigns were implemented such as lucky draws, the enabling of signatures in all languages and exemption of interest revenue from tax. The people managed to save higher percentages of their income even after making the mandatory contributions to the Central Provident Fund (CPF). A more detailed description of the CPF is available in the Appendix to this chapter.

Funds from both the POSB and the CPF were channeled into developmental projects. Goh Keng Swee attributed the rapid growth of Singapore in the late 1960s to the high domestic saving rate (Goh 1995).

In 1972, the POSB ceased operating as a postal service and became a key saving institution. It underwent a major revamp and refurbishment of physical and technological facilities. In 1974, the POSB installed online terminals at physical branches. Various schemes such as automated payment services and Save-As-You-Earn (SAYE) accounts were used to target wage earners. In addition, its subsidiary Credit POSB was launched to encourage homeownership through low-interest rate loans with longer repayment periods. In 1974, the Ministry of Finance took over the running of the POSB.

In the late 1960s and early 1970s, nationwide school saving competitions were held to encourage saving with the POSB. Prizes were awarded to the schools with the highest average saving per student each year. In 1983, these annual saving competitions were adapted in favor of a single designated month for saving. In the same year, the mascot Smiley the

Squirrel was introduced. The squirrel known for its habit of storing food for rainy days was chosen to inspire students to save in a less competitive fashion. Smiley, the mascot, continued to be featured on POSB publicity materials in the 1980s and 1990s.

In the 1980s, the question of over-saving was discussed after Singapore experienced a recession in 1985 while saving continued to increase. A study group headed by the National University of Singapore recommended changes to the CPF. They argued that after provisions for housing and health, the 50% contribution rate to the CPF was too high (Lim 1986). In 1986 and 1987, the CPF contribution rate was lowered. Other empirical studies have supported this conclusion of over-saving. Young (1992) finds that despite Singapore having a higher proportion of saving, both Singapore and Hong Kong had similar growth during this period. His results support the reduction of the CPF contribution rate.

In March 1990, the POSB was renamed POSBank. In 1996, the saving programs targeted at kids expanded to include the First Account program where all newborns were automatically given a bank account with S$1 credit. In 1998, it was further expanded to include all students enrolled in primary schools. In November 1998, POSBank was acquired by a local commercial bank, DBS Bank.

1.3.5 Japan

Due to the *Sakoku* ("closed country") policy from the early 1600s to the 1850s, Japan developed its own concept of thrift.

Early 1880s: Thrift Philosopher

The Japanese role model of diligence, thrift and filial piety was Ninomiya Kinjiro. His teachings of planning (hotoku) and saving with the aim of relieving the poor and sick, contributing to the community and paying taxes were often cited by the authorities (Garon 2012).

1880s–1940s: Thrift as a National Duty

After the 1868 Meiji Restoration, Japanese leaders scoured for leading models of saving that could be adapted to Japan.

In 1872, Samuel Smiles' *Self-Help* was adopted as an approved textbook. The Japanese postal saving system, modeled after the British, was established in 1874. The postal deposits were used to fund public capital investment and the wars.

Japan emerged victorious and prosperous from World War I which lasted from 1914 to 1918. The economy surged in the 1920s but Japanese officials continued to promote thrift as a form of national duty.

Japan took over Manchuria in 1931–1932 and started the China War in 1937. In World War II, Japan attacked European colonies in the Far East. To finance the war, villages and cities were given saving targets and workplace saving programs were put in place.

1940s–1980s: Restoring Japan Through Thrift

Japan's defeat in 1945 and the subsequent inflation destroyed the value of saving in the supposedly guaranteed postal saving system.

From 1945 to 1951, Japan came under the control of the Allied Powers. Japanese leaders urged the people to exercise austerity and save as a form of patriotism as Japan readied itself for independence. In 1952, Allied Occupation ended but the drive to save continued.

As the Japanese economy grew in the 1950s, the proportion of saving increased. While US favored the route of mass consumption, the Japanese favored saving as the way to generate growth.

Saving has become part and parcel of life in Japan. Some attributed it to the salary bonus system; others thought that policies and persuasion played a part; still others believed that culture had a role, and some suggested that the support of political parties and popular organizations helped the cause.

1980s–1990s: Japan's Peak in Thrift and Consumption

In the 1980s, Japan became a role model for the world. High saving and low inflation propelled industrial expansion. US, on the other hand, experienced sluggish saving and investment. Japan's high trade surpluses was a sore point.

Fortunes were turned in 1990 when the Japanese asset price bubble burst. For a decade, Japan experienced little to no growth. The US economy, on the other hand, enjoyed an economic boom amidst financial deregulation and credit expansion.

After 1999, Japan saw a decline in household saving. There were several reasons for this. First, the near zero interest rate was unattractive. Second, income had declined. Third, the population was fast aging.

In 2001, the Japanese government shifted its focus from saving to financial instruments such as stocks, credit cards and derivatives. But the 2008 crisis saw a retreat from the stock market. Although the saving rate had declined, Japan remained ahead of many in terms of net financial assets and wealth (Garon 2012).

1.3.6 Korea

Japan took over Korea from 1905 until the end of World War II in 1945. The Japanese government invested much in Korea in the form of infrastructural development and facilitated on-the-job training for workers, farmers, technicians and military officers.

1905 to 1945: Domestic Saving

The Japanese government introduced the Postal Saving System to the Koreans in 1910 and launched the Saving Bank of Korea in 1928 to collect the small saving of the ordinary people (Chung 2006).

When Japan started its aggressive military campaign in Asia in 1937, Korean households were urged to reduce consumption and later to buy saving bonds.

1950 to 1953: Korean War

After independence from the Japanese, the new regime further ingrained the habit of saving at postal offices. The start of the Korean War between the north (aided by China) and the south (aided by the United Nations with US as the principal participant) in 1950 led to the revival of harsh war saving campaigns.

1954 to 1997: Aftermath of the Korean War

In the aftermath of the Korean War, the South Korean economy floundered. A military coup in 1961 by a Japanese-trained Korean general, Park Chung-hee, mobilized the economy. The new leader re-established diplomatic relations with Japan and promoted domestic saving to finance high growth export-led development (Scher and Yoshino 2004). Household saving rates rose.

1997 to Present: Asian Financial Crisis

The currency cum banking crisis in late 1997 hit South Korea hard. South Korea sought official assistance from the International Monetary Fund to avoid a sovereign default. The US government played a role in helping South Korea resume stability.

In the years following the crisis, South Korea embraced a more consumption-driven economy. The economy revived in 2001 and 2002 on the back of more debt and consumption.

1.3.7 China

In 1919, China Post started postal saving under the Postal Services and Remittance Bureau. During the Chinese Communist Revolution in 1949, China Post was closed. From the 1950s to 1970s, Chinese households saved almost nothing.

The regime eliminated all banks and transferred the assets to the Central People's Bank of China. Household saving rates fell below 1%. Under Communist rule, housing, education, pension and medical services were provided by the government. Goods were in short supply. Any saving was due to unsatisfied consumption (Cristadoro and Marconi 2012).

1980s: Saving Boom

In 1978, plans were made to open up the Chinese economy but for the reform to happen, massive funding was required. The Chinese leaders reopened the postal saving system in 1986 after a 33-year break.

Competing with the postal saving system for retail deposits were the four large state-owned banks, namely, the Industrial and Commercial Bank of China (ICBC), the Agricultural Bank of China (ABC), China Construction Bank (CCB) and the Bank of China (BOC).

Postal saving services were provided by post offices, many of which were situated in far flung rural areas, greatly exceeding the reach of commercial banks. After 1995, depositors at postal services could make withdrawals anywhere in the country. Postal deposits experienced remarkable growth.

The efforts of the Chinese leaders to promote saving was immensely successful. China remained a high-saving society for many years.

1.4 Conclusion of Historical Review

This historical review of organized thrift highlights various economic, social and cultural dimensions under which domestic savings were mobilized. It presents an opportunity to compare and contrast the consequences of a saving-driven economy versus a consumption-driven economy, the ways in which people react to certain policies and the institutional efficiency and effectiveness in galvanizing people to conscientiously set aside funds for specific purposes.

2 Theory

Saving is a key aspect of most economic models that attempt to describe macroeconomic behavior. However, distinct economic models operate under different sets of assumptions which in turn affect how saving is determined. Generally, saving is understood as a transfer of money from households to businesses in the circular flow of income.

In this section, we compare the determination of saving under the Classical, Keynesian and ISLM models.

2.1 Classical Model

The Classical model is rooted in laissez-faire. It suggests that the market can self-regulate and require little government intervention. It is most often associated with the "invisible hand" (Smith 1776). Within classical economics, there exist households and businesses in a circular flow of income (see Fig. 2.1).

The lower loops show the exchange of goods and services between households and businesses for money. The upper loops show the transfer of land, labor and capital between households and businesses for rents, wages, interests and profits. In this model, market equilibrium occurs when the economy is in full employment.

The classical model accounts for both saving and investment in its analysis of the credit or loanable funds market. Any income not spent is saved

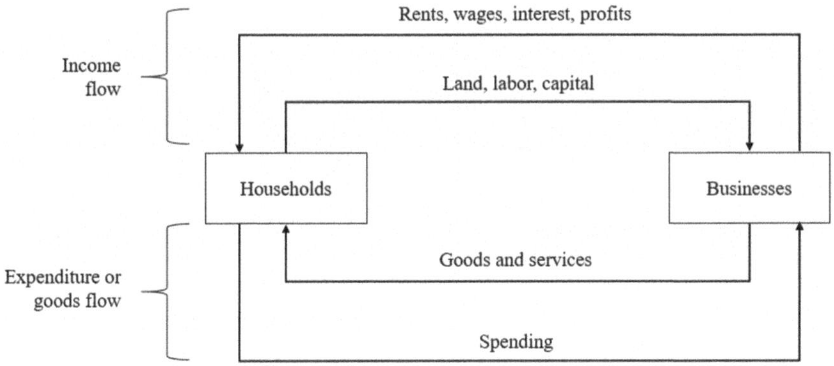

Fig. 2.1 Circular flow of income

by households and will flow into the business sector as investment through the credit or loanable funds market.

The classical model assumes that saving and investment are functions of the rate of interest. Specifically, within the market for loanable funds, there is a transfer of saving from households to businesses. Saving (S) is income (Y) that is not spent where:

$$Y = C + S$$

Saving represent the supply of loanable funds available while investment represent the demand for these loanable funds.

Saving is an increasing function of the interest rate as households are incentivized to save more at higher interest rates. Investment is a decreasing function of the interest rate because businesses are less willing to borrow at higher interest rates (see Fig. 2.2).

Together, the two functions determine the equilibrium level of saving and the rate of interest. At market equilibrium, the amount of saving is equal to the amount of investment. Given that saving is equivalent to total income less expenditures, it is helpful to remember that at equilibrium,

Fig. 2.2 Classical model of saving

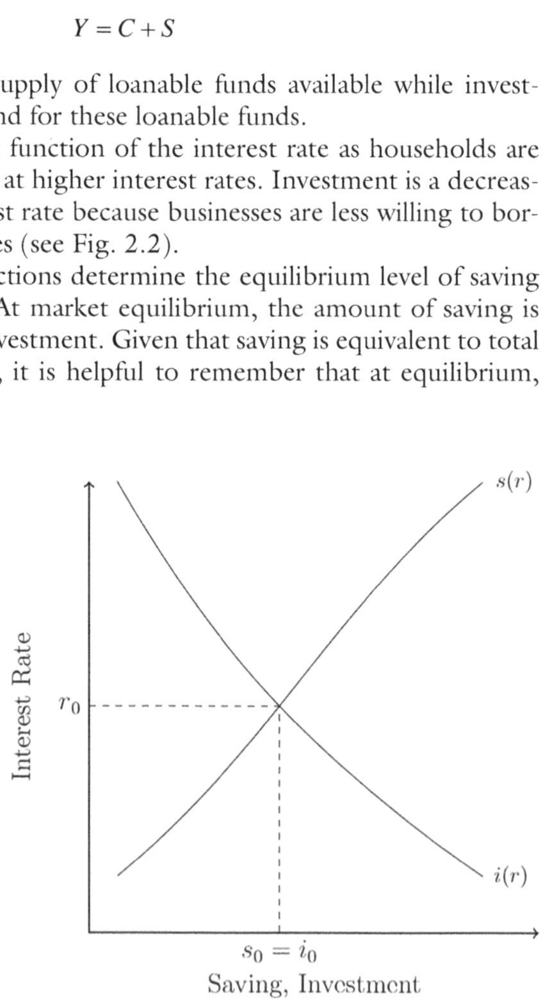

what is saved by some flows into the loanable funds market where it is borrowed and spent by others.

2.2 Keynesian Saving Function

In contrast to the Classical model, Keynes (1936) proposed that market equilibrium occurs when aggregate demand is equal to aggregate supply. This suggests that market equilibrium need not only occur at full employment.

According to Keynesian theory, saving and consumption are based on changes in income, whereas in Classical theory, they are based on changes in interest rates. Keynes considered his explanation more intuitive, for example, a consumer's decision to buy a phone is more likely driven by his income than the current interest rate.

In the simplified version of the Keynesian model, disposable income is the main determinant of saving and consumption. People pay for food, housing and other expenditures and save whatever is left for future use. Disposable income (Y_d) is income after tax.

$$Y_d = C + S,$$

where Y_d is disposable personal income, S is personal saving and C is personal consumption of individuals.

Keynes argued that people are "disposed to increase their consumption as their income increases". Thus, consumption is a function of disposable income.

$$C = f(Y_d)$$

Given that saving is the part of disposable income that is not spent on consumption, saving also increases with disposable income (see Fig. 2.3).

$$S = f(Y_d)$$

The mechanism by which saving and investment is reached in market equilibrium also differs in the Keynesian model. If investment is greater

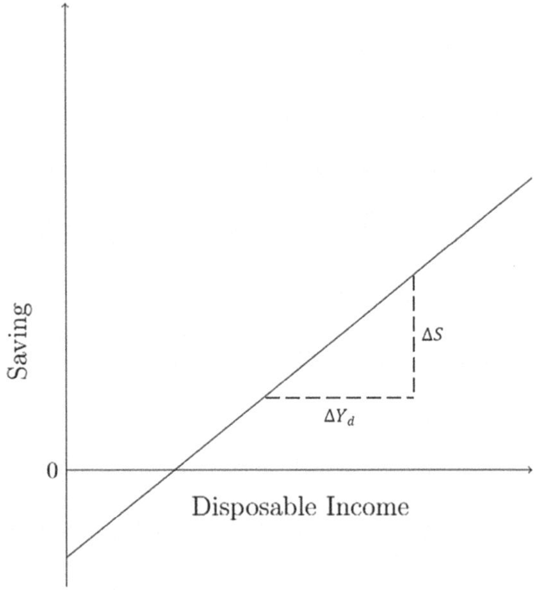

Fig. 2.3 Keynesian saving function

than saving, the increased investment will lead to higher income, which will raise both consumption and saving until equilibrium is achieved.

The Keynesian model characterizes other aspects of saving behavior such as the proportion of income saved and how saving changes with income. The marginal propensity to save (MPS) is the ratio of the change in saving to the change in disposable personal income.

$$\mathrm{MPS} = \frac{\Delta S}{\Delta Y_d}$$

The average propensity to save (APS) is the ratio of total saving to total income. It describes the proportion of income saved.

$$\mathrm{APS} = \frac{S}{Y_d}$$

If consumption exceeds disposable income, APS is negative. If consumption equals disposable income, APS is zero. APS will tend to rise when disposable income increases.

Keynes believed that the MPS is strictly positive and less than one. In addition, the APS always has to be less than the MPS. Keynes explained that the "fundamental psychological law, upon which we are entitled to depend with great confidence both a priori from our knowledge of human nature and from the detailed facts of experience, is that men are disposed, as a rule and on the average, to increase their consumption as their income increases, but not by as much as the increase in their income" (Keynes 1936).

These assumptions about the MPS and APS have important implications for saving behavior. For example, at very low levels of disposable income, consumption can exceed disposable income such that saving is negative. Given that the MPS has to be strictly positive, the lowest value of the MPS is zero when disposable income is very low. Since APS must be less than the MPS based on Keynesian assumptions, APS will be negative when MPS is zero which implies that consumers dissave. Thus, this would suggest that at low levels of disposable income, saving becomes negative.

These assumptions about MPS and APS were explored in many empirical studies and led to the advancement and understanding of saving behavior.

2.3 ISLM Model

Hicks (1937) developed the ISLM (investment-saving liquidity preference money) supply model to summarize Keynes' General Theory. The ISLM model draws an explicit link between saving and consumption from Keynesian economics together with supply and demand in the market for goods and services.

The downward sloping investment-saving curve (IS) represents all combinations of income and real interest rate where the goods market is in equilibrium (see Fig. 2.4). The liquidity preference money supply (LM) curve shows how the goods market interacts with the loanable funds market. Given that the IS curve describes saving in an economy, the remainder of this section will focus on the derivation of the IS curve.

Assume the simplest Keynesian model with two sectors in the economy, namely, the household sector and the business sector. Total spending by

Fig. 2.4 ISLM function

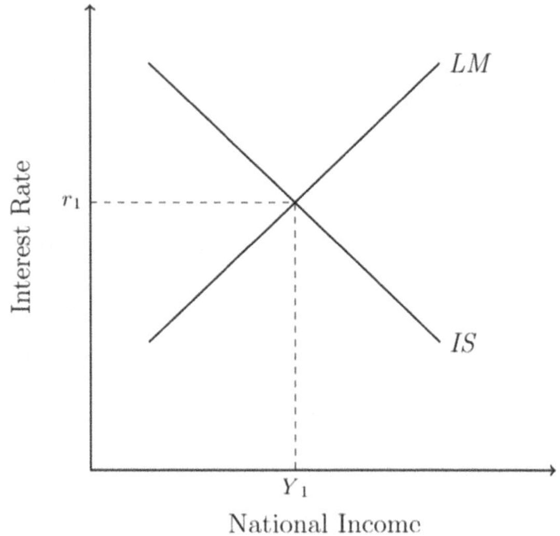

households is consumption (C) and total spending by businesses on plants, equipment and inventories is investment (I). The sum of consumption and investment makes up aggregate expenditure (AE) for goods and services.

$$AE = C + I$$

Similar to the previous models, what is spent by one party is received as income by the counterparty. Thus, AE is equivalent to income (Y) as measured by the sum of consumption (C) and saving (S).

$$Y = C + S$$

In this simplest two-sector economy, investment is a function of income. As the economy grows, businesses will increase their level of investment. Investment decisions also depend on factors such as interest rates, expected inflation and expected profits.

At market equilibrium, the aggregate expenditure (AE) is equal to the income (Y) earned. By putting these two equations together, saving must thus be equal to investment.

$$AE = Y$$
$$C + I = C + S$$
$$I = S$$

The ISLM model enables us to make an explicit link between interest rate, saving and income. If interest rate decreases from r_0 to r_1, businesses will increase their investment from I_0 to I_1 (see Fig. 2.5).

This will cause aggregate expenditure to increase from $AE_0 = C + I_0$ to $AE_1 = C + I_1$, the new equilibrium to move from P_0 to P_1 and income to increase from Y_0 to Y_1 (see Fig. 2.6).

At the equilibrium P_1, the aggregate expenditure AE_1 intersects the income line:

$$AE_1 = C + I_1$$
$$Y_1 = C + S_1$$

Putting the two equations together shows that in the two-sector Keynesian model, the only leakage saving must equal the only injection, investment.

Fig. 2.5 Loanable funds market (rate of interest, planned investments)

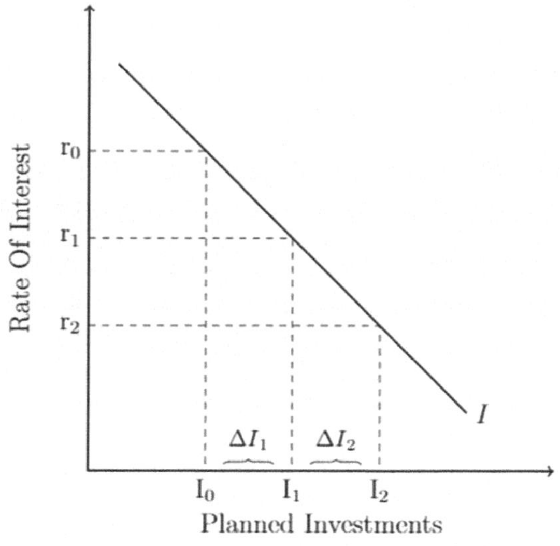

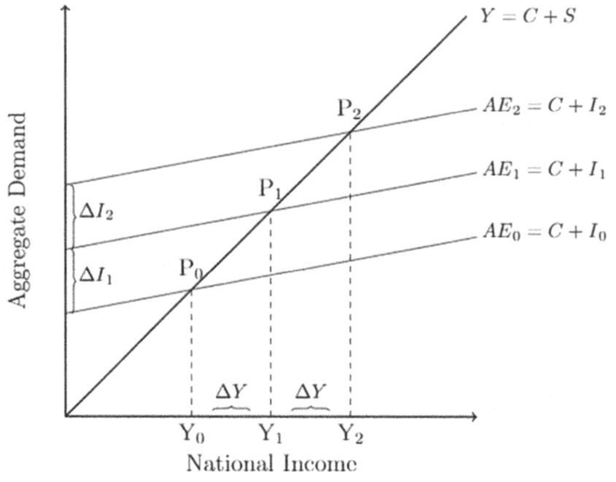

Fig. 2.6 Goods market (aggregate demand, national income)

$$S_1 = I_1$$

In other words, income is at the equilibrium level for a given interest rate when household saving equal investment. Thus, the 45-degree line in Fig. 2.6 is used to reference the different possibilities of market equilibrium in the goods market. This 45-degree line is also known as the Keynesian cross.

In short, as interest rate decreases from r_0 to r_1, income in the goods market increases from Y_0 to Y_1, the new equilibrium moves from A to B (see Fig. 2.7). This is the downward sloping investment-saving (IS) curve which represents the equilibrium in the goods market where aggregate demand is equal to income.

2.3.1 *Early Tests of Keynes' Saving Function*

Initial studies find evidences that support Keynes' saving function: saving rises with income, MPS is less than one and APS rises with income. Most of these initial studies explicitly assume that saving depends on disposable income in the same period. The simple Keynesian model emphasizes the contemporaneous relationship between income and saving.

However, empirical evidences soon show a conflict in the long-run and short-run relationship. There is no rise in the APS as income rises over time (Clark 1945).

Fig. 2.7 Investment-saving (IS) model

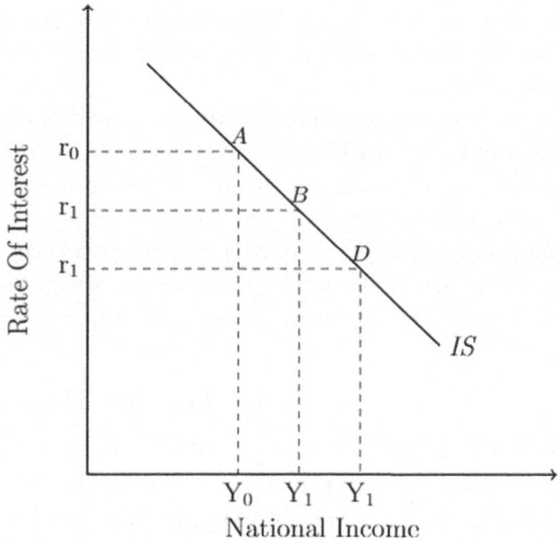

Following these early tests, alternative theories emerged to try and explain saving behavior. In the discussion below, there is no attempt to distinguish between an individual and a household.

2.4 *Permanent Income Hypothesis*

The models of early Keynesian and Classical economists focus on income in a single discrete period. In contrast, Friedman (1957) introduces the permanent income hypothesis (PIH) where saving in any period is determined not by the current level of income, but by the long-term expected income (permanent income).

The PIH is based on two premises: (1) individuals wish to equate their expected marginal utility of consumption across time and (2) individuals are able to respond to income changes by saving and dissaving. They attempt to smooth their consumption over time subject to the inter-temporal or long-term budget constraint. The horizon is infinite in that the stream of income extends beyond the household's lifetime (Hayashi 1997).

The proportion of permanent income saved depends on (1) the rate of interest, (2) the fraction of human wealth and nonhuman wealth in the household's future income and (3) the desire to add to one's wealth. Human wealth refers to the present discounted value of expected future income derived from selling household's labor services. Nonhuman wealth comprises equity shares and tangible assets such as consumer durables and real estate.

As borrowing based on human wealth is more difficult to obtain, the need of saving for future emergencies will be greater the larger the proportion of income in the form of human wealth.

Friedman (1957) argues that transitory income, being temporary in nature, is not likely to have much effect on consumption, that is, the marginal propensity to consume out of transitory income is zero and therefore the marginal propensity to save out of transitory income is one.

2.5 Life Cycle Hypothesis

Modigliani and Brumberg's (1954) theory of the life cycle hypothesis is complementary to the PIH by Friedman (1957). Under PIH, the consumer plans over an infinite period of time. Under the life cycle hypothesis, consumption and saving in any period is determined not just by current income in that period but by lifetime expected income and wealth. Both formulations, PIH and life cycle hypothesis, assume a forward-looking consumer who is certain about the future with point expectations about future income.

According to the life cycle model, lifetime saving has an inverted U-shape (see Fig. 2.8).

The key motivation to save is ultimately to accumulate resources for later consumption. The life cycle hypothesis assumes that saving over the entire lifetime will eventually be spent with no bequests.

The fraction of income saved varies over the individual's lifetime. In his younger years, his consumption is higher than his income. He experiences dissaving, that is, he borrows to fund his consumption. In his working years, his income is higher than his consumption and he starts to save and accumulate wealth for future needs. In his retirement years, his consumption exceeds his income again and as before he experiences dissaving.

2.5.1 Can Life Cycle/Permanent Income Hypothesis Be Applied to Developing Economies?

The life cycle and permanent income theories may be of less relevance in developing economies for several reasons (Deaton 1989).

First, households in developing economies tend to be large and poor. They typically comprise several generations living together. Therefore, it

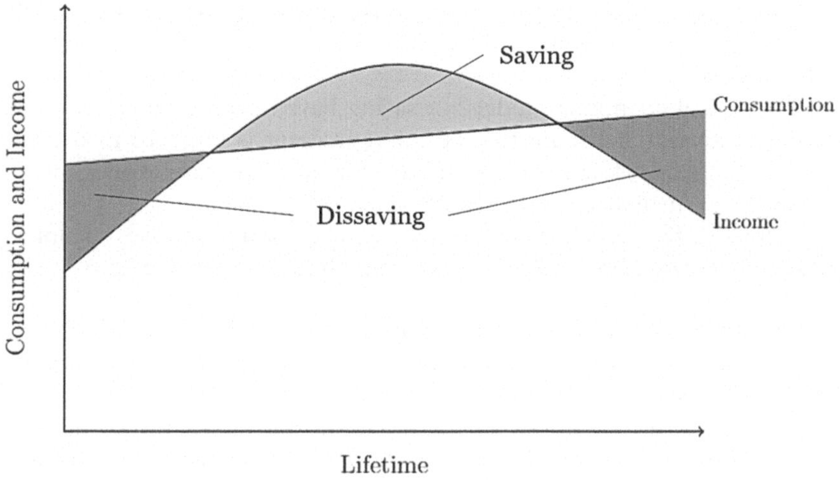

Fig. 2.8 Inverted U-shaped lifetime saving

may not be necessary to save for retirement. Second, uncertain income makes projection of future cash flows difficult. Third, there may be binding credit constraints for the younger households.

Deaton (1989) is of the view that saving in developing economies should be studied separately from saving in developed economies. Households in developing economies save in order to smooth consumption, rather than to accumulate for retirement.

3 Motives of Saving

Keynes (1936) enumerated a list of eight saving motives, some of which are complementary and most of which relate to future consumption needs. They are the inter-temporal substitution motive (to decide between immediate consumption and consumption at a later date), the life cycle motive (to provide for future needs of an individual including retirement), the precautionary motive (to build reserve against unforeseen contingencies such as job loss, illness or accident), the independence motive (to enjoy a sense of independence and the power to do things), the improvement motive (to enjoy an increasing expenditure), the enterprise motive (to secure enough for business projects), the bequest motive (to bequeath to heirs) and the avarice motive (to satisfy pure miserliness).

Browning and Lusardi (1996) added the down payment motive which is to accumulate funds to buy big-ticket items such as houses, cars and other durables.

Theoretical economic models for saving have intrinsic retirement and saving motives. The desire to save for retirement is inherent in the life cycle hypothesis, while the desire to save for the next generation is inherent in the permanent income hypothesis.

Katona (1975) argues that there are six main saving motives spanning emergencies, retirement, children's needs, housing, durable goods and vacations.

Sturm (1983) has a hierarchical approach to saving motives with the desire to save for old age as a primary motive before precautionary, bequest and targeted saving motives.

Lindqvist (1981) argues that there is a hierarchy among the different saving motives. Interestingly, his research finds that financial liquidity and saving for emergencies have priority over saving for old age. However, according to studies that ask respondents to declare their saving motives, retirement motive is the most commonly cited followed by precautionary motive (Katona 1975; Horioka and Watanabe 1997; Lee and Hanna 2015; Xiao and Fan 2002).

Nava et al. (2006) use information from a saving commitment product in a rural Philippines bank to demonstrate how the design of a saving product can significantly affect the type of clients and the amount of saving. Those who opened the Save, Earn, Enjoy Deposits (SEED) account were found to increase their saving after 12 months by 337%. The respondents were asked to state their purpose for saving; 48% stated they were saving for a celebration, 21% for tuition and education and 20% for investments. The study concludes that targeted and specialized products with appropriate and client-focused design are important in mobilizing saving.

Fisher and Anong (2012) examine the impact of saving motive on the consumption and saving patterns of individuals. They find that those with a retirement motive are likely to save more regularly than those with a precautionary motive.

Lee and Hanna (2015) find that households are more likely to save if they have self-actualization and retirement saving goals. These findings support the view that saving motives and saving outcomes are related (Schunk 2009). There is a strong justification, policy wise, to enhance public awareness of the need to save for their retirement needs.

3.1 Inter-temporal Substitution Motive

In the life cycle and permanent income hypothesis, fully rational and forward-looking individuals decide how much to consume based on their total lifetime resources available. They smooth their consumption by borrowing in periods where they have little income and saving in periods where they have higher income, setting aside funds for when they stop working. The main emphasis is the retirement motive of saving.

However, when confronted with data, the basic formulation of the life cycle or PIH cannot explain the sensitivity of consumption to anticipated changes in income.

The voluminous literature on consumption and saving is evidence of the considerable effort in incorporating extensions to the standard model.

3.2 Precautionary Motive

When faced with uncertainty regarding their income, healthcare needs and life span, households save to cushion unexpected events (e.g., unemployment risk), sudden unforeseen expenditures (e.g., health risk) and imperfect annuity markets (e.g., longevity risk) (Hubbard et al. 1995).

In a perfect market setting, households can borrow, lend and smooth resources over their lifetime seamlessly without incurring transaction costs and at a constant interest rate. In practice, households often face liquidity constraints. Even in countries with developed financial systems, young households and low-income households face borrowing constraints. Deaton (1991) and Browning and Lusardi (1996) argue that the presence of liquidity constraints serves to reinforce the precautionary motive of saving. Liquidity constrained households take measures to accumulate assets in good times to meet consumption needs during bad times.

When these liquidity constraints are relaxed, there is less need to save. For example, households receiving overseas remittances invest more (Acosta et al. 2007) and households with better access to credit save less (Butelmann and Gallego 2001).

3.3 Bequest Motive

The evidence that older households continue to save after retirement and retired households have the propensity to hold on to their saving is consistent with the bequest motive (Kotlikoff 1988; Browning and Lusardi 1996; Coleman 1998; Chamon and Prasad 2010).

Horioka (1984) observes that, in Japan, a large percentage of elderly live with their children under the same roof. The children care for them and in return receive a bequest upon their death. In this way, the risk of not having sufficient retirement saving is transferred to their children, who act like insurance agents. This Japanese model is similar to a private pension plan where the bequest is payment for previous services rendered (Ando and Kennickell 1987; Shibuya 1987). The question arises as to why Japanese families enter into such intergenerational arrangements when they could simply buy annuities from insurance companies. The answer appears to be the high price of residences, which makes it economically appealing for the elderly to dwell with their children (Ando and Kennickell 1987).

Dynan et al. (2002) argue that the precautionary life cycle motive and the bequest motive are not mutually exclusive. A dollar of saving can simultaneously serve the precautionary motive and the bequest motive if future contingencies are not as bad as expected and there is money remaining.

4 Factors Affecting Saving

The decision to save is influenced by a host of factors, including institutional, demographic and socio-economic characteristics, for example, the availability of credit, cost of credit, attitude toward debt, demographic age structure, life expectancy, retirement age, family size, saving incentives and investment incentives. In addition, government policies and interventions can affect these factors and alter the saving rate.

4.1 Interest Rate and Saving

There is no fixed relationship between an exogenous change in the interest rate and its impact on saving. This is because a change in the interest rate can affect household saving through the income effect and the substitution effect.

The income effect focuses on how an increase in interest rate reduces saving. The increase in interest rate is seen as an increase in income which reduces the need to save. The substitution effect focuses on how an increase in interest rate leads to a greater desire to save because the opportunity cost for consumption increases. The change in the saving rate that is observed depends on which effect is more dominant.

Generally, there is consensus that a significant relationship exists between the change in interest rate and saving (Wright 1969; Blinder 1975), but the sign of the relationship remains unclear.

4.1.1 Income Effect

Using US data from 1930 to 1965, Weber (1975) finds that the income effect is greater than the substitution effect. An increase in interest rate leads to less saving because individuals can maintain the same level of consumption in the future without saving as much today.

Similarly, Friend and Hasbrouck (1983) note that an increase in the real return increases consumption. Shibuya (1987) finds consistent evidence using Japanese data where capital losses and negative real interest rates led to sharp increases in saving after the 1975 oil crisis.

However, Howrey and Hymans (1978) observe that saving cannot be easily manipulated by policies changing the after-tax rate of return. Hendershott and Peek (1985) also find that the after-tax rate of return does not directly impact saving. Baum (1988) finds that the real rate of interest does not have a significant effect on consumption and saving. Summers et al. (1987) notes that huge rises in rate of interest in the 1980s did not increase private saving.

Using pension withdrawal data from Singapore, Agarwal et al. (2020) find that saving-consumption behavior does not seem to be driven by the rate of return. In Singapore, citizens at age 55 can withdraw some saving from their pension account after setting aside a minimum sum. Despite the pension account having a significantly higher interest rate of 2.5% to 4% per annum, Singaporeans park their withdrawn saving in low-interest bank accounts and choose to forego the higher interest rate that they could have by leaving the funds in their pension accounts. Further analysis shows a modest increase in total card spending (see Fig. 2.9a) with bank account balances declining by one-third at the end of 12 months (see Fig. 2.9b).

The increase in disposable income was also used to reduce credit card debt (see Fig. 2.9c).

In addition, liquidity constrained individuals (those who are in the bottom tercile based on their beginning account balance) are more likely to increase their spending than unconstrained individuals (those who are in the top tercile based on their beginning account balance).

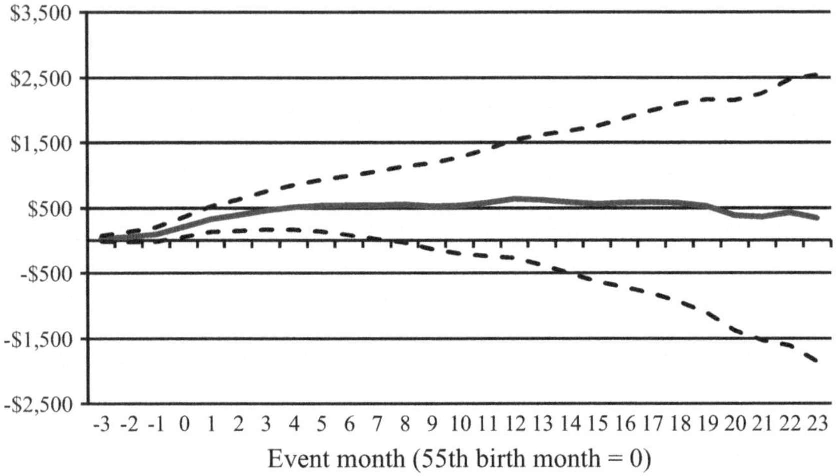

Fig. 2.9a Predicted change in total card spending after age 55. (Note: Dotted lines represent the predictions at 95% confidence intervals. Source: Agarwal et al. 2020)

Agarwal et al. (2020) contend that the evidence of setting aside funds in a low-interest account is consistent with individuals waiting for the right timing and opportunity to invest in the property market.

In contrast, a study into the impact of a reduction in interest rates on household saving, consumption and investment decisions using Indian data finds that households react to the short-term rate cut by rebalancing their asset portfolio, primarily by investing in mutual funds followed by ordinary saving accounts, which supports the hypothesis of "reaching for yield" (Agarwal et al. 2019a).

4.1.2 Substitution Effect

Wright (1969) was among the first to find a positive significant relationship between saving and interest rate. An increase in the real interest rate from 4% to 6% increases saving by up to 10%.

Boskin (1978) also finds a positive relationship between saving and interest rate. The estimated interest elasticity of 0.3 to 0.4 indicates that interest rate can dramatically affect saving and that taxes which reduce the rate of return may discourage wealth accumulation. The results suggest

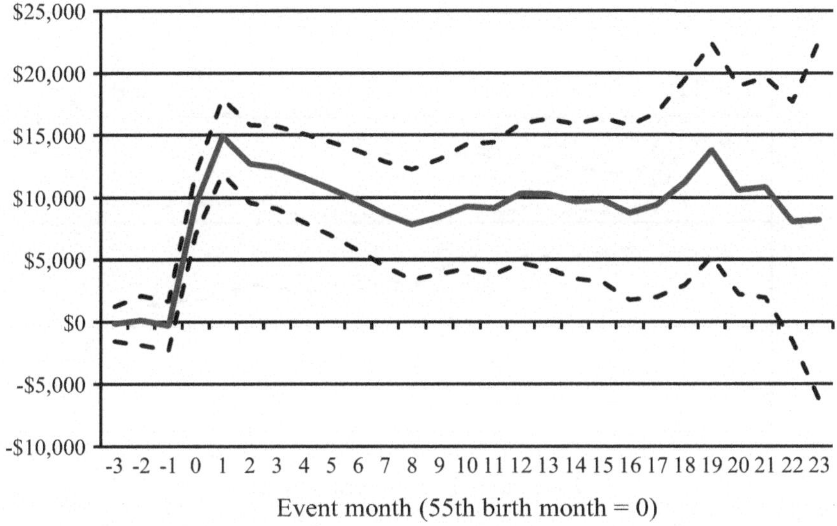

Fig. 2.9b Predicted change in account balances after age 55. (Note: Dotted lines represent the predictions at 95% confidence intervals. Source: Agarwal et al. 2020)

that reducing taxes on interest income can motivate households to save and positively impact long-run income.

Gylfason (1981) observes similar results with an estimated interest elasticity of saving of 0.3 and concludes that consumption and interest rates are inversely related.

Using a sample of eight industrial countries comprising Germany, US, Italy, France, UK, Japan, Belgium and Sweden, Tullio and Contesso (1986) provide support for the hypothesis that a higher after-tax interest rate will enhance saving and reduce consumption.

In a study covering 165 countries from 1981 to 2012, Grigoli et al. (2018) observe that high growth Asian economies have high private saving. By 2012, the average private saving rate of these high growth Asian economies was at 34.7% of gross private disposable income. The study also notes the presence of a substitution effect in high growth Asian economies where a 1% rise in the real deposit rate increases the saving rate by 2.8%.

Using a broad representative sample of individuals from India, Agarwal et al. (2019b) find an asymmetric relationship between stock index returns

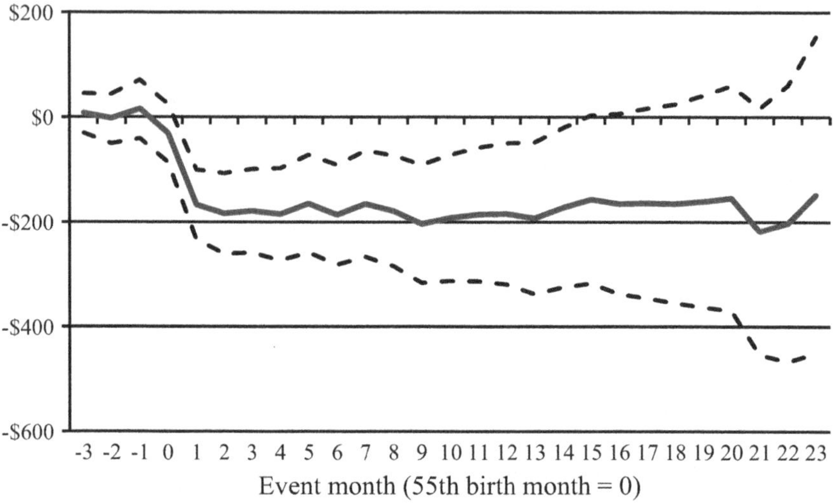

Fig. 2.9c Predicted change in debt after age 55. (Note: Dotted lines represent the predictions at 95% confidence intervals. Source: Agarwal et al. 2020)

and monthly consumption. Following a 1% higher positive return on the 30-stock index SENSEX, individuals decrease overall consumption by 1.7% and increase their investment account balances by 1.7%. They choose to forego consumption of luxuries and durables in order to chase returns. Interestingly, this return chasing effect is not found when SENSEX returns are negative.

The postponement of consumption to chase for yield is also observed through the deposit channel in Turkey, where an unanticipated interest rate hike by the central bank was accompanied by an 8.58% drop in consumption of non-durables and discretionary spending each month in the subsequent six months. Agarwal et al. (2019c) observe that households reduce their checking account balance, which does not accrue interest, and switch out of the banking system into higher yield products following the policy shock. This reflects the substitution effect where higher interest rate leads to lower consumption and higher saving. The response is stronger for households with more liquid assets.

4.2 *Inflation*

There are at least three reasons why inflation may cause saving to increase. First, inflation causes the real value of assets to fall. In response to the loss of wealth, households may save more (Shinohara 1982). Second, inflation causes uncertainty over the level of future income. Therefore, households may save more for precautionary reasons (Grigoli et al. 2018). Howard (1978) finds that inflation affects consumer confidence and encourages personal saving in the US, Japan, the UK and Canada. Third, consumers may postpone purchases when confronted with increased prices.

On the other hand, there may be a substitution effect because the more households save, the more they may lose when faced with an unanticipated drop in the real rate of return. They may decide to hold more real assets rather than currency. This flight from currency will be reflected as a decrease in the measured saving rate.

The overall impact of inflation depends on whether the income effect or the substitution effect is stronger.

4.3 *Corporate Saving and Personal Saving*

When analyzing the factors affecting saving, consideration should also be given to the role played by corporate saving or retained earnings, and the extent to which it is treated as a substitute for personal saving. If capital markets are perfect, corporate saving and personal saving are perfect substitutes as shareholders can borrow against an increase in corporate saving at the return on equity (Montgomery 1986).

Grigoli et al. (2018) touch on the integration of personal and corporate saving behavior. Under the condition that strict assumptions are met, household owners of corporations can "pierce the corporate veil" and substitute higher corporate saving for lower personal saving.

Feldstein (1973) finds that the marginal propensity to consume (MPC) for retained earnings is about 0.5, while the MPC for disposable income is 0.75. This implies that a dollar in retained earnings instead of disposable income can increase saving by $0.25. Feldstein and Fane (1973) show that, for the UK, a pound in retained earning instead of disposable income can increase saving by between 12 pence and 50 pence. These papers imply that, to foster growth, there should be restraint in the taxation of corporate profits.

4.4 Durable and Personal Saving

Durables can be viewed as a form of household saving. As durables increase, other forms of personal saving may decrease.

Households may shift their investment from financial assets to tangible assets when inflation increases, because the value of tangibles does not decline as much with inflation.

Investment in durables will rise with the proportion of young households in the population as they tend to save disproportionately more in the form of durables. This will change the form of saving in the economy, but not necessarily the level of saving.

4.5 Demographic Factors

4.5.1 Age

Many papers note a close association between age and saving behavior. Hayhoe et al. (2012) find that age is negatively associated with regular saving, specifically when age increases by 1 year, the probability of saving decreases by 0.5%. Grigoli et al. (2018) find that a 1% increase in old-age dependency ratio is accompanied by a reduction of 1.13% in private saving rate. Bosworth and Bell (2005) initially find a strong influence of age on saving with households aged between 40 and 60 accounting for more than 75% of all saving, and households aged over 60 experiencing dissaving. However, controlling for education, the age effect on saving is different. They find that the college educated save at a high rate before age 40 and do not dissave after age 60.

4.5.2 Ethnicity and Household Composition

Disparities exist in saving behavior across racial ethnicities. White households are more likely to save than black households (Rha et al. 2006; Yuh and Hanna 2010).

Household composition such as family structure, marriage status and the gender of the breadwinner also affect saving decisions. Browning and Lusardi (1996) observe that saving is highest for married couples without children, lower for households with children and lowest for single parents. Attanasio (1998) finds that, in the US, households headed by males save consistently more while Denizer et al. (2002) find that for transition economies such as Bulgaria, Hungary and Poland, households headed by females save more. Yuh and Hanna (2010) show that married couples are most likely to be savers, while single females are less likely to save than single males.

4.5.3 Employment Status

Employment status affects saving behavior. Those who are self-employed are more likely to save than those who are not, while those who are not retired are more likely to save than those who are (Yuh and Hanna 2010).

4.5.4 Education

The level of education attained has a positive relationship with saving. Those with a college degree are more likely to save than those without, and those who have completed high school are more likely to save than those who have not (Yuh and Hanna 2010).

Fisher and Montalto (2010) examine the motive to save for the education of children and grandchildren, which has yet to be included in any theoretical model of saving. They find a significant negative relationship between this motive and saving over the past year. The results show that households with this motive appear to spend more than save.

4.5.5 Health

Health status affects saving behavior but the results are mixed. Some studies find that households with poor health are more likely to save (Yuh and Hanna 2010), while others find the opposite to be true. Fisher and Montalto (2010) examine saving motives controlling for health status. They find that households with poor health save less, which highlights the need for health insurance. Heckman and Hanna (2015) note that better health is associated with more saving but could not pinpoint the direction of causality.

4.6 Socio-economic Factors

4.6.1 Generations

Attanasio (1998) identifies a "typical age profile" for saving rates which peaks at around age 57. He observes that the profile shift downwards for cohorts born between 1920 and 1939. A plausible explanation is the increase in social security entitlements for these cohorts.

Jappelli (1999) and Kapteyn et al. (2005) examine why different cohorts have different amounts of accumulated wealth. Jappelli (1999) finds shifts in the age-wealth profiles that are consistent with increases in productivity growth across generations. Kapteyn et al. (2005) show that productivity growth can explain differences in household income across cohorts, while productivity growth and social security entitlements can explain differences in net wealth accumulated across cohorts.

4.6.2 *Income*

Generally, household income and saving are positively related (Avery and Kennickell 1991; Chang 1994; Rha et al. 2006; Yuh and Hanna 2010; Henager and Mauldin 2015; Grigoli et al. 2018). Using 5-year surveys in the US from 1995 to 2004, Yuh and Hanna (2010) find that households with a relatively higher income in a regular year are more likely to save, while households with an unusually low income in that year are less likely to save. Homeowners are more likely to save than renters (Fisher and Montalto 2010; Rha et al. 2006; Yuh and Hanna 2010).

Avery and Kennickell (1991), Yuh and Hanna (2010), Mauldin et al. (2016) and Grigoli et al. (2018) find that as household wealth increases, the likelihood of saving increases. However, in reviewing the underlying factors affecting saving, Bovenberg (1988) concludes that improvement in wealth (due to stock portfolios and real estate) is a major reason for the decline in private saving. Similarly, in a time series analysis of Japan for the period 1955 to 1985, Shibuya (1987) finds that the higher the proportion of household assets relative to expected lifetime income, the lower the household saving. He concludes that, in Japan, household wealth substitutes for saving.

4.6.3 *Availability of Credit*

In countries where regulations require huge down payments for large ticket items such as houses and automobiles, households are forced to save. The high down payment ratio of as much as 40% for house purchases contributes to the high saving in Japan (Hayashi 1986). In addition, installment credit for durable consumer goods is not widely used in Japan (Shinohara 1982) which further explains the high saving.

In countries that offer credit readily and allow interest expense deductibility, such as the US, private saving tends to be lower (Sturm 1983; Summers and Carroll 1987; Friend 1986; Grigoli et al. 2018).

4.6.4 *Financial Literacy*

Studies have shown that financial illiteracy affects the ability to make rational saving decisions and may result in financial mistakes (Agarwal et al. 2009; Agarwal et al. 2011; Lusardi and Mitchell 2014). Hung et al. (2009) find that older individuals, men, the more educated (bachelors' degrees and higher) and those with higher income have higher financial literacy. On the other hand, financial illiteracy is widespread among the elderly, women, minorities, the least educated (Lusardi and Mitchell 2011) and those with low income (Lusardi 2008a, b).

There is a vast literature on financial literacy and retirement saving. Broadly, financially literate households are more likely to plan for retirement, and those who plan are more likely to have higher wealth, with causation going from literacy to planning to wealth (Lusardi and Mitchell 2007a).

Lusardi (2004) finds that employees who participated in a retirement seminar at the workplace increased their overall saving. The increase is greatest for those who save the least and those who are the least educated. Using a survey of employers, Bayer et al. (2009) conclude that education programs at the workplace can positively influence employee's participation and contribution to pension funds.

Lusardi and Mitchell (2017) observe that financial literacy is higher in respondents who have been exposed to economics in school and in employer-sponsored programs, and they are more likely to engage in retirement planning.

Lusardi and Mitchell (2007a, b) analyze retired households and find that financial knowledge is associated with successful saving behavior.

Agarwal et al. (2009) study the effect of aging on financial decision making. They find that middle-aged adults make less financial mistakes with the average cost minimizing age at 53.3 (see Table 2.1), while the young and the elderly have the least financial knowledge and cognitive ability and are more predisposed to make financial mistakes. They conclude that the adverse effect of aging dominates the positive effect of experience.

Lusardi et al. (2010) evaluate the financial sophistication of Americans aged 50 and above. Their results show that those who have an acute lack of financial knowledge include women, the least educated, non-whites and those aged above 75.

Using data from India, Agarwal et al. (2015) find that those who are financially literate have better financial planning. Financial planning is

Table 2.1 Age at which financial mistakes are minimized

Financial task	*Age of peak performance (Years)*	*Standard error (Years)*
Home Equity Loans—APR	55.9	4.2
Home Equity Lines—APR	53.3	5.2
Eureka Moment	45.8	7.9
Credit Card—APR	50.3	6
Auto Loans—APR	49.6	5
Mortgage—APR	56	8
Small Business Credit Card—APR	61.8	7.9
Credit Card Late Fee	51.9	4.9
Credit Card Over Limit Fee	54	5
Credit Card Cash Advance Fee	54.8	4.9
Average	53.3	4.3

Source: Agarwal et al. (2009)

found to be higher among the more educated, men and those who are married but is not related to income.

Henager and Mauldin (2015) examine the saving behavior of moderate-income households and find that those who perceive themselves to have financial knowledge save more.

On the other hand, Hilgert et al. (2003) conclude that an increase in financial knowledge may not lead to an improvement in financial management. Instead, the causality may be in the reverse direction—as households save and invest, their financial knowledge improves.

Some studies do not find any relationship between financial knowledge and saving behavior. Mandell and Klein (2009) evaluate 79 high school students who enrolled in a personal financial management module. They find that the students are not more financially literate than those who did not take the module. Heckman and Hanna (2015) examine low-income households and did not find any relationship between financial literacy and saving behavior. Mauldin et al. (2016) study low to moderate income households and find no relationship between their financial knowledge scores and saving behavior.

4.7 Pensions

4.7.1 Public Pensions

It is not clear whether the presence of public pension funds affects household saving positively or negatively.

Some studies find that pension schemes reduce personal saving because they substitute for assets through the wealth effect. Feldstein (1974) observes that pension schemes reduce personal saving by about 50% because of the positive present value from the anticipated benefits net of contribution. Summers and Carroll (1987) find that pension schemes displace personal saving. They suggest that the low US national saving during the 1980s was due to improvements in the well-being of the elderly, availability of credit and improvements in public and private insurance.

Hubbard et al. (1995) show that social insurance can discourage saving by low-income households. Other studies find that social security entitlements depress household saving (Feldstein and Pellechio 1979; Kotlikoff 1979; Diamond and Hausman 1984; Bernheim 1987). In Japan, where social security is low, people save more (Shinohara 1982).

Pension plans can also influence saving through the recognition effect. Barros (1979) observes that public consciousness about the prospect of being financially independent after retirement motivate households to save more. Thus, pension plans may cause other forms of saving to increase (Cagan 1965; Buiter and Tobin 1979). Feldstein (1974) concludes that pension schemes can result in more personal saving because individuals are incentivized to save more with longer retirement periods. In a study of 14 industrial countries, Kopits and Gotur (1980) note that the positive retirement effect (more need to save for a longer retirement period) of old-age transfers outweighs the negative wealth substitution effect (less need to save because pension benefits are deemed as a substitute for personal saving).

There are those who believe that pension schemes have no impact on saving rate. Modigliani and Sterling (1983) show that, for their sample of 21 countries, the net impact of social security is insignificant. Using a sample of 16 industrial countries, Koskela and Viren (1983) find that social security entitlements do not affect household saving. Similarly, Grigoli et al. (2018) conclude that higher public saving do not reduce household saving in their sample of 165 countries.

4.7.2 *Private Pension*

The extent to which private pensions add to total saving depends on whether they are offset by decreases in other household saving.

Munnell (1976), Gultekin and Logue (1979) and Hubbard (1986) find that private pension plans add to total saving. They cite some possible reasons for the increase to saving: (1) positive retirement effect, (2) illiquid pension plans which will not result in a one-to-one substitution for other forms of saving and (3) recognition effect.

4.7.3 *Defined Benefit Versus Defined Contribution*

A defined benefit plan is one that provides a pre-specified income stream to the pension recipient at retirement. A defined contribution plan is one where the contributions are explicit but not the future benefits.

As the retirement pension environment in the US transitions from defined benefit plans to defined contribution plans, and as the demands on social security grow in response to an aging population, there is a perceived shift in responsibility for retirement saving and planning to households (Poterba et al. 2007; Robb and Woodyard 2011).

4.8 *Private Saving Incentives*

Households allocate funds to assets with the highest risk-adjusted real after-tax returns. Thus, saving incentives can alter the composition of saving and possibly increase total saving.

Governments are incentivized to encourage saving behavior as they can alleviate the need for social support later. Examples of incentives used to influence household saving behavior include tax deferral of retirement plans, tax exemptions of retirement plans, education saving plans and long-term saving plans.

Carroll and Summers (1987) conclude that the higher saving rate in Canada compared to US is due to the greater tax incentive for financial saving in Canada, greater tax disincentive for borrowing to purchase tangible assets in Canada and the larger budget deficit in Canada.

Using a sample of 19 OECD countries from 1971 to 1995, Tanzi and Zee (2000) find that total tax, income tax and consumption tax negatively impact the household saving rate and that the negative impact of income tax is greater. This explains the conventional governmental approach to encourage saving through the use of tax deduction for contributions toward retirement account and tax deferral on earnings in retirement accounts. However, this is not attractive for low- and middle-income households who do not pay much income tax in the first place.

Duflo et al. (2006) study the willingness of low-income and middle-income families to contribute to their retirement accounts when they are offered matching contributions of zero, 20% and 50%. This approach of encouraging saving is more attractive as it is independent of the income tax paid. The matching contributions raise participation and contribution levels. The results show that incentives and the availability of information can affect responses to government programs.

Mason et al. (2010) examine the role of financial incentives in encouraging saving in Child Development Accounts (CDAs) in the US. Their results suggest that an initial deposit to seed the CDA (ranging from $0 to $1000), provision of a reward based on a benchmark (financial incentives ranging from $0 to $1000 for achieving goals such as the child making the honor roll) and matching dollars (which are earned at a 1:1 rate on saving ranging from $750 to $3000) encourage contributions to CDAs.

Before 1986, interest paid on all types of household debt was tax deductible. After the US Tax Reform Act of 1986, tax deductible interest expense was phased out because it provided an incentive for consumers to buy consumer durables rather than invest in assets that produce taxable income. In other words, it created an incentive to consume rather than save (Congress of the United States 1987). However, the US Congress chose to retain the residential mortgage interest deduction because one of the government's over-arching goal was to encourage homeownership (Congress of the United States 1987).

Using US data from 1984 to 2007, Hilber and Turner (2014) examine the impact of the favorable tax treatment of mortgage interest on homeownership. They find that the favorable tax treatment has a perverse effect when the supply of housing is inelastic. The increase in house prices cause households constrained by down payments to opt out of the housing market entirely. Thus, Hilber and Turner (2014) conclude that favorable tax treatment of mortgage interest is ineffective in promoting homeownership and improving social welfare. Sommer and Sullivan (2018) find similar results from studying the relationship between mortgage interest payments, equilibrium house prices, rent and homeownership. Their model shows that eliminating the favorable tax treatment of mortgage interest causes house prices to decline, homeownership to increase, mortgage debt to drop and welfare to improve.

Agarwal et al. (2017) estimate changes in consumption and saving resulting from a revision of India's tax policy in 2014. The exogeneous change involves revisions to include mortgage principal payments in the list of exemptions. The study concludes that the exemption causes a large proportion of households with mortgages to increase their mortgage repayment, reduce their consumption and increase their private saving. Comparing households with mortgages (treatment group) against those without mortgages (control group), there is a greater reduction in cash withdrawals, point of sale transactions and total spending among household with mortgages (see Fig 2.10).

Overall, Agarwal et al. (2017) find that the consumption response of the treatment group, relative to the control group, is more pronounced among male, single, younger and lower-income mortgage borrowers.

Schreiner and Sherraden (2007) find that low-income households will save when enough incentives are provided.

4.9 *Other Factors*

4.9.1 *Commitment Strategies*

The use of saving commitment strategies is widespread. They can be found in pension plans, education saving plans, medical saving plans and insurance plans. In recent years, financial institutions have designed saving products with deposit-side and withdrawal-side features that help individuals to commit to save.

Deposit-side features include automatic transfers into investment accounts, automatic deductions from paychecks into retirement or medical saving programs, deadline to enjoy bonus, automatic increases in deposits over time and the use of deposit collectors (Ashraf et al. 2003).

Withdrawal-side features include restrictions on the use of funds (targeted saving for education, healthcare and old age), restrictions on the timing of deposit withdrawal, penalty of a withdrawal fee and implementation of peer monitoring (Ashraf et al. 2003).

4.9.2 *ROSCAs*

Rotating Saving and Credit Associations (ROSCAs) are informal financial saving organizations where members, through a collective mechanism, agree to a schedule of periodic payments in return for a lump sum at a future date without any accumulated interest.

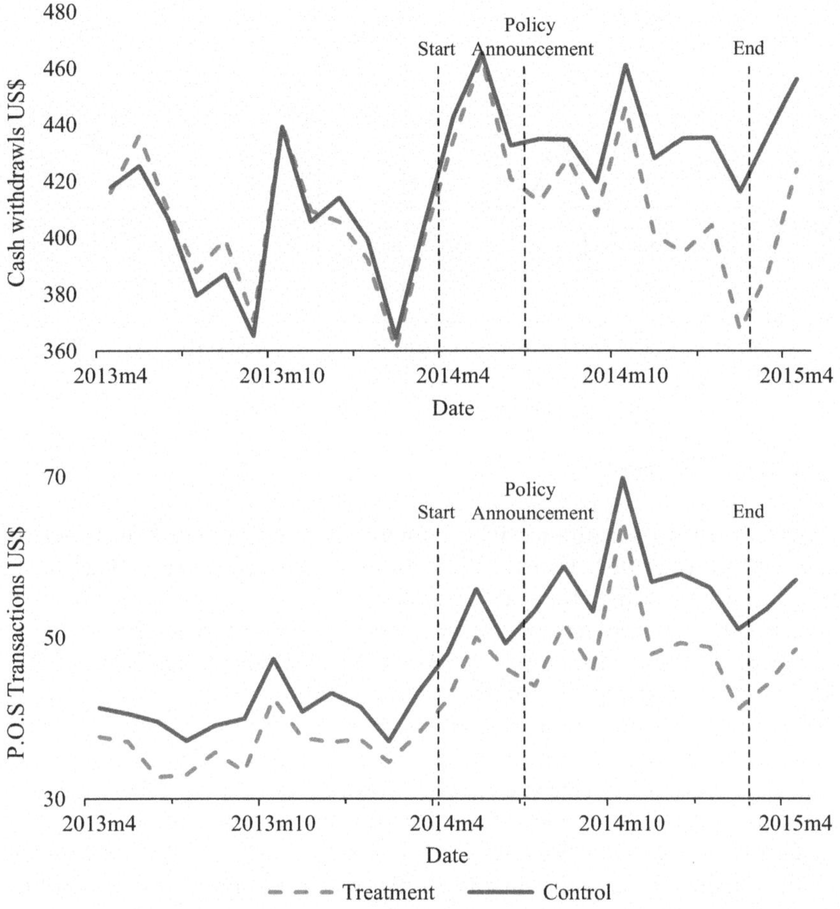

Fig. 2.10 Change in cash withdrawals, P.O.S transactions and total spending before and after policy announcement (Note: Treatment group are households with mortgages, control group are households without mortgages. Source: Agarwal et al. 2017)

ROSCAs perform several functions. First, they help fund indivisible durable purchases by taking advantage of inter-temporal trade among members (Besley et al. 1993). Second, they help to protect household saving from spendthrift spouses (Anderson and Baland 2002). Third, they

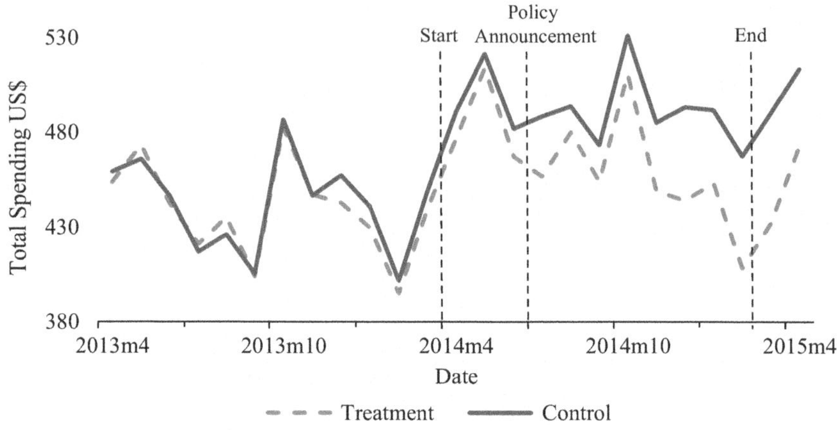

Fig. 2.10 (continued)

provide a form of insurance where members can access cash in times of need (Klonner 2003). Fourth, they commit members to save (Chamlee-Wright 2002). Fifth, they are a collective mechanism for self-control because of the public nature and the inbuilt group enforcement.

Gugerty (2007) examines 70 ROSCAs in Kenya. Members of the ROSCAs meet at regular intervals and contribute funds according to a designated schedule or auction mechanism. Members bear the risk that others do not fulfill their obligations. Although risky, ROSCAs are prevalent in Asia, Latin America, the Caribbean and Africa (Ardener and Burman 1996), often where formal credit markets are absent. They are also found in more developed places such as Taiwan (Levenson and Besley 1996), Japan (Dekle and Hamada 2000) and Argentina (Schreiner 2000).

4.9.3 Lock Box

Another commitment device is the lock box, which functions as a piggy bank. Shipton (1992) and Rutherford (1999) cite the use of lock boxes in Gambia and East Africa, respectively.

4.9.4 Bonus Effect

In countries like Japan, bonus payments make up a substantial portion of a worker's income (Shinohara 1982). Empirical evidence shows that individuals have a lower MPC for bonuses than regular income (Ishikawa and

Ueda 1984). To the extent that bonuses are completely windfall in nature, there is justification to apply the PIH and treat them as transitory income which should not affect consumption, since the MPC for transitory income is zero. However, workers seem to expect these bonuses at regular intervals, thus negating the argument that they are not anticipated. An alternative explanation is the lump sum payment effect where workers who receive a lump sum payment have a lower MPC.

4.9.5 Energy Prices

Higher energy prices may affect expenditures on household appliances such as washing machines, dryers and dish washers. Edelstein and Kilian (2009) show that rising energy prices have a negative effect, but it will take repeated surprise increases in energy prices to have a large effect on household consumption.

4.9.6 Culture

It is tempting to attribute thriftiness to cultural factors. Some argue that the Japanese, Chinese and Koreans are thrifty because of their traditional Buddhism and Confucianism philosophies, where labor and thriftiness are considered virtues (Shinohara 1982).

Friend (1986) examines differences in cross-country saving rates and concludes that, in his judgment, they represent differences in culture and taste.

Strumpel (1975) attributes the higher saving rate observed in Germany to cultural factors such as (1) characteristically pessimistic expectations about the future, (2) a greater satisfaction of wants for the same amount of consumption, and (3) the habit of saving in advance of purchasing large ticket items.

Carroll et al. (1998) test the hypothesis that cultural differences affect saving behavior by examining immigrants to the US from high-saving countries. They conclude that immigrants from high-saving countries do not save more than those from low-saving countries.

4.9.7 Language

Chen (2013) proposes that because languages differ in the way time is encoded, such as whether speakers have to specify the timing of events or can leave timing unsaid, they can influence how households choose to save. The study separates languages into two categories of future time reference (FTR), namely, weak FTR and strong FTR. It concludes that weak FTR speakers are 31% more likely to save and accumulate 39% more wealth by retirement. Chen (2013) attributes the results to two causal mechanisms. First, a constant need to distinguish between the present and the future makes the temporal future seems further away and therefore deters saving. Second, strong FTR speakers have more precise beliefs about time which leads to more precise beliefs about rewards which again deters saving.

In a follow-up paper, Roberts et al. (2015) test whether Chen's (2013) findings can be rejected after controlling for how different languages are related to each other. The effect of FTR on saving behavior diminishes after accounting for language relatedness. In addition, comparing the FTR model against a null model without FTR shows that although the FTR variable is significant, the FTR model does not significantly increase the amount of explained variation in saving behavior. The study concludes that FTR does not affect future-oriented behavior such as saving.

4.9.8 *Insurance*

Summers and Carroll (1987) suggest that the availability and accessibility of insurance may have contributed to the drop in private saving. Life insurance, disability insurance and annuities serve to protect against the insured's premature death, permanent disability and longevity risk, respectively.

4.9.9 *Health and Longevity*

Improvement in longevity will increase the length of retirement and therefore the need for more retirement saving. The impact of improved health on saving is less clear because although better health should lead to longer working lives and higher saving, much depends on the institutional arrangement and the legislated retirement age.

Bloom et al. (2003) find that longer life expectancy leads to higher saving. Their results can explain the surge in saving in East Asia during 1950–1990 which is a period of rising life expectancy and the decline in saving in Uganda where life expectancy fell sharply after 1980 to only 41 by 1990.

4.9.10 *Differences Across Countries*

Saving rates vary considerably across countries and over time. Using panel data on 36 countries, Edwards (1996) finds that per capita income growth is the most important determinant of saving and that government-provided social security benefits tend to crowd out household saving.

Loayza et al. (2000) investigate the policy and non-policy factors behind the saving disparities of 49 developing countries. They find that private saving (1) rises with real per capita income, (2) has an inverse relationship with dependency ratio which is consistent with the standard life cycle model of consumption, (3) is positively related to inflation (consistent with precautionary motive), (4) reduces with credit availability and (5) is not related to real interest rates.

5 Conclusion

The cornerstone of Keynesian saving function is the relationship between consumption and income in the same period.

Under the life cycle model and permanent income model, saving in any period is determined not by current level of income but by lifetime resources.

Households save for various reasons including the inter-temporal substitution motive, life cycle motive, precautionary motive, independence motive, improvement motive, enterprise motive, bequest motive, avarice motive and the down payment motive.

Notwithstanding the motives, there are factors that affect household saving behavior to varying degrees. These include the rate of return, inflation, corporate saving, durable purchases, demographic and socio-economic characteristics, financial literacy, health and longevity, private saving incentives and the availability of credit, pension funds and insurance.

Appendix: Singapore's Central Provident Fund

In 1955, the colonial British government founded the Central Provident Fund (CPF). It was originally designed as a state pension scheme to provide account holders with a lump sum for their retirement needs. On attaining self-government in June 1959, the state pension scheme was rejected in favor of an endowment scheme based on the defined contribution principle.

The CPF scheme, in its present form, is highly regarded as a model of social security for several reasons. First, the funds are accumulated from the earnings of the account holder and thus will not be a drain on the public budget. Second, the account holder is responsible for his own retirement needs and is encouraged to improve himself so that he can set aside more for his own use later. In his memoirs, Lee Kuan Yew, who was the first Prime Minister of Singapore, said that having each generation/person to save for its/his own pension is fairer and sounder (Lee 2000).

In the early years, the Singapore government assumed a paternalistic role where major decisions over the use of the funds were entrusted to the state.

CPF Structure

The efficacy of the CPF in meeting the retirement needs of Singaporeans is an oft-debated subject. Despite being ranked the best in Asia and seventh best globally in 2018 by the Melbourne Mercer Global Pension Index, the CPF attracts much scrutiny from naysayers.

A good pension system should, at the most basic level, meet the housing, healthcare and consumption needs of an individual. In Singapore, these requirements are achieved holistically through the CPF. Every employee has a CPF saving account which is divided into three components, namely, the Special account, the Ordinary account and the Medisave account.

The Special account is intended for retirement use and can only be withdrawn at age 55 after setting aside a minimum sum. The Ordinary account can be used for housing and asset enhancement purposes. The Medisave account is meant to defray healthcare cost. Initially, Medisave was not compulsory for the self-employed but this has since changed in January 1998.

The CPF, thus structured, supports the three basic needs of housing, healthcare and retirement. The contributions enjoy risk-free interest rates of up to 5% for account holders below 55 years old and up to 6% for those aged 55 and above. Funds in the Ordinary account are guaranteed an interest rate of 2.5%, while funds in the Special account and Medisave account earn 4%. The first $60,000 of combined balances of which $20,000 comes from the Ordinary account earns an extra 1%. From 2016, an additional 1% is paid on the first $30,000 of combined balances for all account holders aged 55 and above.

Every month, employees and employers contribute a fixed percentage of the employee's gross salary into the CPF. The contribution rates have changed over time (see Table 2.2). The total contribution rates hit a

Table 2.2 Employer and employee CPF contribution rates since 1955

Year	*Employee contribution (%)*		*Employer contribution (%)*		*Total contribution (%)*	
	Minimum	*Maximum*	*Minimum*	*Maximum*	*Minimum*	*Maximum*
1955	5	5	5	5	10	10
1968	6.5	6.5	6.5	6.5	13	13
1970	8	8	8	8	16	16
1971	10	10	10	10	20	20
1972	10	10	14	14	24	24
1973	11	11	15	15	26	26
1974	15	15	15	15	30	30
1975	15	15	15	15	30	30
1977	15.5	15.5	15.5	15.5	31	31
1978	16.5	16.5	16.5	16.5	33	33
1979	16.5	16.5	20.5	20.5	37	37
1980	18	18	20.5	20.5	38.5	38.5
1981	22	22	20.5	20.5	42.5	42.5
1982	23	23	22	22	45	45
1983	23	23	23	23	46	46
1984	23	25	23	25	46	50
1985	25	25	25	25	50	50
1986	25	25	10	10	35	35
1988	18	24	8	12	26	36
1989	11	23	6	15	17	38
1990	5	23	5	16.5	10	39.5
1991	5	22.5	5	17.5	10	40
1992	5	22	5	18	10	40
1993	5	21.5	5	18.5	10	40
1994	5	20	5	20	10	40
1999	5	20	2	10	7	30
2000	5	20	2.5	12	7.5	32
2001	5	20	3.5	16	8.5	36
2002	5	20	3.5	16	8.5	36
2003	5	20	3.5	13	8.5	33
2004	5	20	3.5	13	8.5	33
2005	5	20	3.5	13	8.5	33
2006	5	20	3.5	13	8.5	33
2007	5	20	5	14.5	10	34.5
2010	5	20	5.5	15	10.5	35
2011	5	20	6	16	11	36
2012	5	20	6.5	16	11.5	36
2014	5	20	6.5	16	11.5	36

(*continued*)

Table 2.2 (continued)

Year	*Employee contribution (%)*		*Employer contribution (%)*		*Total contribution (%)*	
	Minimum	*Maximum*	*Minimum*	*Maximum*	*Minimum*	*Maximum*
2015	5	20	7.5	17	12.5	37
2016	5	20	7.5	17	12.5	37

Source: Singapore Central Provident Fund

Note: The contribution rates are based on the age of the account holder

Table 2.3 CPF contribution rates across different age groups as at December 2018

Age group (years)	*Ordinary account (%)*	*Special account (%)*	*Medisave account (%)*	*Total (%)*
Below 35	23	6	8	37
36–45	21	7	9	37
45–50	19	8	10	37
46–55	15	11.5	10.5	37
56–60	12	3.5	10.5	26
61–65	3.5	2.5	10.5	16.5
Above 65	1	1	10.5	12.5

Source: Singapore Central Provident Fund

maximum of 50% in 1984 and 1985, comprising 25% from the employee and 25% from the employer.

The contribution rates have, on occasion, been adjusted to manage business cost and export competitiveness (note the adjustments in 1986, 1999 and 2003).

The contributions and the interest earned are completely exempted from income tax. The contribution rates vary by age groups and are divided into the three component accounts, with the bulk going into the Ordinary account (see Table 2.3).

Liberalization

Over time, account holders were given greater control over the investment of their saving to enhance the return. The liberalization, however, threatened to undermine the ability of the CPF to meet the original purpose of funding retirement needs.

In 1968, account holders were allowed to use their Ordinary account for the purchase of public housing and the servicing of monthly mortgage installments. In 1981, this was expanded to include private property. The scheme was very successful in promoting homeownership.

In 1984, a separate account to finance personal health care, known as the Medisave account, was launched under the Medisave scheme. Funds in the Medisave account could be used to pay for approved medical treatments. Subsequently, this was modified to include premiums for approved insurance schemes. In 1989 and 1990, premiums for life insurance under the Dependants' Protection Scheme and health insurance under the Medishield Scheme could also be deducted from the Medisave account.

In 1989, account holders could use their Ordinary accounts to pay for their own, their spouses' and their children's tuition fees at local tertiary institutions.

In the mid-1980s, the CPF Investment Scheme was introduced. It allowed account holders to diversify into non-residential properties, gold and approved stocks. In 1993, more equities, government bonds, bank deposits and managed funds were appended to the list of permissible products.

From January 2001, account holders were allowed to invest their Special account funds in retirement-related instruments such as bank deposits, endowment insurance products, government bonds as well as approved unit trusts and insurance-linked products (Ng 2000). The then Minister for Manpower, Dr Lee Boon Yang, explained that the government wanted Singaporeans to take greater responsibility for their retirement planning but he also warned that the goal of higher returns had to be balanced against the fact that the Special account is the basic safety net and therefore should only be invested in safe products (Channel News Asia 2000).

Problems of Liberalization

Volatility of the Housing Market

The property market underwent a decade-long boom from the mid-1980s amidst strong economic growth. It attracted first-time buyers, existing homeowners who wished to upgrade to bigger residences and people who bought multiple properties. The pre-occupation with housing led to inflationary prices. The property price index doubled from Q1 1991 to peak in Q2 1996.

In May 1996, the government implemented a series of anti-speculation measures aimed at stabilizing the overheated property market. The measures included an 80% loan-to-value financing restriction, a 30-month project completion period (PCP) for private developments under the Qualifying Certificate scheme (meant to prevent foreign developers from hoarding land or buying land for speculation), a 5% per annum penalty imposition for PCP extension, an imposition of stamp duty on sales of uncompleted properties, a new seller stamp duty on residential properties sold within three years of purchase and a capital gains tax on properties sold within three years of purchase.

These anti-speculation measures and the onset of the 1997 Asian Financial Crisis saw the market falling sharply from Q3 1996 to Q4 1998 (see Fig. 2.11). Many who bought during the property boom were in negative equity, that is, the market price of their property could not cover the outstanding balance of their mortgage.

The government implemented two rounds of stimuli to help the real estate market ride out the downturn, namely, the November 1997 surprise

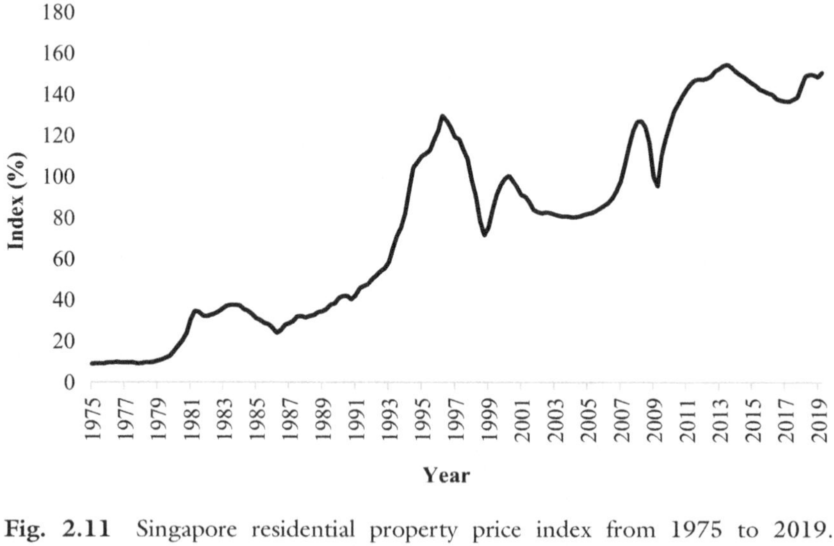

Fig. 2.11 Singapore residential property price index from 1975 to 2019. (Source: Singapore Urban Redevelopment Authority)

package (deferral of government land sale, extended PCP for residential projects and suspension of stamp duty surcharge on sale of properties within 3 years of purchase) and a package of off-budget measures worth S$2 billion in June 1998 (suspension of government land sale and deferral of stamp duty payments on purchases until completion of properties).

In addition, the employers' CPF contributions were lowered in January 1999 to help them cope with the crisis. Some CPF account holders who had relied on their monthly CPF contributions to pay for their mortgage faced shortfalls in their installment payments. These affected homeowners were allowed to dip into their special account. Following this episode, the government took steps to prevent excessive speculation in the property market.

The market revived at the end of 1998. Unfortunately, less than two years later, it experienced a prolonged decline from Q3 2000 to Q1 2004 (see Fig. 2.11). In 2002, the government placed limits on CPF withdrawals for housing purposes so as to avoid over concentration of household assets in properties (Phang 2007).

To stimulate the economy, two more rounds of stimuli were implemented, namely, the December 2002 extension of off-budget measures (suspension of government land sale and rebates on property tax) and the April 2003 S$230 million SARS (severe acute respiratory syndrome) Relief Package which includes additional property tax rebates for commercial properties.

The market recovered in 2004. In July 2005, the Ministry of National Development, which oversees the property market, made some policy changes to facilitate the purchase of properties. For example, the loan-to-value (LTV) ratio was increased from 80% to 90%, the cash down payment was reduced from 10% to 5% and unrelated singles were allowed to jointly use CPF saving to buy private residential properties.

Another speculative housing bubble started to form. On 16 December 2006, the government decided to withdraw the concession which allowed buyers to defer stamp duty payment until the property is completed. With the withdrawal, buyers of new properties would have to pay stamp duty within 14 days of making a purchase. Previously, they could defer paying until the project is conferred the Temporary Occupation Permit.

The growth of the property market was interrupted by the 2008 subprime crisis.

In Q3 2009, the market rebounded sharply and hit a peak in Q3 2013. From September 2009 to December 2013, the government implemented ten rounds of cooling measures to ensure a stable and sustainable property market.

Round 1, on 14 September 2009, witnessed the removal of the interest absorption scheme (where the developer absorbed the interest payments until the units are completed) and interest-only mortgages (where the borrower makes only interest payments with no repayments of the loan principal for a period of time).

Round 2, on 20 February 2010, saw the introduction of a seller's stamp duty (SSD) on residential properties and land sold within a year of purchase (see Table 2.4) and the reduction of the LTV ratio to 80% on all housing loans except loans for Housing Development Board (HDB) flats.

Round 3, on 30 August 2010, evidenced the extension of the SSD period to properties sold within three years, the raising of the requirement of minimum cash payment from 5% to 10% for buyers with one or more outstanding housing loans and the reduction of the LTV for the second property to 70%. In addition, the minimum occupation period of HDB flats, before they can be sold, was revised from three to five years.

Round 4, on 14 January 2011, revealed further extension of the SSD period to four years, the raising of SSD rates (see Table 2.4), the reduction of the LTV for the second loan to 60% and the introduction of a LTV for non-individual borrowers at 50%.

Round 5, on 8 December 2011, saw the imposition of an additional buyer's stamp duty (ABSD) over and above the current buyer's stamp duty (see Table 2.5).

Table 2.4 Seller's Stamp Duty (SSD)

Residential property	*Sold in Year 1*	*Sold in Year 2*	*Sold in Year 3*	*Sold in Year 4*
SSD rate since Feb 2010	Same as basic buyer stamp duty	N/A	N/A	N/A
SSD rate since Aug 2010	Same as basic buyer stamp duty	2/3 of basic buyer stamp duty	1/3 of basic buyer stamp duty	N/A
SSD rate since Jan 2011	16%	12%	8%	4%
SSD rate since Mar 2017	12%	8%	4%	N/A

Source: Singapore Property Market Cooling Measures by Singapore Real Estate Exchange

Table 2.5 Additional Buyer's Stamp Duty (ABSD)

Citizenship	*ABSD Rate on primary home*	*ABSD Rate on secondary home*	*ABSD Rate on tertiary and subsequent homes (%)*
Singapore citizens	N/A	N/A	3
Permanent residents	N/A	3%	3
Foreigners and non-individuals	10%	10%	10

Source: Singapore Property Market Cooling Measures by Singapore Real Estate Exchange

Table 2.6 Additional Buyer's Stamp Duty (ABSD) revised in January 2013

Citizenship	*ABSD Rate on primary home*	*ABSD Rate on secondary home*	*ABSD Rate on tertiary and subsequent homes*
Singapore citizens	N/A	0% revised to 7%	3% revised to 10%
Permanent residents	0% revised to 5%	3% revised to 10%	3% revised to 10%
Foreigners and non-individuals	10% revised to 15%	10% revised to 15%	10% revised to 15%

Source: Singapore Property Market Cooling Measures by Singapore Real Estate Exchange

Round 6, on 6 October 2012, restricted the loan tenure for all loans to 35 years and lowered the LTV for non-individual borrowers from 50% to 40%.

Round 7, on 12 January 2013, saw an increase in the ABSD (see Table 2.6) and a further tightening of the LTV.

Round 8, on 29 June 2013, featured the introduction of a total debt servicing ratio (TDSR), which is the percentage of total monthly debt obligations to gross monthly income.

Round 9, on 27 August 2013, witnessed the reduction of the maximum loan term for HDB flats from 30 years to 25 years and the mortgage servicing ratio limit from 35% to 30% of the borrower's gross monthly income.

Round 10, on 9 December 2013, saw the introduction of resale levy for second-time HDB applicants and the revision of mortgage servicing ratio for purchasers of executive condominiums, which are higher end flats sold by the HDB.

The ten rounds of cooling measures from 2009 to 2013 managed to put a damper on the market.

Table 2.7 Additional Buyer's Stamp Duty (ABSD) adjusted on 6 July 2018

Citizenship	*ABSD Rate on primary home*	*ABSD Rate on secondary home*	*ABSD Rate on tertiary and subsequent homes*
Singapore citizens	N/A	7% revised to 12%	10% revised to 15%
Permanent residents	5%	10% revised to 15%	10% revised to 15%
Foreigners	15% revised to 20%	15% revised to 20%	15% revised to 20%
Non-individuals	15% revised to 25%	15% revised to 25%	15% revised to 25%

Source: Singapore Property Market Cooling Measures by Singapore Real Estate Exchange

In March 2017, more than three years after the last round of cooling measures, the government relaxed rules on TDSR and reduced the SSD on residential properties by 4% for each tier (see Table 2.4).

However, when data showed that private home prices had risen to its highest point in four years in Q2 2018, the ABSD rates were adjusted upward (see Table 2.7) and the LTV limits were tightened by 5% across the board (see Table 2.8) in July 2018.

The numerous rounds of cooling measures point to the extensive involvement of the Singapore government in the transformation of the property market. The intervention via the government land sale program, buyer and seller stamp duties and macro-prudential tools such as LTV limits, TDSR and CPF withdrawals were aimed at achieving socio-economic goals and political stability.

Poor Returns from Equity Market

Following the introduction of the CPF Investment Scheme, the Singapore stock market rose and peaked in 1996. The 1997 Asian Economic Crisis and the 2001 to 2003 recession saw share prices plunged (see Fig. 2.12). Many account holders who had withdrawn their CPF saving to invest in equities lost money. Data released by the CPF Board (Chow 2001) showed that nearly three in five people in 2000 would have been better off leaving their money in their CPF account, that is, they made less than the 2.5% guaranteed rate for ordinary accounts.

More recent data confirmed that most account holders did not make good investment decisions. Of those who had invested through the CPF Investment Scheme between 2004 and 2013, 47% incurred losses, 35%

Table 2.8 Restrictions on loan-to-value (LTV) ratios

Feb-2010	For all loans, the LTV values revised down from 90% to 80%, to reduce speculative buys in the market.
Aug-2010	For the first loan, the LTV remains at 80% and for the second loan revised down to 70%.
Jan-2011	For the second loan, the LTV further reduced to 60%. Additional, new restriction introduced for non-individuals, requiring maximum 50% LTV.
Oct-2012	First loan down to 80% and second loan down to 60%. For non-individuals, revised down to 40%.
Jan-2013	First loan down to 80%, second loan down to 50% and third loan down to 40%. For non-individuals, revised down to 20%.
July-2018	First loan down to 75%, second loan down to 45% and third loan down to 35%. For non-individuals, revised down to 15%.

Source: Singapore Property Market Cooling Measures by Singapore Real Estate Exchange

Fig. 2.12 Straits Times Industrial index from 1990 to 2019. (Source: Thomson Reuters)

generated returns no greater than 2.5% and only 18% outperformed the 2.5% guaranteed rate (Teh 2014). In other words, 82% would have been better off or just as well off if they had left their money in their CPF accounts.

Other Developments

National Annuity Scheme

In 2009, the CPF introduced an annuity scheme known as CPF Life after data showed that many Singaporeans live beyond the age of 85 when their monthly payouts under the Old Retirement Sum Scheme would have run out.

The old scheme was simple. It required the account holder to set aside a minimum sum at age 55 from which he would draw monthly amounts from age 65 to 85. If he passed on before age 85, any remaining balance would go to his beneficiaries.

Instead of a fixed 20-year horizon, the new scheme provides lifelong income. The account holder's minimum sum is commingled with those of other retirees. There is pooling of risk. The actual payout will depend on the longevity of all account holders covered. If more people live longer, the payout may be less than projected. The longer the account holder lives, the higher the difference in the cumulative payment compared to the old scheme.

CPF Life has numerous available configurations based on affordability level, payout needs and the account holder's appraisal of his own mortality. The basic plan has lower payouts but larger bequest for loved ones. The standard plan, which is the default, has higher payouts but lower bequest. The escalating plan, designed to hedge against inflation, has lower initial payouts but grows at a fixed annual rate of 2%.

CPF Transfers to Loved Ones

The CPF also allows account holders to transfer their Ordinary account saving to their spouses, siblings, parents, parents-in-law, grandparents and grandparents-in-law, if it does not affect their own retirement adequacy support.

From Q4 2018, account holders can help their elders if they have set aside the required basic retirement sum and have sufficient property pledge to make up the full retirement sum of S$176,000. Before the change, CPF account holders can only make transfers to their loved ones after they have set aside the full retirement sum.

Retirement Income Adequacy

In Singapore, the healthcare, housing and retirement needs of an individual are achieved through the CPF system.

All Singaporeans have medical insurance coverage under Medishield Life, which is paid via the Medisave account. This means that the bulk of medical expenses are taken care of.

Singapore has one of the highest homeownership rates in the world. More than 90% of Singaporeans and more than 80% of the lowest income group are homeowners. To unlock the value of their homes, retirees can access schemes such as reverse mortgage and lease buyback.

All Singaporeans are covered by the CPF Life annuity program, which provides a reliable stream of income for as long as they live. The monthly quantum, however, is small. Many are not convinced that the annuities are adequate to meet the basic needs of retirees. Of those who are eligible to receive their CPF payouts as of December 2018, 74% get less than S$500 monthly (see Table 2.9) (Teo 2019).

However, for most Singaporeans, the CPF annuity is unlikely to be the only source of support in retirement. They have other forms of investments such as shares, bonds, mutual funds and private annuities. The Singapore pension system encourages self-reliance and personal responsibility.

For the low-income elderly, the Silver Support Scheme provides an average monthly supplement of S$200. In addition, there are other forms of social assistance schemes like ComCare.

Table 2.9 Average monthly payouts of CPF members as at December 2018

Age band	*Number of account holders*	*Average monthly payout*
65–69	116,000	S$450
70–79	130,000	S$290
80–87	19,000	S$220

Source: Teo (2019)

Challenges

Singapore's CPF system is based on full employment. This has been challenged by a series of crisis and downturns, the aging demographics as well as structural changes caused by globalization and information communication technology.

Some have suggested creative steps to fine-tune CPF as a provider of old-age security such as (1) raising the minimum sum to be set aside for CPF Life, (2) delaying CPF payout which is now at age 65, (3) making the system more flexible so that account holders can try and earn higher return themselves depending on their risk appetites, (4) allowing account holders to start investing earlier and (5) finding ways to lower the administrative cost.

Based on past experiences, however, few individuals can outperform the CPF's minimum guaranteed interest rate. A less risky alternative would be to see whether the CPF Board can do better and offer account holders a higher return.

References

Acosta, Pablo A., Pablo R. Fajnzylber, and Humberto Lopez. 2007. The Impact of Remittances on Poverty and Human Capital: Evidence from Latin American Household Surveys. World Bank Policy Research Working Paper No. 4247.

Agarwal, Sumit, John C. Driscoll, Xavier Gabaix, and David Laibson. 2009. The Age of Reason: Financial Decisions over the Life Cycle and Implications for Regulation. *Brookings Papers on Economic Activity* Fall: 51–101.

Agarwal, Sumit, Gene Amromin, Itzhak Ben-David, Souphala Chomsisengphet, and Douglas D. Evanoff. 2011. Financial Counseling, Financial Literacy, and Household Decision-Making. In *Financial Literacy: Implications for Retirement Security and the Financial Marketplace*, ed. Olivia S. Mitchell and Annamaria Lusardi, 181–205. Oxford and New York: Oxford University Press.

———. 2015. Financial Literacy and Financial Planning: Evidence from India. *Journal of Housing Economics* 27: 4–21.

Agarwal, Sumit, Souphala Chomsisengphet, Pulak Ghosh, and Man Zhang. 2017. Consumption and Saving Response to a Tax-Subsidized Saving Policy: Evidence from India. *SSRN*. Accessed March 23, 2020. https://papers.ssrn.com/sol3/papers.cfm?abstract_id=3020062.

Agarwal, Sumit, Yeow Hwee Chua, Pulak Ghosh, and Changcheng Song. 2019a. Consumption and Investment Response to Monetary Policy: Evidence of the Heterogeneous Agent New Keynesian (HANK) channel: 1–39. Paper presented at the 2019 Singapore Management University Summer Finance Research Camp, June 25–26.

Agarwal, Sumit, Ben Charoenwong, and Pulak Ghosh. 2019b. Foregone Consumption and Return-Chasing Investments. *SSRN*. Accessed March 22, 2020. https://papers.ssrn.com/sol3/papers.cfm?abstract_id=3428811.

Agarwal, Sumit, Souphala Chomsisengphet, Yildiray Yildirim, and Jian Zhang. 2019c. Interest Rate Pass-Through and Consumption Response: the Deposit Channel. Unpublished Paper, National University of Singapore.

Agarwal, Sumit, Jessica Pan, and Wenlan Qian. 2020. Age of Decision: Pension Savings Withdrawal and Consumption and Debt Response. *Management Science* 66 (1): 43–69.

Alger, Horatio. 1868. *Ragged Dick, or, Street Life in New York with the Boot-Blacks*. Boston: Loring.

Anderson, Siwan, and Jean-Marie Baland. 2002. The Economics of Roscas and Intra-household Resource Allocation. *Quarterly Journal of Economics* 117 (3): 963–995.

Ando, Kazuya A., and Arthur B. Kennickell. 1987. How Much (or Little) Life Cycle Is There in Micro Data? The Cases of the United States and Japan. In *Macroeconomics and Finance*, ed. Rudiger Dornbusch, Stanley Fischer, and John Bossons. Cambridge, MA: MIT Press.

Ardener, Shirley, and Sandra Burman. 1996. *Money-Go-Rounds: The Importance of Rotating Savings and Credit Associations for Women*. Washington: Berg Publishers.

Ashraf, Nava, Nathalie Gons, Dean S. Karlan, and Wesley Yin. 2003. A Review of Commitment Saving Products in Developing Countries. Asian Development Bank Economics and Research Department Working Paper 45.

Attanasio, Orazio P. 1998. Cohort Analysis of Saving Behavior by US Households. *The Journal of Human Resources* 33 (3): 575–609.

Avery, Robert B., and Arthur B. Kennickell. 1991. Household saving in the U.S. *Review of Income and Wealth* 37 (4): 409–430.

Barros, David. 1979. Private Saving and Provision of Social Security in Britain 1946–75. In *Social Security versus Private Saving*, ed. George M. von Furstenberg. Cambridge: Ballinger.

Baum, Donald N. 1988. Consumption, Wealth and the Real Rate of Interest: A Reexamination. *Journal of Macroeconomics* 10 (1): 83–102.

Bayer, Patrick J., Douglas B. Bernheim, and John Karl Scholz. 2009. The Effects of Financial Education in the Workplace: Evidence from a Survey of Employers. *Economic Inquiry* 47 (4): 605–624.

Bernheim, Douglas B. 1987. Ricardian Equivalence: An Evaluation of Theory and Evidence. In *NBER Macroeconomics Annual 1987*, ed. Stanley Fischer. Cambridge, MA: MIT Press.

Besley, Timothy, Stephen Coate, and Glen Loury. 1993. The Economics of Rotating Savings and Credit Associations. *American Economic Review* 83 (4): 792–810.

Blinder, Alan S. 1975. Distribution Effects and the Aggregate Consumption Function. *Journal of Political Economy* 83: 447–475.

Bloom, David E., David Canning, and Bryan S. Graham. 2003. Longevity and Life-Cycle Savings. *Scandinavian Journal of Economics* 105: 319–338.

Boskin, Michael J. 1978. Taxation, Saving, and the Rate of Interest. *Journal of Political Economy* 86: S3–S27.

Bosworth, Barry P., and Lisa Bell. 2005. The Decline in Household Saving: What Can We Learn from Survey Data? *The Brookings Institution* 27: 1–31.

Bovenberg, Lans A. 1988. Private Saving: Measurement and Analysis of Recent Trends. Washington, International Monetary Fund Working Paper.

Browning, Martin, and Annamaria Lusardi. 1996. Household Saving: Micro Theories and Micro Facts. *Journal of Economic Literature* 34: 1797–1855.

Buiter, Willem H., and James Tobin. 1979. Debt Neutrality: A Brief Review of Doctrine and Evidence. In *Social Security versus Private Saving*, ed. George M. Von Furstenberg. Cambridge: Ballinger.

Butelmann, Andrea, and Francisco Gallego. 2001. Household Saving in Chile (1988 and 1997): Testing the Life Cycle Hypothesis. *Cuadernos de Economía* 38 (113): 3–48.

Cagan, Phillip. 1965. *The Effect of Pension Plans on Aggregate Saving: Evidence from a Sample Survey*. New York: National Bureau of Economic Research.

Carroll, Christopher D., and Lawrence H. Summers. 1987. Why Have Private Saving Rates in the United States and Canada Diverged? *Journal of Monetary Economics* 20: 249–279.

Carroll, Christopher D., Byung-Kun Rhee, and Changyong Rhee. 1998. Does Cultural Origin Affect Saving Behavior? Evidence from Immigrants. NBER Working Paper #6568.

Chamlee-Wright, Emily. 2002. Savings and Accumulation Strategies of Urban Market Women in Harare, Zimbabwe. *Economic Development and Cultural Change* 50 (4): 979–1006.

Chamon, Marcos D., and Eswar S. Prasad. 2010. Why are Saving Rates of Urban Households in China Rising? *American Economic Journal: Macroeconomics* 2 (1): 93–130.

Chang, Regina Y. 1994. Saving behavior of U.S. households in the 1980s: Results from the 1983 and 1986 Survey of Consumer Finances. *SSRN*. Accessed March 22, 2020. https://papers.ssrn.com/sol3/papers.cfm?abstract_id=5713.

Channel News Asia. 2000. CPF Special Account Now Available for Investments. *Channel News Asia*, Singapore.

Chen, Keith M. 2013. The Effect of Language on Economic Behavior: Evidence from Savings Rates, Health Behaviors, and Retirement Assets. *The American Economic Review* 103 (2): 690–731.
Child, Lydia M. 1832. *The American Frugal Housewife: Dedicated to Those Who Are Not Ashamed of Economy.* Boston: Carter and Hendee.
Chow, Hugh. 2001. CPF Investors—3 in 5 Make Losses. *The Straits Times*, Singapore.
Clark, Colin. 1945. Post-War Savings in the USA. *Bulletin of the Oxford University Institute of Statistics* 7: 97–103.
Coleman, Andrew. 1998. Household Savings: A Survey of Recent Microeconomic Theory and Evidence. New Zealand Treasury. Treasury Working Paper Series 98/08.
Congress of the United States. 1987. General explanation of the Tax Reform Act of 1986. *The Joint Committee on Taxation.*
Consulton Research Bureau. 1977. *The First Hundred Years of the Post Office Savings Bank of Singapore.* Singapore: Post Office Savings Bank.
Cristadoro, Ricardo, and Daniela Marconi. 2012. Household Savings in China. *Journal of Chinese Economic and Business Studies* 10 (3): 275–299.
Deaton, Angus. 1989. Saving in Developing Countries: Theory and Review. *The World Bank Economic Review* 3: 61–96.
———. 1991. Saving and Liquidity Constraints. *Econometrica* 59 (4): 1221–1248.
Defoe, Daniel. 1726. *The Complete English Tradesman.* Edinburgh: W. and R. Chambers.
———. 1999. *An Essay upon Projects.* New York: AMS Press.
Dekle, Robert, and Koichi Hamada. 2000. On the Development of Rotating Credit Associations in Japan. *Economic Development and Cultural Change* 49 (1): 77–90.
Denizer, Cevdet, Holger C. Wolf, and Yvonne Ying. 2002. Household Savings in the Transition. *Journal of Comparative Economics* 30: 463–475.
Diamond, Peter A., and Jerry Hausman. 1984. Individual Retirement and Savings Behavior. *Journal of Public Economics* 23: 81–114.
Duflo, Esther, William Gale, Jeffrey Liebman, PIeter Orszag, and Emmanuel Saez. 2006. Saving Incentives for Low- and Middle-Income Families: Evidence from a Field Experiment with H&R Block. *The Quarterly Journal of Economics* 121 (4): 1311–1346.
Dynan, Karen E., Jonathan Skinner, and Stephen P. Zeldes. 2002. The Importance of Bequests and Life-Cycle Saving in Capital Accumulation: A New Answer. *American Economic Review* 92 (2): 274–278.
Edelstein, Paul, and Lutz Kilian. 2009. How Sensitive Are Consumer Expenditures to Retail Energy Prices? *Journal of Monetary Economics* 56: 766–779.

Edwards, Sebastian. 1996. Why are Latin America's Savings Rates So Low? An International Comparative Analysis. *Journal of Development Economics* 51 (1): 5–44.

Feldstein, Martin S. 1973. Tax Incentives, Corporate Saving and Capital Accumulation in the United States. *Journal of Public Economy* 2: 159–171.

Feldstein, Martin S. 1974. Social Security, Induced Retirement, and Aggregate Capital Accumulation. *Journal of Political Economy* 82 (5): 905–926.

Feldstein, Martin S., and George Fane. 1973. Taxes, Corporate Dividend Policy and Personal Savings: The British Postwar Experience. *The Review of Economics and Statistics* 55 (4): 399–411.

Feldstein, Martin S., and Anthony Pellechio. 1979. Social Security and Household Wealth Accumulation: New Microeconomic Evidence. *Review of Economics and Statistics* 61 (3): 361–368.

Ferguson, Niall. 1998. *World's Banker: The History of the House of Rothschild*, 941–946. London: Weidenfeld & Nicolson.

Fisher, Patti J., and Sophia Anong. 2012. Relationship of Saving Motives to Saving Habits. *Journal of Financial Counseling and Planning* 23 (1): 63–79.

Fisher, Patti J., and Catherine P. Montalto. 2010. Effect of Saving Motives and Horizon on Saving Behaviors. *Journal of Economic Psychology* 31: 92–105.

Franklin, Benjamin. 1963. *The Autobiography, and Other Writings: With Selections from Poor Richard's Almanac and Papers Relating to the Junto*. New York: Dodd, Mead.

Friedman, Milton. 1957. *A Theory of the Consumption Function*. Princeton, NJ: National Bureau of Economic Research.

Friend, Irwin. 1986. The Policy Options for Stimulating National Saving. In *Savings and Capital Formation*, ed. Gerard F. Adams and Susan M. Wachter. Lexington, MA: D.C. Heath.

Friend, Irwin, and Joel Hasbrouck. 1983. Saving and After-Tax Rates of Return. *The Review of Economics and Statistics* 65 (4): 537–543.

Galbraith, John K. 1958. *The Affluent Society*. Boston: Houghton Mifflin.

Garon, Sheldon. 2012. *Beyond Our Means: Why America Spends While the World Saves*. Princeton University Press.

Goh, Keng Swee. 1995. *Wealth of East Asian Nations. Singapore Federal Publications* 78.

Great Britain Post Office. 1911. *The Post Office: An Historical Summary*, 113. London: His Majesty's Stationery Office.

Grigoli, Francesco, Alexander Herman, and Kalus Schmidt-Hebbel. 2018. Saving in the World. *World Development* 104: 257–270.

Gugerty, Mary K. 2007. You Can't Save Alone: Commitment in Rotating Savings and Credit Associations in Kenya. *Economic Development and Cultural Change* 55 (2): 251–282.

Gultekin, Bulent N., and Dennis E. Logue. 1979. Social Security and Personal Saving: Survey and New Evidence. In *Social Security versus Private Saving*, ed. George M. von Furstenberg. Cambridge: Ballinger.

Gylfason, Thorvaldur. 1981. Interest Rates, Inflation, and the Aggregate Consumption Function. *Review of Economics and Statistics* 63: 233–245.

Hayashi, Fumio. 1986. Why is Japan's Saving Rate so Apparently High? In *NBER Macroeconomics Annual 1986*, ed. Stanley Fischer, 147–210. Cambridge, MA: The MIT Press.

———. 1997. *Understanding Saving: Evidence from the United States and Japan*. Cambridge, MA: The MIT Press.

Hayhoe, Celia R., Soo Hyun Cho, Sharon A. Devaney, Sheri Lokken Worthy, Kim Jinhee, and Gorham Elizabeth. 2012. How Do Distrust and Anxiety Affect Saving Behavior? *Family and Consumer Sciences Research Journal* 41 (1): 69–85.

Heckman, Stuart J., and Sherman D. Hanna. 2015. Individual and Institutional Factors Related to Low-Income Household Saving Behavior. *Journal of Financial Counseling and Planning* 26 (2): 187–199.

Henager, Robin, and Teresa Mauldin. 2015. Financial Literacy: The Relationship to Saving Behavior in Low- to Moderate-Income Households. *Family and Consumer Sciences Research Journal* 44 (1): 73–87.

Hendershott, Patric H., and Joe Peek. 1985. Household Saving: An Econometric Investigation. In *The Level and Composition of Household Saving*, ed. Patric H. Hendershott. Cambridge, MA: Ballinger Publishing Co.

Hicks, John R. 1937. Mr. Keynes and the Classics: A Suggested Interpretation. *Econometrica* 5 (2): 147–159.

Hilber, Christian A., and Tracy M. Turner. 2014. The Mortgage Interest Deduction and Its Impact on Home Ownership Decisions. *Review of Economics and Statistics* 96 (4): 618–637.

Hilgert, Marianne A., Jeanne M. Hogarth, and Sondra G. Beverly. 2003. Household Financial Management: The Connection between Knowledge and Behavior. *Federal Reserve Bulletin* 89: 309–332.

Horioka, Charles Y. 1984. The Applicability of the Life-Cycle Hypothesis to Japan. *Kyoto University Economics Review* 54: 31–56.

Horioka, Charles Yuji, and Wako Watanabe. 1997. Why Do People Save? A Micro-analysis of Motives for Household Savings in Japan. *The Economic Journal* 107 (442): 537–552.

Howard, David H. 1978. Personal Saving Behavior and the Rate of Inflation. *The Review of Economics and Statistics* 60 (4): 547–554.

Howrey, Eugene Philip, and Saul H. Hymans. 1978. The Measurement and Determination of Loanable-Funds Saving. *Brookings Papers on Economic Activity* 1978 (3): 655–685.

Hubbard, Glenn R. 1986. Pension Wealth and Individual Saving: Some New Evidence. *Journal of Money, Credit and Banking* 18 (2): 167–178.

Hubbard, Glenn R., Jonathan Skinner, and Stephen P. Zeldes. 1995. Precautionary Saving and Social Insurance. *Journal of Political Economy* 103 (2): 360–399.

Hung, Angela A., Andre M. Parker, and Joanne K. Yoong. 2009. Defining and Measuring Financial Literacy. RAND Working Paper.

Ishikawa, Tsuneo, and Kazuo Ueda. 1984. The Bonus Payment System and Japanese Personal Saving. In *The Economic Analysis of the Japanese Firm*, ed. Masahiko Aoki, 133–192. North–Holland, Amsterdam: Elsevier Science Publishers.

Jappelli, Tullio. 1999. The Age-Wealth Profile and the Life-Cycle Hypothesis: A Cohort Analysis with a Time Series of Cross-Sections of Italian Households. *Review of Income and Wealth* 45 (1): 57–75.

Kapteyn, Arie, Rob Alessie, and Annamaria Lusardi. 2005. Explaining the Wealth Holdings of Different Cohorts: Productivity Growth and Social Security. *European Economic Review* 49: 1361–1391.

Katona, George. 1975. *Psychological Economics*. Oxford: Elsevier.

Keynes, John Maynard. 1936. *The General Theory of Employment, Interest and Money*. London: Macmillan.

Klonner, Stefan. 2003. Rotating Savings and Credit Organizations When Participants Are Risk Averse. *International Economic Review* 44 (3): 979–1006.

Kopits, George, and Padma Gotur. 1980. The Influence of Social Security on Household Savings: A Cross-Country Investigation. *Washington. Staff Papers, International Monetary Fund (Washington)* 27 (1): 161–190.

Koskela, Erkki, and Matti Viren. 1983. Social Security and Household Saving in an International Cross Section. *American Economic Review* 73 (1): 212–217.

Kotlikoff, Laurence J. 1979. Testing the Theory of Social Security and Life Cycle Accumulation. *The American Economic Review* 69 (3): 396–410.

———. 1988. Intergenerational Transfers and Savings. *Journal of Economic Perspectives* 2 (2): 41–58.

Lee, Kuan Y. 2000. *From Third World to First: The Singapore Story, 1965–2000*, 105. New York: Harper Collins.

Lee, Jae M., and Sherman D. Hanna. 2015. Savings Goals and Saving Behavior in the Context of Maslow's Hierarchy of Needs. *Journal of Financial Counseling and Planning* 26 (1): 129–147.

Levenson, Alec R., and Timothy Besley. 1996. The Anatomy of an Informal Financial Market: Rosca Participation in Taiwan. *Journal of Development Economics* 51: 45–68.

Lim, Chong Y. 1986. Report of the Central Provident Fund Study Group. *Singapore Economic Review: Special Issue* 31: 1–103.

Lindqvist, Alf. 1981. A Note on Determinants of Household Saving Behavior. *Journal of Economic Psychology* 1: 37–59.

Loayza, Norman, Klaus Schmidt-Hebbel, and Luis Serven. 2000. What Drives Private Saving Across the World? *The Review of Economics and Statistics* 82 (2): 165–181.

Lusardi, Annamaria. 2004. Savings and the Effectiveness of Financial Education. In *Pension Design and Structure: New Lessons from Behavioral Finance*, ed. Olivia S. Mitchell and Stephen Utkus, 157–184. Oxford: Oxford University Press.

———. 2008a. Financial Literacy: An Essential Tool for Informed Consumer Choice? *SSRN*. Accessed March 23, 2020. https://papers.ssrn.com/sol3/papers.cfm?abstract_id=1336389.

———. 2008b. Household Saving Behavior: The Role of Financial Literacy, Information, and Financial Education Programs. NBER Working Paper #14084.

Lusardi, Annamaria, and Olivia S. Mitchell. 2007a. Financial Literacy and Retirement Preparedness: Evidence and Implications for Financial Education. *Business Economics* 42: 35–44.

———. 2007b. Baby Boomer Retirement Security: The Roles of Planning, Financial Literacy, and Housing Wealth. *Journal of Monetary Economics* 54 (1): 205–224.

———. 2011. Financial Literacy and Planning: Implications for Retirement Wellbeing. NBER Working Paper #17078.

———. 2014. The Economic Importance of Financial Literacy: Theory and Evidence. *Journal of Economic Literature* 52 (1): 5–44.

———. 2017. How Ordinary Consumers Make Complex Economic Decisions: Financial Literacy and Retirement Readiness. *Quarterly Journal of Finance* 7 (3): 1–31.

Lusardi, Annamaria, Olivia S. Mitchell, and Vilsa Curto. 2010. Financial Literacy among the Young. *Journal of Consumer Affairs* 44(2): 358–380.

Mandell, Lewis, and Linda S. Klein. 2009. The Impact of Financial Literacy Education on Subsequent Financial Behavior. *Journal of Financial Counseling and Planning* 20 (1): 15–24.

Mason, Lisa R., Yunju Nam, Margaret Clancy, Youngmi Kim, and Vernon Loke. 2010. Child Development Accounts and Saving for Children's Future: Do Financial Incentives Matter? *Children and Youth Services Review* 32: 1570–1576.

Mauldin, Teresa A., Robin Henager, Cathy F. Bowen, and Michael Cheang. 2016. Barriers and Facilitators to Saving Behavior in Low- to Moderate-Income Households. *Journal of Financial Counseling and Planning* 27 (2): 231–251.

Modigliani, Franco, and Richard H. Brumberg. 1954. Utility Analysis and the Consumption Function: An Interpretation of Cross-Section Data. In *Post Keynesian Economics*, ed. K.K. Kurihara. New Brunswick, NJ: Ruthers University Press.

Modigliani, Franco, and Arlie Sterling. 1983. Determinants of Private Saving with Special Reference to the Role of Social Security. In *The Determinants of National Saving and Wealth*, ed. Franco Modigliani and Richard Hemming. New York: St. Martin's Press.

Montgomery, Edward. 1986. Where Did All the Saving Go? A Look at the Recent Decline in the Personal Saving Rate. *Economic Inquiry* 24 (4): 681–697.

Munnell, Alicia H. 1976. Private Pensions and Saving: New Evidence. *Journal of Political Economy* 84: 1013–1032.

Nava, Ashraf, Dean Karlan, and Wesley Yin. 2006. Tying Odysseus to the Mast: Evidence from a Commitment Savings Product in the Philippines. The Quarterly Journal of Economics 121(2): 635-672.

Ng, Serena. 2000. Government Makes Major Changes to CPF Scheme. *The Business Times*, Singapore.

Packard, Vance O. 1957. *The Hidden Persuaders*. New York: Pocket Books.

Phang, Sock Y. 2007. The Singapore Model of Housing and the Welfare State. *Research Collection School of Economics*: 15–44.

Poterba, James, Joshua Rauh, Steven Venti, and David Wise. 2007. Defined Contribution Plans, Defined Benefit Plans, and the Accumulation of Retirement Wealth. *Journal of Public Economics* 91 (10): 2062–2086.

Rha, Jong-Youn, Catherine P. Montalto, and Sherman D. Hanna. 2006. The Effect of Self-Control Mechanisms on Household Saving Behavior. *Journal of Financial Counseling and Planning* 17 (2): 3–16.

Robb, Cliff A., and Ann Woodyard. 2011. Financial Knowledge and Best Practice Behavior. *Journal of Financial Counseling and Planning* 22 (1): 60–70, 86–87.

Roberts, Sean G., James Winters, and Keith Chen. 2015. Future Tense and Economic Decisions: Controlling for Cultural Evolution. *PloS One* 10 (7): e0132145.

Rutherford, Stuart. 1999. Savings and the Poor: The Methods, Use and Impact of Savings by the Poor of East Africa. *MicroSave*.

Scher, Mark J., and Naoyuki Yoshino. 2004. *Small Savings Mobilization and Asian Economic Development: The Role of Postal Financial Services*. New York M.E: Sharpe Armonk.

Schreiner, Mark. 2000. Formal Roscas in Argentina. *Development in Practice* 10 (2): 229–232.

Schreiner, Mark, and Michael Sherraden. 2007. *Can the Poor Save? Saving and Asset Building in Individual Development Accounts*. New York: Routledge.

Schunk, Daniel. 2009. What Determines Household Saving Behavior? An Examination of Saving Motives and Saving Decisions. *Journal of Economics and Statistics* 229 (4): 467–491.

Shibuya, Hiroshi. 1987. Japan's Household Saving Rate: An Application of the Life Cycle Hypothesis. International Monetary Fund Working Paper 87/15.

Shinohara, Miyohei. 1982. The Determinants of Post-war Savings Behavior in Japan. In *The Determinants of National Saving and Wealth*, ed. Franco Modigliani, and Richard Hemming, 201–218. London: The Macmillan Press Ltd. Proceedings of a Conference held by the International Economic Association at Bergano, Italy.
Shipton, Parker. 1992. The Rope and the Box: Group Savings in the Gambia. In *Informal Finance in Low-Income Countries*, ed. Dale W. Adams and Delbert Fitchett. Boulder, CO: Westview.
Smiles, Samuel. 1859. *Self-help: With Illustrations of Character and Conduct*. London: Ward Loc.
———. 1875. *Thrift*. London: John Murray.
Smith, Adam. 1776. *An Inquiry into the Nature and Causes of the Wealth of Nations: In Three Volumes*. London.
Sommer, Kamila, and Paul Sullivan. 2018. Implications of US Tax Policy for House Prices, Rents and Home Ownership. *American Economic Review* 108 (2): 241–274.
Strumpel, Burkhard. 1975. Saving Behavior in Western Germany and the United States. *American Economic Review* 65 (2): 210–216.
Sturm, Peter H. 1983. Determinants of Saving: Theory and Evidence. *OECD Economic Studies* 1: 147–196.
Summers, Lawrence, Chris Carroll, and Alan S. Blinder. 1987. Why Is U.S. National Saving So Low?; Comments and Discussion. *Brookings Papers on Economic Activity* 2: 607.
Tanzi, Vito, and Howell H. Zee. 2000. Taxation and the Household Saving Rate: Evidence from OECD Countries. *Banca Nazionale Del Lavoro Quarterly Review* 53 (212): 31.
Teh, Shi Ning. 2014. Hunt for Higher CPF Yields Entails Trade-Offs, Risks. *The Business Times*, Singapore.
Teo, Josephine. 2019. Written Answer by Mrs Josephine Teo, Minister of Manpower, to Parliamentary Question on CPF Payouts. Notice Paper No. 1558.
Tullio, Giuseppe, and Francesco Contesso. 1986. Do After-Tax Interest Rates Affect Private Consumption and Savings? Empirical Evidence for 8 Industrial Countries: 1980–83. *Economic Papers, Commission of the European Communities* 51.
Weber, Warren E. 1975. Interest Rates, Inflation and Consumer Expenditures. *American Economic Review* 65 (5): 843–858.
Wright, Colin. 1969. Saving and the Rate of Interest. In *The Taxation of Income from Capital*, ed. Arnold C. Harberger and Martin J. Bailey. Washington: The Brookings Institution.
Xiao, Jing J., and Jessie X. Fan. 2002. A Comparison of Saving Motives of Urban Chinese and American Workers. *Family and Consumer Sciences Research Journal* 30: 463–495.

Young, Alwyn. 1992. A Tale of Two Cities: Factor Accumulation and Technical Change in Hong Kong and Singapore. *NBER MacroEconomics Annual* 1992 (7): 13–63.

Chung,Young-Iob. 2006. *Korea under Siege, 1876–1945: Capital Formation and Economic Transformation*. Oxford University Press.

Yuh, Yoonkyung, and Sherman D. Hanna. 2010. Which Households Think They Save? *The Journal of Consumer Affairs* 44 (1): 70–97.

CHAPTER 3

Consumption

1 Introduction

Consumption plays an important role in the economy. First, it involves the demand for labor and materials in production and the demand for final goods and therefore has implications for employment. Second, economists are interested in the relationship between national consumption and national income and its effect on growth. Third, people are interested in the spending on public goods such as transportation, defense and schooling and how policy changes and countercyclical spending can stimulate or rein in economic growth.

The chapter starts with the standard models of the consumption function formalized by Keynes, the Permanent Income Hypothesis (PIH) and the Life Cycle Hypothesis, and further augment the discussion to include market imperfections, consumer preferences as well as behavioral factors.

2 Theories

Economic theories about consumption are generally inextricable from saving. This is because saving is defined as the residual part of income or what is left after accounting for consumption. However, the saving function was formalized first and followed, much later, by the consumption function. Keynes built upon what the classical economists had theorized about national income and the role of the consumer to lay the foundation of consumption. This was further developed by Modigliani and Brumberg

S. Agarwal et al., *Household Finance*,
https://doi.org/10.1007/978-981-15-5526-8_3

(1954) through the life cycle hypothesis and Friedman (1957) through the permanent income hypothesis.

2.1 Early Theories on Consumption

Classical economists focus on the role of the consumer and the amount of intervention necessary to achieve a certain level of national income.

2.1.1 Consumer Sovereignty

Adam Smith (1723–1790) is best known for his two books, "*The Theory of Moral Sentiments*" (Smith 1759) and "*An Inquiry into the Nature and Causes of the Wealth of Nations*" (Smith 1776). The former discusses human nature, while the latter dwells on the economic belief of consumer sovereignty through social philosophy.

In "*An Inquiry into the Nature and Causes of the Wealth of Nations*", Smith argued in favor of consumer sovereignty which proposes that consumers as careful spenders should be empowered with the freedom to manage their own economic affairs.

> *Consumption is the sole end and purpose of production; and the interest of production ought to be attended to only so far as it may be necessary for promoting that of the consumer.* (Smith 1776)

Consumer sovereignty is closely related to the concept of laissez faire. While consumer sovereignty refers to the role that consumers play in the free market system, laissez faire refers to the free market system itself (Vatter 1965). Although Smith never explicitly referred to laissez faire in his works (Naggar 1977), consumer sovereignty where the consumer is king is widely understood as support for laissez faire.

Smith's ideology of consumer sovereignty was a detraction from societal structures at the time because it was believed that there should be a separate group regulating consumption in the economy. Mercantilism and central planning, for example, suggest that it is best for the government or aristocrats to assume control.

Smith argued that because consumers are able to individually pursue decisions to meet honest needs and wants, they will naturally steer resources toward healthy economic development. Thus, government intervention will not be required under the assumption that consumers will seek high-quality products at reasonable prices, a concept famously termed as the "invisible hand".

In addition to consumer sovereignty, Smith focused on the division of labor, specialization and market exchange. Under this model of capitalism, the living conditions of many indeed improved but there were some who suffered extreme poverty because they could not find work.

Consumer sovereignty was also popularized by the French economist Jean Baptiste Say (1767–1832). Say believed that self-regulating markets can help produce rapid economic progress. His "*A Treatise on Political Economy*" (Say et al. 1803) assured economists that if markets are left alone, periods of unemployment will be temporary and minor under the assumption that production will always create its own demand. This became known as Say's law.

> *It is worthwhile to remark that a product is no sooner created, than it, from that instant, affords a market for other products to the full extent of its own value. When the producer has put the finishing hand to his product, he is most anxious to sell it immediately, lest its value should vanish in his hands. Nor is he less anxious to dispose of the money he may get for it; for the value of money is also perishable. But the only way of getting rid of money is in the purchase of some product or other. Thus, the mere circumstance of the creation of one product immediately opens a vent for other products.* (Say et al. 1803)

Government intervention will not be necessary as the market will operate to remove unemployment. If a product is over produced, its price will fall and the resources will flow elsewhere. This is precisely Smith's concept of an invisible hand that will direct the economy to prosperity.

In contrast, Karl Marx (1818–1883), who was a widely known critic of laissez faire markets, argued that if markets are allowed to self-regulate, workers will be exploited to subsistence levels. However, despite the conditions of the poor and the presence of critiques, laissez faire capitalism flourished.

2.1.2 Mixed Economy

In the late nineteenth and early twentieth century, the US suffered repeated economic downturns. In the 1920s, Keynes challenged the notion that free markets will always result in the greatest social good in his essay "*The End of Laissez Faire*" (Keynes 1927).

Keynes rejected Say's law that supply will always create its own demand. He argued that sustained periods of unemployment occurred because profitable investment opportunities dried up and capital flowed to increasingly risky areas. As more investments failed, consumer spending and investor confidence waned. The lowered confidence led to more saving and unspent money in the financial sector and thus to more unemployment. In place of laissez faire, Keynes advocated for a mixed economy where the state assumes some responsibility to avoid chronic unemployment and economic instability.

Beginning in the 1930s, many countries began to adopt Keynes' idea of a mixed economy. The free markets were allowed to work but when public interests were violated, the government would step in with selective regulations. It was recognized that ignoring violations of public interests could result in huge social costs.

2.1.3 *Is the Consumer Rational?*

In his *Manual of Political Economy* (1906), Vilfredo Pareto (1848–1923) assumed an ideal rational economic man. A *homo economicus* is a perfectly rational agent who has complete information and clear goals with the capacity to scan all of his options. He is able to make prudent and logical decisions to consistently maximize his utility over time.

In reality, however, the consumer is often indecisive, embattled, confused, faced with incomplete information and overwhelmed by lapses in self-control.

In the interest of isolating optimizing behaviors, economic theory adopts the simplifying assumption of *homo economicus.*

2.2 *Keynesian Consumption Function*

Prior to Keynes, consumption was viewed as the passive residual of income remaining after saving. In this view, households save and hence consume as a function of the interest rate (Bunting 2001).

Keynes observed that "(t)here are not many people who will alter their way of living because the rate of interest has fallen from 5 to 4 percent" (Keynes 1936). His "fundamental psychological law" of consumption was proposed in his General Theory.

> *The fundamental psychological law, upon which we are entitled to depend with great confidence both a priori from our knowledge of human nature and from*

the detailed facts of experience, is that men are disposed, as a rule and on the average, to increase their consumption as their income increases, but not by as much as the increase in their income.

Keynes postulated that households consume more goods and services as their absolute income increases. Thus, the Keynesian consumption function is also known as the absolute income hypothesis.

A basic tenet of the Keynesian consumption function is that households determine the proportion of income that is devoted to consumption based on the absolute level of income. In the Keynesian model, the consumption function is an increasing function of disposable income (See Fig. 3.1). As disposable income rises, consumer spending will increase. The classic Keynesian consumption function assumes that household spending is wholly determined by current income and changes in income.

According to the absolute income hypothesis, consumption is based on present disposable income as represented by the following equation where C is consumption, Y_d is disposable income and b is the marginal propensity to consume (MPC):

$$C = a + bY_d$$

Fig. 3.1 Keynesian consumption function

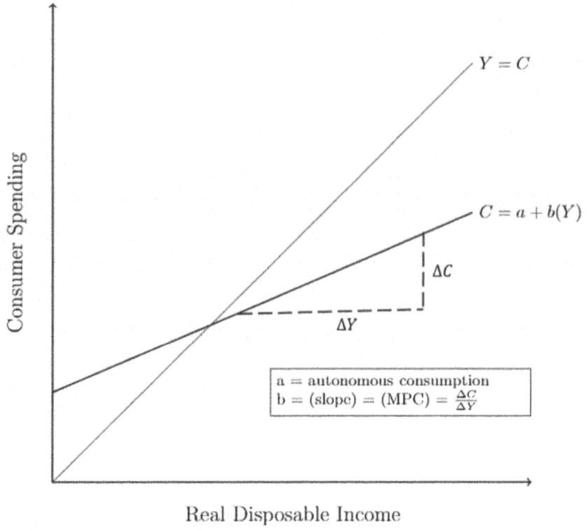

Households' average propensity to consume (APC) declines as the level of income increases. APC is the proportion of income that is devoted to consumption.

At low income, households will spend a higher proportion of their income. The APC can be one, which means households spend all their income, or greater than one. As income rises, households save a higher proportion of their income. Their consumption increases at a lower rate than disposable income. Thus, households with higher income have a lower APC.

This implies that if the government cuts income tax of low-income households who have a higher MPC, the extra income will lead to a larger increase in spending. On the contrary, households with high income have a lower MPC and therefore will save a greater proportion of the extra income.

The Keynesian consumption function can be represented by a parallel shift or non-parallel shift. An upward (downward) parallel shift in the consumption function indicates that households are spending a higher (lower) percentage of their total income (see Fig. 3.2). This can be due to changes in the prices of properties, stocks or bonds.

A non-parallel shift in the consumption function reflects a change in the MPC (see Fig. 3.3). A steeper slope means the MPC is higher, that is, households are spending a higher percentage of their additional income.

Fig. 3.2 Shifts in Keynesian consumption function

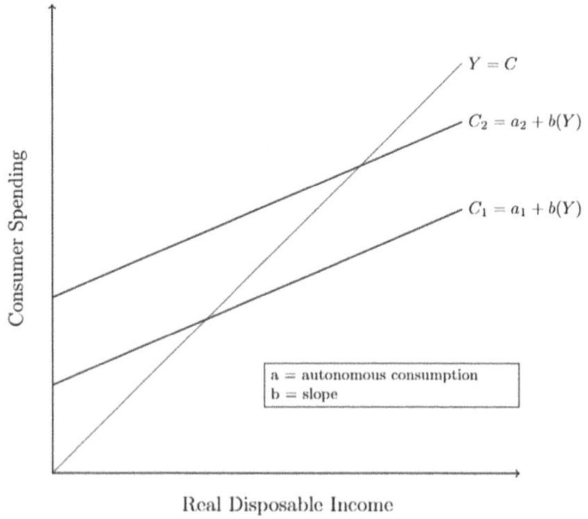

Fig. 3.3 Change in slope of Keynesian consumption function

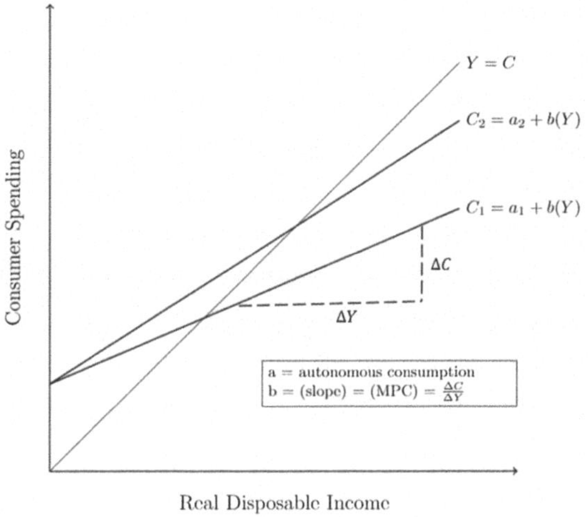

This can be due to rising confidence, lower saving or greater availability of credit.

The Keynesian consumption function was confronted by an empirical puzzle. Given that the APC is expected to decrease with income, it should diminish continuously as national income grows over time. While empirical studies find that APC decreases in the short run, it is not true in the long run.

Using a five-year moving average of consumption spending, Kuznets (1946) found that the US economy was characterized by a constant aggregate APC. With the exception of the Great Depression, the APC in the US fluctuated narrowly between 0.84 and 0.89 over the period 1869 to 1938. Although total income rose over the years, total consumption accounted for a fairly stable share of total income. This empirical result was contradictory to the Keynesian absolute income hypothesis. It is known as the Kuznets puzzle or the consumption puzzle (Friedman 1957).

There were attempts to rationalize this empirical puzzle in a way that is still consistent with Keynes' theory. Keynesian advocates argue that the short-run and long-run consumption functions behave differently. In the short run, the consumption function is non-proportional. Upward shifts in the non-proportional consumption function from C_1 to C_2 are caused by factors other than income (see Fig. 3.4). One possible explanation is habit persistence which implies a gradual adaptation and can therefore

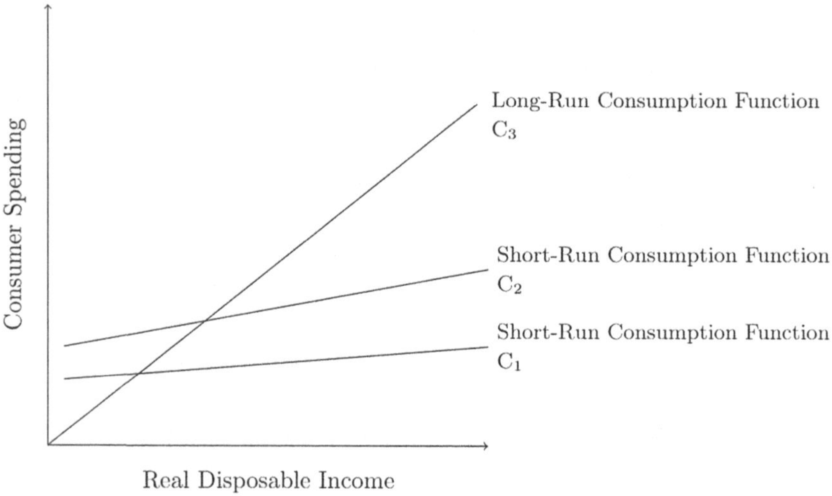

Fig. 3.4 Short-run and long-run Keynesian consumption function

explain the slow reaction to changes in income. Over the long run, however, these shifts in the short run produce a proportional relationship between C and Y as shown by C_3 and a constant APC.

2.3 Permanent Income Hypothesis

In response to the empirical puzzle, Friedman (1957) proposed his permanent income hypothesis (PIH) as an alternative to the absolute income hypothesis.

The PIH theorizes that household consumption is determined by permanent income. Permanent income is defined as the annuity value of lifetime income and wealth. Friedman (1957) argues that using permanent income adds a forward dimension to consumption theory that can reconcile the differences between short-run and long-run APCs observed in the consumption puzzle.

Under the PIH, changes in income can be permanent or temporary. In the Keynesian consumption function, it makes no difference whether the change in income is permanent or temporary. Under the PIH, if households interpret an increase in income as permanent, they will increase their consumption. On the other hand, if households interpret the increase as temporary, they will not increase their consumption. Thus, the effectiveness of fiscal policies (e.g., tax rebates and changes in taxes) will hinge on whether households view these policy changes as permanent or temporary.

A household's permanent income (Y_p) is determined by the expected income to be received over a long period of time into the future. In any year, the difference between measured income (Y_m) and permanent income (Y_p) is transitory income (Y_t), which may be positive or negative.

$$Y_m = Y_p + Y_t$$

Transitory income is the part of income that is produced by influences that are considered random and therefore not accounted for in the planning of a household's budget. For example, if a worker wins a lottery and does not expect to win again, the additional income is interpreted as a positive transitory income. The lottery increases his Y_m above his Y_p. If he is in between jobs, the income loss is a negative transitory income which has the effect of reducing his actual income below his permanent income. Another example of a positive (negative) transitory income is the higher (lower) income that a farmer receives because of an unusually good (bad) harvest.

Similar to income, the observed consumption (C_m) of a household may be divided into a permanent component (C_p) and a transitory component (C_t). Transitory consumption can be positive or negative. An unexpected doctor bill and a purchase made because of an attractive discount are examples of positive transitory consumption. A purchase postponed because of the unavailability of the good is an example of a negative transitory consumption.

$$C_m = C_p + C_t$$

According to the PIH, permanent consumption is determined by the level of permanent income Y_p, where permanent consumption is equal to a constant proportion of permanent income Y_p. In other words, the MPC out of permanent income is constant and equal to the APC out of permanent income.

$$C_p = nY_p \left(0 < n < 1\right)$$

Under the PIH, only permanent income affects changes in permanent consumption. There is no relationship between transitory and permanent income, between transitory and permanent consumption and between transitory consumption and transitory income. A key takeaway is that the MPC out of transitory income is zero, an implication that is later used by Friedman to reconcile differences between short-run and long-run consumption.

Assume that at time t, there is no transitory income, so measured income and permanent income are equal $Y_m = Y_p$ and consumption is at L (see Fig. 3.5).

At time t_{t+1}, the measured income rises from Y_M to Y_1. According to the absolute income hypothesis, consumption should increase from L to B. Under PIH, there is a transitory and permanent aspect to the change in the measured income (Friedman 1957). The increase from Y_P to Y_{P1} is due to permanent income. The increase from Y_{P1} to Y_1 represents transitory income. Under PIH, only the increase in permanent income affects consumption which explains why consumption will increase from L to N. The relationship between C_p and Y_p is proportional.

A decrease in measured income can be interpreted in a similar manner. At time $t + 1$, the measured income may decrease from Y_M to Y_2 where the decrease from Y_P to Y_{P2} is due to permanent income. Similarly, the decrease between Y_{P2} and Y_2 represents transitory income. Given that consumption only responds to changes in permanent income, consumption will decrease from L to M.

Fig. 3.5 Long-run relationship between permanent income and permanent consumption

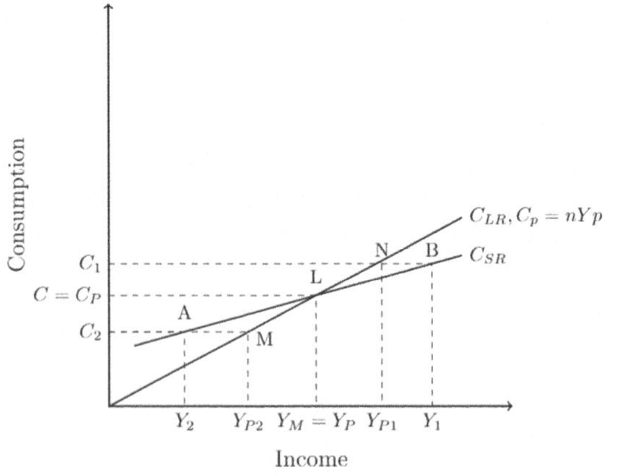

By joining M, L and N, points which indicate short-run consumption strictly due to changes in permanent income, we obtain a long-run consumption function (C_{LR}), where permanent consumption is proportional to permanent income ($C_p = n\Upsilon_p$). By making a distinction between permanent and transitory income, Friedman (1957) demonstrates why consumption and income are non-proportional in the short run.

There are criticisms of the PIH. First, the PIH postulates a constant APC. Friend and Kravis (1957) argue that households with low levels of permanent income should have higher APC than high-income households, that is, the APC should decline as permanent income increases.

Second, under PIH, MPC of transitory income is assumed to be zero. Empirical evidences suggest that the MPC of transitory income is lower than for permanent income, but not zero. For example, analysis of windfall income shows moderate increase in consumption.

Third, PIH does not address income uncertainty. Households may choose to save as a precaution against uncertain income shocks. The greater the income uncertainty, the less they will consume, the more they will save and accumulate wealth. By accumulating saving, they can more easily spread resources over the life cycle. Fortunately, the contribution of precautionary saving to wealth accumulation is not very large (Lusardi 1998).

Fourth, the PIH assumes that households have perfect knowledge, but this is not likely to be true given uncertainties such as longevity risk.

2.4 Life Cycle Hypothesis

The life cycle hypothesis by Modigliani and Brumberg (1954) is another response to the consumption puzzle. It assumes that individuals seek to maintain the same level of consumption throughout their lifetime. The amount available for consumption is the sum of the household's net worth at the beginning of the period plus the present value of its income minus the present value of planned bequests. In this model, individuals have complete knowledge about their consumption spending in the future, which includes future family size, life expectancy, emergencies, opportunities, social pressure and availability of credit.

In principle, the life cycle hypothesis and the PIH are similar because they assume that individuals plan their consumption on the basis of long-term income expectation, not current income. The life cycle hypothesis and PIH are equivalent when the individual's net worth and permanent income are the same. The necessary assumptions for equivalence are a zero interest rate and the absence of liquidity constraints.

In the life cycle hypothesis, individuals maintain the same level of consumption by choosing to save, taking on debt or liquidating their assets.

To illustrate consumption smoothing in the life cycle hypothesis, assume an individual who expects to live for *T* years, has an initial wealth *w*, expects an annual income *y* and expects to retire in *R* years' time.

Assuming the interest rate of saving is zero, the resources which an individual use to smooth his consumption will consist of the initial wealth endowment *w* and lifetime earnings $R \times y$. The individual will seek to maintain a constant level of consumption *c* throughout his lifetime of *T* years, as follows:

$$c = \frac{\text{Net Worth}}{\text{Life Time}} = \frac{w + R * y}{T} = \frac{1}{T} w + \frac{R}{T} y$$

Under the life cycle hypothesis, a one-time increase in income will have the same effect as a one-time increase in wealth. This one-time increase in income will be spread out over the consumption period. However, an increase in income that is expected to persist will have a greater impact on consumption. The increase in *y* will continue for the remaining *R* years denoted by $R \times y$ and will be spread out over the lifetime of *T* years.

On an aggregate basis, consumption (*C*) in the whole economy is a function of wealth (*W*) and income (*Y*).

$$C = aW + bY$$

where *a* is the MPC for wealth and *b* is the MPC for income.

The APC is determined by the proportion of present consumption to disposable income.

$$\text{APC} = \frac{C}{Y} = a\frac{W}{Y} + b$$

In the short run, wealth is not likely to change proportionately with income. Thus, as income increases, wealth remaining constant, higher income will lead to a lower APC. In the long run, wealth and income increase in a proportional manner such that W/Y converges to a constant APC.

There are various criticisms of the life cycle hypothesis.

The life cycle model fails to recognize the presence of liquidity constraints. Households are assumed to be able to freely borrow against future labor income to finance current consumption (Gross and Souleles 2002). However, some may have difficulty borrowing on the basis of expected future income. They may face liquidity constraints because of credit rationing or differential interest rates (Hayashi 1987). Comparing younger and older households, younger households with liquidity constraints may be much more responsive to a change in income. The consumption of older households with more accumulated wealth and therefore less liquidity constraints may not be as responsive to a change in income.

There are various implications of liquidity constraints on consumption.

First, the timing of income is important (Jappelli and Pistaferri 2017). In a model without liquidity constraints, households can smooth consumption by borrowing before the anticipated income is received. In a model with liquidity constraints, households cannot smooth anticipated increases in income by borrowing. Instead, they must collect the increase in income first before they can spend. Thus, the inter-temporal transfer of resources is hindered such that income and consumption can only be matched in the period when income is received. This delay in consumption leads to excess sensitivity.

Second, Deaton (1991) proposes that liquidity constraints will lead to precautionary saving among households, where households save in order to avoid having to curtail consumption during difficult times.

These implications have led to studies investigating the intensity of liquidity constraints and how households seek to overcome them. For example, durable goods can be used as collaterals to overcome liquidity constraints.

Empirical studies show that households do not smooth consumption over their lifetime. Instead, consumption tends to rise through middle age and fall after retirement. This may be due to uncertainty about income and lifespan. Individuals do not know exactly how long they will live and how much they will earn. Thus, they are unable to plan the smoothing of their consumption.

In addition, the elderly do not use their saving during retirement to smooth consumption. There are two possible reasons. Retirees are worried that they may live longer than expected or that they may have health issues so they put aside precautionary saving. In addition, retirees may wish to leave bequests to their children.

Other criticisms of the life cycle model include the belief that households have complete knowledge of their consumption needs in the future and the assumption of certainty-equivalent preferences where households can make objective decisions between certain and uncertain outcomes by fairly weighing payoffs.

3 Empirical Studies

Both the PIH and life cycle hypothesis embrace the view that households smooth their consumption. Consumption will not vary unless long-term expectations of income change, whereupon households will seek to smooth the changes in their income by borrowing or saving.

However, studies have shown that consumption responds excessively to increases in income. Parker (1999) finds that households change their consumption in response to anticipated income increases from changes in the social security tax, where a $1 increase in income results in a $0.20 increase in non-durable consumption. Souleles (1999a) examines the response of household consumption to income tax refunds and finds them to be excessive as well. Souleles (1999b), using data from pre-announced tax cuts, finds that the increase in household consumption exceeds what is predicted. Stephen Jr (2003) and Mastrobuoni and Weinberg (2009) observe that the consumption of food stamp beneficiaries rise on receipt of payment and decline until the receipt of the next payment.

Some attribute this excessive response to liquidity constraints. Standard theories assume that increases in permanent income can be smoothed by borrowing. However, not all households have easy access to credit. Across countries, there are large differences in the degree to which consumption responds to expected changes in income (Jappelli and Pagano 1989). The excess sensitivity of consumption to income is higher in countries where household debt is lower. Jappelli and Pagano (1989) believe that the low level of household debt is due to capital market imperfection and propose liquidity constraints as a possible explanation for the excess sensitivity.

Although liquidity constraint may be a tempting catch-all explanation for the excess sensitivity, it cannot explain why consumption decreases excessively when income decreases. Households can smooth decreases in consumption by simply saving. Some studies find that even after controlling for liquidity constraints, consumption respond excessively to increases in income. This suggests that there are other contributing factors.

3.1 *Liquidity Constraints*

An individual is liquidity constrained if he cannot borrow as desired. Liquidity constraints can arise because it is difficult to sell claims to future labor income. The limitation to borrow inhibits the ability of households to smooth their consumption. A key caveat is that liquidity constraints can explain why consumption changes excessively with increases in income but cannot explain why consumption changes excessively with decreases in income.

There are various implications of liquidity constraints on consumption. First, in the presence of liquidity constraints, the timing of income affects the timing of consumption (Jappelli and Pistaferri 2017). In a model without liquidity constraints, households will smooth their consumption by increasing consumption at the announcement of an increase in income. However, households with liquidity constraints are forced to delay their consumption until they receive the increased income. Second, it may lead to precautionary saving (Deaton 1991).

The sub-sections review studies that examine how consumption responds to (1) anticipated and unanticipated changes in income and (2) increases and decreases in income.

In the presence of borrowing constraints, a regression of consumption growth on anticipated income increases and declines should give a significantly positive coefficient on the former (anticipated income increase), while the coefficient on the latter should not be statistically different from zero.

3.1.1 *Anticipated Changes in Income*

These studies investigate whether excessive changes in consumption arising from anticipated changes in income are attributable to liquidity constraints.

Using data from Panel Study of Income Dynamics (PSID), Shea (1995) finds that the coefficient of anticipated income increase from negotiated collective wage bargaining agreements was insignificant, while the coefficient for anticipated income decline was significant. These results suggest that the excessive change in consumption cannot be attributable to liquidity constraints.

Jappelli and Pistaferri (2000) examine subjective income expectations of Italian households and find no evidence of excess sensitivity with respect to either income increase or decrease.

Parker et al. (2018) test the consumption responses of US households to anticipated tax refunds and payments which they interpret as an increase and decrease in income, respectively. They find that households do not cut consumption when making tax payments but increase spending when receiving tax refunds which is indicative of liquidity constraints.

Other studies examine anticipated income increase and anticipated income decline separately.

3.1.2 *Anticipated Increase in Income*

The following papers find evidence of excess sensitivity in consumption arising from an anticipated increase in income and attribute it to liquidity constraints.

Using data from the UK Family Expenditure Survey, Stephens Jr (2006) examines consumption responses to monthly paycheck receipt. Since the amount and arrival date are known in advance, consumption should not respond to paycheck arrival. In the study, liquidity constraints are measured by wealth and age. Using reported asset income as an indication for wealth, the study finds a significant increase in non-durables and food consumption upon paycheck arrival for households who do not own assets. Using the median age of the primary earner as an indication for age, the study finds that there is a stronger response from households where the primary earner's median age is below 39 than where the median age is above 39. The paper concludes that liquidity constraints can explain the consumption response to paycheck receipt.

Johnson et al. (2006) examine how households respond to income tax rebate in 2001 where a single sum of $300 to $600 was sent to approximately two-thirds of US households. According to the PIH, this single rebate should have little effect on consumption. However, the results show that 20% to 40% of the tax rebate was spent on non-durable goods during the three-month period in which it was received. There was evidence of excess sensitivity and liquidity constraints as households with the least liquidity and lowest income registered the largest expenditure.

Similarly, Agarwal et al. (2007) analyze how households respond to the same 2001 income tax rebate. They find that households initially saved part of the rebate but increased their spending afterwards. The spending increased most for households who are most likely to be liquidity constrained, while debt declined the most for unconstrained households.

Stephens Jr (2008) examines the consumption response to predicted increases in discretionary income following the final payment of a vehicle loan using data from Consumer Expenditure Survey. He observes that a 10% increase in discretionary income led to a 2% to 3% increase in nondurable consumption, which is suggestive of liquidity constraints.

Parker (2017) evaluates how consumption changes in response to a $25 million randomly distributed stimulus payment. Despite knowledge about the payment, the stimulus caused significant spending increases. The significant increase in consumption was almost entirely due to households who were the most liquidity constrained.

Shapiro and Slemrod (1995, 2003, 2009) use survey data to measure how consumption responds to changes in US tax policies. They find little evidence of liquidity constraints.

Shapiro and Slemrod (1995) examine the impact of a temporary reduction in income tax withholding by Bush in 1992 to stimulate the economy. Given that this was temporary, lifetime income would be unchanged. Thus, only households who are liquidity constrained would increase their consumption. From telephone interviews, 43% of respondents had plans to spend their extra income, but the reasons were not related to liquidity constraints. The paper suggests that households were not behaving rationally and the changes in consumption were due to preference nonseparability or rule of thumb behavior.

Shapiro and Slemrod (2003) conduct a follow-up study based on the tax rebates announced by President George Bush in 2001. The tax rebates were substantial. Singles would receive up to $300 in tax rebates and couples up to $600. From telephone surveys, 21.8% of households planned to increase their spending but the actual spending rate was closer to zero. This was surprising as some of the households interviewed were likely to be liquidity constrained.

In a third paper, Shapiro and Slemrod (2009) study how low-income households, who were likely to be liquidity constrained, react to a 2008 tax stimulus payment by President George Bush. Individuals who filed tax returns would receive between $300 and $600, while those who filed joint returns would receive between $600 and $1200. Parents with children under 17 would receive an additional $300 per child. Higher income households would receive smaller rebates or nothing at all. Of the survey respondents, only 19.9% said that they would increase spending. Most respondents said they would save or pay off their debts. The transitory tax rebate did not increase consumption and there was no evidence of liquidity constraints.

3.1.3 *Anticipated Income Decline*

Most studies about a decline in anticipated income focus on how consumption changes at retirement. There is overwhelming evidence that consumption declines after retirement, which is contrary to the PIH and life cycle hypothesis (Banks et al. 1998; Bernheim et al. 2001). This change cannot be attributable to liquidity constraints because in response to an anticipated decline in income, households can always save (Jappelli and Pistaferri 2017).

An explanation for the observed decline in consumption that is still consistent with the PIH and the life cycle hypothesis is that the retirement was not anticipated (Haider and Stephens 2007). Olafsson and Pagel (2018) find that Icelandic households decrease work expenses, leisure and increase saving after retirement. They conclude that the decline in consumption is indicative of the inability to plan adequately for retirement. Stephens Jr and Toohey (2018) find that food expenditure, caloric and nutrient intake decrease after retirement. This is consistent with inadequate retirement saving and failure among households to plan for their retirement. Ganong and Noel (2019) find that households cut consumption by 13% when they lose their eligibility for unemployment benefits. The drop in spending cannot be explained by rational models but can be explained by behavioral models with hand-to-mouth consumers or inattentive consumers.

Another possibility is that retirement increases the amount of time available for shopping for cheaper goods or the same goods at lower prices (Aguiar and Hurst 2007a). Yet, another possible explanation is home production (Hurd and Rohwedder 2003; Aguiar and Hurst 2005, 2007b) which suggests that retirees produce their own goods at home because they have more time. Li et al. (2015) find that non-durable expenditures of Chinese households decrease after retirement. They attribute the decline to reduced work-related expenditures and reduced food expenditures which were the result of more time spent shopping and home production.

Baxter and Jermann (1999) find that the omission of home production in previous models may have led to evidence of excess sensitivity of consumption responses to expected income growth.

3.1.4 Unanticipated Changes in Income

While the literature on anticipated shocks is very extensive, very few papers study unanticipated shocks, mainly because of the difficulty in identifying income shocks that are genuinely exogenous and unanticipated (Jappelli and Pistaferri 2017).

Unanticipated income changes can be either transitory or permanent in nature. Examples of transitory shocks are bonuses, lottery prizes and bequests. Examples of permanent shocks are job losses, promotions and severe health shocks.

It is important to distinguish between these various types of shocks because theory has a clear prediction that households should respond to the announcement of an unanticipated permanent shock. Consumption should change almost one-to-one in response to permanent income shocks (positive or negative). Friedman argues that the MPC out of transitory income should be small (Friedman 1957).

Bodkin (1959) finds that war veterans who received unexpected dividend payments from the National Service Life Insurance have a high MPC of transitory income of 0.72. Therefore, the theoretical prediction of the PIH that there is zero correlation between transitory income and transitory consumption is not supported.

Browning and Crossley (2001) examine how unemployment shocks affect the consumption of unemployed Canadian workers who possess unemployment insurance. The consumption smoothing benefit of the unemployment insurance is especially significant for liquidity constrained households who would otherwise not be able to consume in a manner consistent with their expected future income. For 90% of all respondents, small changes in unemployment insurance benefits do not lead to changes in total expenditure. However, for households who have little assets or access to credit, total expenditure is very sensitive to the level of unemployment benefits. These results are suggestive of liquidity constraints.

Agarwal and Qian (2014) study how Singaporeans respond to an unanticipated cash payment from the Singapore government Growth Dividend Program in 2011. On average, the treatment group (locals who receive the Growth Dividend) has a higher total spending than the control group (foreigners who are ineligible for the Growth Dividend) (see Fig. 3.6). The consumption response is through the increased usage of credit cards. This reveals the role of consumer credit in facilitating consumption before the disbursement of the unanticipated income.

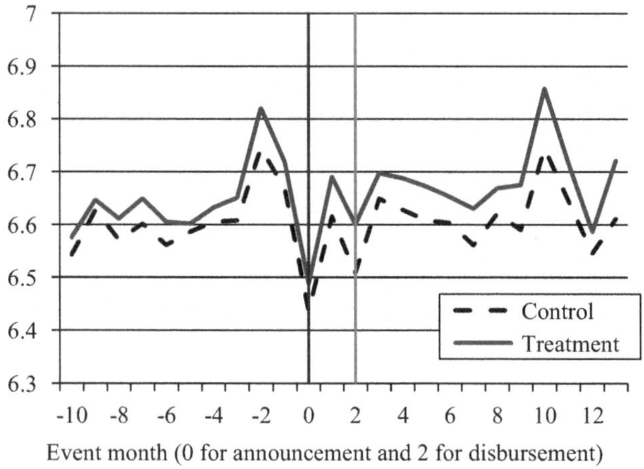

Fig. 3.6 Announcement effect and disbursement effect. (Note: Y-axis represents total spending. Treatment group represents Singaporeans affected by Growth Dividend Program. Control group represents Foreigners. Source: Agarwal and Qian (2014))

Given that the dividend was announced two months before it was disbursed, the study can test separately for an announcement effect and a disbursement effect. Agarwal and Qian (2014) find both a significant announcement effect and a significant disbursement effect.

The significant announcement effect is consistent with the life cycle model where households smooth the unanticipated increase in income by spending. In addition, consumers with low liquid assets or with low credit card limit experienced stronger consumption responses, which implies that liquidity constraints are important in considering consumption response to income shock.

Di Maggio et al. (2017) examine unanticipated income changes using home mortgages in the US between 2005 and 2007. Their findings are broadly consistent with the predictions of the life cycle hypothesis where households with lower income and wealth tend to be more responsive to positive income shocks. The mortgages were subject to an automatic mortgage rate reset after five years, where the change in mortgage rate was interpreted as an unanticipated income change for the households. The increase in disposable income that came from an average $940 decrease in mortgage payments saw an average increase in consumption of durables (car purchase) by about \$108 per month and an average deleveraging response (partial repayment of mortgage debt) of about \$90 per month. Borrowers with lower income and wealth were significantly more responsive to the reduction in mortgage payment compared to more endowed and wealthy households.

Gelman et al. (2018) test whether government employees smooth their consumption during the US federal government shutdown in 2013, which led to a 40% paycheck cut for affected employees. The government shutdown had affected only the timing of the payments. It was an unanticipated and temporary shock to liquidity. Employees had knowledge that they would be fully compensated for lost pay within two weeks. Using non-government employees as a control group, the paper finds that the shutdown did not cause a drop in consumption. Respondents smoothed their consumption by choosing to reschedule their recurrent expenditures such as mortgage and credit card payments which imposed little to no penalty. This suggests that individuals smooth consumption by borrowing, which is consistent with the life cycle model.

In contrast, using another dataset related to the same 2013 government shutdown, Baker and Yannelis (2017) find that consumption was affected by the government shutdown. They find excess sensitivity of consumption to temporary changes in income that violates the PIH. Households respond to the change in the amount of leisure time by changing the level and composition of their spending allocations and increasing home production. There is evidence that the excess sensitivity is largely driven by liquidity and credit constraints.

Fuster et al. (2018) use survey responses from interviewing US households about their consumption responses to unanticipated changes in income in various scenarios. They find that the consumption response to unanticipated losses is larger than unanticipated gains and that many households act as if they expect to be hand-to-mouth although they have substantial liquid wealth. Fuster et al. (2018) could not attribute the results to short-term liquidity constraints as they find that households do not seem to respond to a one-year interest-free loan. The study concludes that the consumption response is more consistent with a precautionary saving model.

Christelis et al. (2019) test the consumption responses of Dutch households to a hypothetical, unanticipated change in income. They find evidence consistent with consumption models in the presence of liquidity constraints. First, the MPC of negative income shocks is greater than positive income shocks. Second, the size of income shocks also matters. For large increases (decreases) in income, they find that the MPC is smaller (larger).

In recent years, there is an increasing prevalence of wealthy hand-to-mouth households who own a significant amount of illiquid assets like property but have little to no liquid assets. These households are important because they have large consumption responses to transitory income shocks which are crucially important for fiscal interventions. Their consumption responses are similar to poor hand-to-mouth households although intrinsically they are different because they can use illiquid assets to buffer large negative shocks (Kaplan et al. 2014).

3.2 *Bounded Rationality*

According to bounded rationality, consumers tend to smooth consumption when expected changes to income are large, but less so when the changes are small because the disutility from not smoothing consumption is small. For example, households may want to increase their consumption in response to an anticipated increase in income but they face difficulties in borrowing. If the increase in utility from consumption is small relative to the cost of negotiating a loan, no adjustment to consumption will be made.

Browning and Collado (2001) examine how Spanish households respond to institutionalized extra wage payments in June and December of every year. These wage payments are interpreted as unanticipated changes in income as the amount of wage payment is only known upon receipt and can vary in amount every year. They did not find excess sensitivity in consumption where households expect the income changes to be insignificant. They explain that because of bounded rationality, individuals choose to smooth consumption if there are large income changes but that they will not bother to adjust to small income changes since the utility loss is small. They suggest that excess sensitivity found in other studies may be due to bounded rationality as the income changes were large and ignoring them would impose a large welfare cost.

Using credit card spending and mortgage payments, Scholnick (2009) seeks to determine whether changes in consumption depend on the size of the final mortgage payment where the final mortgage payment represents an anticipated shock to disposable income. The evidence supports the magnitude hypothesis which states that the smoothing of consumption occurs if the predictable income shock is large enough.

3.3 *Income Uncertainty*

Income uncertainty prompts consumers to defer their consumption. This suggests that those with more volatile income streams will save more and consume less.

In the standard case, the consumption function is assumed to be linear. As income decreases, income risk increases at an increasing rate, leading to more precautionary saving and less consumption which gives rise to a concave function (Carroll and Kimball 1996).

Ben-David et al. (2018) find that US households with greater income uncertainty are more pessimistic which lead to precautionary behaviors such as reduced consumption.

Dominitz and Manski (2006) show that income uncertainty varies with age. Younger persons are less confident that social security will continue to exist when they retire. They are concerned that the social security system will collapse entirely and perceive more uncertainty than older persons.

Consumers closer to retirement have more financial wealth (the value of labor earnings earned thus far) relative to human wealth (the expected present discounted value of future labor earnings), hence the response of their consumption to permanent shocks in income is less sharp. The more prudent the individuals, the less sharp their response as they have accumulated more wealth to smooth the impact.

3.4 *Lifetime Uncertainty*

Apart from income risk, health and longevity risk can provide useful insights into the wealth holdings of households. With lifetime uncertainty, households with a longer life span may outlive their retirement saving.

In the life cycle model, wealth is assumed to be completely depleted at the time of death. With uncertainty about lifespan, this is no longer true. Households may leave unintended bequests (Yaari 1965) or be left penniless and dependent on handouts.

Hubbard et al. (1995) show that a combination of social insurance programs and income risk can explain heterogeneity in wealth accumulation and the minimal accumulation of wealth by individuals at the bottom of the income distribution. These social insurance programs guarantee households a minimum level of consumption. Their model suggests that some households choose not to save in order to remain eligible for social insurance.

3.4.1 Financial Products: Annuities and Reverse Mortgages

In order to protect against longevity risks, individuals can rely on financial products such as annuities or reverse mortgages to smooth consumption.

In exchange for a lump sum premium, annuities enable individuals to avoid the risk of depleting all their wealth before they die through a guaranteed payout that is disbursed for as long as they live. Reverse mortgages are loans secured by housing equity which allow individuals to continue residing in their home, while they are still alive.

Although annuities should be popular because of increasing life expectancy, the demand remain low. There are various reasons for the limited demand including the preference for lump sum payment, unfavorable pricing (Mitchell et al. 1999), bequest motives (Lockwood 2018), alternative sources of annuity income such as Social Security (Inkmann et al. 2011), risk sharing among couples who may inherit the spouse's remaining resources (Brown and Poterba 2000), inertia and lack of financial sophistication (Benartzi et al. 2011).

3.5 Bequest Motives

Bequest can be voluntary or involuntary.

Involuntary bequests are closely related to lifetime uncertainty. They are involuntary because they are accidental (Yaari 1965). An individual is unable to use up all his wealth as he is unsure how long he will live.

Voluntary bequests can arise from altruism or from strategic intent. Altruistic individuals choose to leave behind bequests because they gain satisfaction from knowing that heirs will enjoy their inherited wealth, for example, parents who leave the family home to their children. Strategic bequests are those made when individuals condition their bequests on the actions of potential beneficiaries, for example, parents who reward more attentive children.

There is mixed evidence on the prevalence of voluntary bequests. According to Kotlikoff and Summers (1981), an estimated 80% of US wealth accumulation is due to intergenerational transfers, whereas Modigliani (1988) finds that the fraction is closer to 20%.

There is indication that voluntary bequests based on altruism are rare. To be truly altruistic, voluntary bequests should be made while the giver is still alive when the beneficiary is credit constrained or most in need. In addition, the tax treatment of inter-vivo transfers is more favorable than bequests made at death.

Controlling for households with access to family networks, gifts and loans, Engelhardt (1996) finds that most first-time US home buyers use their own saving for down payments with no more than 20% getting help from relatives. The small proportion of households who received assistance suggests that there is little inter-vivo transfers made out of altruism.

Bernheim et al. (1985) test for voluntary bequests arising from strategic intent. They compare visitation rates of households with one child and those with two or more children. They find that visitation rates increase where there is substantial bequeathable wealth and in families with two or more children. The study concludes that parents can use bequests to influence their children in areas such as education, marriage and migration and to create competition for bequests, couples should have more than one child.

3.6 Inter-temporal Non-separability

Inter-temporal non-separability is the inability to make consumption decisions based on discrete time periods. In theory, the consumption of an individual in one period should not affect his consumption in the next period. However, in reality, inter-temporal non-separability can arise due to habits, cue theory, durable goods and home purchase.

3.6.1 Habits

With habit formation, the marginal utility derived from present consumption depends on past consumption. Thus, observation of excessive change in consumption may be due to slow adjustment to changes in income because habits reduce the variability of consumption across time.

Habit formation can be either myopic or rational. In myopic habit formation, households are not aware of how their current consumption decisions affect their future marginal rate of substitution between goods. As a result, their behavior may seem inconsistent over time. In rational habit formation, households are aware of the effects of their habit on consumption and will seek to maximize their utility consistently over time.

There are mixed results in the empirical tests of habit formation. Guariglia and Rossi (2002) observe that, among British households, the addition of habit formation and labor income uncertainty to the standardized consumption model can explain the excessive changes in consumption observed. Alessie and Teppa (2010) find evidence of habit formation using household-level data from the Netherlands, but the magnitude of the habit formation is small compared to labor income uncertainty which also affects consumption behavior of these Dutch households.

In contrast, Meghir and Weber (1996) note that allocation of expenditure on food, transport and services is inter-temporally separable among US households. After controlling for employment status, working and non-working spouses, food out of the home, clothing and fuel, Dynan (2000) notes that habit formation has limited impact on food consumption. Rhee (2004) finds similar results in the food expenditures of Korean households.

3.6.2 *Cue Theory*

An alternative explanation for inter-temporal non-separability is cue theory. Cue theory suggests that some individuals receive additional marginal utility of consumption from pairing of a cue and the consumption of a good.

Under cue theory, the mind unconsciously picks up on available cues by filling the blanks with a perceived image or pattern. According to the cue model, small changes in cues give rise to large changes in marginal utility of consumption (Laibson 2001), which may explain the observed excessive consumption.

Environmental cues such as the scent of beer or the sight of drug (for an addict) can create positive feelings of pleasure and increase the marginal utility of consumption.

There are instances where cue theory and habit formation coexist, for example, if the act of a previous consumption leads to a cue that increases the marginal utility of consumption.

3.6.3 *Durable Goods*

By definition, the services of a durable good last for more than a period. The purchase of a durable good in one period affects consumption in subsequent periods. For example, a car provides services over a number of years. Some durable goods can serve as collateral for loans.

Fernandez-Villaverde and Krueger (2011) compare the consumption of durable and non-durable goods over the life cycle of US households. They find that expenditure on housing, appliances, furniture, vehicles, books and electronic equipment continue to increase despite a substantial buildup of such durables over time. Alessie and De Ree (2009) come to a similar conclusion but find that durable consumption drops dramatically after age 60.

However, Browning et al. (2016) find that the demand for consumer electronics rises with age among British households. They attribute this to the luxurious nature of the goods and the change in lifetime wealth.

Adams et al. (2009) find that for lower income households, demand for auto loans increase during tax rebate season. These purchases are highly sensitive to down payment constraints.

Aaronson et al. (2012) estimate the response to a minimum-wage hike. They find that minimum-wage households (those with annual income below S$20,000) increase their spending by more than the wage hike and increase their debt substantially. In comparison, debt of higher wage households remain unchanged (see Fig. 3.7). The spending response is concentrated in a small number of households who purchase vehicles after the wage increase. The result is consistent with an augmented buffer stock model where a small income increase can generate small down payments for large durable goods.

Home Ownership and Mortgage

Households face borrowing constraints in the mortgage market because of the large quantum involved. They may have to provide a sizeable down payment. Such imperfections in the credit market often raise the age of first home ownership.

Chiuri and Jappelli (2003) show that increases in down payments negatively affect home ownership. Countries with higher down payment like Italy and Austria are associated with 5% to 8% less home ownership among the young compared to countries like Australia and France.

It is argued that if credit markets work well, desired consumption is equal to actual consumption. Gerardi et al. (2010) find that mortgage markets have become less imperfect since the early 1980s with the development of the secondary mortgage market.

Households who refinance their mortgages and cash out equity from their homes spend them on consumption, home improvements and repaying other debts. Brady et al. (2000) find that funds raised through

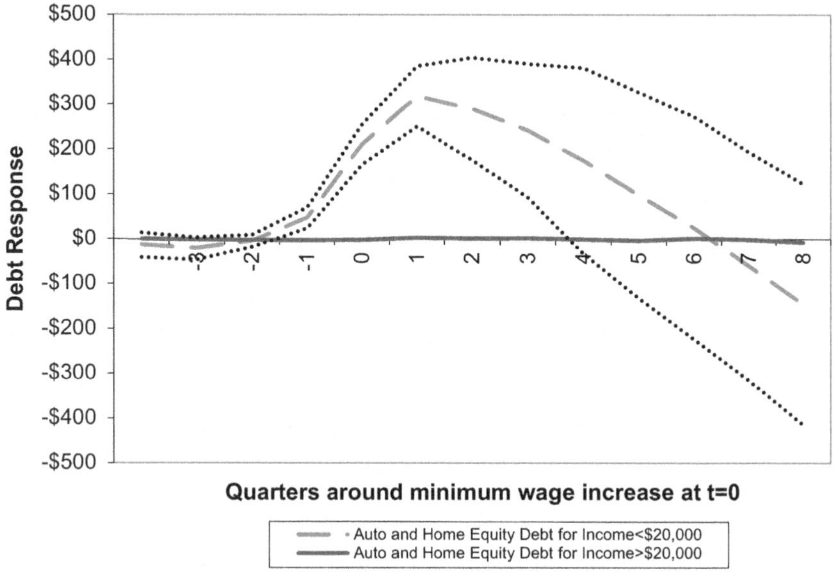

Fig. 3.7 Debt response of minimum- and non-minimum-wage households. (Note: Dotted lines represent estimates at 90% confidence intervals. Source: Aaronson et al. (2012))

mortgage refinancing are used for home improvements, consumer expenditures, stock market investments and real estate investments. Canner et al. (2002) find similar results. Greenspan and Kennedy (2008) find that home owners use the additional funds to acquire assets, improve their homes and repay non-mortgage consumer debt.

3.7 *Intra-temporal Non-separability*

Intra-temporal non-separability is the inability to separate utility from different types of goods within a discrete time period.

3.7.1 *Leisure*

Contrary to the life cycle theory which predicts smoothing of consumption and therefore no relationship between income and consumption, some find a strong relationship between income and consumption and attribute it to market imperfections.

Heckman (1974) has an alternative explanation for the strong relationship between income and consumption that does not involve market imperfections. Instead of the standard life cycle model which assumes that the hours of work is institutionally fixed, he allows individuals to decide on their hours of work, that is, he introduces a labor-leisure choice. If wage rates change over the life cycle, the hours worked may vary and affect labor supply. Heckman views earnings as a result of the labor supply decision. If the price of leisure is high (wage is high) at a certain age, an individual will tend to consume less leisure at that age and work more. He will consume less of goods that are complements to leisure such as vacation. He will consume more of goods that are substitutes to leisure such as work clothes. Heckman points out that the consumption of leisure and certain goods will be pushed to the latter part of the life cycle. He concludes that there is non-separability between consumption and leisure.

In a more recent paper, Blundell et al. (2016) find strong evidence of consumption smoothing in the presence of permanent wage shocks. They study the mechanisms behind the smoothing of household consumption to wage shocks. The mechanisms include the credit market, family labor supply, progressive taxation on joint family earnings, saving, government transfers and external insurance. They find that female labor supply helps to insure against wage shocks faced by the husband both on the intensive margin (from part-time to full-time) and on the extensive margin (from not working to working). In addition, the various mechanisms were able to explain consumption smoothing in response to wage shocks. Further the decision of whether to work (extensive margin) and the number of hours to work (intensive margin) affect consumption. Some goods are complements with work, while others are substitutes for work. They find that the co-movement of consumption and hours worked depends on the type of wage shock (whether temporary or permanent), the type of consumption good (whether work related) and the labor supply (whether at the intensive margin or extensive margin).

3.7.2 Home Production

Standard models do not consider that households have the option of home production. Home production refers to the production of goods and services by a household for its own consumption such as farming, childcare, cooking and gardening.

Aguiar and Hurst (2005) find that home production is significant and can explain why consumption declines after retirement. They investigate the extent to which food expenses outside the home are replaced by meals prepared at home after retirement. They conclude that retirees are able to smooth consumption by substituting their time for food expenditures. They conclude that food consumption do not decline at retirement. About 80% of the reduction in spending after retirement is due to home production. The remaining 20% is due to more intensive shopping, where the additional time enables retirees to find the same goods at lower prices.

However, Been et al. (2020) explore the extent to which home production can smooth a wealth shock during the recession from 2007 to 2009. They find that home production, defined to include housekeeping, gardening, home repair, dining out and vehicle maintenance services, is unlikely to smooth wealth shocks because of the low proportion of goods that are substitutable by home production. They find that only 11% of total consumption spending on goods and services are potentially substitutable by home production. The other 89%, such as utilities, do not have home produced counterparts.

3.7.3 *Unitary Models*

The standard approach to modeling household behavior is based on the "unitary" approach where the household is treated as a single decision maker, regardless of the fact that household members may not all agree with the decisions made. For example, husband and wife may not agree on what to do with a government cash rebate at the end of the year.

In addition, the different sources of income within the household is aggregated and treated as one single amount at the household's disposal. The household is considered as a single entity. In some countries, married couples are jointly taxed which is aligned to this standard approach. However, in many other countries, married couples can choose to be taxed independently.

If it is important to understand the intra-household power dynamics, then more complicated models will be needed (Chiappori and Mazzocco 2017).

3.8 *Behavioral Factors*

In the standard model, households are assumed to have certainty-equivalent preferences, to be fully informed and to make choices independently of other consumers. In the real world, some of these assumptions may not hold because of mental accounting, hyperbolic preferences, present bias and social influences.

3.8.1 *Mental Accounting*

Individuals who practice mental accounting are more willing to spend certain sources of income or assets than others. While people should value money in the same way regardless of how it is earned or stored, some households behave as if money is not fungible and saving levels can be influenced by mere framing of decisions (Shefrin and Thaler 1988). For example, if resources are shifted from high temptation accounts (such as checking) to low temptation accounts (such as retirement saving), they are more likely to be saved. With this in mind, governments can influence household consumption and saving through preferential tax treatment of such accounts.

Thaler (1990) and Tversky and Kahneman (1981) find that households have different MPCs for different assets. They are more willing to spend money from tax refunds and lotteries than from their regular paychecks.

Levin (1998) tests the problem of self-control across ten different goods. The MPC for liquid assets is greater than the MPC for real estate wealth which suggests some form of mental accounting. The results show that assets are not fungible and consumers enforce liquidity constraints on themselves because of either financial or psychological transaction costs.

Baker et al. (2007) find that the MPC of dividend income is disproportionately higher than the MPC of capital gains among US households. They attribute the differences in MPCs to mental accounting.

Di Maggio et al. (2018) repeat the study using Swedish households. While they also find that the MPC of dividend income is higher than the MPC of capital gains, they observe that dividend income changes more persistently than capital gains which suggests that dividend income and capital gains are independent of each other. Thus, they conclude that households are behaving rationally and there is no evidence of mental accounting.

3.8.2 *Hyperbolic Preferences*

An individual with hyperbolic preferences is impatient, lacks self-control and have difficulty carrying out his good intentions. Hyperbolic preference is a cognitive bias. It refers to the tendency where people choose a smaller-sooner reward over a larger-later reward when the delay occurs sooner rather than later in time. That is, people avoid waiting more as the wait nears the present.

For example, they prefer $100 now to $110 in a day but are willing to wait if offered $100 in 30 days to $110 in 31 days. They do not mind waiting one day for $10 if the wait happens a month from now. There are several reasons why people might rationally choose a smaller reward now over a larger reward later. They may have an urgent need such as hunger or rent payment.

However, when the 30 days have passed, many of the same people will reverse their preferences and now choose the immediate $100 rather than wait a day for an additional $10. In short, people act impulsively in the short term but exhibit greater patience in the longer term.

Hyperbolic preferences can explain anomalies such as undersaving and a sharp decline in consumption at retirement (Laibson 1998). To avoid the temptation of immediate gratification, such individuals turn to illiquid assets such as pensions, certificates of deposits or housing as a form of commitment. Assets with this golden egg property provide substantial benefits in the long run that are impossible to realize immediately (Laibson 1997). However, too much illiquid assets can be problematic for households who seek to smooth their consumption.

3.8.3 *Present Bias*

Present bias increases the desire for instant gratification, which may drive households to borrow from expensive sources like credit cards to fund their purchases.

Using administrative data on borrowing, Meier and Sprenger (2010) find evidence of present bias at the individual level. The study shows that those who exhibit present bias are 15% more likely to have credit card debt and to have higher amount of credit card debt.

3.8.4 *Social Influences*

In the standard model, the utility of an individual's consumption depends only on his personal consumption. With social influences, it also depends on the average peer consumption.

Grinblatt et al. (2008) demonstrate the impact of social influences on consumption using automobile purchases among Finnish households. The study finds that the type of automobile bought is influenced by the purchases of their neighbors.

Studies about social influences and their effect on consumption focus on identifying peer groups and explaining the underlying peer effect (Maurer and Meier 2008). These peer groups are often defined based on demographic factors such as racial group (Charles et al. 2009), neighborhood (Kuhn et al. 2011) and cities (Ravina 2007).

The underlying peer effect can be broadly described by three models. First, "Keeping up with the Joneses" focuses on the competitive desire of an individual who compares his consumption to his neighbor as a benchmark of social class (Duesenberry 1948). Second, the risk sharing model involves the smoothing of consumption by relying on reference groups such as friends and family. Third, conspicuous consumption involves the purchase of goods such as jewelry, luxury cars and watches which serve as status symbols of self-worth (Veblen 1953).

De Giorgi and Pistaferri (2016) test the three models using panel data on Danish co-workers, controlling for occupation, education and time spent together. Their results show that peer effects are significant and are more in line with "Keeping up with the Joneses" than the other two models.

3.9 Government Stimulus

Since 1994, Singapore has an indirect government stimulus program in the form of an annual nationwide shopping promotion held during the summer holidays. The Great Singapore Sales (GSS), started jointly by the Singapore Tourism Board and the Singapore Retailers Association, is a concerted effort to attract tourists and boost consumer spending.

While consumption seems to increase during the GSS, it is unclear whether consumers merely delay or bring forward their purchases.

Agarwal et al. (2016) study the shopping behavior four weeks before the GSS and one week after. The first three weeks serve as the reference period for comparison against the spending one week before and one week after the GSS. They find that consumers spend more on shopping products during the GSS than before and after the GSS but spend less on non-shopping products during the GSS than before the GSS. This implies that consumers are savvy and know how to substitute by spending more on items discounted during the sale and less on items not related to the sale. People who are financially stronger are more disciplined; they spend more during the early part of the GSS. People who have low credit limit, low account balance or low income increase their spending throughout the entire GSS. This implies that the stimulus program has a greater impact on the shopping behavior of consumers with financial concerns.

Agarwal et al. (2017) find that households increase spending on apparel items during US sales tax holidays and that this increase in spending is not offset in the periods before or after the tax holiday. In addition, higher income households and those with more access to credit gain more from the tax break. The study suggests that other policies which temporarily decrease taxes may also be successful in increasing demand.

4 Conclusion

The consumption function was first formalized by Keynes who explicitly modeled how consumption changes with current income. This was followed by the PIH and life cycle which assume that households plan their consumption based on long-term income expectations.

These standard consumption models have been augmented to include other significant features of consumers' preferences as well as imperfections in the financial market such as liquidity constraints, precautionary saving, income uncertainty, lifetime uncertainty, bequest motive, intertemporal non-separability, intra-temporal non-separability as well as behavioral factors such as mental accounting, hyperbolic preferences and social influences.

There remains an ongoing debate about the role of consumption in generating economic growth and the optimal mix of state intervention and consumer sovereignty required for the economy to thrive.

References

Aaronson, Daniel, Sumit Agarwal, and Eric French. 2012. The Spending and Debt Response to Minimum Wage Hikes. *American Economic Review* 102 (7): 3111–3139.

Adams, William, Liran Einav, and Jonathan Levin. 2009. Liquidity Constraints and Imperfect Information in Subprime Lending. *American Economic Review* 99 (1): 49–84.

Agarwal, Sumit, and Wenlan Qian. 2014. Consumption and Debt Response to Unanticipated Income Shocks: Evidence from a Natural Experiment in Singapore. *American Economic Review* 104: 4205–4230.

Agarwal, Sumit, Chunlin Liu, and Nicholas S. Souleles. 2007. The Reaction of Consumer Spending and Debt to Tax Rebates—Evidence from Consumer Credit Data. *Journal of Political Economy* 115: 986–1019.

Agarwal, Sumit, Qian Wenlan, and Kang Mo Koo. 2016. Shop Till You Drop or When You Run Out of Cards. Economic Affairs. *The Straits Times.*

Agarwal, Sumit, Nathan Marwell, and Leslie McGranahan. 2017. Consumption Responses to Temporary Tax Incentives: Evidence from State Sales Tax Holidays. *American Economic Journal: Economic Policy* 9 (4): 1–27.

Aguiar, Mark, and Erik Hurst. 2005. Consumption vs. Expenditure. *Journal of Political Economy* 133 (5): 919–948.

———. 2007a. Lifecycle Prices and Lifecycle Production. *American Economic Review* 97 (5): 1533–1559.

———. 2007b. Measuring Trends in Leisure: The Allocation of Time over Five Decades. *Quarterly Journal of Economics* 122: 969–1006.

Alessie, Rob, and Joppe de Ree. 2009. Explaining the Hump in Lifecycle Consumption Profiles. *Economist-Netherlands* 157 (1): 107–120.

Alessie, Rob, and Federica Teppa. 2010. Saving and Habit Formation: Evidence from Dutch Panel Data. *Empirical Economics* 38 (2): 385–407.

Baker, Scott, and Constantine Yannelis. 2017. Income Changes and Consumption: Evidence from the 2013 Federal Government Shutdown. *Review of Economic Dynamics* 23: 99–124.

Baker, Malcolm, Nagel Stephen, and Wurgler Jeffrey. 2007. The Effect of Dividends on Consumption. *Brookings Papers on Economic Activity* 2007 (1): 231–276.

Banks, James, Richard Blundell, and Sarah Tanner. 1998. Is There a Retirement-Savings Puzzle? *American Economic Review* 88: 769–788.

Baxter, Marianne, and Urban J. Jermann. 1999. Household Production and the Excess Sensitivity of Consumption to Current Income. NBER working paper #7046.

Been, Jim, Susann Rohwedder, and Michael Hurd. 2020. Does Home Production Replace Consumption Spending? Evidence from Shocks in Housing Wealth in the Great Recession. *Review of Economics and Statistics.* 102 (1): 113–128.

Benartzi, Shlomo, Alessandro Previtero, and Richard H. Thaler. 2011. Annuitization Puzzles. *Journal of Economic Perspectives* 25: 143–164.

Ben-David, Itzhak, Elyas Fermand, Camelia M. Kuhnen, and Geng Li. 2018. Expectations Uncertainty and Household Economic Behavior. NBER working paper #25336.

Bernheim, Douglas B., Andrei Schleifer, and Lawrence H. Summers. 1985. The Strategic Bequest Motive. *Journal of Political Economy* 93: 1045–1076.

Bernheim, Douglas B., Jonathan Skinner, and Steven Weinberg. 2001. What Accounts for he Variation in Retirement Wealth among U.S. Households? *American Economic Review* 91: 832–857.

Blundell, Richard, Luigi Pistaferri, and Itay Saporta-Eksten. 2016. Consumption Inequality and Family Labor Supply. *American Economic Review* 106 (2): 387–435.

Bodkin, Ronald G. 1959. Windfall Income and Consumption. *American Economic Review* 49: 602–614.

Brady, Peter J., Glenn B. Canner, and Dean M. Maki. 2000. The Effects of Recent Mortgage Refinancing. *Board of Governors of the Federal Reserve System* 86 (7): 441–450.

Brown, Jeffrey R., and James M. Poterba. 2000. Joint Life Annuities and Annuity Demand by Married Couples. *Journal of Risk and Insurance* 67: 527–553.

Browning, Martin, and Maria Dolores Collado. 2001. The Response of Expenditures to Anticipated Income Changes: Panel Data Estimates. *American Economic Review* 91: 681–192.

Browning, Martin, and Thomas F. Crossley. 2001. Unemployment Insurance Benefit Levels and Consumption Changes. *Journal of Public Economics* 80 (1): 1–23.

Browning, Martin, Thomas F. Crossley, and Melanie Luhrmann. 2016. Durable Purchases over the Later Life Cycle. *Oxford Bulletin of Economics and Statistics* 78 (2): 145–169.

Bunting, David. 2001. Keynes' Law and Its Critics. *Journal of Post Keynesian Economics* 24: 149–163.

Canner, Glenn B., Dynan Karen, and Passmore Wayne. 2002. Mortgage Refinancing in 2001 and early 2002. *Board of Governors of the Federal Reserve System* 88 (12): 469–481.

Carroll, Christopher D., and Miles S. Kimball. 1996. On the Concavity of the Consumption Function. *Econometrica* 64: 981–992.

Charles, Kerwin K., Erik Hurst, and Nikolai Roussanov. 2009. Conspicuous Consumption and Race. *Quarterly Journal of Economics* 124 (2): 425–467.

Chiappori, Pierre-Andre, and Maurizio Mazzocco. 2017. Static and Intertemporal Household Decisions. *Journal of Economic Literature* 55 (3): 985–1045.

Chiuri, Maria C., and Tullio Jappelli. 2003. Financial Market Imperfections and Home Ownership: A Comparative Study. *European Economic Review* 47 (5): 857–875.

Christelis, Dimitris, Dimitris Georgarakos, Tullio Jappelli, Luigi Pistaferri, and Maarten Van Rooij. 2019. Asymmetric Consumption Effects of Transitory Income Shocks. *The Economic Journal* 129 (622): 2322–2341.

De Giorgi, Anders F., and Luigi Pistaferri. 2016. Consumption Network Effects. NBER working paper #22357.

Deaton, Angus S. 1991. Saving and Liquidity Constraints. *Econometrica* 59: 1221–1248.

Di Maggio, Marco, Amir Kermani, Benjamin J. Keys, Tomasz Piskorski, Rodney Ramcharan, Amit Seru, and Vincent Yao. 2017. Interest rate Pass-Through:

Mortgage Rates, Household Consumption, and Voluntary Deleveraging. *American Economic Review* 107 (11): 3550–3588.
Di Maggio, Marco, Amir Kermani, and Kaveh Majlesi. 2018. Stock Market Returns and Consumption. NBER working paper #24263.
Dominitz, Jeff, and Charles F. Manski. June 2006. Measuring Pension-benefit Expectations Probabilistically. *Labor* 20 (2): 201–236.
Duesenberry, James S. 1948. Income-Consumption Relations and their Implications. In *Income, Employment and Public Policy: Essays in Honor of Alvin H. Hansen*, ed. Lloyd A. Metzler, 54–81. New York: W.W. Norton.
Dynan, Karen E. 2000. Habit Formation in Consumer Preferences: Evidence from Panel Data. *American Economic Review* 90 (3): 391–406.
Engelhardt, Gary V. 1996. House Prices and Home Owner Saving Behavior. *Regional Science and Urban Economics* 26: 313–336.
Fernandez-Villaverde, Jesus, and Dirk Krueger. 2011. Consumption and Saving over the Life Cycle: How Important are Consumer Durables? *Macroeconomic Dynamics* 15 (5): 725–770.
Friedman, Milton. 1957. *A Theory of the Consumption Function*. Princeton: Princeton University Press.
Friend, Irwin, and Irving B. Kravis. 1957. Consumption Patterns and Permanent Income. *The American Economic Review* 5 (2): 536–555.
Fuster, Andreas, Basit Zafar, and Greg Kaplan. 2018. What Would you do with $500? Spending Responses to Gains, Losses, News and Loans. NBER working paper #23486.
Ganong, Peter, and Pascal J. Noel. 2019. Consumer Spending During Unemployment: Positive and Normative Implications. NBER working paper #25417.
Gelman, Michael, Shachar Kariv, Matthew D. Shapiro, Dan Silverman, and Steven Tadelis. 2018. How Individuals Respond to a Liquidity Shock: Evidence from the 2013 Government Shutdown. NBER working paper #21025.
Gerardi, Kristopher S., Harvey S. Rosen, and Paul S. Willen. 2010. The Impact of Deregulation and Financial Innovation on Consumers: The Case of the Mortgage Market. *The Journal of Finance* 65 (1): 333–360.
Greenspan, Alan, and James Kennedy. 2008. Sources and Uses of Equity Extracted from Homes. *Oxford Review of Economic Policy* 24 (1): 120–144.
Grinblatt, Mark, Matti Keloharju, and Seppo Ikaheimo. 2008. Social Influence and Consumption: Evidence from the Automobile Purchases of neighbors. *The Review of Economics and Statistics* 90 (4): 735–753.
Gross, David B., and Nicholas S. Souleles. 2002. Do Liquidity Constraints and Interest Rates Matter for Consumer Behavior? Evidence from Credit Card Data. *Quarterly Journal of Economics* 107: 149–185.

Guariglia, Alessandra, and Mariacristina Rossi. 2002. Consumption, Habit Formation, and Precautionary Saving: Evidence from the British Household Panel Survey. *Oxford Economic Papers* 54 (1): 1–19.

Haider, Steven J., and Melvin Stephens Jr. 2007. Is There a Retirement-Consumption Puzzle? Evidence Using Subjective Retirement Expectations. *Review of Economics and Statistics* 89 (2): 247–264.

Hayashi, Fumio. 1987. Tests for Liquidity Constraints: A Critical Survey and Some New Observations. In *Advances in Econometrics: Fifth World Congress*, ed. Truman F. Bewley, 91–120. Cambridge University Press.

Heckman, James J. 1974. Life Cycle Consumption and Labor Supply: An Explanation of the Relationship between Income and Consumption over the Life Cycle. *American Economic Review* 64 (1): 188–194.

Hubbard, Glenn R., Jonathan Skinner, and Stephen P. Zeldes. 1995. Precautionary Saving and Social Insurance. *Journal of Political Economy* 103 (2): 360–399.

Hurd, Michael D., and Susann Rohwedder. 2003. The Retirement-Consumption Puzzle: Anticipated and Actual Declines in Spending at Retirement. NBER working paper #9586.

Inkmann, Joachim, Paula Lopes, and Alexander Michaelides. 2011. How Deep is the Annuity Market Participation Puzzle? *Review of Financial Studies* 24 (1): 279–319.

Jappelli, Tullio, and Marco Pagano. 1989. Consumption and Capital Market Imperfections. *American Economic Review* 79: 1088–1105.

Jappelli, Tullio, and Luigi Pistaferri. 2000. Using Subjective Income Expectations to Test the Excess Sensitivity of Consumption to Predicted Income Changes. *European Economic Review* 44: 337–358.

———. 2017. *The Economics of Consumption: Theory and Evidence*. New York NY: Oxford University Press.

Johnson, David S., Jonathan A. Parker, and Nicholas S. Souleles. 2006. Household Expenditure and the Income Tax Rebates of 2001. *American Economic Review* 96: 1589–1610.

Kaplan, Greg, Giovanni L. Violante, and Justin Weidner. 2014. The Wealthy Hand-to-Mouth. *Brookings Papers on Economic Activity* 45 (1): 77–153.

Keynes, John M. 1927. *The End of Laissez-faire*. Dubuque, Iowa: W. C. Brown Reprint Library.

———. 1936. *The General Theory of Employment, Interest and Money*. New York: Harcourt, Brace.

Kotlikoff, Laurence J., and Lawrence H. Summers. 1981. The Role of Intergenerational Transfers in Aggregate Capital Accumulation. *Journal of Political Economy* 89: 706–732.

Kuhn, Peter, Peter Kooreman, Adriann Soetevent, and Arie Kapteyn. 2011. The Effects of Lottery Prizes on Winners and their neighbors: Evidence from the Dutch Postcode Lottery. *American Economic Review* 101 (5): 2226–2247.

Kuznets, Simon. 1946. *National Product Since 1869*. Assisted by L. Epstein and E. Zenks. New York: National Bureau of Economic Research.
Laibson, David. 1997. Golden Eggs and Hyperbolic Discounting. *Quarterly Journal of Economics* 112 (2): 443–477.
———. 1998. Life-cycle Consumption and Hyperbolic Discount Functions. *European Economic Review* 42 (3–5): 861–871.
———. 2001. A Cue-Theory of Consumption. *The Quarterly Journal of Economics* 116 (1): 81–119.
Levin, Laurence. 1998. Are Assets Fungible? Testing the Behavioral Theory of Life-Cycle Savings. *Journal of Economic Behavior and Organization* 36: 59–83.
Li, Hongbin, Xinzheng Shi, and Binzhen Wu. 2015. The Retirement Consumption Puzzle in China. *The American Economic Review* 105 (5): 437–441.
Lockwood, Lee M. 2018. Incidental Bequests and the Choice to Self-insure Late-life Risks. *The American Economic Review* 108 (9): 2513–2550.
Lusardi, Annamaria. 1998. On the Importance of the Precautionary Saving Motive. *The American Economic Review* 88 (2): 449–453.
Mastrobuoni, Giovanni, and Matthew Weinberg. 2009. Heterogeneity in Intra-monthly Consumption Patterns, Self-Control, and Savings at Retirement. *American Economic Journal: Economic Policy* 1 (2): 163–189.
Maurer, Jurgen, and Andre Meier. 2008. Smooth it Like the Joneses? Estimating Peer-Group Effects in Intertemporal Consumption Choice. *The Economic Journal* 118 (527): 454–476.
Meghir, Costas, and Guglielmo Weber. 1996. Intertemporal Non-Separability or Borrowing Restrictions? A Disaggregate Analysis Using a US Consumption Panel. *Econometrica* 64: 1151–1182.
Meier, Stephan, and Charles Sprenger. 2010. Present-Biased Preferences and Credit Card Borrowing. *American Economic Journal: Applied Economics* 2 (1): 193–210.
Mitchell, Olivia S., James M. Poterba, Mark J. Warshawsky, and Jeffrey R. Brown. 1999. New Evidence on Money's Worth of Individual Annuities. *American Economic Review* 89 (5): 1299–1318.
Modigliani, Franco. 1988. The Role of Intergenerational Transfers and Life Cycle Saving in the Accumulation of Wealth. *The Journal of Economic Perspectives* 2 (2): 15–40.
Modigliani, Franco, and Richard H. Brumberg. 1954. *Utility Analysis and the Consumption Function: An Interpretation of Cross-section Data*, 388–436. Edited by Kenneth K. Kurihara. New Brunswick, NJ. Rutgers University Press.
Naggar, Tahany. 1977. Adam Smith's Laissez Faire. *The American Economist* 21 (2): 35–39.
Olafsson, Arna, and Michaela Pagel. 2018. The Retirement-consumption Puzzle: New Evidence from Personal Finances. NBER working paper #24405.

Parker, Jonathan A. 1999. The Reaction of Household Consumption to Predictable Changes in Social Security Taxes. *The American Economic Review* 89 (4): 959–973.

———. 2017. Why Don't Households Smooth Consumption? Evidence from a $25 million Experiment. *American Economic Journal: Macroeconomics* 9 (4): 153–183.

Parker, Jonathan A., Brian Baugh, Itzhak Ben-David, and Hoonsuk Park. 2018. Asymmetric Consumption Response of Households to Positive and Negative Anticipated Cash Flows. NBER Working Paper #25086.

Ravina, Enrichetta. 2007. Habit Persistence and Keeping Up with the Joneses: Evidence from Micro Data. *SSRN*. Accessed March 19, 2020. http://repec.org/sed2005/up.23090.1107140609.pdf.

Rhee, Wooheon. 2004. Habit Formation and Precautionary Saving: Evidence from the Korean Household Panel Studies. *Journal of Economic Development* 29 (2): 1–19.

Say, John B., Charles R. Prinsep, and Clement C. Biddle. 1803. *A Treatise on Political Economy: Or the Production, Distribution, and Consumption of Wealth.* Philadelphia: Grigg & Elliot.

Scholnick, Barry. 2009. Credit Card Use After the Final Mortgage Payment: Does the Magnitude of Income Shocks Matter? European Central Bank Working Paper Series No. 1142.

Shapiro, Matthew D., and Joel Slemrod. 1995. Consumer Response to the Timing of Income: Evidence from a Change in Tax Withholding. *American Economic Review* 85: 274–283.

———. 2003. Consumer Response to Tax Rebates. *American Economic Review* 93: 381–396.

———. 2009. Did the 2008 Tax Rebates Stimulate Spending? *American Economic Review* 99: 374–379.

Shea, John. 1995. Union Contracts and the Life-Cycle Permanent Income Hypothesis. *American Economic Review* 85: 186–200.

Shefrin, Hersh M., and Richard H. Thaler. 1988. The Behavioral Life-Cycle Hypothesis. *Economic Inquiry* 26(4): 609–643.

Smith, Adam. 1759. *The Theory of Moral Sentiments.* London: Printed for A. Millar, and A. Kincaid and J. Bell.

———. 1776. *An Inquiry into the Nature and Causes of the Wealth of Nations.* London: Methuen & Co., Ltd.

Souleles, Nicholas S. 1999a. The Response of Household Consumption to Income Tax Refunds. *The American Economic Review* 89 (4): 947–958.

———. 1999b. Consumer Response to the Reagan Tax Cuts. *Journal of Public Economics* 85: 99–120.

Stephens, Melvin Jr. 2003. "3rd of the month": Do Social Security Recipients Smooth Consumption between Checks? *American Economic Review* 93 (1): 406–422.

———. 2006. Paycheck Receipt and the Timing of Consumption. *The Economic Journal* 116 (513): 680–701.

———. 2008. The Consumption Response to Predictable Changes in Discretionary Income: Evidence from the Repayment of Vehicle Loans. *Review of Economics and Statistics* 90: 241–252.

Stephens, Melvin Jr., and Desmond Toohey. 2018. Changes in Nutrient Intake at Retirement. NBER working paper #24621.

Thaler, Richard H. 1990. Anomalies: Saving, Fungibility and Mental Accounts. *Journal of Economic Perspectives* 4 (1): 193–205.

Tversky, Amos, and Daniel Kahneman. 1981. The Framing of Decisions and the Psychology of Choice. *Science* 211: 453–458.

Vatter, Harold G. 1965. Another Look at the Theory of 'consumer choice'. *Challenge* 13 (3): 35–39.

Veblen, Thorstein. 1953. *The Theory of the Leisure Class (Mentor)*. New York: Times Mirror.

Vilfredo, Pareto. 1906. *Manual of Political Economy*. Edited by Aldo Montesano, Alberto Zanni, Luigino Bruni, John S. Chipman, and Michael McLure. Oxford University Press.

Yaari, Menachim E. 1965. Uncertain Lifetime, Life Insurance, and the Theory of Consumer. *Review of Economic Studies* 32: 137–150.

CHAPTER 4

Investment

1 Introduction

Consumption has opposing effects on the economy. On the one hand, increased consumption increases demand for labor and income which generates more consumption and therefore prosperity. On the other hand, high consumption may preclude saving and investment which can potentially undermine prosperity in the long run. Thus, it is important to have a balanced amount of consumption and adequate saving for investment. For this reason, an examination of investment follows naturally after the saving and consumption chapters.

In this chapter, we review (1) macroeconomic models and the theory underlying investment, (2) factors affecting investment decisions and (3) empirical studies on investments.

2 Theory

Under Classical Economics, the saving investment equality is brought about by the rate of interest. If saving exceeds investment, the rate of interest will fall. This discourages saving and encourages investment until saving equals investment. On the other hand, if investment exceeds saving, the rate of interest will rise. The equilibrium, where saving equals investment, is achieved at full employment.

S. Agarwal et al., *Household Finance*,
https://doi.org/10.1007/978-981-15-5526-8_4

2.1 Keynesian Models

Under Keynes, the saving investment equality is not due to the rate of interest but to changes in income. Keynes' best known explanation for the business cycle explores the connection between consumption expenditure and income.

The mechanism to explain changes in the business cycle have been formalized into the two-sector, three-sector and four-sector models which consider how different sectors in the economy affect national income.

2.1.1 Two-Sector Model

In the simplest two-sector Keynesian model, there is the household sector and the business sector.

Under Keynes' General Theory, the equality between saving and investment is due to changes in income. If investment exceeds saving, for example, saving is at \$10 while investment is at \$20 and national income is at Y_1 (see Fig. 4.1), the higher investment will through the multiplier increase aggregate income to Y where saving is equal to investment at \$50 and the equilibrium income is \$400.

On the other hand, if investment is lower than saving, national income will fall from Y_2 to Y so that investment is equal to saving at \$50 at the equilibrium income of \$400. The saving investment equality can happen at less than full employment.

This helps to explain Keynes' paradox of thrift or paradox of saving, where personal saving is a drag on the economy during a recession. If everyone cuts current consumption and save more than what investors think it worthwhile to invest, the demand for consumer and producer goods will be stifled. Production will be curtailed and national income will fall. The proper response to an economic recession is therefore more spending and less saving. This is a paradox.

Paul Samuelson, the first American to win a Nobel Prize in economics, explains the paradox of thrift by comparing classical economists and Keynesian thought: "It is a paradox because in kindergarten we are all taught that thrift is always a good thing. Benjamin Franklin's *Poor Richard's Almanac* never tired of preaching the doctrine of saving. And now comes a new generation of alleged financial experts who seem to be telling us that black is white and white is black, and that the old virtues may be modern sins" (Samuelson 1958).

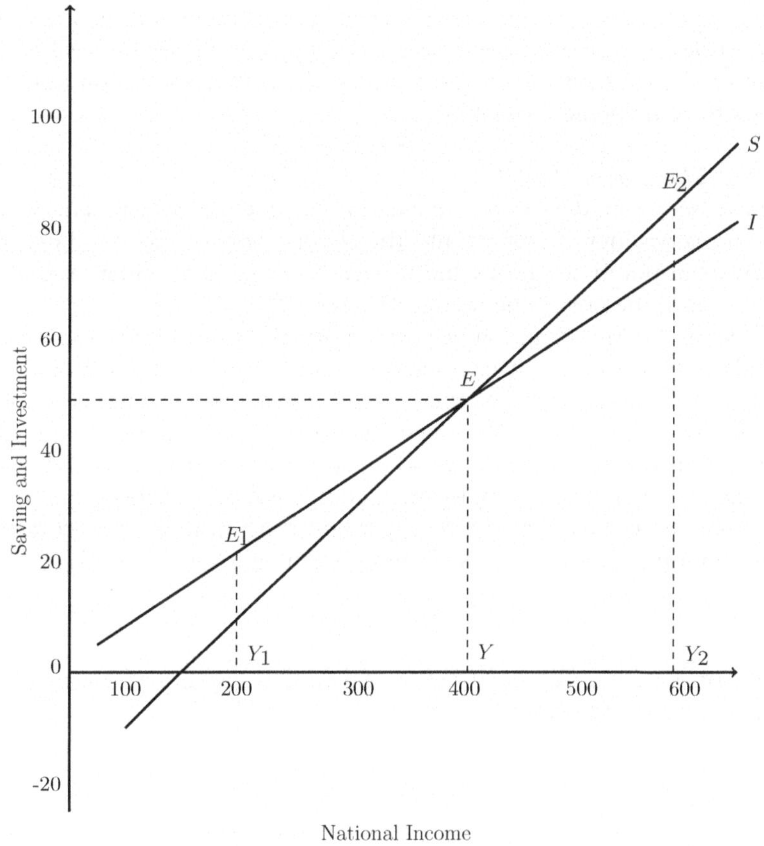

Fig. 4.1 Equilibrium in a two-sector model

The key feature of the saving investment theory propounded by Keynes is the shift from a model where "a dog called savings wagged his tail labelled investment" to a model where "a dog called investment wagged his tail labelled savings" (Meade 1975). Before Keynes, the theory starts with saving: if saving goes up, more funds are available so the cost of borrowing falls and accordingly more is spent on investment. Under Keynes, however, the reasoning starts with investment expenditure as an injection from outside, generating income through the waves of demand for consumption goods until the leakage (saving) is equal to the original injection of investment. Thus, the greater the level of investment and the lower the proportion of people's income saved, the higher will be the level of the resulting demand for goods and services, the higher the output and the higher the employment of labor.

2.1.2 *Three-Sector Model*

The two-sector model can be expanded to include the government, which introduces two new elements into the circular flow of income. First, the government purchases goods and services through government spending (G). Second, the government collects taxes (T).

Government spending can be part of normal operations or initiatives to stimulate the economy. It encompasses a wide variety of goods and services such as computers, weapons, road construction materials, police vehicles, stationery, law enforcement and general government administration. Government spending does not include transfer payments, for example, veterans' benefits, unemployment compensation and food stamps.

In the three-sector economy, aggregate expenditures (AE) comprise consumption (C), investments (I) and government spending (G)

$$AE = C + I + G$$

National income (Y) measured by real GDP is the sum of consumption (C), saving (S) and taxes (T).

$$Y = C + S + T$$

Given that disposable income (Y_d) is the sum of consumption and saving, national income can be rewritten as

$$Y = Y_d + T$$

In equilibrium, AE equals aggregate output Y and S + T equal I + G. In this three-sector economy, S + T are leakages, while I + G are injections.

$$Y = AE$$
$$C + S + T = C + I + G$$
$$S + T = I + G$$

2.1.3 Four-Sector Model

A four-sector model includes foreign trade, which introduces another two new elements into the circular flow of income. Funds flow into the economy when goods and services are exported (X), and funds flow out of the economy when goods and services are imported (M).

In dealing with these flows, the term net exports (X–M) is used. If net exports is positive, funds flow into the economy and national income (Y) increases. If net exports is negative, funds flow out of economy and national income (Y) decreases.

Aggregate expenditures (AE) in this four-sector model is equal to the sum of consumption (C), investment (I), government spending (G) and net exports (X–M).

$$AE = C + I + G + (X - M)$$

National income measured by real GDP is the sum of consumption (C), saving (S) and taxes (T).

$$Y = C + S + T = Y_d + T$$

In equilibrium, AE equals Y such that S + T + M equal I + G + X.

$$\begin{aligned} Y &= AE \\ C + S + T &= C + I + G + (X - M) \\ S + T &= I + G + (X - M) \\ S + T + M &= I + G + X \\ \text{Leakages} &= \text{Injections} \end{aligned}$$

In Keynes' four-sector model, injections comprise private investment, government spending and exports, while leakages are made up of saving, taxes and imports. The equilibrium level of income is at the point where AE intersects the 45° line (see Fig. 4.2) and all leakages out of the economy denoted by S + T + M equal all injections into the economy denoted by I + G + X.

The expression can be rearranged to show the problems that government budget deficit brings

$$G - T = S - I - (X - M)$$

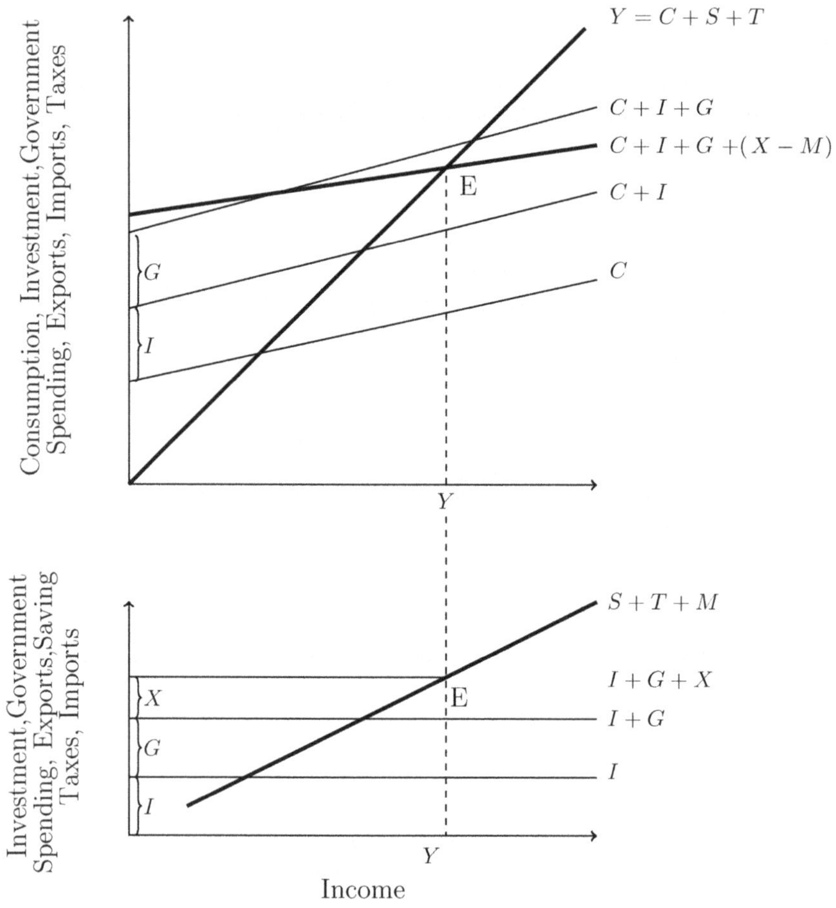

Fig. 4.2 Equilibrium in a four-sector model

If taxes (receipts) are less than government expenditures, there is a deficit. If the deficit is chronic, then government expenditures will have to be funded by private or public savings which leaves less for private investment. Alternatively, the government can borrow from foreign citizens or institutions.

2.1.4 *Balancing Consumption and Investment*

Keynes taught that prosperity, measured by GDP, is supported largely by consumer spending. Assuming a linear consumption function,

$$C = a + bY$$

where C = domestic consumption, Y = national income = value of goods and services produced in a year often known as the GDP, and b = MPC = ratio of a change in consumption to a change in income.

In a four-sector model, the value of goods and services produced (Y) equal AE at the equilibrium:

$$Y = C + I + G + (X - M)$$

If demand exceeds supply, then inventories fall, employers will hire more workers and pay more income, GDP will rise until inventories stabilize. If supply exceeds demand, then inventories will rise and firms will lay off employees and income will fall until value of goods and services produced equal the value demanded.

Combining the two equations and making Y the subject of the equation gives:

$$\begin{aligned} Y &= a + bY + I + G + (X - M) \\ Y - bY &= a + I + G + (X - M) \\ Y(1 - b) &= a + I + G + (X - M) \\ Y &= \frac{a + I + G + (X - M)}{(1 - b)} \end{aligned}$$

The above shows that if consumer spending increases (either because a rises or b rises), equilibrium income will increase. It amplifies the contributions of investment, export and government spending. Income rises by a multiple of any initial change in I or G or X–M through the multiplier effect.

Keynes argued that, in the short run, aggressive consumption can boost the economy. However, in the long run, high consumption can undermine investment and compromise economic growth. Hence, a vibrant economy must balance its consumption and devote resources to investment.

3 Factors Affecting Investing

While saving and investing go hand in hand, they are distinct activities. Saving has to do with refraining from consumption, which requires discipline. Investing involves buying assets, including stocks, bonds, mutual funds and real estate. Successful investing requires diligence and careful attention to changing asset values.

Households face challenges when making investment decisions. First, they must premise the decision around personal limitations such as an uncertain future. Second, their investment decisions must also consider asset allocation and diversification. However, they have the option of using intermediaries such as financial advisors.

Household investment problems have many notable features. Households must plan over a lifetime, not just a single short period. This means they must consider not only risks to their wealth but also the rate of return at which their wealth can be reinvested. In addition, the largest component of wealth for most household is human capital, which refers to the expected present discounted value of future labor earnings. Human capital is non-tradable, that is, it cannot be sold or hedged easily. This reduces the willingness of households to take financial risk.

3.1 Asset Allocation

Using information from the 2001 Survey of Consumer Finance, Campbell (2006) examines how households allocate their assets across broad categories such as safe assets (checking, saving, money market, certificate of deposits and saving bonds), vehicles, real estate, public equity and private business. He finds that the wealthy have a disproportionate influence on aggregate statistics and asset pricing models. Households in the bottom quartile of the wealth distribution largely hold safe assets and vehicles, with less in public equity (risky assets) and real estate. Households in the middle of the wealth distribution have a propensity to hold real estate. Wealthy households have a large stake in private business, followed by equity and real estate.

3.2 *Market Efficiency*

All investors are looking for good deals. However, in an efficient market, all public information pertaining to the value of a stock or bond is quickly reflected in its market price. It will be difficult to find good deals that will lead to a trading strategy more profitable than simply "buy and hold" a diversified portfolio. Only insiders will have information that give them an edge over others.

In an efficient market, investors will be compensated for bearing systematic risk (market risk) which is measured by beta. The higher the beta of the portfolio, the higher will be the expected return. Investors have to determine the level of risk they are willing to bear. Generally, when an investor approaches retirement, his risk appetite will decrease and his investments will comprise mainly safe assets.

3.3 *Diversification*

Given that investors are risk averse and have certainty-equivalent preferences, they will only bear risk if they are adequately compensated for it. Thus, it is sensible for investors to diversify away unsystematic risk. This explains the saying "Do not put all your eggs in one basket". Instead, investors should spread their investments in assets that are not perfectly correlated so that they can diversify away unsystematic risk.

3.4 *Financial Advisors*

A financial advisor (or investment advisor) is a professional who assists an investor in making informed financial decisions. In principle, financial advisors have economies of scale in portfolio management and in information acquisition because they can spread their costs across many investors. The economies of scale and superior financial practices they bring can potentially improve portfolio performance. As investment advice is expensive, the question is whether it is worth the fee.

4 Empirical Studies

Empirical evidence is not particularly flattering to households, many of whom make investment decisions that are contrary to what is prescribed in theory. Some under-diversify or do not participate in equity markets.

Others exhibit behavioral biases such as overconfidence and the disposition effect. There are also those who suffer from inattention.

4.1 Non-participation in Equity Markets

According to standard financial theory, all households should hold some equities since equity premium is positive. The non-participation in equity markets is a "stockholding puzzle". Some have attributed the puzzle to the failure of one or more of the standard assumptions (Bertaut and Haliassos 2000; Heaton and Lucas 2000; Barberis et al. 2006).

4.1.1 Lack of Awareness

One possible explanation for the stockholding puzzle is that households lack awareness about financial assets.

In a survey of Italian households, Guiso and Jappelli (2005) find that 35% of them are unaware of stocks as an asset class and 50% are unaware of mutual funds. The study finds that awareness is positively correlated with education, income, wealth, banking relationship, social interaction and newspaper readership. They note that wealthy and educated households are more likely to interact and learn from one another, leading to social learning. The study highlights that the lack of awareness can help explain home equity bias, especially if it is expensive to disseminate information over long distances.

4.1.2 Fixed Costs

Another possible reason for non-participation is the presence of fixed costs such as entry cost or ongoing participation costs, which are not accounted for in standard theory. These costs can be explicit such as trading costs and management fees or implicit such as the time spent to assess risk and returns.

Fixed costs can explain why wealthier households are more likely to participate in stock markets. Vissing-Jorgensen (2003) notes that a cost of $55, in 2003 prices, is sufficient to explain 50% of non-participation among US households. Many of the non-participants have little or no financial wealth to invest.

Guiso et al. (2003a) examine stock market participation among households in France, Germany, Italy, the Netherlands, Sweden, US and the United Kingdom. They document that stockownership correlates positively with wealth and education. In addition, they find that participation improves over time with the lowering of participation costs.

However, not all wealthy households hold stocks so fixed costs are unlikely to be the only reason for non-participation (Vissing-Jorgensen 2003).

4.1.3 Proprietary Income Risk

In some wealthy households, private business assets substitute for public equity (Heaton and Lucas 2000). However, these private business assets have significant idiosyncratic risks which are largely non-diversifiable. This unhedgeable risk increases the risk aversion of entrepreneurs so they are less willing to bear another risk. They offset their high proprietary income risk by investing more conservatively in other risky assets.

4.1.4 Social Interaction

Social interaction may increase stock market participation because households through their participation in such social activities become better informed.

Hong et al. (2004) study how social behaviors affect stock market participation of US households using data from the Health and Retirement Study. Their model comprises "non-social" and "social" investors. The "social" investors are those who interact with their neighbors or attend church and therefore have a lower fixed cost of participation because they learn about investing from their peers through word of mouth or observation learning and/or from the enjoyment of talking to fellow market participants. The "non-social" investors face a fixed cost of participation which can be idiosyncratic (low financial literacy) and/or systematic (low access to brokers). The study shows that social households are more likely to participate in the stock market and they are more likely to participate if the stock market participation rate is high.

Duflo and Saez (2003) conduct an experiment on employees of a university to assess their responses to some tax deferred annuity retirement plans (TDAs) after attending an information fair. Employees in the treatment group received invitations promising a $20 incentive to attend the fair. The treatment was administered to a subset of departments. The results show that (1) treated employees are five times more likely to attend the fair than the control (non-treated employees from non-treated departments) and (2) non-treated employees from treated departments are three times more likely to attend the fair than the control. In other words, there is a spill-over social effect on colleagues within the treated departments. In addition, (3) all employees, including those who were not offered the $20, in the treated departments are more likely to enroll in TDAs than the control, and (4) all employees in the treated departments are just as likely to enroll in TDAs. Duflo and Saez conclude that (3) and (4) could be due to social effect, differential treatment effect and/or motivational reward effect.

4.1.5 *Trust*

When making investments, households need to trust the reliability of the information used for their risk-return assessment and have confidence that the financial market is fair. Trust depends on objective characteristics in the financial system such as enforcement of investment protection as well as the subjective characteristics of the individual such as religious upbringing (Guiso et al. 2003b) and educational background (Guiso et al. 2004).

An advantage of using trust to explain stock market participation is that it affects all household and can be used to account for non-participation among the wealthiest households.

Using the World Values Survey that covers 66 countries from 1981 to 1997, Guiso et al. (2003b) analyze the effect of religion on attitudes toward (1) neighbors from different races or countries, (2) the government, police and armed forces, (3) pay inequality and competition, (4) cheating on taxes and transportation fares and (5) offering of bribes. The results show that religious people trust others more, trust the government more, have a positive attitude toward the market economy, are less willing to break rules but are more racist.

In another paper, Guiso et al. (2004) analyze how social capital affects financial development. The study uses social capital measured by electoral participation and blood donation as a proxy for trust in the community. In regions of Italy where social capital is high, households are more likely to use checks, borrow from financial institutions and invest in stocks. In addition, households rely more on social capital when they are less educated and where legal enforcement is weaker.

Using a sample of 1943 households from the Dutch National Bank Household Survey, Guiso et al. (2008) use their calibrated model to demonstrate that trusting households are 50% more likely to buy stock. The trust-based explanation of stock market participation can explain why a significant fraction of the wealthy do not invest in stocks, why some investors exhibit local and regional bias in picking stocks and why employees are biased in favor of their employer's stock.

4.1.6 Trading Experience

Past trading experiences can explain the low stock market participation and why some households quit the stock market.

Linnainmaa (2011) tests whether Finnish households are motivated to invest because they wish to learn and whether investors increase trade sizes after successful trades and decrease trade sizes or quit after unprofitable trades. The study finds that trading intensity increases with good performance and investors learn from their personal trading experiences.

Malmendier and Nagel (2011) examine whether past personal macroeconomic experiences affect the risk attitudes of individuals, whether more recent experiences have a stronger impact and whether experiences during one's formative years affect risk attitudes. Using household asset allocation data from the Survey of Consumer Finances from 1960 to 2007, they find that households that have experienced low stock returns are less likely to participate in the stock market. Households that have experienced low bond returns are less likely to invest in bonds. While more weight is placed on recent experiences, distant experiences (several decades ago) continue to have some impact on current risk taking.

In another paper, Malmendier and Nagel (2016) find that inflation expectation is affected by personal past experiences of inflation.

4.1.7 Demographic Characteristics

In addition, demographic characteristics such as socio-economic status, cognitive ability and financial literacy can explain the willingness of investors to participate in the stock market and how they learn from their experience.

Socio-economic Status

Kuhnen and Miu (2017) examine whether the manner in which individuals learn from financial information is related to their socio-economic status, which is measured based on their parents' income and education, their family size and closeness of family ties. The study finds that students from low socio-economic status underestimate gains of equity investments with good payoffs and overestimate losses of equity investments with bad payoffs. The results suggest that economically disadvantaged individuals form more pessimistic assessments about financial outcomes of investments. Kuhnen and Miu (2017) conclude that the lower participation of individuals with lower income or lower education is, in part, driven by pessimistic expectations about stock returns.

Das et al. (2020) show that income and education have a strong influence on how individuals form beliefs about macroeconomic conditions. Individuals with higher income and higher education are more optimistic about future macroeconomic conditions. These expectations, in turn, influence their decisions to invest in stocks and real estate. Their findings suggest that differences in macroeconomic expectations across people with different socio-economic standing can potentially contribute to wealth inequality in the population.

Cognitive Ability

Higher cognitive ability measured by standardized test scores or education can help to explain the stockholding puzzle.

Benjamin et al. (2006) find that high-school students, who scored higher on cognitive ability, are more likely to participate in the financial market.

Using revisions to compulsory schooling laws from 1914 to 1978, Cole et al. (2014) study how education affects financial market participation, investment income and credit management. They find that an exogenous increase in education results in less bankruptcy, less foreclosure, higher credit score and fewer delinquent credit card debt. Their results show that education can explain participation in the stock market and can also affect saving outcomes as less educated households are more likely to make financial mistakes.

Grinblatt et al. (2011) examine the relationship between Finnish stock market participation and intellectual quotient (IQ) scores. They find a high correlation between stock market participation rate and IQ, even among the rich who can afford to invest. Low-IQ investors have fewer stocks, are less likely to hold mutual funds and tend to bear more non-systematic risk.

In another paper, Grinblatt et al. (2011) show that high-IQ investors outperform low-IQ investors, experience lower trading costs and are less subject to the disposition effect (the tendency to sell winners and keep losers).

Financial Literacy

Generally, most studies find that financial illiteracy is widespread. Lusardi and Mitchell (2007) note that financial illiteracy is common in developed countries including Europe, Australia and New Zealand.

Lusardi and Mitchell (2011) conclude that, in the US, illiteracy is acute among women, the elderly and less educated.

Van Rooij et al. (2011) document that Dutch households who have little financial knowledge are more likely to rely on friends and family for financial advice and are less likely to participate in the stock market. They construct two indices of financial literacy, one based on basic knowledge about investing and the other based on more advanced financial knowledge relating to stocks, financial markets and other financial instruments. They find that while the majority of households have some grasp of basic financial concepts such as interest compounding, inflation and the time value of money, very few understand risk diversification, the difference between stocks and bonds and the relationship between interest rates and bond prices.

Anantanasuwong et al. (2019) separately estimate the ambiguity preferences and perceived ambiguity of different financial assets for a sample of Dutch investors. They find that perceived ambiguity is lower for investors with higher financial literacy and better education. They conclude that policies aimed at improving peoples' financial literacy and knowledge of financial markets can help increase equity market participation.

4.2 *Under-Diversification*

Using data from the 1983 Survey of Consumer Finance, Kelly (1995) confirms that households are not well diversified. The median US stockholder holds one single stock which is often that of the employer. Of the households in the top 2 percentile of income distribution, the median number of stocks held is 10. The poor diversification is pervasive.

The literature finds that the demographic predictors of under-diversification are similar to the predictors of non-participation.

Goetzmann and Kumar (2008) test for demographic predictors of under-diversification. They find that older investors are more diversified than younger investors, high-income investors are more diversified than low-income investors and experienced investors (those who engage in short selling and options) are more diversified than inexperienced investors. In terms of occupations, investors holding professional jobs (technical or managerial positions) are more diversified than non-professionals, while the retired are the most diversified. Overconfidence, local bias and trend-following behavior are associated with lower diversification. Those who are less diversified hold stocks that are volatile, riskier (high beta), have higher turnover and greater skewness. The portfolio return and Sharpe ratio increase with diversification and alphas are higher for the better diversified (who have better stock picking ability). The evidences suggest that there are active (high turnover) successful investors who choose to under-diversify because they have superior stock picking skills.

4.2.1 *Information Advantage*

Although standard finance theory suggests investors should diversify away all unsystematic risk, information advantage can explain why they choose to under-diversify, particularly if they believe the information will enable them to beat the market.

Van Nieuwerburgh and Veldkamp (2010) argue that when an investor can choose what information to acquire before he invests, he may deviate from a diversified portfolio strategy based on the information advantage that he has acquired.

After controlling for differences in investment abilities, Ivkovic et al. (2008) find that households with concentrated portfolios outperform those with diversified portfolios. In addition, they find that the better performance is larger for stocks that are likely to have greater information asymmetries, which suggests that households with concentrated portfolios have superior information processing skills. However, they also note that while concentrated portfolios outperform, these portfolios bear increased total risk and have lower Sharpe ratios (worse return-risk tradeoff) than diversified portfolios.

Korniotis and Kumar (2013) explore whether investors, who hold concentrated portfolios, trade actively and prefer local stocks, possess informational advantage or suffer from psychological biases. Given that standard finance theory predict that investors should have diversified portfolios, trade infrequently and trade objectively, the study defines "smart" investors as those who trade infrequently, have diversified portfolios and do not have a bias for local stocks. They define "dumb" investors as those who trade actively, have concentrated portfolios and exhibit a preference for local stocks. Using an ex ante model administered in 11 European countries to individuals aged 50 and above, they find that smart investors make decisions that reflect an informational advantage.

4.2.2 *Familiarity*

The preference to stick with the familiar such as local stocks and employer stocks can lead to under-diversification.

Local Stocks

Huberman (2001) show that households choose to invest in companies familiar to them by comparing the geographic distribution and investments of households who purchase shares in Regional Bell Operating Companies (RBOC). In 1984, a national US telecommunication company was split into seven separate RBOCs. Although the RBOCs are equally accessible, have large market capitalizations and trade on the NYSE, RBOC customers tend to hold more of their local RBOC shares than other RBOCs. The propensity to invest in the familiar is consistent with the avoidance of foreign stocks (home bias) and the bias in favor of employer stock, which all conflict with portfolio diversification.

Grinblatt and Keloharju (2001a) examine three familiarity attributes, namely, language, culture and physical distance from the investor. They focus on open market purchases and sales of 97 firms in Finland, where the two official languages are Finnish and Swedish. The culture of the firm is based on the name and native language of the CEO. The physical distance from the investor is measured as the distance between the investor's municipality and the firm's HQ. The study shows that Finnish-speaking investors prefer to invest in firms that report in Finnish, while Swedish-speaking investors prefer to invest in firms that report in Swedish. Investors also show preference for firms of the same culture and firms that are closer. The results carry over to investors who are more sophisticated, albeit weaker. The study concludes that investors generally prefer to invest in firms that they are familiar with.

Graham et al. (2009) study the link between competence, trading frequency and home bias. Their results show that male, more educated, overconfident investors and those with larger portfolios are more likely to perceive themselves as competent. They conclude that investors who are comfortable about their investment skills trade more frequently and are more internationally diversified.

Grullon et al. (2004) find that firms that spend more on advertising have a larger number of both individual and institutional investors, greater stock market liquidity and higher equity value. This result is consistent with home equity bias where households are more likely to invest in firms familiar to them. The results support the existence of familiarity bias and suggest advertising as a new channel through which to affect firm value.

While there is evidence that investors exhibit a preference for stocks that they are familiar with, the question is whether they outperform.

Ivkovic and Weisbenner (2005) examine investments made by 78,000 US retail investors through a discount broker from 1991 to 1996. They find that households prefer local stocks and successfully exploit information asymmetries about local firms to earn excess returns.

Massa and Simonov (2006) use Swedish data from 1995 to 2000 and consider three measures of familiarity: professional proximity (work in same industry), geographical proximity (distance between zip code of residence and company) and the holding period of the stock. They report that investors show preference for familiar stocks and are able to achieve higher returns. They argue that familiarity is information driven.

On the contrary, Seasholes and Zhu (2010), who study the trades of US investors in a large discount brokerage firm over the period 1991 to 1996, find that portfolios of local stocks do not generate abnormal returns. They conclude that investors do not have value-relevant information about local stocks.

Employer Stocks

The motivation for employers to offer their stocks as part of their employees' retirement plan include aligning interests, increasing worker productivity, increasing employee morale and putting stocks in friendly hands (Mitchell and Utkus 2003).

Conventional reasons for employees to hold employer stocks include their better understanding of the firm, the appeal of owning part of the firm they worked for, the stock's good past performance, tax incentives and not having to pay brokerage commissions (Mitchell and Utkus 2003).

According to a Vanguard (2001) survey, employees underestimate the risk of their employer stocks and rate them as less risky than money market funds and bond funds.

In the wake of Enron's demise, Poterba (2003) reviews the excessive concentration of 401(k) retirement plans and their potential impact on employees. He recommends that a limit be placed on the amount of employer stock that can be held in retirement accounts until the individual has sufficient funds for his retirement.

4.3 *Behavioral Biases*

4.3.1 Overconfidence

Barber and Odean (2000) analyze the trading activity of 66,465 households at a large discount brokerage firm from 1997 to 2003. They find that, net of transaction costs, households underperform a passive investment strategy of buying and holding a value-weighted market index. The poor performance of active investment strategies can be traced to costs associated with excessive trading. The aggregate turnover in the sample was 70% compared to the 50% aggregate turnover on the NYSE during the sample period. The evidence supports the view that overconfident investors trade excessively.

Robinson and Anderson (2018) find that Swedish pension investors who mistakenly believe they are financial literate are more prone to investment mistakes. The study documents the type of mutual funds that pensioners choose after a review that mandates that they invest a set sum into mutual funds. The pensioners were allowed to choose from a large number of mutual funds. Those who did not make a choice were allocated to a default low-fee, well-diversified global index fund. They find that investors who mistakenly believe they are financially literate were more likely to opt out of the default fund and choose a fund with higher fees.

4.3.2 Disposition Effect

The disposition effect relates to the tendency of investors to sell assets that have increased in value, while keeping assets that have dropped in value. This can lead to underperformance because investors cling to loss making investments that may not turn around.

Grinblatt and Keloharju (2001b) track five domestic investor classes, namely, non-financial corporations, finance and insurance institutions, governmental organizations, non-profit institutions and households. They find that the two major determinants behind the propensity to sell are the disposition effect (sell winners) and tax-loss selling. All investor types have the tendency to hold on to losers especially for losses exceeding 30%. There is evidence of the disposition effect for all five investor classes, but the effect is more obvious for the least sophisticated investor classes, namely, households, government organizations and non-profit institutions.

Grinblatt et al. (2012) examine how IQ, measured by standardized test scores of Finnish Armed Forces entrance tests, affects trading behavior. They document that high-IQ investors enjoy higher after-tax returns than low-IQ investors and have a relatively greater tendency to sell loss making stocks, to engage in tax-loss selling and to sell (hold) a stock at a 30-day high (low). These results suggest that high-IQ investors are less susceptible to disposition effects, are more rational about minimizing taxes, have superior market-timing abilities and are better at picking stocks.

Feng and Seasholes (2005) study the effect of experience on the disposition effect using data from a national brokerage firm in China. They find that sophistication and trading experience can reduce the disposition effect but there is an asymmetry. Although sophistication/experience can eliminate the reluctance to realize losses, it only reduces the propensity to realize gains by 37%.

4.3.3 *Trading Experience*

Korniotis and Kumar (2011) examine whether investors make better investment choices as they age. While their choices should improve with the investment experience gained, there is a need to consider the tradeoff from cognitive aging. The study analyzes 62,387 investors at a US discount brokerage over the period 1991 to 1996. The mean and median number of stocks in a portfolio are four and three, respectively. The wealth peaks in the 65–69 age range; annual income peaks in the 47–52 age range, portfolio size increases monotonically with age and investment performance peaks at age 42 with a sudden significant drop at age 70. They document that older investors own less risky stocks, are more diversified, trade less frequently, have a greater propensity to engage in tax-loss selling, have a weaker disposition effect and a weaker local bias. The evidence suggests that older investors are more conservative and have more investment knowledge. In terms of risk-adjusted performance, investors' stock selection skills decline with age and the adverse effects of aging are more pronounced for older investors with lower income. The study concludes that investment experience and cognitive aging significantly affect investment performance. It is consistent with the stockholding puzzle as younger investors refrain from investing due to their lack of experience, while older investors are less willing to participate because of their declining cognitive abilities.

Using transaction-level data from a German retail bank, Pagel and Meyer (2019) explore how individuals reinvest after realizing capital gains and losses from a forced liquidation of mutual funds. Theoretically, if individuals hold optimized portfolios, the marginal propensity to reinvest out of forced sales should be 100%. Pagel and Meyer (2019) find that individuals reinvest 83% of their proceeds if the forced sale resulted in a gain but reinvest only 40% of their proceeds if the forced sale resulted in a loss. Such differential treatment of gains and losses is inconsistent with active rebalancing or tax considerations but consistent with mental accounting. It also shows that individuals do not learn rationally from their experiences in the stock market.

4.4 *Foreign Versus Domestic Investors*

There is mixed evidence of how foreign investors perform compared to local investors.

Using Finnish data, Grinblatt and Keloharju (2000) show that foreign investors outperform domestic investors. They document that foreign investors tend to use momentum strategies, while domestic investors tend to use contrarian strategies (buying losers and selling winners). The study concludes that foreign investors are the most sophisticated players in the Finnish stock market.

Similarly, Seasholes (2000) using Taiwanese data find that foreign investors are informed traders. The study compares how foreign investors trade in response to earning announcements. Foreign investors accumulate shares of companies before positive announcements and sell shares of companies before negative announcements. These results challenge the assumption that foreigners are at an information disadvantage.

On the other hand, Dvorak (2005) using Indonesian data reports that domestic investors perform better than foreign investors. Comparing local and foreign clients of global brokerages, the study reports that domestic clients perform better in the short and medium term. They conclude that domestic investors successfully leverage on the informational advantage of local businesses and their global brokers to make more profitable investments.

However, Agarwal et al. (2009) have an alternative explanation for the underperformance of foreign investors in the Indonesia stock market. At an aggregate level, they find that foreign investors perform worse than domestic investors. However, further analysis show that foreign investors only underperform domestic investors in non-initiated orders but not for initiated trades. Initiated orders are trades initiated by the buyer, while non-initiated orders are those matched by incoming initiated orders. In non-initiated buys, foreign investors pay 33 basis points more than domestic investors. In non-initiated sells, foreign investors receive 40 basis points less than domestic investors. The findings are inconsistent with the information disadvantage hypothesis because if foreign investors have worse information, then their profits should always be lower. The paper concludes that the underperformance of the foreign investors is due to their aggressive trading behavior, not due to any information advantage that domestic investors have over them.

4.5 *Investor Inattention*

According to standard finance theories, households should rebalance their portfolios to smooth consumption. Inertia or inaction on the part of investors would suggest departure from these standard theories.

Bilias et al. (2010) study inertia in stockholding participation and trading. They find that stock market participation does not seem to increase during downswings and there are limited changes in trading activity in the sample period. In addition, many households including those already invested in financial markets are insensitive to stock market conditions. There is widespread inertia in relation to investing, particularly among the less educated and less well-off. The findings strengthen the case for built-in trading provisions to overcome investor inattention in retirement accounts and funds.

4.5.1 Rational Inattention

In the presence of significant observation costs measured by the time required to gather, monitor and process information related to investments, households respond by practicing rational inattention. They choose to be inattentive to their portfolio when the costs of monitoring outweigh the benefits.

Abel et al. (2013) calibrate a model to show that information costs defined by costs to gather, process and act on information about stocks induce selective inattentive behaviors.

Along the same lines, Alvarez et al. (2012) conclude that information costs on the part of investors to monitor equity value and on the part of firms to monitor production costs induce rational inattention.

4.5.2 *Selective Inattention and Preference-Based Models*

There are findings that cannot be explained by "rational inattention". The literature on information-dependent and belief-dependent utility examine incentives to avoid paying attention to information.

One specific form of selective inattention is the ostrich effect. Karlsson et al. (2009) describe how investors pay less attention to their finances after bad news than good news. Sicherman et al. (2015) find evidence of an ostrich effect where US investors pay less attention when the market declines and when the volatility index is high.

Olafsson and Pagel (2017) find evidence of an ostrich effect among Icelandic households by comparing online logins and account balances of current, saving and credit cards. They find that attention decreases with more spending and overdrafts, while attention increases with cash holdings. Individuals are willing to pay to not receive information when bad news hurt more than good news please them. The inattention is highly selective and driven by information or belief rather than rational costs and benefits.

The preference-based literature provides another alternative explanation for results that cannot be explained by "rational inattention".

Andries and Haddad (2017) propose a disappointment aversion model, where investors decrease attention during turbulent times because they choose to remain uninformed and want to stay away from stressful information.

Pagel (2018) considers the news-utility preferences model, as developed by Koszegi and Rabin (2009), where investors dislike bad news more than they like good news. The model generates inattention on the part of investors who choose to delegate the rebalancing to expensive portfolio managers. The model is consistent with evidence on non-participation in the stock market, lower portfolio share of stocks compared to standard preferences, presence of mental accounting, inattention to portfolio rebalancing and willingness to pay for delegation.

Peijnenburg et al. (2018) explore a probability weighting model, where investors place a greater emphasis on lower probability events such as positively skewed returns or risk of small losses. These choices reflect their preferences and are associated with more under-diversification.

4.5.3 Overcoming Investor Inattention

Households can overcome investor inattention by relying on financial advisors or passive investment strategies.

Financial Advisors

The following studies explore whether financial advisors help investors improve their portfolio performance.

Comparing direct-sold funds and broker-sold funds, where more fees are paid for the latter because of additional broker advice, Bergstresser et al. (2009) find that broker-sold funds do not outperform direct-sold funds. Financial advisors do not show any evidence of superior market-timing ability compared to direct-sold funds and they deliver lower risk-adjusted returns on a pre-distribution fee basis. These results suggest financial advisors do not help investors to overcome their informational constraints. Since broker-sold funds do not outperform, it is a puzzle why they continue to exist when they cost more and provide no incremental benefit. The study concludes that investors prefer to use financial advisors because of intangible benefits which are not measurable such as saving time, help in customizing portfolios to risk tolerances and help in assuring them of their investment choices. The alternative explanation is that financial advisors act out of their own self-interests to increase their compensation and other broker incentives.

Hackethal et al. (2012) study whether financial advisors help investors improve performance. They find that portfolios managed by advisors deliver lower net returns, have worse Sharpe ratios and have higher portfolio turnovers. In addition, they document that financial advisors are matched with richer, older, experienced and female investors. The results suggest that financial advisors play the role of babysitters because the investors who use financial advisors seem qualified to make better investments on their own, without the need for the service. This is similar to parents who are able to take care of their children on their own but choose to hire a babysitter.

Del Guercio and Reuter (2014) compare direct-sold and broker-sold mutual funds in the US. Within the direct-sold segment, actively managed funds do not underperform passive funds. Within the broker-sold segment, actively managed funds underperform index funds by 112 to 132 basis points. Given that the underperformance is limited to the broker-sold segment, Del Guercio and Reuter (2014) conclude that investors in the broker-sold segment are likely ignorant of the underperformance.

With the compelling evidence that financial advisors do not improve portfolio performance, the following studies explore why households continue to pay high fees to them.

Intelligence

Grinblatt et al. (2016) show that high-IQ investors tend to hold low-fee funds. Using standardized test scores from the Finnish Armed Forces from 2004 to 2008, they find that high-IQ investors avoid fund categories that charge high fees such as actively managed funds, balanced funds and service-intensive funds. In addition, a business education is associated with lower-fee funds, even among low-IQ investors. Finance professionals are associated with lower-fee funds. The study concludes that intellectual ability, financial literacy and career-related expertise are related with lower-fee funds.

Kim et al. (2019) investigate how cognitive ability and financial literacy shape demand for financial advice among Americans aged above 50. Their results show that cognitive ability and financial literacy are positively correlated with advice-seeking on financial matters. They tend to seek financial advice from professionals outside of family members but those who are more cognitively able tend to be overconfident (distrust others' advice).

Advertising Effort

The interest in delegated portfolio management could also be due to advertising effort. Gallaher et al. (2015) find that more advertising is associated with more flows into mutual funds at the industry level (even for funds that do not advertise), fund family level and individual fund level. At the individual fund level, the flow is mainly due to reduction in redemptions by existing shareholders rather than increase in purchases. This implies that advertising serves a persuasion function primarily for existing shareholders. In addition, at the individual fund level, advertising can dampen the flow out of the worst performing mutual funds and enhance the flow into the top performing mutual funds.

Search Costs

Yet another possible explanation for why investors pay high fees is search costs. Hortacsu and Syverson (2004) investigate whether non-portfolio fund differences (measured by characteristics such as fund age, tax exposure, number of funds in the fund family) and search costs can explain the dispersion in the fees charged by passive mutual funds tracking the S&P

500. Although the funds are rather homogeneous, the dispersion in the fees is enormous. Among the 85 retail funds, the highest annualized fee is 268 basis points, while the lowest is 9.5 basis points. Hortacsu and Syverson (2004) observe that reasonable magnitudes of search cost can explain the dispersion in the fees. In addition, the widening of the search cost distribution coincides with the increase in first-time mutual fund investors, likely novices, who gravitate toward funds bundled with financial advisory services.

Peer Effects

Han et al. (2018) offer a social approach to investment decision making. They explain that biases in conversations can promote superficially appealing personal investing strategies and suggest that active investment strategies persist because investors possess systematic biases when promoting their personal investing strategies to their social networks. The self-enhancing transmission process, which recounts wins rather than losses, ends up promoting active over passive investing. The study shows that the strategy an investor adopts depends on who he is connected to and his sociability. In addition, a shift in the social acceptability of discussing one's investment success and investing strategy can have large effects on risk taking and active investing.

Ambuehl et al. (2018) study the effect of peer advice on the quality of financial decision making among undergraduates from a UK university. In a laboratory experiment, students make decisions about investments that accrue compound interest. While peer-to-peer communication generally improves financial decision making compared to a control group that was left alone, peer advice is most effective when peers are equally uninformed, rather than when an informed decision maker teaches an uninformed peer.

Passive Investment Strategies

Some studies document that passive investment strategies outperform active strategies. This means that an investor can increase his average annual return by switching to a lower-fee passive portfolio. If this is true, it is a puzzle why investors continue with active investment strategies.

French (2008) finds that an investor who holds a passive portfolio outperforms the value-weighted average return of all investors by 67 basis points annually over the period from 1980 to 2006. The study offers a few reasons for why investors choose active investing: (1) they understand from the popular press that active investing is profitable, (2) they are overconfident and believe that they can outperform, (3) they want to brag about achieving superior returns and owning individual accounts and (4) they are indeed superior investors who can beat the market.

Fama and French (2010) conclude that mutual funds on aggregate underperform the Capital Asset Pricing model, three-factor and four-factor benchmarks. In their sample of 3156 mutual funds, some do very well but some do very poorly. Their simulation tests show that few active funds have the skill to cover cost and that the better active funds are no better than passive funds.

Choi and Robertson (2018) investigate the key factors that influence individuals' decision regarding the fraction of their portfolio to invest in stocks. The factors extensively discussed in academic literature include background risks, investment horizon, rare disasters, transactional factors and fixed costs of stock market participation. The largest drivers for investing in active equity mutual funds are professional advice, the belief that active funds will outperform passive funds, the belief that good mutual fund performance is due to good stock picking skills and the belief that fund managers will continue to perform just as well when they manage more assets.

Private Retirement Accounts

Ahmed et al. (2018) test how an investor's choice of retirement schemes affects his payoffs. The study concludes that households always benefit more from private retirement accounts, with or without choice, than the social security system.

4.6 Financial Innovation

Financial products that reward sophisticated decision making leave much room for expensive mistakes. There are calls for financial instruments that are simpler. However, there is inertia in financial innovation for several reasons.

First, it is expensive to reach and explain to unsophisticated or naïve households who tend to follow the lead of relatives and neighbors.

Second, it is hard to recoup the costs of advertising and the requisite costs of financial education.

Third, sophisticated households have little reason to switch to new products as existing products often involve cross-subsidies from naïve households.

Fourth, innovators may have the perverse incentive to mislead naïve households by offering confusing products with high fees. For example, financial institutions may reduce upfront payment to attract naïve households and raise hidden costs. This is an example of a "shrouded equilibrium" where households are unaware of the hidden costs.

Other business practices that encourage the shrouded equilibrium can be observed in advertising. For example, retail stores may introduce a low base price to increase store traffic in the hope of selling add-ons at high unadvertised or unobservable prices (Ellison 2005). Hotels, for instance, typically do not include phone calls, minibar items and breakfasts in their quoted prices. As another illustration, cheaper models of personal computers often require additional memory cards and upgrades at the time of purchase.

Gabaix and Laibson (2006) discuss the inefficiency that shrouding creates and explain why it continues to flourish even in highly competitive markets. Naïve households may be exploited by advertising schemes that shroud high-priced add-ons, while sophisticated households benefit from the cross-subsidy. It does not pay for innovators to reveal the hidden costs if sophisticated households have the ability to avoid them while purchasing the cheaper products because of the revenue provided by naïve households. This impedes financial innovation and the introduction of simpler lower cost options.

4.7 Cross-Country Comparison

Using household surveys from Australia, Europe, Canada and US, Bandarinza et al. (2016) compare household balance sheets across 13 developed countries. They document certain patterns in household behavior that are consistent across the sample. Many households do not participate in equity markets (inclusive of direct equity holdings, indirect equity holdings in retirement accounts and mutual funds). Among households who participate, mutual funds, bonds and stocks account for a relatively small fraction of their portfolios. The dominant non-financial asset category, in all countries, is the household's primary residence. This is particularly so in southern European countries such as Greece, Spain and Italy. The second largest category of non-financial asset, in all countries except Greece, Spain and Finland, is vehicle and other consumer durables. Households that have higher income, education and wealth participate more actively and efficiently in financial markets, holding more diversified portfolios and paying lower fees. Although stock market participation increases with wealth, there are non-participants even among the wealthy. In all countries, an estimated 10% of households own businesses. These tend to be the wealthiest households.

Campbell (2016) made a similar comparison of household balance sheets but for a smaller sample of eight developed countries. Participation rates in direct and indirect equity range from 23.2% in Italy to 72.3% in Canada. Participation rates in direct and indirect risky assets range from 31.4% in Italy to 72.7% in Canada. Home ownership rate also varies considerably from a low of 44.2% in Germany to a high of 82.7% in Spain. It appears that non-financial assets are more important than financial assets in all countries, particularly so in southern Europe. The heterogeneity across countries implies that national financial regulation and culture may have a strong influence.

4.7.1 Culture

The refugee and migrant crisis in Europe is a rich bed for testing whether cultural differences in behavior exist and, if they do, whether they will diminish through exposure to host institutions in the country.

Using panel data from the Swedish Longitudinal Individual Database (LINDA) on migrants from different European countries for the observation period 1999 to 2007, Haliassos et al. (2017) examine whether stockholding participation differs significantly between migrants and locals, after controlling for household characteristics, and whether they converge over time. The results show that stockholding differs significantly between the two but there is convergence with exposure to host institutions, albeit with a delay if the migrants are exposed to original (home) institutions.

D'Acunto et al. (2019) test whether the historical specialization of Jews in financial services, paired with persistent historical discrimination against Jews (antisemitism), helps to explain variation in the demand for financial services across German counties. They find that financial development is lower in German counties where historical antisemitism is higher. Households in counties with high historical antisemitism have similar savings rates but invest less in stocks, hold lower bank deposits, are less likely to get a mortgage and express lower trust in finance. The results show that historical ethnic tensions, such as discrimination against Jews in the past, continue to have long-run effects on financial decision making in the present day.

5 Conclusion

Given the complexity of the financial planning problem, it is not surprising that households make investment mistakes such as non-participation in risky asset markets, under-diversification of risky portfolios, misuse of complicated products and have behavioral biases.

The unwillingness to assume financial risk may be due to the lack of awareness about financial assets, high fixed costs of entry, high proprietary income risk, lack of information, lack of trust, bad experiences and disadvantaged socio-economic status.

Holding a concentrated portfolio may be reasonable if investors have information advantage about certain stocks or possess superior information processing skills. Other not so logical reasons include behavioral biases such as overconfidence, local bias and employer bias.

The disposition effect, which runs counter to rational decision making, afflicts even sophisticated investors. Factors that mitigate its effect include IQ and experience. There is a tension between experience accumulated through investing in the stock market over time and stock picking skills which decline with age.

It is a puzzle why active funds continue to exist although they generally underperform passive funds. Some reasons put forth include bragging rights, mistaken belief due to marketing efforts and overconfidence.

Another puzzle is the high fees paid to hire expensive portfolio managers. Explanations provided include bundled financial advice, search costs and financial illiteracy.

Yet another puzzle is the presence of complex financial products. The lack of financial innovation is partly explained by shrouded equilibrium and the presence of cross-subsidies from naïve investors.

References

Abel, Andrew B., Janice C. Eberly, and Stavros Panageas. 2013. Optimal Inattention to the Stock Market with Information Costs and Transaction Costs. *Econometrica* 81 (4): 1455–1481.

Agarwal, Sumit, Sheri Faircloth, Chunlin Liu, and Ghon S. Rhee. 2009. Why Do Foreign Investors Underperform Domestic Investors in Trading Activities? *Journal of Financial Markets* 12 (1): 32–53.

Ahmed, Javed, Brad M. Barber, and Terrance Odean. 2018. Made Poorer by Choice: Worker Outcomes in Social Security versus Private Retirement accounts. *Journal of Banking and Finance* 92: 311–322.

Alvarez, Fernando, Luigi Guiso, and Francesco Lippi. 2012. Durable Consumption and Asset Management with Transaction and Observation Costs. *American Economic Review* 102 (5): 2272–2300.

Ambuehl, Sandro, Douglas B. Bernheim, Fulya Ersoy, and Donna Harris. 2018. Peer Advice on Financial Decisions: A Case of the Blind Leading the Blind? NBER Working Paper #25034.

Anantanasuwong, Kanin, Olivia S. Mitchell, Roy Kouwenberg, and Kim Peijnenberg. 2019. Ambiguity Attitudes about Investments: Evidence from the Field. NBER Working Paper #25561.

Andries, Marianne, and Valentin Haddad. 2017. Information Aversion. NBER Working Paper #23958.

Bandarinza, Cristian, John Y. Campbell, and Tarun Ramadorai. 2016. International Comparative Household Finance. *Annual Review of Economics* 8: 111–144.

Barber, Brad M., and Terrance Odean. 2000. Trading is Hazardous to Your Wealth: The Common Stock Investment Performance of Individual Investors. *Journal of Finance* 55: 773–806.

Barberis, Nicholas, Ming Huang, and Richard H. Thaler. 2006. Individual Preferences, Monetary Gambles, and Stock Market Participation: A Case for Narrow Framing. *The American Economic Review* 96 (4): 1069–1090.

Benjamin, Daniel J., Brown Sebastian Andres, and Shapiro Jesse M. 2006. Who is 'Behavioral'? Cognitive Ability and Anomalous Preferences. *SSRN*. Accessed March 19, 2020. https://papers.ssrn.com/sol3/papers.cfm?abstract_id=675264.

Bergstresser, Daniel, John M.R. Chalmers, and Peter Tufano. 2009. Assessing the Costs and Benefits of Brokers in the Mutual Fund Industry. *The Review of Financial Studies* 22 (10): 4129–4156.

Bertaut, Carol C., and Michael Haliassos. 2000. Why Do So Few Hold Stocks? *The Economic Journal* 105 (432): 1110–1129.

Bilias, Yannis, Dimitris Georgarakos, and Michael Haliassos. 2010. Portfolio Inertia and Stock Market Fluctuations. *Journal of Money, Credit and Banking* 42 (9): 715–742.

Campbell, John Y. 2006. Household Finance. *Journal of Finance* 61 (4): 1553–1604.

———. 2016. Restoring Rational Choice: The Challenge of Consumer Financial Regulation. *American Economic Review: Papers & Proceedings* 106 (5): 1–30.

Choi, James J., and Adriana Z. Robertson. 2018.What Matters to Individual Investors? Evidence from the Horse's Mouth. NBER Working Paper #25019.

Cole, Shawn, Anna Paulson, and Gauri Shastry. 2014. Smart Money? The Effect of Education on Financial Outcomes. *Review of Financial Studies* 27 (7): 2022–2051.

D'Acunto, Francesco, Marcel Prokopczuk, and Michael Weber. 2019. Historical Antisemitism, Ethnic Specialization, and Financial Development. *The Review of Economic Studies* 86 (3): 1170–1206.

Das, Sreyoshi, Camelia M. Kuhnen, and Stefan Nagel. 2020. Socioeconomic Status and Macroeconomic Expectations. *The Review of Financial Studies* 33 (1): 395–432.

Del Guercio, Diane, and Jonathan Reuter. 2014. Mutual Fund Performance and the Incentive to Generate Alpha. *Journal of Finance* 69 (4): 1673–1704.

Duflo, Esther, and Emmanuel Saez. 2003. The Role of Information and Social Interactions in Retirement Plan Decisions: Evidence from a Randomized Experiment. *The Quarterly Journal of Economics* 118 (3): 815–842.

Dvorak, Tomáš. 2005. Do Domestic Investors have an Information Advantage? Evidence from Indonesia. *Journal of Finance* 60: 817–839.

Ellison, Glenn. 2005. A Model of Add-on Pricing. *Quarterly Journal of Economics* 120 (2): 585–637.

Fama, Eugene F., and Kenneth R. French. 2010. Luck versus Skill in the Cross-Section of Mutual Fund Returns. *The Journal of Finance* 65 (5): 1915–1947.

Feng, Lei, and Mark Seasholes. 2005. Do Investor Sophistication and Trading Experience Eliminate Behavioral Biases in Financial Markets? *Review of Finance* 9: 305–351.

French, Kenneth R. 2008. Presidential Address: The Cost of Active Investing. *The Journal of Finance* 63 (4): 1537–1573.

Gabaix, Xavier, and David Laibson. 2006. Shrouded Attributes, Consumer Myopia, and Information Suppression in Competitive Markets. *Quarterly Journal of Economics* 121: 505–540.

Gallaher, Steven, Ron Kaniel, and Laura T. Starks. 2015. Advertising and Mutual Funds: From Families to Individual Funds. *SSRN*. Accessed March 19, 2020. https://papers.ssrn.com/sol3/papers.cfm?abstract_id=2554403.

Goetzmann, William N., and Alok Kumar. 2008. Equity Portfolio Diversification. *Review of Finance* 12 (3): 433–463.

Graham, John R., Campbell R. Harvey, and Hai Huang. 2009. Investor Competence, Trading Frequency, and Home Bias. *Management Science* 55 (7): 1094–1106.

Grinblatt, Mark, and Matti Keloharju. 2000. The Investment Behavior and Performance of Various Investor-types: A Study of Finland's Unique Data Set. *Journal of Financial Economics* 55: 43–67.

———. 2001a. How Distance, Language, and Culture Influence Stockholdings and Trades. *Journal of Finance* 56 (3): 1053–1073.

———. 2001b. What Makes Investors Trade? *Journal of Finance* 56 (2): 589–616.

Grinblatt, Mark, Matti Keloharju, and Juhani Linnainmaa. 2011. IQ and Stock Market Participation. *Journal of Finance* 66 (6): 2121–2164.

———. 2012. IQ, Trading Behavior and Performance. *Journal of Financial Economics* 104 (2): 339–362.
Grinblatt, Mark, Seppo Ikaheimo, Matti Keloharju, and Samuli Knupfer. 2016. IQ and Mutual Fund Choice. *Management Science* 62 (4): 924–944.
Grullon, Gustavo, George Kanatas, and James P. Weston. 2004. Advertising, Breadth of Ownership and Liquidity. *The Review of Financial Studies* 17 (2): 439–461.
Guiso, Luigi, and Tullio Jappelli. 2005. Awareness and Stock Market Participation. *Review of Finance* 9 (4): 537–567.
Guiso, Luigi, Michael Haliassos, and Tullio Jappelli. 2003a. Stockholding in Europe: Where Do We Stand, and Where Do We Go? *Economic Policy* 36: 123–170.
Guiso, Luigi, Paola Sapienza, and Luigi Zingales. 2003b. People's Opium. The Economic Effects of Religion. *Journal of Monetary Economics* 50: 225–282.
———. 2004. The Role of Social Capital in Financial Development. *American Economic Review* 94: 526–556.
———. 2008. Trusting the Stock Market. *Journal of Finance* 63 (6): 2557–2600.
Hackethal, Andreas, Michael Haliassos, and Tullio Jappelli. 2012. Financial Advisors: A Case of Babysitters? *Journal of Banking and Finance* 36: 509–524.
Haliassos, Michael, Thomas Jansson, and Yigitcan Karabulut. 2017. Incompatible European Partners? Cultural Predispositions and Household Financial Behavior. *Management Science* 63 (11): 3780–3808.
Han, Bing, Johan Walden, and David Hirshleifer. 2018. Social Transmission Bias and Investor Behavior. NBER Working Paper #24281.
Heaton, John, and Deborah Lucas. 2000. Portfolio Choice and Asset Prices: The Importance of Entrepreneurial Risk. *Journal of Finance* 55: 1163–1198.
Hong, Harrison, Jeffrey D. Kubik, and Jeremy Stein. 2004. Social Interaction and Stock-Market Participation. *Journal of Finance* 59: 137–163.
Hortacsu, Ali, and Chad Syverson. 2004. Product Differentiation, Search Costs, and Competition in the Mutual Fund Industry: A Case Study of S&P 500 Index Funds. *Quarterly Journal of Economics* 119: 403–456.
Huberman, Gur. 2001. Familiarity Breeds Investment. *Review of Financial Studies* 14: 659–680.
Ivkovic, Zoran, and Scott Weisbenner. 2005. Local Does as Local Is: Information Content of the Geography of Individual Investors' Common Stock Investments. *Journal of Finance* 60 (1): 267–306.
Ivkovic, Zoran, Clemens Sialm, and Scott Weisbenner. 2008. Portfolio Concentration and the Performance of Individual Investors. *Journal of Financial and Quantitative Analysis* 43 (3): 613–655.
Karlsson, Niklas, George Loewenstein, and Duane Seppi. 2009. The Ostrich Effect: Selective Attention to Information. *Journal of Risk and Uncertainty* 38 (2): 95–115.

Kelly, Morgan. 1995. All their Eggs in One Basket: Portfolio Diversification of U.S. Households. *Journal of Economic Behavior and Organization* 27: 87–96.

Kim, Hugh Hoikwang, Olivia S. Mitchell, and Raimond Maurer. 2019. How Cognitive Ability and Financial Literacy Shape the Demand for Financial Advice at Older Ages. NBER Working Paper #25750.

Korniotis, George M., and Alok Kumar. 2011. Do Older Investors Make Better Investment Decisions? *The Review of Economics and Statistics* 93 (1): 244–265.

———. 2013. Do Portfolio Distortions Reflect Superior Information or Psychological Biases? *Journal of Financial and Quantitative Analysis* 48 (1): 1–45.

Koszegi, Botond, and Matthew Rabin. 2009. Reference-Dependent Consumption Plans. *American Economic Review* 99 (3): 909–936.

Kuhnen, Camelia M., and Andrei C. Miu. 2017. Socioeconomic Status and Learning from Financial Information. *Journal of Financial Economics* 124 (2): 349–372.

Linnainmaa, Juhani T. 2011. Why Do (Some) Households Trade So Much? *The Review of Financial Studies* 24 (5): 1630–1666.

Lusardi, Annamaria, and Olivia S. Mitchell. 2007. Financial Literacy and Retirement Preparedness: Evidence and Implications for Financial Education Programs. *Business Economics* 42: 35–44.

———. 2011. Financial Literacy and Planning: Implications for Retirement Wellbeing. NBER Working Paper #17078.

Malmendier, Ulrike, and Stefan Nagel. 2011. Depression Babies: Do Macroeconomic Experiences Affect Risk-Taking? *Quarterly Journal of Economics* 126 (1): 373–416.

———. 2016. Learning from Inflation Experiences. *Quarterly Journal of Economics* 131 (1): 53–87.

Massa, Massimo, and Andrei Simonov. 2006. Hedging, Familiarity and Portfolio Choice. *Review of Financial Studies* 19 (2): 633–685.

Meade, James. 1975. The Keynesian Revolution. In *Essays on John Maynard Keynes*, ed. J.M. Keynes. Cambridge University Press.

Mitchell, Olivia S., and Stephen P. Utkus. 2003. The Role of Company Stock in Defined Contribution Plans. In *The Pension Challenge: Risk Transfers And Retirement Income Security*, ed. Olivia S. Mitchell and Kent Smetters. Oxford University Press.

Olafsson, Arna, and Michaela Pagel. 2017. The Ostrich in Us: Selective Attention to Financial Accounts, Income, Spending, and Liquidity. NBER Working Paper #23954.

Pagel, Michaela. 2018. A News-Utility Theory for Inattention and Delegation in Portfolio Choice. *Econometrica* 86 (2): 491–522.

Pagel, Michaela, and Steffen Meyer. 2019. Fully Closed: Individual Responses to Realized Gains and Losses. NBER Working Paper #25542.

Peijnenburg, Kim, Olivia S. Mitchell, Roy Kouwenberg, and Stephen G. Dimmock. 2018. Household Portfolio Underdiversification and Probability Weighting: Evidence from the Field. NBER Working Paper #24928.

Poterba, James M. 2003. Employer Stock and 401(k) Plans. *American Economic Review* 93 (2): 398–404.

Robinson, David T., and Anders Anderson. 2018. Who Feels the Nudge? Knowledge, Self-awareness and Retirement Savings Decisions. NBER Working Paper No. #2561.

Samuelson, Paul A. 1958. *Economics*. New York: McGraw-Hill.

Seasholes, Mark S. 2000. Empirical Studies in International Finance. PhD diss., Harvard University.

Seasholes, Mark S., and Ning Zhu. 2010. Individual Investors and Local Bias. *Journal of Finance* 65 (5): 1987–2010.

Sicherman, Nachum, Loewenstein George, Duane J. Seppi, and Stephen P. Utkus. 2015. Financial Attention. *Review of Financial Studies* 29 (4): 863–897.

Van Nieuwerburgh, Stijn, and Laura Veldkamp. 2010. Information Acquisition and Under-Diversification. *The Review of Economic Studies* 77 (2): 779–805.

Van Rooij, Maarten, Annamaria Lusardi, and Rob Alessie. 2011. Financial Literacy and Stock Market Participation. *Journal of Financial Economics* 101 (2): 449–472.

Vanguard Group. 2001. Expecting Lower Returns in the Short Run. Vanguard Center for Retirement Research.

Vissing-Jorgensen, Annette. 2003. Perspectives on Behavioral Finance: Does "Irrationality" Disappear with Wealth? Evidence from Expectations and Actions. *NBER Macroeconomics Annual* 18: 139–194.

CHAPTER 5

Housing

1 Introduction

In his 1989 Presidential Address at the American Real Estate and Urban Economics Association, James R Follain noted that:

> *Mortgage choice is also the topic of this address because it is a challenging problem ripe for additional study.* (Follain 1990)

Since then, much research has been conducted and there is now an extensive literature in the areas of mortgage demand, mortgage instrument, mortgage refinancing and mortgage default.

Housing or real estate plays an important role in the economy of most countries as it is usually the largest component of household net wealth.

> *Households typically hold a highly exposed nondiversified portfolio, where housing is by far the most important asset. Indeed, at time of purchase, a household may convert nearly all of its wealth into housing equity.* (Plaut 1987)

It is often the most expensive consumer durable good since house prices generally are equivalent to a multiple of annual household incomes. Fluctuations in house prices tend to affect household behavior, consumption and investment, thereby directly impacting the level of macroeconomic activity.

S. Agarwal et al., *Household Finance*,
https://doi.org/10.1007/978-981-15-5526-8_5

Real estate is important to the banking sector as well since mortgages and home equity loans constitute a large fraction of bank credit. Fluctuations in house prices can affect the value of collateral and hence the financial soundness of lending institutions. In 2017, out of the US$14.6 trillion in US household debt, US$9.8 trillion or 67% comprise mortgage loans (Beshears et al. 2018).

The real estate sector creates jobs for many not only when the house is being built but also after it has been purchased. New homeowners spend on furniture, appliances and landscaping generating a multiplier effect on other sectors of the economy.

In addition, land sales and stamp duties on real estate transactions are important sources of government revenue.

2 Housing for Consumption

2.1 *House Versus Housing*

Although the terms house and housing are usually used loosely and interchangeably to mean the same thing, there is a distinction between the two: one is a stock, while the other is a flow. A house is a durable good, relatively unique and immobile. Housing, on the other hand, is the service provided by a house. The price of a house is its market value, while the price of housing is rent.

Whether a house is rented or owned, it generates housing and therefore rent. For a tenant, the rent is an out-of-pocket expense. For an owner-occupant, the rent is a form of income known as implicit rental income and the cost of housing is the sum of several components comprising interest, maintenance, property taxes, utilities, insurance and depreciation.

A house can appreciate in value and most have done so over the years, serving as a good hedge against inflation. In some cases, the appreciation has been so great as to offset the cost of housing. This has led many to believe that privately owned houses are sure to appreciate.

2.2 *Buy or Rent*

All households start with a "short" position in housing services since they need to live somewhere—if they do not own a house, they will have to rent. Owning a house is risky as house prices fluctuate (asset price risk) but renting is also risky as rentals likewise fluctuate (rent risk). The difference lies in the fact that asset price risk occurs in the future when the homeowner moves or sells his house. If the homeowner's expected length of stay (also known as horizon) is long, then the asset price risk is further in the future and will be heavily discounted. The demand for homeownership therefore increases with longer horizons. Rent risk, on the other hand, depends on rent fluctuations. The demand for homeownership will increase with rent volatility.

There is considerable heterogeneity in the correlation between house prices across different housing markets in the US, with a median of only 0.35. If the homeowner sells his home and moves to a correlated housing market, the repurchase price is partially hedged by the sale price, thereby reducing total asset price risk (Sinai and Souleles 2005). Sinai and Souleles (2013) show that households tend to move between highly correlated housing markets with correlation of 0.60 or greater and their decision to rent versus own is sensitive to the moving-hedge benefit of owning. Households with higher expected correlation in the house prices between their current market and possible future markets where they will relocate are more likely to buy. Ortalo-Magne and Prat (2016) find that higher expected correlation between markets yields higher house prices and reduces the demand for stocks that are correlated with housing markets.

Agarwal et al. (2016a) examine the influence of house price growth (measured using the house price index [HPI]) on the demand for first home purchases over the life cycle. They find stronger positive correlation between homeownership rates and average house price growth for individuals aged 25 to 34 than older age groups (Fig. 5.1).

In explaining this relationship, they argue that house price growth has two offsetting effects on the demand for houses. The first is the liquidity constraint channel where an individual will postpone buying a first home when house prices increase substantially and consumption may have to be sacrificed to pay for the down payment. The second is the expectation channel where the individual will buy a first home earlier as he expects house prices to rise even faster in the future. The results show that, consistent with the expectation channel, an individual tends to buy a house earlier in his life cycle by as much as five years if he lives in a location that has experienced high local house price growth. This can be observed from Fig. 5.2 where the likelihood of home purchase at any given age (hazard rate) is generally higher in cities with faster house price growth.

Adelino et al. (2018) study the effect of perceptions of house price risk on current and future intentions to buy or rent. They find that people who

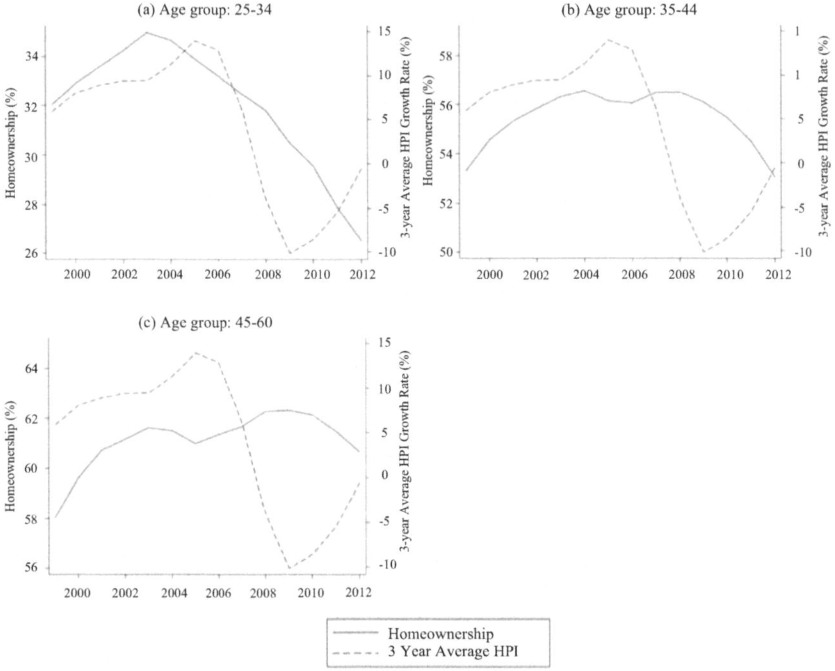

Fig. 5.1 Probability of homeownership by age groups between 1999 and 2012. (Source: Agarwal et al. 2016a)

perceive housing as risky investments are 12% more likely to be renters than owners. The gap persists even after controlling for differences in risk exposure such as labor income risk, expected mobility and local rental price volatility. Perceptions of house price risk correlate with past local house price changes and local house price volatility measures, suggesting that people's beliefs about house price risks are shaped by recent experiences in the past 12 months. In addition, renters adjust house price expectations less often than owners, causing them to lag in their response thus increasing their vulnerability to price movements.

Apart from asset price risk, rent risk and moving-hedge benefit, there are other factors to consider when deciding to buy or rent. Renters are more mobile. They can easily move to another location for better job opportunities and can avoid plumbing costs, roofing costs, home insurance and general upkeep of the premises, which are the responsibility of

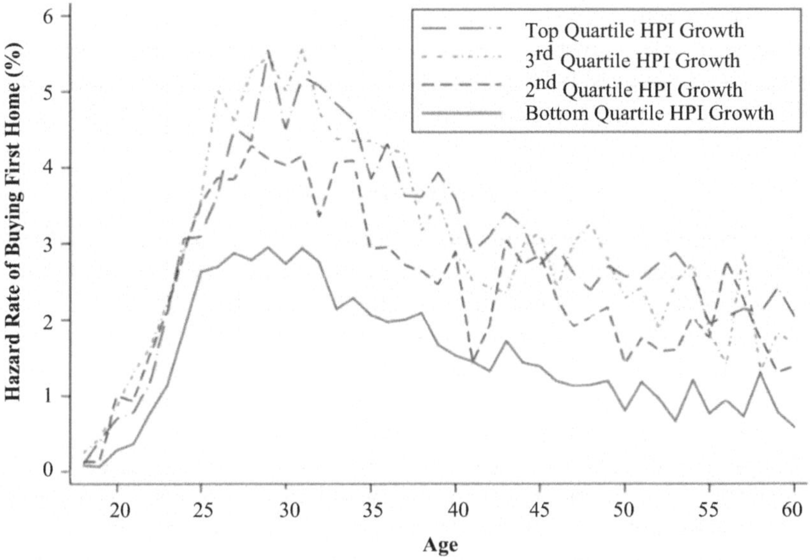

Fig. 5.2 Hazard rate of buying first home by age. (Source: Agarwal et al. 2016a)

the landlord. They do not need to worry about mortgage qualification checks, school district problems or safety issues within the community.

Homeowners generally have large mortgages. Leveraging amplifies the return to equity when house value appreciates and the loss to equity when the house value falls. In many countries, like the US, homeowners receive favorable tax treatment. Special preferences are granted to owner-occupied houses through mortgage interest deduction and capital gains tax exemption.

Even at the pretax level, Somerville et al. (2007) find that homeowners (by paying down mortgages) amass more wealth than renters (who invest the down payment and the difference in the periodic cost borne by the owner versus the renter) because they are forced to save. In order for renters to be ahead, they have to be extremely disciplined in investing the cost differences into high-yield instruments.

Homeownership enhances the well-being of the community as homeowners care about their neighborhoods (Soderlind 2001). While this positive externality is commonly used by supporters of home mortgage interest deduction, evidence shows that mortgage interest deduction has no effect on homeownership even in the long run (Glaeser and Shapiro 2003; Gruber et al. 2017). Instead, Gruber et al. (2017) find that the tax subsidy changes homeowners' behavior on the intensive margin by inducing them to buy larger and more expensive houses.

2.3 *The Housing Ladder*

The phenomenon of changing status from a renter to an owner and the purchase or upgrading of houses over time is known as the housing ladder or property ladder. Using data from the UK and the US, Banks et al. (2015) conclude that the housing ladder, where a steep incline is seen between age 20 and 40 and a plateau at around age 50, can be explained by changing demographics over the life cycle as individuals go through marriage, parenthood and the empty nest syndrome.

Banks et al. (2015) show that house price volatility incentivizes homeownership and movements up the housing ladder. Their study revolves around the idea that households demand for housing early in life as a form of insurance against fluctuation in house prices so that they can afford to climb the housing ladder over the course of their lives to meet changing housing needs. They find that individuals living in areas with volatile house prices buy their first home at a younger age, live in bigger homes and are less likely to refinance for the purpose of financing consumption. This suggests that houses do not only serve the conventional functions of consumption and investment, but insurance as well.

3 Housing for Investment

Classical economic theory suggests that households should diversify their investment portfolio within and between asset classes to minimize risk exposure. However, households invest in ways that do not align with predictions of traditional economic theory.

According to Arrondel et al. (2014), the main residence accounts for 51% of an European household's total gross assets. Other real estate forms the second largest asset category, while safe and risky financial assets constitute on average 8% and 4% of total gross assets, respectively.

3.1 *Motives for Household Demand for Assets*

Kimball (1991) expounds on three types of precautionary motives related to a household's demand for assets. The first is prudence where the household responds to a risk by reducing exposure and accumulating more wealth. The second is temperance where the household seeks to moderate total exposure to risk when faced with an unavoidable risk by hedging. The third is precautionary demand for liquidity where the household reacts by holding more money.

In a study of Italian households, Guiso et al. (1996) find supporting evidence for the prudence argument as subjective expectations of labor income uncertainty 12 months ahead reduces the share of risky financial assets held.

Heaton and Lucas (2000) observe that entrepreneurs with high and variable business income hold less wealth in stocks.

However, using data from households in the Netherlands, Hochguertel (2002) concludes that precautionary motives in the presence of income uncertainty play a limited role in explaining low risk taking and stockholding. Other variables such as age, education and tax incentives are more important.

Unavoidable risks such as medical expenditures affect portfolio allocation decisions. According to Ayyagari and He (2016), individuals are more likely to hold risky investments when they are eligible for a medical expenditure insurance because their health cost risk is lowered.

In recent years, there is an increasing prevalence of wealthy hand-to-mouth households who own a significant amount of illiquid assets like property but have little to no liquid assets (Kaplan et al. 2014). They exhibit negative marginal propensity to consume when planning to upgrade or have just upgraded their homes (De Francisco 2019). This is due to the large initial down payment which depletes their saving. It is difficult for them to adjust to small shocks by moving to a cheaper dwelling because of the high transaction costs involved so they cut back on their non-durable consumption instead.

3.2 *Homeownership or Stockholding*

In the light of positive equity premium, it is hard to explain non-participation in the stock market.

Intuitively it could be because households are risk-averse or are not inclined to assume stockholding risk in addition to labor income risk and health cost risk. However, according to standard economic theory, even risk-averse households should invest in stocks in order to maximize utility. Further confounding the stockholding puzzle is Piazzesi and Schneider's (2007) finding that large changes in stock return expectations are required to shift household portfolio shares.

With reference to Kimball's (1991) three precautionary motives, previous works by Bertaut and Haliassos (1997), Gollier and Pratt (1997), Viceira (2001) and Heaton and Lucas (1996) have shown that the unavoidable risk in labor income uncertainty and hence prudence is too small to explain the stockholding puzzle. Instead, Fratantoni (1998) finds that committed expenditure risk (the risk of committing to fixed nominal payments over a long horizon) associated with homeownership is inversely correlated with stockholding and sufficiently explains the stockholding puzzle. This gives strength to the argument for precautionary demand for liquidity. Though not empirically proven, temperance, in principle, could also be an explanation for the stockholding puzzle.

Household residential real estate differs from other financial assets in that it serves a dual purpose of consumption and investment. It is both a durable consumption good from which the owner derives utility and an investment vehicle that allows the owner to hold home equity. Although housing services is a necessary good, the associated level of homeownership may not be optimal from a portfolio point of view. For example, households with identical risk preferences and perceptions of risk and return may hold different portfolio of financial assets because of the different constraints imposed by their house. The lumpy nature of housing services may also contribute to the overestimation of a household's demand for such services.

Compared with stocks and bonds, a house is often highly leveraged and relatively illiquid. For many on the verge of retirement, housing wealth may be a crucial component of net worth. This is true across educational levels and across all ethnic groups (Lusardi and Mitchell 2007).

Some have noted that if the value of home equity keeps appreciating, it may be a good way to finance retirement. However, a study of the elderly in Singapore shows that housing equity does not significantly impact non-durable consumption (Chen et al. 2019). Results are consistent across different age of household head, house type and the number of properties owned. Even a novel housing equity monetization scheme (Lease

BuyBack Scheme) that allows the elderly to sell a portion of their property lease to fund their retirement increases non-durable consumption by only an insignificant 0.69% (Chen et al. 2019).

Despite the high weight of a house in the portfolio of a household, it is largely ignored by financial advisors. Of the literature on efficient portfolios, only a few papers incorporate it as a component asset (Goetzmann and Ibbotson 1990; Goetzmann 1993). The main reason is the difficulty of dealing with frictions such as collateral requirement and liquidation cost in the real estate market.

The ratio of house value to net worth varies over the homeowner's life cycle. It manifests as a high ratio in young households, which together with the high leverage results in high portfolio risk. In response, young households invest less in stocks and more in safe assets. On the other hand, older households who have accumulated more wealth will have a lower house value to net worth ratio and will find stocks relatively more attractive (Marjorie and Yamashita 2002).

3.3 Boom and Bust in House Prices

House prices can have an impact on work incentives. Gu et al. (2018) study its impact on individuals' shirking behavior at work, as measured by their tendency to attend to personal needs during work hours. They find that individuals increase their use of credit cards for non-work-related transactions during work hours. The impact is greater for those with higher housing wealth and those with lower work incentives. They conclude that increases in house price raise shirking behavior and lower labor productivity.

Credit conditions and expectations may also affect house prices (Piazzesi and Schneider 2016).

Cox and Ludvigson (2018) observe that changes in credit supply are positively related with house price growth and riskier non-conforming debt, while beliefs and expectations are unrelated.

On the other hand, Kaplan et al. (2017) find that the housing boom-bust leading up to the subprime mortgage crisis is best explained by shifting expectations about future house price growth. These boom-bust in house prices are responsible for half of the fluctuations in non-durable expenditures, while labor income accounts for the other half. They argue that even with timely and adequately large debt forgiveness programs such as the Home Affordable Modification Program (HAMP) and Home

Affordable Refinance Program (HARP), the collapse of house prices and aggregate demand could not have been prevented.

Gao et al. (2019) study the housing boom-bust between 2004 and 2009 in the US. They find that speculation amplifies house price appreciation, drives economic expansion in terms of increased employment, raises payroll and per capita income and increases the number of business establishments. Speculation also creates demand for construction between 2004 and 2006. It is a double-edged sword as it magnifies the drop in house price during the housing bust, with corresponding declines in employment, income and business establishments. The declines in the construction and non-construction sectors can be explained by the supply overhang channel and the local household demand channel, respectively.

The supply overhang channel suggests that excessive capital invested in the construction sector results in overbuilding during the boom and a subsequent reallocation of resources to other sectors during the bust (Rognlie et al. 2018).

The local household demand channel highlights the wealth shocks following the housing collapse with the highest cut in consumption for the poorer and more levered households (Mian et al. 2013).

4 Mortgages

A mortgage is a large long-term loan collateralized by the property financed. It plays a crucial role in enabling households to buy homes. The lender's obligation is immediately performed by providing the loan. The remaining contractual performance rests wholly upon the borrower to make the interest and capital repayments. The focus of contractual failure is therefore on the borrower.

The lender's exposure is mitigated in several ways. First, the house serves as a collateral. In the event of a default, the lender can repossess and sell the borrower's home. Second, the lender can spread the risk of default through the process of securitization. Third, the lender can cover its funding costs by adjusting interest rates.

The borrower is being held hostage by the awful prospect of default and losing the home if mortgage payments are not made (Clarke and Kohler 2005). The extended loan repayment period presents the risk that circumstances may change to jeopardize the ability of the borrower to meet his obligations such as illness, loss of job, economy downturn and relationship break down. Even the most stringent sales standards cannot eliminate unforeseen risks (Nield 2015).

In a perfectly competitive, no arbitrage Modigliani and Miller world where different mortgage instruments are priced accurately to reflect their risks, borrowers will be indifferent between them. In the real world, however, mortgage choices are relevant because of capital market imperfections, regulatory constraints and asymmetric information (Campbell and Cocco 2003).

The literature pertaining to mortgage is extensive covering (1) mortgage demand, (2) the choice of mortgage instrument, (3) the decision to refinance the mortgage, (4) the determinants of mortgage default and (5) access to home equity.

4.1 Mortgage Demand

Early theoretical models assume that homeowners borrow up to the limit of their housing collateral. These models implicitly assume that non-mortgage debts are either unavailable or too costly (Hendershott and Lemmon 1975; Rothenberg 1983).

An alternative formulation seeks the optimal strategy of minimizing mortgage borrowing (Ranney 1981). Subsequent models incorporate market imperfections to arrive at debt positions that are larger or smaller than the debt minimization optimum (Jones 1993).

Brueckner (1994) links the demand for mortgage debt to the house value and level of saving where households choose the largest mortgage size available if the rate of return on saving is greater than the mortgage interest rate (after accounting for tax subsidies). However, this is only true under conditions where future income, interest rates, house prices and other asset prices are known with certainty.

In reality, borrowers face an uncertain environment when making mortgage decisions. The analysis of mortgage demand under uncertainty is complex, which explains the recourse to empirical analysis.

One important consideration is labor income uncertainty (Naoi et al. 2013). As markets are incomplete, households cannot borrow against future income or eliminate labor income risk via insurance.

Other considerations include movement in house prices (Piskorski and Tchistyi 2011), interest rate expectations (Leece 2001), the degree of flexibility in mortgage contracts (Campbell and Cocco 2003), affordability issues (Bramley and Watkins 2009) and tax savings associated with interest deductions.

Several factors explain cross-country variations in the size and economic significance of mortgage contracts. These include economic conditions, demographics, house prices, legal and regulatory framework, mortgage market institutions, interest rate expectations and down payment constraint.

In a world with perfect capital markets where an individual can borrow and lend over his life cycle, the decision to purchase a house will have no effect on the lifetime consumption-saving pattern. However, in the presence of a liquidity constraint (e.g., a down payment requirement), purchasing a house may create a distortion in the lifetime consumption-saving decision. A higher down payment requirement may induce households to postpone consumption early in the life cycle in order to build up enough resources to qualify for homeownership. It may affect the timing of entry into owner occupation (Slemrod 1982; Hayashi et al. 1988), the supply of labor by inducing people to work harder, the timing of marriage and the desire to save. In countries with higher down payment constraints, the proportion of owner occupancy among the young is relatively low (Chiuri and Jappelli 2003). The down payment constraint may not be binding if intergenerational transfers and gifts can help in the financing (Engelhardt and Mayer 1998). Using Italian data, Guiso and Jappelli (2002) find that gifts are inadequate to overcome credit market imperfections.

La Porta et al. (1998) suggest that enforcement costs in mortgage markets, measured by the length of the foreclosure process, can affect the required down payment ratio. The lengthier and less efficient the process, the higher will be the down payment ratio. They find that countries with less efficient courts such as Belgium, Germany, Italy and Spain have higher down payment ratios. On the other hand, countries that have shorter foreclosure process have less restrictive down payment requirements.

High transaction costs, relatively higher house prices and imperfect capital market cause Japanese households to save more toward the down payment and to defer homeownership to later in the life cycle (Hayashi et al. 1988).

Further, cross-country comparison on demographic change shows that population decline and population aging depress real house prices and mortgage borrowing (Levin et al. 2009). This is the case in Japan where there is low fertility, high aging rates, excess supply of housing and low household borrowing (Naoi et al. 2019). Although fertility is also on the decline in Australia and the UK, the population is growing due to migration, causing the demand for houses and mortgage debt to rise (Naoi et al. 2019).

Bailey et al. (2019) investigate how homebuyers' belief about future house price changes affect the amount of mortgage leverage they take on. They propose two mechanisms through which a relationship may exist. The expected return mechanism suggests that optimistic homebuyers will take on high leverage to maximize their investment. The down payment protection mechanism posits that pessimistic homebuyers will choose lower down payment and thus higher leverage to limit potential losses on their investment. Using data from the US housing market, Bailey et al. (2019) find that when housing is viewed purely as an investment, expected return mechanism dominates. However, when housing is meant for consumption, the mortgage leverage choice is fully driven by the down payment protection mechanism.

Using interest expense on mortgage debt, consumer debt and other types of loans as a proxy for household financial decisions, Gruber et al. (2017) find that mortgage interest deduction induces households to increase indebtedness by buying larger and more expensive houses. They conclude that tax incentives distort the housing and debt demand of homeowners.

4.2 *Choice of Mortgage Instrument*

The conventional fixed-rate mortgage (FRM) has fixed interest payments over the term of the loan. The adjustable-rate mortgage (ARM) has fixed interest payments initially but adjusts after a specified interval to a new interest rate that is based on the prime rate at the time. The initial rate is comparatively low which increases its appeal.

These contract choices have major implications for risk sharing between lenders and borrowers. The proportion of FRM and ARM is of great importance for macroeconomic policy decision making as interest rate shocks affect FRM and ARM differently with potential impact upon the real estate market (Koblyakova et al. 2014).

Mortgage choices vary across countries. FRMs are popular in Germany and the US, while ARMs are used widely in Australia, Ireland, the UK and Southern Europe (Campbell 2013). The wide variation in the use of ARMs across countries is influenced by factors such as the historical inflation volatility (Campbell 2013), the subsidy afforded by the regulatory system (e.g., US policy subsidizes FRMs) and the bank's funding arrangements (Foa et al. 2016).

To understand the determinants of cross-country variation in the market share of ARMs, Badarinza et al. (2017) study a panel of nine countries. They find that households do not seem to anticipate longer-term rate movements, relying instead on the current rate spread in their mortgage choice. In tight lending markets, liquidity-constrained households seek low rates in order to maintain their current level of consumption and the maximum level of mortgage debt.

Botsch and Malmendier (2017) find that individuals who have experienced higher inflation in the past prefer FRMs over ARMs as they expect higher future inflation and higher nominal interest rates.

Koblyakova et al. (2014) present evidence of regional variation of mortgage choice within the UK, with ARMs more likely to occur in areas with lower incomes and lower affordability such as Northern England, Scotland and Wales. This could be due to lower initial payment on ARMs but borrowers who opt for ARMs end up paying a higher price.

Borrowers from regions in the UK with higher house prices enjoy better mortgage rates, which is consistent with the perspective that lenders factor in expectations of future price increases into the lending criteria (Besley et al. 2010). Higher risk and older borrowers are more heavily penalized by lenders (Besley et al. 2010).

Brueckner and Follain (1988) find that interest rate differential is the most important determinant in the choice between ARM and FRM. When interest rates are high, borrowers prefer ARM, which is consistent with the expectation of mean reversion in interest rates. Borrowers who are less likely to be credit constrained (high-income borrowers) prefer ARM. Borrowers who are likely to move (and prepay their loan) also prefer ARM.

Campbell and Cocco (2003) find that ARM is generally attractive but exposes borrowers to income risk, while FRM exposes borrowers to wealth risk. They conclude that households with smaller houses, more stable income, lower risk aversion, more lenient treatment in bankruptcy and higher probability of moving are more likely to use ARM. These results are consistent with Dhillon et al. (1987) who observe that households with stable income and who are likely to move are more likely to use ARM.

On the contrary, Naoi et al. (2013, 2019) and Koblyakova et al. (2014) conclude that FRM borrowers are less risky than ARM borrowers because they borrow less, have lower income risk, lower unemployment risk and plan ahead.

Paiella and Pozzolo (2007) find that the individual characteristics that can explain the choice between ARM and FRM are the age of the head and the presence of children, which both reduce the probability of using ARM.

Households' mortgage choices have macroeconomic consequences. ARM is more sensitive to interest rate shocks. Some argue that mortgage markets with more ARMs are more vulnerable to policy rate changes and therefore are less financially stable. For instance, the widespread use of ARMs in the UK saw households subject to severe liquidity squeeze when mortgage rates rose (Chinloy 1995).

Others hold a more positive view and regard ARMs to be more responsive to policy changes with higher pass-through to households in the transmission of monetary policy. In a recession, for example, a reduction in interest rate is more effective in an ARM system, where the interest rates are automatically adjusted and incorporated into mortgage payments.

During the financial crisis, regions in the US that have higher concentration of ARM relative to FRM experienced a larger increase in consumption when interest rates decline (Di Maggio et al. 2014).

Agarwal et al. (2012a) find that ARM has significantly lower default rates than FRM, but hybrid-ARM (mortgage with an initial fixed interest rate period followed by an adjustable rate period) has significantly higher default rates than FRM.

The latitude to tilt mortgage payments toward the early years of the debt can help unconstrained borrowers to minimize cost (Miles 1994). On the other hand, liquidity-constrained households can benefit from flexible repayment schemes to meet life cycle spending and saving needs. Flexible repayment scheduling can have an impact on the demand for houses and mortgage (Plaut 1986).

Campbell and Cocco (2003) investigate the welfare properties of inflation-indexed mortgage contracts. They find that there are large welfare gains arising from the reduced mortgage payments in the initial years, as implied by constant real payments instead of constant nominal payments.

Gurun et al. (2016) show that naïve consumers are persuaded by advertising to take expensive mortgages. Lenders that advertise more, charge higher mortgage rates especially where there are borrowers who are less informed and more susceptible to manipulation, such as racial minorities, less educated consumers and low-income consumers.

Using pre-crisis data, Agarwal et al. (2016b) find that borrowers who are rejected by lenders but are subsequently approved by their affiliates (steered borrowers) are led to take up mortgages with features that are considered highly profitable in the mortgage industry (high-margin mortgage products). The mortgage types include interest-only mortgage, option ARM, mortgage with prepayment penalty and low documentation mortgage (where little documentation on the borrower's income is required). Single female borrowers residing in low- and moderate-income areas are more likely to be steered. These are borrowers with lower levels of financial sophistication and are less likely to shop around.

Another form of steering is where predatory lenders steer low-risk borrowers into piggyback loans in order to circumvent regulations requiring primary mortgage insurance (PMI) for loans with loan-to-value (LTV) ratio above 80%. Borrowers accept the offer to break the loan into a first lien mortgage not exceeding 80% and a second lien home equity loan, if the cost of the extra interest on the second lien is lower than the insurance premium. Banks, in turn, offer this piggyback mortgage option to low-risk borrowers because the extra risk assumed is capped by the premium on the PMI (Agarwal et al. 2017a).

Even with the decline in popularity for piggyback lending, PMI itself is a moral hazard. According to Bhutta and Keys (2018), PMI companies do not only fail to provide restrain but rather encourage expansion of risky lending. They underprice risk during good times to capture market share causing undercapitalization for future potential claims, a behavior reflective of the moral hazard inherent in the insurance industry.

Some banks offer lower initial rate on ARMs to attract naïve borrowers. According to Agarwal et al. (2017b), banks use price discounts to attract naïve borrowers into exploitative contracts. These contracts shroud add-on attributes such as back-loaded resetting rates which are included in the contract to offset the bank's potential losses from the initial price discount offered.

4.3 Mortgage Refinancing

In the US, a majority of the mortgage contracts are FRMs that amortize over 15 to 30 years. Most mortgages can be repaid in full at any time without penalties by taking a new loan backed by the same property, also known as refinancing.

Mortgage refinancing allows borrowers to benefit from declines in the cost of credit. This is especially relevant for FRMs. A borrower with a FRM is unaffected when interest rates go up. If, however, interest rates move significantly downward, he will benefit by paying off the old mortgage (known as a prepayment) and taking out a new fixed-rate loan at the lower prevailing rate.

With favorable economic conditions, steady employment, credit scores and house prices between 2002 and 2006, the refinancing market grew rapidly allowing equity extraction.

During the refinancing process, borrowers may make errors of commission and omission. An example of an error of commission is refinancing at a rate that is not sufficiently below the initial mortgage rate. An example of an error of omission is failing to refinance at the optimal time.

There are those who advocate that borrowers should refinance when the value of interest saved exceeds the cost of refinancing. This rule ignores the loss in value from exercising the option to refinance today rather than in the future (Agarwal et al. 2013). The optimal point to refinance should be where the interest saved by refinancing equals the sum of refinancing costs and the option value of refinancing.

Agarwal et al. (2013) provide the first optimal closed-form solution to the borrower's refinancing problem based on the difference between the borrower's contract rate and the current mortgage interest rate. Their solution requires the consideration of a large number of parameter values. However, given a reasonable set of parameter values, they find that interest rates must fall by 100 to 200 basis points for refinancing to be optimal.

Anecdotal evidences suggest that many households fail to refinance, even though potential savings are large (Campbell et al. 2011a). The literature termed these borrowers as "woodheads".

Some borrowers do not actively monitor mortgage rates and do not immediately refinance even if they notice that the rates have reached the trigger rate because they are too busy (Agarwal et al. 2013). For these busy borrowers, the delay or rational inattention may be the optimal response (Reis 2006).

Agarwal et al. (2016c) investigate the time-varying option value of refinancing and find that over half of borrowers who refinance do so at a suboptimal time. They conclude that the error of commission and omission is correlated with the borrower's financial sophistication. Financially sophisticated borrowers (as proxied by larger FICO (Fair Isaac Corporation) credit scores and higher income) make smaller mistakes, refinancing at rates closer to the optimal rate and waiting less after the trigger rate is reached. Agarwal et al. (2016c) confirm that borrowers make smaller mistakes when the mortgage is important to them (as proxied by a high ratio of mortgage to borrower's income). In addition, borrowers learn from their refinancing experiences, making smaller mistakes on their second refinancing.

Using Danish data, Andersen et al. (2015) find that older households and households with lower income and education tend to make refinancing mistakes, while households with larger mortgage on their balance sheet are more likely to refinance. Similarly, Keys et al. (2016) find that less educated and less wealthy households are less likely to refinance when interest rates decline.

However, some argue that it is naïve to conclude that a borrower is acting sub-optimally if he fails to refinance. The ability to refinance may be constrained by factors such as (1) unemployment, (2) costs to re-evaluate the household's financial position, (3) costs to re-value the house, (4) credit scores, (5) homeowner's equity position, (6) decrease in property value, (7) plans to relocate, (8) expectations about future interest rate changes and (9) current mortgage balance.

A borrower considering refinancing must first qualify for a new mortgage. A fall in income or the value of the collateral makes it difficult to qualify for a new mortgage (Archer et al. 1996). Those with poor credit history and low equity position in the property are often blocked from obtaining replacement financing to prepay their existing mortgage (Peristiani et al. 1997). When adverse economic shocks cause property value to decrease, the negative impact on the collateral makes it impossible for some homeowners to obtain new mortgages (Caplin et al. 1997).

Johnson et al. (2016) find that some households do not refinance because they have suspicions about the motives of financial institutions. Specifically, households expect there to be a catch and are concerned about hidden costs. In situations where borrowers do not trust the financial provider, it is important to develop different interventions to nudge borrowers into refinancing and unlock savings.

One suggestion is to have fixed-rate mortgages that adjust automatically when rates decline (Campbell 2013). Such innovative products will remove the cross-subsidization of sophisticated homeowners who refinance when rates decline. However, there is no incentive for banks to introduce such easier-to-use products because the "shrouded equilibrium" benefits the sophisticated customers, who are subsidized by the less sophisticated households.

4.4 *Mortgage Default*

When borrowers are unable to keep up with the mortgage payments and lenders choose to foreclose, the total amount of the loan becomes immediately due. If the borrower fails to pay, the lender can sell the property to satisfy the debt.

Individual borrowers' risk characteristics play an important role in predicting default rates. Borrowers with better credit scores are less likely to default. Borrowers with lower loan-to-value (LTV) ratios are associated with lower default risk. Agarwal et al. (2012a) find that subprime mortgages are 1.3 times more likely to default than prime mortgages, and borrowers with low or no documentation are 1.8 and 2.4 times more likely to default than those who provide documentation.

A number of studies indicate that foreclosures have a negative spill-over effect on the value of surrounding properties ranging from 1% (Immergluck and Smith 2006; Campbell et al. 2011b) to 8.7% (Lin et al. 2009). However, the clustering of subprime lending in a neighborhood and their decay do not lead to greater default risks for surrounding borrowers (Agarwal et al. 2012a), although the share of subprime mortgages in the area is highly correlated with prime mortgage default rates (Agarwal et al. 2015).

Guren and McQuade (2019) argue that foreclosures exacerbate housing downturns through three channels. First, capital constraint and reduced equity push lenders to ration mortgage credit, preventing buyers from obtaining pre-approved loans. Second, foreclosed homeowners are prevented from further purchases due to the foreclosure flagged on their credit. Third, buyers of distressed properties are more selective in their purchase. Cumulatively, these channels reduce the number of transactions in the housing market, prolonging housing downturns. Guren and McQuade (2019) evaluate three government policies meant to stem foreclosures. They find that the most effective is a government facility to purchase distressed homes, followed by equity injections and principal reduction.

Default behavior crucially depends on the type of mortgage used. Mortgages in the UK, Australia and Japan are recourse type of loans where a defaulting household that is in negative equity will still be liable for the outstanding balance. In other words, the lender can foreclose any asset in addition to the mortgaged property to recover outstanding amounts. In such markets, households borrow less (Naoi et al. 2019).

Cho et al. (2012) find that regional differences in economic conditions in the UK give rise to different underlying mortgage risks. This is reflected in the equilibrium relationship between mortgage default rates and macroeconomic variables such as household income, mortgage rates and unemployment rates.

The literature on mortgage default emphasizes the role of house prices and home equity accumulation. However, many borrowers do not default as soon as home equity becomes negative; they prefer to wait because default is irreversible and there is a chance that house prices may increase. Most defaults can be traced to shocks such as illnesses and unemployment, which result in illiquidity. Elul et al. (2010) find that both the negative equity factor and illiquidity factor (as measured by high credit card utilization) are significantly associated with mortgage default, with both factors interacting with each other.

Gerardi et al. (2018) study the relative importance of negative equity and ability to pay on the likelihood of default. They find that job loss has the equivalent effect as a 35% decline in home equity on the likelihood of default. They also study the importance of strategic motives on default probability. Strategic defaulters have the ability to pay but choose to default because the home value has fallen below the loan amount. These account for 38% of defaulting households. A jump in loan-to-value (LTV) ratio from 75% to 125% increases the probability of default by two and seven percentage points for high- and low-income borrowers, respectively. The study finds that most mortgage borrowers are reluctant to default. Approximately 80% of households that need to cut their consumption to make their mortgage payments continue to make their mortgage payments. Consequently, Gerardi et al. (2018) conclude that policies reducing monthly mortgage payments can decrease incidences of foreclosures.

The onslaught of mortgage defaults and foreclosures during the 2008 financial crisis were attributed to many factors including rapid expansion of credit (Mian and Sufi 2009), improper rating of mortgage-backed securities (Ospina and Uhlig 2018), the belief that house prices will keep rising (Adelino et al. 2016; Foote et al. 2016), the impact of government-backed programs (Agarwal et al. 2012b) and illiquidity (Elul et al. 2010). These factors are further elaborated in Sect. 5 "Causes of the Subprime Crisis".

4.5 Access to Home Equity

Home equity is the worth of a homeowner's unencumbered interest in his property, that is, the difference between the fair market value and the outstanding balance of all liens on the property. Home equity increases as the borrower makes payments against the mortgage balance and as the property value appreciates.

There are several ways of accessing home equity—sell the property outright in the market, refinance the property, borrow via home equity credit and take up reverse mortgages (Agarwal et al. 2016c; Hurst and Stafford 2004).

Although home equity credit is collateralized, it is subordinated to the first mortgage. In the event of a foreclosure, the collateral property will be sold and the first mortgage has to be paid in full before the home equity lender can recover anything. If the home equity lender suffers a loss, then the balance of the loan will be converted into a personal unsecured liability.

Under the US tax law, interest expenses on mortgages and on home equity loans are tax deductible. This favorable treatment affects the size of mortgage debt and leads many to borrow against their home equity. Home equity credit constitutes a significant fraction of household leverage from 2002 to 2006 and defaults from 2006 to 2008.

Home equity credit can be classified into home equity loan and home equity line. A home equity loan is a closed-end loan for a term of 10 to 20 years, with fixed interest rates and monthly installment repayments of interest and principal. It is a form of consumer credit that offers tax deductibility on interest expense and reduces monthly debt service payments by lengthening loan maturities. A home equity credit line is an open-ended, variable rate, revolving credit facility that allows the borrower to take a loan of up to a predetermined amount.

Borrowers who need financing for current spending will choose home equity loans. Borrowers who anticipate future spending or future credit shocks will prefer home equity lines since they do not need to pay interest on unnecessary credit and will have access to credit when they are in need (Agarwal et al. 2006a).

Borrowers who choose home equity lines are typically high-income earners with relatively expensive homes, higher home equity and greater access to credit (Canner et al. 1998; Agarwal et al. 2006b). Borrowers who tap on home equity loans have lower credit scores and higher loan-to-value (LTV) ratios (Agarwal et al. 2006b), are younger and have high credit card utilization rates (Mian and Sufi 2012).

Hard information gathered for loan approvals includes credit score, income, existing debt, age, occupation status and purpose of loan. Soft information is gathered through the loan officer's interaction with the borrower. Agarwal et al. (2011a) examine the use of soft information in the design of counteroffers in the home equity credit market and confirm that soft information is effective in reducing overall ex post portfolio credit losses. A counteroffer that lowers the annual percentage rate (APR) reduces the default risk ex post, while a counteroffer that raises the APR increases the default risk ex post. Although borrowers with the higher APR counteroffer are more likely to default, the higher default rate is offset by the higher APR charged.

Using the same set of loan applications, Agarwal et al. (2016d) find that the traditional rationale that joint liability lending per se lowers credit risk is not true. They observe that jointly liable borrowers have lower default risk than single liability borrowers only in cases where the joint borrowers have similar credit scores. If the joint borrowers have divergent credit scores, the risk of default is actually higher than the risk associated with single borrowers.

Agarwal et al. (2006b) find that both home equity lines and home equity loans prepay and refinance when interest rates decline, but home equity loans are twice as sensitive to financial saving resulting from lower rates. On the other hand, households with home equity lines are thrice as likely to prepay when home prices appreciate, suggesting that they are more sensitive to equity accumulation. When faced with unemployment, households increase the utilization of their home equity lines to counter the negative income shock.

Agarwal and Qian (2017) examine a negative shock to home equity access in Singapore in August 2010, when the minimum occupation period for resale flats in the public housing market was extended from 3 years to 5 years. The policy change was an effort to cool down the overheated housing market and to reduce speculative activities. They find that the negative shock did not decrease house prices but affect homeowners' ability to access home equity, which is manifested in a significant negative consumption response.

Reverse mortgages also facilitate the monetization of home equity by allowing homeowners to borrow against home equity and receive either a lump sum or monthly disbursement. The demand for reverse mortgage products is low in high-income countries such as Australia (Jefferson et al.

2017), Italy (Fornero et al. 2016), the Netherlands (Dillingh et al. 2017) and the US (Davidoff et al. 2017).

The seemingly low take-up rate of reverse mortgage products can be improved with better product knowledge and more targeted marketing. Hanewald et al. (2019) note that older homeowners and their adult children show interest in a pilot reverse mortgage program in China that was redesigned and reframed.

5 Causes of the Subprime Crisis

Overinvestment and speculative activity in the property markets of many countries including Spain, Ireland and Britain, together with the burst of the US housing bubble, triggered a near collapse of the financial system during the subprime crisis. This was quickly followed by a fiscal crisis to deal with unemployment, foreclosures and to bail out banks.

Most of the explanations for the causes of the subprime crisis are drawn from theories of why credit markets malfunction but that is limiting because financial innovation, deregulation and re-regulation also played a part (Immergluck 2009).

The deregulatory phase in the US during the 1980s facilitated the growth of mortgage debt. The Depository Institutions Deregulation and Monetary Control Act (DIDMCA) of 1980 removed the cap on interest rates. The Alternative Mortgage Transaction Parity Act (AMTPA) of 1982 permitted the use of adjustable mortgages, balloon payment mortgages and interest-only mortgages. The Tax Reform Act (TRA) of 1986 prohibited the interest deduction on consumer loans but allowed interest deduction on mortgages for a primary residence and an additional home (Chomsisengphet and Pennington-Cross 2006). This makes mortgage debt cheaper than many consumer loans. It encourages the borrower to refinance when interest rate is low by assuming a new loan that is larger than the old loan and receiving the difference in cash (also known as cash-out refinancing).

Subprime mortgages became popular in the early 1990s when falling interest rates made them appealing as a means to finance a first home, refinance existing mortgages, consolidate debt and finance home improvements. It made homeownership possible for some who might not have qualified previously. It also provided access to home equity through refinances and second mortgages. The main difference between prime and subprime mortgages lies in the risk profile of the borrower.

Subprime lending grew earnestly after 1995. Between 1998 and 2000, there was a downturn in subprime originations for two reasons. First, there were delinquent payments and loan defaults arising from earlier subprime loans. Second, the 1997 Asian financial crisis increased the cost of borrowing and reduced loan originations.

During this period, some subprime originators failed, others merged and yet others were acquired. The consolidation resulted in a subprime industry dominated by large firms. From 2000, the origination of subprime loans resumed its momentum in response to low interest rates. According to Chomsisengphet and Pennington-Cross (2006), most of the subprime loans from 2000 to 2004 were from the more credit worthy borrowers (with higher credit scores). In addition, loans that presented more risk to the lenders had larger down payments or lower loan-to-value (LTV) ratios. The evidence is consistent with a reduction of risk exposure in the subprime market.

The US government re-regulated the mortgage market and made trading of mortgage-backed securities (MBS) possible, delinking investment from the property. The securitization succeeded in increasing the supply of credit (Mian and Sufi 2009) but was credited with undesired outcomes such as the housing bubble (Mian and Sufi 2009), lax borrower screening (Keys et al. 2010) and lower renegotiation rates in the aftermath of the crisis (Piskorski et al. 2010).

The mortgage market and the housing market fueled one another—the expansion of the mortgage market resulted in higher house prices, which meant even bigger mortgage loans. Post origination, subprime loans were packaged and sold to investors. By selling MBS, lenders offloaded the risk from their balance sheets and used the money to grant even more loans.

Subprime mortgages are more common in areas with rising house prices (Mayer and Pence 2008). Apart from higher default risk, subprime mortgages also have higher prepayment risk because, over time, these borrowers may qualify for lower interest rates and therefore have much to gain from refinancing (Pennington-Cross 2003).

There were concerns that lenders had retained higher quality loans on their balance sheets while securitizing inferior quality loans. Agarwal et al. (2012c) find that in the pre-crisis period when the market was doing well and prepayment risk was prevalent, lenders of prime loans exercised a profitable strategy where they sold loans with lower default risk (to satisfy the stringent criteria) but higher prepayment risk to government-sponsored enterprises (GSEs) such as Fannie Mae and Freddie Mac. Therefore, there was adverse selection with respect to prepayment risk during years of high refinancing and low default. Conversely, as the crisis approached and default risk became a concern, the same lenders of prime loans were less willing to retain higher default risk for lower prepayment risk. Compared to prime loans, subprime loans do not face the same degree of adverse selection. Agarwal et al. (2012c) attribute it to higher scrutiny by investors.

Things started to fall apart in the second half of 2007 when financial conditions weakened, interest rates rose and house prices declined. Between 2007 and 2017, there were an estimated six million foreclosures, with 25% of affected homeowners owning multiple homes (Piskorski and Seru 2019). These foreclosures displaced homeowners, causing most to move at least once, with only 25% foreclosed households regaining homeownership after an average of four years (Piskorski and Seru 2019). As of 2017, it was found that half the zip codes in the US have yet to restore house price, consumption and employment to pre-crisis levels, while those that recovered took four to five years on average (Piskorski and Seru 2019).

The US subprime crisis affected the local economy through the housing market and the financial markets. It affected the whole world through the financial markets, not just through mortgage-backed securities but also through the lack of liquidity. The widespread damage motivated extensive research into factors contributing to the crisis so that preventive measures can be put in place to avoid a recurrence.

5.1 *Credit Growth Through Subprime Mortgage*

Mian and Sufi (2009) argue that the rapid expansion of mortgage credit to subprime zip codes is the main cause of the sharp rise in house prices from 2001 to 2005 and the subsequent spike in mortgage defaults from 2005 to 2007. They find that 2002 to 2005 was the only period in 18 years where mortgage growth and income growth were negatively correlated. They attribute the expansion in credit supply to the shift toward "disintermediation", where originators sell mortgages in the secondary market shortly after origination. They find that disintermediation leads to higher default rates when originators sell bad loans to unaffiliated institutions lacking the skills to screen loan quality.

In a subsequent study, Mian and Sufi (2018) point to credit-fueled speculation as the critical channel through which mortgage securitization contributed to the housing boom-bust. They find that individuals who buy and sell properties quickly accounted for 80% of the rise in transaction volumes in zip codes with more mortgage securitization. Home buyers drawn into the housing market are younger, have lower average credit scores and default ex post at significantly higher rates, highlighting the role of speculation in the housing boom-bust.

5.2 *Improper Credit Ratings*

Even while the risk escalated, credit rating agencies continued to bestow good ratings. There are several possible reasons for the lapse on the part of the rating agencies. First, some rating agencies believed that house prices would keep rising. Second, the rating agencies were paid to rate the securities by issuers rather than investors. If a major part of their income was from rating complex products, then they might compromise their rating integrity by inflating their ratings (Mathis et al. 2009). Third, the rating agencies did not understand the complex products that they rated. Fourth, competition between rating agencies led to compromised ratings (Bolton et al. 2012; Becker and Milbourn 2011; Griffin et al. 2013).

In defense of credit rating agencies, Ospina and Uhlig (2018) who evaluate data from non-agency Residential Mortgage-Backed Securities (RMBS) conclude that these RMBS were not bad investments and that the ratings issued were not wrong. They rationalize that agency-backed securities were explicitly backed by the Federal Reserve Bank which meant that their role was a matter of policy. On the other hand, the performance of non-agency RMBS was completely at the disposal of the market hence studying them would more accurately portray the role of credit rating agencies. Ospina and Uhlig (2018) find that the mis-rating, if any, was modest and the allegations of improper ratings on the part of credit rating agencies were untrue.

5.3 *House Price and House Price Expectations*

Contrary to the broadly accepted narrative that financial innovation and deregulation led to the expansion of subprime credit, Adelino et al. (2017) argue that house price and house price expectations play a larger role. They examine the distribution of loan-to-value (LTV) ratios of new purchases to show that lenders extended loans in response to increased house prices instead of relaxed collateral constraints. They find that credit expansion by homeowners in areas with rapid house price increase was achieved through faster turnover rate for houses and cash-out refinances among the middle- and upper-income households. These middle- and high-income borrowers made up the majority of mortgage originations and accounted for a larger fraction of delinquencies especially in areas where house prices dropped more, suggesting that they were buying into high house price expectations (Adelino et al. 2016). The higher default rates exhibited by the middle- and high-income borrowers post-crisis also strengthened the house price expectations argument (Adelino et al. 2017).

Albanesi et al. (2017) expand on these findings. They observe that the mortgage delinquencies were due to credit growth in the prime segment between 2001 and 2007. The individuals with low credit score did not increase their borrowing. In fact, their mortgage delinquencies fell from 40% to 30%, while their fraction of foreclosures fell from 70% to 35% during the crisis. Albanesi et al. (2017) note that the credit growth was concentrated in the middle and top credit score distribution, which defaulted disproportionately during the crisis, with real estate investors exclusively accounting for the rise in delinquencies. Their findings were derived from up to eight quarters of lagged credit scores as opposed to the 1996 and 1997 credit scores used by Mian and Sufi (2009) and Mian and Sufi (2015) to identify subprime individuals. Albanesi et al. (2017) argue that their more recent credit scores took into account life cycle demand for credit. That is, subprime individuals identified using 1996 and 1997 credit scores might have experienced a rise in income, change in the pattern of borrowing and credit scores over time, which may invalidate the earlier conclusions.

5.4 *Government-Backed Housing Program*

Some feel that government-backed housing program is partly responsible for the poor-quality mortgage loans. An example is the 1977 Community Reinvestment Act (CRA), which is at the core of the US affordable housing mission. Banks have to meet their lending quotas of CRA loans. Compliance with CRA can help banks with their applications for new bank branches as well as for mergers and acquisitions. For example, the merger between Citibank and Washington Mutual was stalled until they pledged more loans for poor minorities. From 2001 to 2007, Fannie and Freddie bought roughly half of all CRA home loans, most carrying subprime features.

Agarwal et al. (2012b) examine the impact of CRA on the quality of the loans approved. They find that CRA led to riskier lending by banks with loans defaulting about 15% more often.

6 Market Review Post-Crisis

The subprime crisis resulted in loan defaults, extensive foreclosures, MBS collapse and insolvency of several financial institutions (Beshears et al. 2018). The extent of the crisis triggered a major rethink of the appropriate balance of responsibility among all stakeholders.

6.1 Debt Relief and Foreclosure Prevention: Home Affordable Modification Program (HAMP)

When the housing crisis erupted in 2007, the number of foreclosures in the US reached unparalleled dimensions. In order to stem the significant negative externalities, the US government provided sizeable financial incentives to lenders to renegotiate distressed residential mortgages by launching the Home Affordable Modification Program (HAMP) in February 2009. The underlying assumption of the debt relief program is that enhancing mortgage affordability will reduce default.

HAMP managed to forestall a substantial number of foreclosures but reached only one-third of the targeted households. Agarwal et al. (2017c) find that the shortfall was due to inadequate pre-existing organizational and infrastructure capacity in terms of staff strength, staff training effort and servicing capability. They believe that the program might have been more successful if the distressed mortgages had been transferred to organizations better equipped to conduct renegotiations.

Another argument for the less than ideal performance of HAMP was securitization. Piskorski et al. (2010) find that securitized loans have a higher rate of foreclosure than portfolio-held loans. Securitization hampers mortgage renegotiation.

Similarly, Agarwal et al. (2011b) note that securitization lowers renegotiation rates, even for high-quality loans where information asymmetry is low. They find that re-default is less likely if mortgages become more affordable after renegotiation, which is consistent with the motivation behind HAMP.

In contrast, Adelino et al. (2013) did not find any difference in the renegotiation rates of portfolio-held and securitized loans. They conclude that securitization does not impede renegotiation. Instead, they attribute the low renegotiation rates to information asymmetries between borrowers and lenders, where lenders expect to recover more from a foreclosure than a renegotiated loan because of self-cure risk and risk of re-default.

Piskorski and Seru (2019) identified organizational capacity of financial intermediaries, mortgage contract rigidity and refinancing constraints as factors affecting recovery across the US. Alleviating these frictions could reduce foreclosures by more than 50% and hasten recovery in house prices, consumption and employment by up to two times.

6.2 Government Credit Guarantee: Home Affordable Refinancing Program (HARP)

With the economic downturn, rising unemployment rates and sinking house prices, a large number of mortgages exceed the LTV ratio of 80%. Many borrowers want to take advantage of the lower interest rates available but had problems refinancing.

The Home Affordable Refinancing Program (HARP) allowed households with insufficient equity to refinance their mortgages through a credit guarantee on loans that exceed the usual LTV of 80%. The LTV limit, initially capped at 105%, was later increased to 125% and finally removed under HARP 2.0.

According to Agarwal et al. (2017d), more than three million eligible borrowers with primarily FRM refinanced under HARP but a significant number did not do so although the program was well advertised. They attribute the muted response to the lack of competitive pressure on the lenders. Regions that were more exposed to the program saw a decline in foreclosure rates, faster recovery in house prices and a sizeable increase in consumption. If not for the competitive friction which hampered the adoption of HARP, the impact on consumption would have been much greater given that the liquidity-constrained households likely have high marginal propensity to consume.

6.3 *Financial Counseling, Regulation and Predatory Lending*

In the wake of the subprime crisis, regulators were urged to tighten oversight and require mandatory financial counseling of borrowers (President Obama's Homeownership Affordability and Stability Plan of 2009).

Empirical evidences suggest that households with lower levels of financial literacy are more likely to have costly mortgages (Moore 2003), and households may borrow too much at high rates without realizing the consequences (Agarwal et al. 2009). However, there is less consensus that counseling and regulation will be effective in helping households make informed choices.

Agarwal et al. (2020) evaluate the impact of a mortgage counseling program implemented in Chicago in 2006. They find that borrowers altered mortgage contract choice to avoid being subjected to counseling, and lenders with predatory characteristics exited the market to avoid scrutiny from regulators. The volume of loan applications and originations declined by 51% and 61%, respectively. They believe that a counseling session earlier in the mortgage origination process will enhance the probability of better loan terms at origination and the presence of a regulator will improve the quality of the originated mortgages.

The setting also provided an opportunity to examine the proposition that predatory lending played a central role in creating the housing bubble through subprime loan originations (Financial Crisis Inquiry Commission 2011; Center for Responsible Lending 2009). Predatory lending are loans that imposed unfair and abusive loan terms on borrowers through aggressive sales tactics or that contain terms and conditions that potentially harm borrowers (FDIC 2006). Agarwal et al. (2014) find that eliminating bad lenders have a greater effect on defaults than eliminating bad loans. The remaining lenders made less risky loans that were of better credit quality. However, default rates remained high, suggesting that the loans eliminated may have been aggressive rather than predatory and that predatory lending may have played a relatively limited role in causing the crisis.

6.4 *Mortgage Market Review in the UK*

In the UK, the Mortgage Market Review conducted by the Financial Services Authority (FSA) concluded that the crisis was caused by (1) access to funds (credit boom), (2) availability of wholesale money markets and

(3) widespread use of MBS which fueled irrational lending giving rise to a housing bubble (FSA 2012).

Over reliance on mortgage collateral in the belief that house prices would continue to rise and the ability to offload risk via securitization led to the failure to conduct due diligence on the ability of borrowers to service loan repayments, often relying on self-certification of income. The incentive structure with performance-based pay and commission tied to sales targets resulted in a proliferation of subprime mortgages to borrowers with low credit scores (Appleyard 2011). Increasing house prices made homeowners feel wealthier and consume more (Buiter 2010). The overly optimistic belief that house prices will continue to trend upward and the rapid growth of interest-only mortgages contributed to the descent into irrationality (Gerardi et al. 2008; Mayer et al. 2009; Foote et al. 2012; Kuchler and Zafar 2018).

The review found that irresponsible lending and borrowing contributed to the unsustainable housing prices (FSA 2009). In order to minimize the risk of mortgage default, it recommended a shift in responsibility to mortgage providers who should take preemptive steps to evaluate the suitability of their financial products (FSA 2012).

Nield (2015) suggests that a coherent response to the crisis should include mediating strategies, safety nets and housing alternatives to manage the disruption caused by borrower defaults. For example, premature exercise of repossession should be avoided in favor of forbearance, and housing alternatives such as sale and leaseback, private rental and social housing should be explored to help exiting homeowners.

6.5 Housing Boom in China

Between 2003 and 2013, China's housing prices appreciated significantly, albeit unequally. First-tier cities such as Beijing, Shanghai, Guangzhou and Shenzhen saw prices grew at an average 13.1% per year, while second- and third-tier cities grew at 10.5% and 7.9%, respectively (Fang et al. 2016). Rapid growth in house prices stoked fears that a housing market meltdown in China might have spill-over effects.

Fang et al. (2016) argue that a financial crisis in China is unlikely for several reasons. First, banks in China are protected against a decline of up to 30% in house prices, as down payment on mortgage loans are typically about 40%. Second, rapid house price growth is accompanied by comparable growth in households' disposable income, providing justification for the housing boom. Third, participation of low-income households in the housing market is stable, suggesting that credit conditions are reasonable and do not lean in favor of borrowers with low credit scores.

7 Post-Crisis Policy Measures

Following the financial crisis, international financial institutions like the International Monetary Fund (IMF) and Bank for International Settlements (BIS) published papers detailing the policy options and their effectiveness in avoiding a similar crisis in the future.

As the housing boom-bust cycle was associated with high leverage in both the real and financial sectors, Crowe et al. (2011) argue that future policies should (1) prevent housing booms associated with build-up of leverage in the household and banking sectors and (2) increase the resilience of the financial system to a meltdown in the housing market.

In addition, policy makers should consider how macro-prudential policies can be coordinated with monetary and fiscal policy tools more effectively to prevent the incidence of another financial crisis (Gadanecz and Jayaram 2016; Lim et al. 2011).

7.1 Controlling Credit Supply Through Macro-prudential Policies

The role of the credit boom in fueling the housing bubble and the subsequent financial crisis show that one way to cool down an overheated market is to control credit supply. Macro-prudential policies control credit supply through three sets of measures: (1) capital requirements, (2) dynamic provisioning and (3) tightening of eligibility criteria through the LTV and debt-to-income (DTI) ratios (Crowe et al. 2011).

Capital requirements and dynamic provisioning force banks to hold more capital during economic boom to build buffer for bad times. However, as these measures are targeted at preventing a banking collapse in an event of a bust, they have limited effect on curbing credit growth and household leverage. Furthermore, they hurt the competitiveness of domestically regulated banks causing lending to shift to unregulated financial intermediaries and banks abroad (Crowe et al. 2011).

LTV limits reduce leverage and vulnerabilities as a larger drop in real estate prices is needed to fall into negative equity. DTI limits reduce the purchasing power of borrowers and increase their resilience to falling income or temporary unemployment. Both ratios directly affect the affordability of real estate, housing demand and prices (Crowe et al. 2011).

Agarwal et al. (2018) examine the impact of a collateral tightening policy implemented by the Monetary Authority of Singapore to reduce the LTV ratio from 80% to 70% and to raise the cash down payment from 5% to 10% of the estimated property value for borrowers with a mortgage loan outstanding. The policy was binding for all financial institutions, all types of borrowers and all types of properties. The intervention happened in August 2010 after the mortgage market had grown at above 20% for two years. The aim was to moderate house price appreciation by discouraging high LTV mortgage lending. The study finds that, in response to the excess resources freed up by the tougher LTV restrictions, there was an adjustment of lending standards on the part of banks toward riskier borrowers. The assumption that risky and over-optimistic borrowers will leave the market did not materialize.

Kuttner and Shim (2016) study the effectiveness of macro-prudential policies on housing credit and house prices. Using data from 57 countries over three decades, they find that an incremental tightening of the DTI ratio decelerate credit growth by four to seven percentage points over the following year.

7.2 *Curbing Debt-Financed Homeownership Through Fiscal Policies*

As tax regimes in most countries are designed in favor of debt-financed homeownership, theoretically, the tax structure can be tweaked to prevent the housing market from overheating. Transaction tax, capital gains tax and property tax are common ways to partially offset the bias toward homeownership, but mortgage interest tax relief is often large enough to undo the offset (Crowe et al. 2011).

Transaction taxes are sometimes imposed to discourage speculation. In 1973, James Tobin proposed a tax to curb speculative trading and market volatility after the dissolution of the Bretton Woods system in 1973 (Tobin 1978). Thereafter, the term "Tobin tax" has been applied to many forms of financial taxes.

In 2010, as the financial crisis dragged on, a group of 350 economists from 35 nations signed a petition urging the G20 to implement an international Tobin tax.

This tax is an idea that has come of age. The financial crisis has shown us the dangers of unregulated finance, and the link between the financial sector and society has been broken. It is time to fix this link and for the financial sector to give something back to society. This money is urgently needed. The crises of poverty and of climate change require an historic transfer of billions of dollars from the rich world to the poor world, and this tax would offer a clear way to help fund this.

Although the idea of taxing financial transactions was popular, the weak political will and massive coordination efforts required proved unsurmountable.

The empirical relationship between the level of transaction tax and house price movement is ambiguous (Crowe et al. 2011). While Belgium and Japan both have high transaction taxes, house price movement was modest in Belgium but went through a boom-bust in Japan.

On the other hand, transaction taxes that change with real estate conditions help to stabilize the market in a down turn through the use of tax breaks in the US and the UK and help to discourage speculation in a boom through the use of higher stamp duties in China and Hong Kong (Crowe et al. 2011).

In 2006, the Singapore government withdrew a concession which allowed buyers to defer stamp duty payment until the property was completed. The policy change effectively raised the transaction cost of short-term speculators. It managed to deter speculative trading activities but instead of promoting price stability, it did the reverse. It discouraged informed speculators more than noise speculators, leading to the unintended consequence of lower price stability and reduced informativeness (Fu et al. 2016).

Property tax increases the cost of homeownership. According to Crowe et al. (2011), high property tax in the US limits housing boom and short-run volatility around an upward trend in prices. However, they also caution against the generalization of its effectiveness as property tax has to be suitably high to have any impact.

8 Conclusion

A home is a highly leveraged and illiquid asset. It typically constitutes a significant fraction of a household's portfolio and is funded by a long-term mortgage. The committed expenditure risk associated with homeownership can help explain the stockholding puzzle.

In a perfect market, mortgage market economics would be a matter of indifference. However, in the presence of capital market imperfections, empirical evidences provide insights into mortgage demand, mortgage choices, refinancing decisions and mortgage default.

Financial innovation, deregulation, re-regulation and failure to control new mortgage products are some contributing factors to the subprime crisis. Following the crisis, the US government implemented programs such as HAMP to cope with foreclosures and HARP to help households with refinancing.

The crisis prompted a major rethink of how macro-prudential policies can more effectively prevent a similar crisis through better control of credit supply and implementation of fiscal policies.

References

Adelino, Manuel, Kristopher Gerardi, and Paul S. Willen. 2013. Why Don't Lenders Renegotiate More Home Mortgages? Redefaults, Self-Cures and Securitization. *Journal of Monetary Economics* 60 (7): 835–853.

Adelino, Manuel, Antoinette Schoar, and Felipe Severino. 2016. Loan Originations and Defaults in the Mortgage Crisis: The Role of the Middle Class. *The Review of Financial Studies* 29 (7): 1635–1670.

———. 2017. Dynamics of Housing Debt in the Recent Boom and Great Recession. NBER Working Paper #23502

———. 2018. Perception of House Price Risk and Homeownership. NBER Working Paper #25090.

Agarwal, Sumit, and Wenlan Qian. 2017. Access to Home Equity and Consumption: Evidence from a Policy Experiment. *Review of Economics and Statistics* 99 (1): 40–52.

Agarwal, Sumit, Brent W. Ambrose, and Chunlin Liu. 2006a. Credit Lines and Credit Utilization. *Journal of Money, Credit, and Banking* 38 (1): 1–22.

Agarwal, Sumit, Brent W. Ambrose, Souphala Chomsisengphet, and Chunlin Liu. 2006b. An Empirical Analysis of Home Equity Loan and Line Performance. *Journal of Financial Intermediation* 15: 444–469.

Agarwal, Sumit, John C. Driscoll, Xavier Gabaix, and David Laibson. 2009. The Age of Reason: Financial Decisions over the Life Cycle and Implications for Regulation. Brookings Papers on Economic Activity Fall, 51–101.

Agarwal, Sumit, Brent W. Ambrose, Souphala Chomsisengphet, and Chunlin Liu. 2011a. The Role of Soft Information in a Dynamic Contract Setting: Evidence from the Home Equity Credit Market. *Journal of Money, Credit and Banking* 43 (4): 633–655.

Agarwal, Sumit, Gene Amromin, Itzhak Ben-David, Souphala Chomsisengphet, and Douglas D. Evanoff. 2011b. The Role of Securitization in Mortgage Renegotiation. *Journal of Financial Economics* 102 (3): 559–578.

Agarwal, Sumit, Brent W. Ambrose, Souphala Chomsisengphet, and Anthony B. Sanders. 2012a. Thy Neigbor's Mortgage: Does Living in a Subprime Neigborhood Affect One's Probability of Default? *Real Estate Economics* 40 (1): 1–22.

Agarwal, Sumit, Efraim Benmelech, Nittai Bergman, and Amit Seru. 2012b. Did the Community Reinvestment Act Lead to Risky Lending? NBER Working Paper #18609: 1-45.

Agarwal, Sumit, Yan Chang, and Abdullah Yavas. 2012c. Adverse Selection in Mortgage Securitization. *Journal of Financial Economics* 105: 640–660.

Agarwal, Sumit, John C. Driscoll, and David Laibson. 2013. Optimal Mortgage Refinancing: A Closed Form Solution. *Journal of Money, Credit and Banking* 45 (4): 591–622.

Agarwal, Sumit, Gene Amromin, Itzhak Ben-David, Souphala Chomsisengphet, and Douglas D. Evanoff. 2014. Predatory Lending and the Subprime Crisis. *Journal of Financial Economics* 113 (1): 29–52.

Agarwal, Sumit, Brent W. Ambrose, and Yildiray Yildirim. 2015. The Subprime Virus. *Real Estate Economics* 43 (4): 891–915.

Agarwal, Sumit, Luojia Hu, and Xing Huang. 2016a. Rushing into the American Dream? House Prices Growth, Timing of Homeownership and Adjustment of Consumer Credit. *Review of Finance* 20 (6): 2183–2218.

Agarwal, Sumit, Gene Amromin, Itzhak Ben-David, and Douglas D. Evanoff. 2016b. Loan Product Steering in Mortgage Market. NBER Working Paper #22696

Agarwal, Sumit, Richard J. Rosen, and Vincent W. Yao. 2016c. Why do Borrowers make Mortgage Refinancing Mistakes? *Management Science* 62 (12): 3494–3509.

Agarwal, Sumit, Brent W. Ambrose, Souphala Chomsisengphet, and Chunlin Liu. 2016d. Joint Liability Lending and Credit Risk: Evidence from the Home Equity Market. *Journal of Housing Economics* 32: 47–66.

Agarwal, Sumit, Brent W. Ambrose, and Vincent W. Yao. 2017a. Lender Steering in Residential Mortgage Markets. *Real Estate Economics* 50: 1–30.

Agarwal, Sumit, Changcheng Song, and Vincent W. Yao. 2017b. Banking Competition and Shrouded Attributes: Evidence from the US Mortgage Market. Georgetown McDonough School of Business Research Paper #2900287.

Agarwal, Sumit, Gene Amromin, Itzhak Ben-David, Souphala Chomsisengphet, Tomasz Piskorski, and Amit Seru. 2017c. Policy Intervention in Debt Renegotiation: Evidence from the Home Affordable Modification Program. *Journal of Political Economy* 125 (3): 654–712.

Agarwal, Sumit, Gene Amromin, Souphala Chomsisengphet, Tim Landvoigt, Tomasz Piskorski, Amit Seru, and Vincent Yao. 2017d. Mortgage Refinancing, Consumer Spending, and Competition: Evidence from the Home Affordable Refinancing Program. NBER Working Paper #21512.

Agarwal, Sumit, Cristian Badarinza, and Wenlan Qian. 2018. The Effectiveness of Housing Collateral Tightening Policy. *SSRN*. Accessed March 23, 2020. https://papers.ssrn.com/sol3/papers.cfm?abstract_id=2917308.

Agarwal, Sumit, Amromin Gene, Itzhak Ben-David, Souphala Chomsisengphet, and Douglas D. Evanoff. 2020. Financial Education Versus Costly Counseling: How to Dissuade Borrowers from Choosing Risky Mortgages? *American Economic Journal: Economic Policy* 12 (1): 1–32.

Albanesi, Stefania, Giacomo De Giorgi, and Jaromir Nosal. 2017. Credit Growth and the Financial Crisis: A New Narrative. NBER Working Paper #23740.

Andersen, Steffen, John Y. Campbell, Kasper Meisner Nielsen, and Tarun Ramadorai. 2015. Inattention and Inertia in Household Finance: Evidence from the Danish Mortgage Market. NBER Working Paper #21386.

Appleyard, Lindsey. 2011. Review Article: Household Finances Under Pressure: What is the Role of Social Policy? *Social Policy and Society* 11 (1): 131–140.

Archer, Wayne R., David C. Ling, and Gary A. McGill. 1996. The Effect of Income and Collateral Constraints on Residential Mortgage Termination. *Regional Science and Urban Economics* 26: 235–261.

Arrondel, Luc, Laura Bartiloro, Pirmin Fessler, Peter Lindner, Thomas Y. Matha, Cristiana Rampazzi, Frederique Savignac, et al. 2014. How do Households Allocate Their Assets? Stylised Facts from the Eurosystem Household Finance and Consumption Survey. European Central Bank Working Paper Series #1722

Ayyagari, Padmaja, and Daifeng He. 2016. The Role of Medical Expenditure Risk in Portfolio Allocation Decisions. *Health Economics* 26 (11): 1447–1458.

Badarinza, Cristian, John Y. Campbell, and Tarun Ramadorai. 2017. What Calls to ARMs? International Evidence on Interest Rates and the Choice of Adjustable Rate Mortgages. *Management Science* 64 (5): 2275–2288.

Bailey, Michael, Eduardo Davila, Theresa Kuchler, and Johannes Stroebel. 2019. House Price Beliefs and Mortgage Leverage Choice. *Review of Economic Studies* 86: 2403–2452.

Banks, James, Richard Blundell, Zoe Oldfield, and James P. Smith. 2015. House Price Volatility and the Housing Ladder. NBER Working Paper #21255.

Becker, Bo, and Todd Milbourn. 2011. How Did Increased Competition Affect Credit Ratings? *Journal of Financial Economics* 101: 493–514.

Bertaut, Carol C., and Michael Haliassos. 1997. Precautionary Portfolio Behavior from a Life-cycle Perspective. *Journal of Economic Dynamics and Control* 21 (8–9): 1511–1542.

Beshears, John, James J. Choi, David Laibson, and Brigitte C. Madrian, 2018. Behavioral Household Finance. NBER Working Paper #24854.

Besley, Timothy, Neil Meads, and Paolo Surico. 2010. Risk Heterogeneity and Credit Supply: Evidence from the Mortgage Market. Bank of England Discussion Paper #29.

Bhutta, Neil, and Benjamin J. Keys. 2018. Eyes Wide Shut? The Moral Hazard of Mortgage Insurers during the Housing Boom. NBER Working Paper #24844.

Bolton, Patrick, Xavier Freixas, and Joel Shapiro. 2012. The Credit Ratings Game. *The Journal of Finance* 67 (1): 85–112.

Botsch, Matthew J., and Ulrike M. Malmendier. 2017. Inflation Experiences and Contract Choice—Evidence from Residential Mortgages. Paper presented at the American Economic Association Expectations, Learning, and Household Choices Paper session. Philadelphia, January 6

Bramley, Glen, and David Watkins. 2009. Affordability and Supply: The Rural Dimension. *Planning Practice and Research* 24 (2): 185–210.

Brueckner, Jan K. 1994. The Demand for Mortgage Debt: Some Basic Results. *Journal of Housing Economics* 3: 1–21.

Brueckner, Jan K., and James R. Follain. 1988. The Rise and Fall of the ARM: An Econometric Analysis of Mortgage Choice. *The Review of Economics and Statistics* 70: 93–102.

Buiter, Willem H. 2010. Housing Wealth Isn't Wealth. *Economics* 4 (22): 1-29A.

Campbell, John Y. 2013. Mortgage Market Design. *Review of Finance* 17: 1–33.

Campbell, John Y., and Joao F. Cocco. 2003. Household Risk Management and Optimal Mortgage Choice. *Quarterly Journal of Economics* 118: 1449–1494.

Campbell, John Y., Howell E. Jackson, Brigitte C. Madrian, and Peter Tufano. 2011a. Consumer Financial Protection. *Journal of Economic Perspectives* 25 (1): 91–114.

Campbell, John Y., Stefano Giglio, and Parag Pathak. 2011b. Forced Sales and House Prices. *American Economic Review* 101 (5): 2108–2131.

Canner, Glenn B., Thomas A. Durkin, and Charles A. Luckett. 1998. Recent Developments in Home Equity Lending. Federal Reserve Bulletin, Washington.

Caplin, Andrew, Charles Freeman, and Joseph Tracy. 1997. Collateral Damage: Refinancing Constraints and Regional Recessions. *Journal of Money, Credit and Banking* 29 (4): 496–516.

Center for Responsible Lending. 2009. Restoring Integrity to the Financial System Predatory Lending and the Economic Crisis. Centre for Responsible Lending.

Chen, Lipeng, Jiang Liang, Phang Sock Yong, and Yu Jun. 2019. Housing Equity and Household Consumption in Retirement: Evidence from the Singapore Life Panel. Singapore Management University Research Collection School of Economics: 1-27. Working Paper.

Chinloy, Peter. 1995. Privatised Default Risk and Real Estate Recessions: the UK Mortgage Market. *Real Estate Economics* 23: 401–420.

Chiuri, Maria Concetta, and Tullio Jappelli. 2003. Financial Market Imperfections and Home Ownership: A Comparative Study. *European Economic Review* 47 (5): 857–875.

Cho, Youngha, Soosung Hwang, and Steve Satchell. 2012. The Optimal Mortgage Loan Portfolio in UK Regional Residential Real Estate. *The Journal of Real Estate Finance and Economics* 45 (3): 645–677.

Chomsisengphet, Souphala, and Anthony Pennington-Cross. 2006. The Evolution of the Subprime Mortgage Market. *Federal Reserve Bank of St Louis Review* 88 (1): 31–56.

Clarke, Alison, and Paul Kohler. 2005. *Property Law: Commentary and Materials*. Cambridge University Press.

Cox, Josue, and Sydney C. Ludvigson. 2018. Drivers of the Great Housing Boom-Bust: Credit Conditions, Beliefs or Both. NBER Working Paper #25285.

Crowe, Christopher, Giovanni Dell'Ariccia, Deniz Igan, and Pau Rabanal. 2011. How to Deal with Real Estate Booms: Lessons from Country Experiences. International Monetary Fund Working Paper #11/91.

Davidoff, Thomas, Patrick Gerhard, and Thomas Post. 2017. Reverse Mortgages: What Homeowners (Don't) Know And How It Matters. *Journal of Economic Behavior & Organization* 133: 151–171.

De Francisco, Eva. 2019. Housing Choices and Their Implications for Consumption Heterogeneity. Board of Governors of the Federal Reserve System International Finance Discussion Papers #1249.

Dhillon, Upinder S., James D. Shilling, and C.F. Sirmans. 1987. Choosing between Fixed and Adjustable Rate Mortgages. *Journal of Money, Credit and Banking* 19 (2): 260–267.

Di Maggio, Marco, Amir Kermani, and Rodney Ramcharan. 2014. Monetary policy pass-through: Household Consumption and Voluntary Deleveraging. Columbia Business School Research Working Paper 14-24: 1–77.

Dillingh, Rik, Henriette Prast, Mariacristina Rossi, and Cesira Urzi Brancati. 2017. Who Wants To Have Their Home And Eat It Too? Interest In Reverse Mortgages in the Netherlands. *Journal of Housing Economics* 38: 25–37.

Elul, Ronel, Nicholas S. Souleles, Souphala Chomsisengphet, Dennis Glennon, and Robert Hunt. 2010. What 'Triggers' Mortgage Default? *American Economic Review: Papers and Proceedings* 100 (2): 490–494.

Engelhardt, Gary V., and Christopher J. Mayer. 1998. Intergenerational Transfers, Borrowing Constraints and Saving Behavior: Evidence from the Housing Market. *Journal of Urban Economics* 44: 135–157.

Fang, Hanming, Gu Quanlin, Wei Xiong, and Li-An Zhou. 2016. Demystifying the Chinese Housing Boom. *National Bureau of Economic Research Macroeconomics Annual* 30 (1): 105–166.

Federal Deposit Insurance Corporation. 2006. Challenges and FDIC Efforts Related to Predatory Lending. Report by the Office of Inspector General.

Financial Crisis Inquiry Commission. 2011. *The Financial Crisis Inquiry Report: Final Report of the National Commission on the Causes of the Financial and Economic Crisis in the United States.* New York, NY: Public Affairs.

Financial Services Authority. 2009. The Turner Report: A Regulatory Response to the Banking Crisis. Financial Services Authority, London.

———. 2012. Mortgage Market Review. Financial Services Authority London: PS12/16.

Foa, Gabriele, Leonardo Gambacorta, Luigi Guiso, and Paolo Emilio Mistrulli. 2016. The Supply Side of Housing Finance. Bank of Italy Working Paper #1044: 1-61.

Follain, James R. 1990. Mortgage Choice. *American Real Estate and Urban Economics Association Journal* 18 (2): 125–144.

Foote, Christopher L., Kristopher Gerardi, and Paul S. Willen. 2012. Why Did So Many People Make So Many Ex-Post Bad Decisions? The Causes of the Foreclosure Crisis. Federal Reserve Bank of Boston Public Policy Discussion Papers No. 12(2).

Foote, Christopher L., Lara Loewenstein, and Paul S. Willen. 2016. Cross-Sectional Patterns of Mortgage Debt during Housing Boom: Evidence and Implications. Federal Reserve Bank of Boston Working Paper.

Fornero, Elsa, Mariacristina Rossi, and Maria Cesira Urzi Brancati. 2016. Explaining Why, Right or Wrong (Italian) Households Do Not Like Reverse Mortgages. *Journal of Pension Economics & Finance* 15 (2): 180–202.

Fratantoni, Michael C. 1998. Homeownership and Investment in Risky Assets. *Journal of Urban Economics* 44: 27–42.

Fu, Yuming, Wenlan Qian, and Bernard Yeung. 2016. Speculative Investors and Transactions Tax: Evidence from the Housing Market. *Management Science* 62 (11): 3254–3270.

Gadanecz, Blaise, and Kaushik Jayaram. 2016. Macroprudential Policy Frameworks, Instruments and Indicators: A Review. In *Combining Micro and Macro Data for Financial Stability Analysis*, vol. 41. Bank for International Settlements.

Gao, Zhenyu, Michael Sockin, and Wei Xiong. 2019. Economic Consequences of Housing Speculation. NBER Working Paper #26457.

Gerardi, Kristopher, Andreas Lehnert, Shane M. Sherlund, and Paul S. Willen. 2008. *Making Sense of the Subprime Crisis.* Brookings Papers on Economic Activity: 69–145.

Gerardi, Kristopher, Kyle F. Herkenhoff, Lee E. Ohanian, and Paul Willen. 2018. Can't Pay or Won't Pay? Unemployment, Negative Equity, and Strategic Default. *Review of Financial Studies* 31 (3): 1098–1131.

Glaeser, Edward L., and Jesse M. Shapiro. 2003. The Benefits of the Home Mortgage Interest Deduction. In *MIT Press Tax Policy and the Economy*, vol. 17, 37–82. MIT Press.

Goetzmann, William N. 1993. The Single Family Home in the Investment Portfolio. *Journal of Real Estate Finance and Economics* 6 (3): 201–222.

Goetzmann, William N., and Roger G. Ibbotson. 1990. The Performance of Real Estate as an Asset Class. *Journal of Applied Corporate Finance* 3 (1): 65–76.

Gollier, Christian, and John W. Pratt. 1997. Risk Vulnerability and the Tempering Effect of Background Risk. *Econometrica* 64: 1109–1123.

Griffin, John M., Jordan Nickerson, and Dragon Yongjun Tang. 2013. Rating Shopping or Catering? An Examination of the Response to Competitive Pressure for CDO Credit Ratings. *The Review of Financial Studies* 26 (9): 2270–2310.

Gruber, Jonathan, Aalie Jensen, and Henrik Kleven. 2017. Do People Respond to the Mortgage Interest Deduction? Quasi-Experimental Evidence from Denmark. NBER Working Paper #23600.

Gu, Quanlin, He Jia, and Qian Wenlan. 2018. Housing Booms and Shirking. *SSRN*. Accessed March 23, 2020. https://papers.ssrn.com/sol3/papers.cfm?abstract_id=3189933.

Guiso, Luigi, and Tullio Jappelli. 2002. Private Transfers, Borrowing Constraints and the Timing of Home Ownership. *Journal of Money, Credit and Banking* 34: 315–340.

Guiso, Luigi, Tullio Jappelli, and Daniele Terlizzese. 1996. Income Risk, Borrowing Constraints and Portfolio Choice. *American Economic Review* 86 (1): 158–172.

Guren, Adam M., and Timothy J. McQuade. 2019. How do Foreclosures Exacerbate Housing Downturns? NBER Working Paper #26216.

Gurun, Umit G., Gregor Matvos, and Amit Seru. 2016. Advertising Expensive Mortgages. *Journal of Finance* 71 (5): 2371–2416.

Hanewald, Katja, Hazel Bateman, Hanming Fang, and Shang Wu. 2019. Is there a Demand for Reverse Mortgages in China? Evidence from Two Online Surveys. NBER Working Paper #25491.

Hayashi, Fumio, Takatoshi Ito, and Joel Slemrod. 1988. Housing Finance Imperfections, Taxation and Private Saving: A Comparative Simulation Analysis of the United States and Japan. *Journal of the Japanese and International Economies* 2: 215–238.

Heaton, John, and Deborah Lucas. 1996. Market Frictions, Saving Behavior, and Portfolio Choice. *Macroeconomic Dynamics* 1 (1): 76–101.

———. 2000. Portfolio Choice and Asset Prices: The Importance of Entrepreneurial Risk. *Journal of Finance* 55 (3): 1163–1198.

Hendershott, Patric H., and Richard C. Lemmon. 1975. The Financial Behavior of Households: Some Empirical Estimates. *Journal of Finance* 30: 733–759.

Hochguertel, Stefan. 2002. Precautionary Motives and Portfolio Decisions. *Journal of Applied Econometrics* 18 (1): 61–77.

Hurst, Erik, and Frank Stafford. 2004. Home is Where the Equity is: Mortgage Refinancing and Household Consumption. *Journal of Money, Credit and Banking* 36 (6): 985–1014.

Immergluck, Dan. 2009. *Foreclosed: High Risk Lending, Deregulation, and the Undermining of America's Mortgage Market.* New York: Cornell University Press.

Immergluck, Dan, and Geoff Smith. 2006. The External Costs of Foreclosure: The Impact of Single-Family Mortgage Foreclosures on Property Values. *Housing Policy Debate* 17 (1): 57–79.

Jefferson, Therese, Siobhan Austen, Rachel Ong, and Marietta E.A. Haffner. 2017. Housing Equity Withdrawal: Perceptions of Obstacles among Older Australian Home Owners and Associated Service Providers. *Journal of Social Policy* 46 (3): 623–642.

Johnson, Eric, Stephan Meier, and Olivier Toubia. 2016. Leaving Money on the Kitchen Table: Exploring Sluggish Mortgage Refinancing Using Administrative Data, Surveys, and Field Experiments. In *Advances in Consumer Research*, ed. Page Moreau and Stefano Puntoni, vol. 44, 179–184. Duluth, MN: Association for Consumer Research.

Jones, Lawrence D. 1993. The Demand for Home Mortgage Debt. *Journal of Urban Economics* 33: 10–28.

Kaplan, Greg, Giovanni L. Violante, and Justin Weidner. 2014. The Wealthy Hand-to-Mouth. *Brookings Papers on Economic Activity* 45 (1): 77–153.

Kaplan, Greg, Kurt Mitman, and Giovanni L. Violante. 2017. The Housing Boom and Bust: Model Meets Evidence. NBER Working Paper #23694.

Keys, Benjamin J., Tanmoy Mukherjee, Amit Seru, and Vikrant Vig. 2010. Did Securitization Lead to Lax Screening? Evidence from Subprime Loans. *Quarterly Journal of Economics* 125 (1): 307–362.

Keys, Benjamin J., Devin G. Pope, and Jaren Pope. 2016. Failure to Refinance. *Journal of Financial Economics* 122 (3): 484–499.

Kimball, Miles S. 1991. Precautionary Motives for Holding Assets. NBER Working Paper #3586 MA: 1–7.

Koblyakova, Alla, Norman Hutchison, and Piyush Tiwari. 2014. Regional Differences in Mortgage Demand and Mortgage Instrument Choice in the UK. *Regional Studies* 48 (9): 1499–1513.

Kuchler, Theresa, and Basit Zafar. 2018. Personal Experiences and Expectations about Aggregate Outcomes. *The Journal of Finance* 74 (5): 2491–2542.
Kuttner, Kenneth N., and Ilhyock Shim. 2016. Can Non-Interest Rate Policies Stabilise Housing Markets? Evidence From A Panel of 57 Economies. *Journal of Financial Stability* 26: 31–44.
La Porta, Rafael, Florencio Lopez-de-Silanes, Andrei Shleifer, and Robert W. Vishny. 1998. Law and Finance. *Journal of Political Economy* 106 (6): 1113–1155.
Leece, David. 2001. Regressive Interest Rates Expectations and Mortgage Instrument Choice in the United Kingdom housing market. *Real Estate Economics* 29: 589–614.
Levin, Eric, Alberto Montagnoli, and Robert E. Wright. 2009. Demographic Change and the Housing Market: Evidence from a Comparison of Scotland and England. *Urban Studies* 46 (1): 27–43.
Lim, Cheng Hoon, Francesco Columba, Alejo Costa, Piyabha Kongsamut, Akira Otani, Mustafa Saiyid, Torsten Wezel, et al. 2011. Macroprudential Policy: What Instruments and How to Use Them? Lessons from Country Experiences. International Monetary Fund Working Paper #11/238.
Lin, Zhenguo, Eric Rosenblatt, and Vincent W. Yao. 2009. Spillover Effects of Foreclosures on Neighborhood Property Values. *The Journal of Real Estate Finance and Economics* 38 (4): 387–407.
Lusardi, Annamaria, and Olivia S. Mitchell. 2007. Baby Boomer Retirement Security: The Roles of Planning, Financial Literacy, and Housing Wealth. *Journal of Monetary Economics* 54: 205–224.
Marjorie, Flavin, and Takashi Yamashita. 2002. Housing and Portfolio Composition. *The American Economic Review* 92 (1): 345–362.
Mathis, Jerome, James McAndrews, and Jean-Charles Rochet. 2009. Rating the Raters: Are Reputation Concerns Powerful Enough to Discipline Rating Agencies? *Journal of Monetary Economics* 56 (5): 657–674.
Mayer, Christopher J., and Karen M. Pence. 2008. Subprime Mortgages: What, Where, and to Whom? NBER Working Paper #14083.
Mayer, Christopher, Karen Pence, and Shane M. Sherlund. 2009. The Rise in Mortgage Defaults. *Journal of Economic Perspectives* 23 (1): 27–50.
Mian, Atif, and Amir Sufi. 2009. The Consequences of Mortgage Credit Expansion: Evidence from the US Mortgage Default Crisis. *Quarterly Journal of Economics* 124: 1449–1496.
———. 2012. House Prices, Home Equity-Based Borrowing, and the US Household Leverage Crisis. *American Economic Review* 89: 959–973.
———. 2015. Household Debt and Defaults from 2000 to 2010: Facts from Credit Bureau Data. University of Chicago Law School Kreisman Working Paper Series in Housing Law and Policy #28.

———. 2018. Credit Supply and Housing Speculation. National Bureau of Economic Research Working Paper #24823.

Mian, Atif, Kamalesh Rao, and Amir Sufi. 2013. Household Balance Sheets, Consumption, and the Economic Slump. *Quarterly Journal of Economics* 128 (4): 1687–1726.

Miles, David. 1994. *Housing, Financial Markets and the Wider Economy*. John Wiley & Sons.

Moore, Danna L. 2003. Survey of Financial Literacy in Washington State: Knowledge, Behavior, Attitudes, and Experiences. Washington State Department of Financial Institutions 03-39.

Naoi, Michio, Yoko Moriizumi, and Norifumi Yukutake. 2013. Income Risk and Mortgage Choice among Japanese Households. *SSRN*. Accessed March 23, 2020. https://papers.ssrn.com/sol3/papers.cfm?abstract_id=2211396

Naoi, Michio, Piyush Tiwari, Yoko Moriizumi, Norifumi Yukutake, Norman Hutchison, Alla Koblyakova, and Jyoti Rao. 2019. Household Mortgage Demand: A Study of the UK, Australia and Japan. *International Journal of Housing Markets and Analysis* 12 (1): 110–130.

Nield, Sarah. 2015. Mortgage Market Review: Hard-Wired Common Sense? *Journal of Consumer Policy* 38: 139–159.

Ortalo-Magne, Francois, and Andrea Prat. 2016. Spatial Asset Pricing: A First Step. *Economica* 83: 130–171.

Ospina, Juan, and Harald Uhlig. 2018. Mortgage-Backed Securities and the Financial Crisis of 2008: a Post Mortem. NBER Working Paper #24509.

Paiella, Monica, and Alberto F. Pozzolo. 2007. Choosing between Fixed and Adjustable Rate Mortgages. In *Household Credit Usage*, ed. Sumit Agarwal and Brent W. Ambrose, 219–236. Palgrave Macmillan.

Pennington-Cross, Anthony. 2003. Credit History and the Performance of Prime and Nonprime Mortgages. *The Journal of Real Estate Finance and Economics* 27 (3): 279–301.

Peristiani, Stavros, Paul Bennett, Gordon Monsen, Richard Peach, and Jonathan Raiff. 1997. Credit, Equity, and Mortgage Refinancings. *Federal Reserve Bank of New York Economic Policy Review* 3 (2): 83.

Piazzesi, Monika, and Martin Schneider. 2007. Asset Prices and Asset Quantities. *Journal of the European Economic Association* 5 (2–3): 380–389.

———. 2016. Housing and Macroeconomics. NBER Working Paper #22354.

Piskorski, Tomasz, and Amit Seru. 2019. Debt Relief and Slow Recovery: A Decade after Lehman. NBER Working Paper #25403.

Piskorski, Tomasz, and Alexi Tchistyi. 2011. Stochastic House Appreciation and Optimal Mortgage Lending. *The Review of Financial Studies* 24 (5): 1407–1446.

Piskorski, Tomasz, Amit Seru, and Vikrant Vig. 2010. Securitization and Distressed Loan Renegotiation: Evidence from the Subprime Mortgage Crisis. *Journal of Financial Economics* 97 (3): 369–397.

Plaut, Steven E. 1986. Mortgage Design in Imperfect Capital Markets. *Journal of Urban Economics* 20: 107–119.

———. 1987. The Timing of Household Tenure Transition. *Journal of Urban Economics* 21: 312–322.

Ranney, Susan I. 1981. The Future Price of Houses, Mortgage Market Conditions and the Returns to Homeownership. *American Economic Review* 71: 323–333.

Reis, Ricardo. 2006. Inattentive Producers. *Review of Economic Studies* 73 (3): 793–821.

Rognlie, Matthew, Andrei Shleifer, and Alp Simsek. 2018. Investment Hangover and the Great Recession. *American Economic Journal: Macroeconomics* 10 (2): 113–153.

Rothenberg, Jerome. 1983. Housing Investment, Housing Consumption and Tenure Choice. In *The Urban Economy and Housing*, ed. R.E. Grieson. Toronto: Lexington Books.

Sinai, Todd, and Nicholas S. Souleles. 2005. Owner-occupied Housing as a Hedge against Rent Risk. *The Quarterly Journal of Economics* 120: 763–789.

———. 2013. Can Owning a Home Hedge the Risk of Moving? *American Economic Journal: Economic Policy* 5 (2): 282–312.

Slemrod, Joel. 1982. Down-Payment Constraints: Tax Policy Effects in a Growing Economy with Rental and Owner Occupied Housing. *Public Finance Quarterly* 10: 193–217.

Soderlind, Steven D. 2001. *Consumer Economics: A Practical Overview*. Armonk New York: ME Sharpe.

Somerville, Tsuriel C., Paulina Teller, Michael Farrell, Yosh Kasahara, and Li Qiang. 2007. Do Renters Miss the boat? Homeownership, Renting, and Wealth Accumulation. In *Household Credit Usage*, ed. Sumit Agarwal and Brent W. Ambrose, 203–217. Palgrave Macmillan.

Tobin, James. 1978. A Proposal for International Monetary Reform. *Eastern Economics Journal* 4: 153–159.

Viceira, Luis M. 2001. Optimal Portfolio Choice for Long-Horizon Investors with Nontradable Labor Income. *Journal of Finance* 56 (2): 433–470.

CHAPTER 6

Payment

1 Introduction

The payment function has to do with the transfer of money for the purchase of goods and services. Despite its routine nature, the act of paying evokes positive and negative emotions.

1.1 Acquisition and Transaction Utility

To incorporate psychology into the buying process, Thaler (1985) postulates two types of utility.

The acquisition utility is the excess utility over and above the value of the next best alternative use of the money paid. A purchase provides acquisition utility if the buyer values it more than what the market does.

The transaction utility is the perceived merit of the purchase compared to a reference price or an expected price. The transaction utility is negative if the buyer feels that he has been fleeced. It is positive if the buyer feels that he has secured a good deal. Positive transaction utility mitigates the "pain of payment" (Prelec and Loewenstein 1998).

The most important factor in determining the reference price is fairness. Fairness may depend on the cost of similar products, the last price paid or the cost to the seller. If a much higher price is charged than a well-established reference price, there is negative transaction utility. A seller who cares about a long-term relationship with a buyer will have to weigh

S. Agarwal et al., *Household Finance*,
https://doi.org/10.1007/978-981-15-5526-8_6

the gains associated with a higher price charged against the long-run loss of goodwill.

Zellermayer (1996) studies the emotions felt by buyers and the effect on their behavior. He concludes that the pain of paying holds buyers in check but the pain depends on contextual factors. When contextual factors mitigate the pain of paying, buyers may spend against their best interests. If the pain of paying is too intense, buyers may not spend even when spending benefits them.

1.1.1 Factors Influencing Transaction Utility

While it seems intuitive that transaction utility will be higher during a price promotion, Lee and Tsai (2013) observe that price promotion in fact reduces consumption enjoyment. They explain that when a buyer pays a discounted price, he is less attentive when consuming. For instance, a buyer who pays full price for a concert ticket is more motivated to get the most out of the experience. This effect is further influenced by the time gap between payment and consumption. A longer delay makes the consumption of a positive item less desirable and a negative item less undesirable.

An identity-linked price promotion targets buyers based on their social identity (e.g., a discount for tertiary students). According to Dalton and Li (2014), a buyer is more likely to recall the identity-linked promotion when reminded of his social identity. His memory of the identity-linked promotion depends on how strongly he identifies with it, suggesting that the same identity-linked promotion brings greater utility to a buyer who identifies strongly with the social identity. However, identity-linked promotions may motivate unnecessary consumption, diminishing overall utility derived from the purchase.

A study by Yang et al. (2012) shows that owning more goods within a product category can dampen satisfaction, contrary to the conventional belief that those who own closets of clothes and shoes or multiple televisions necessarily have higher satisfaction than those who have fewer possessions.

1.2 Buffering Hypothesis

According to the buffering hypothesis, the pain of paying is cushioned or lessened by the act of consumption (Prelec and Loewenstein 1998). The enjoyment of consumption and the pain of paying are interdependent. While payment may affect the delight of consumption, the consumption may mitigate the pain of paying. When the consumer feels that the purchase is worth it, for example, paying for dinner with a dream date, the consumption buffers the payment. On the other hand, if the consumer feels that the food and the service do not warrant the payment, then it becomes painful to pay.

1.2.1 Factors Influencing Buffering Effect

Buffering is influenced by the degree of coupling between payment and consumption. When the benefits and costs are tightly coupled or closely associated, the more painful the payment and therefore the more likely the customer will consume the good despite poor weather conditions or poor health (Soman and Gourville 2018).

Price bundling, such as ordering a value meal at a restaurant, having optional features on a new car or buying a football season ticket, leads to a disassociation or decoupling of the benefits and costs. People who purchase a bundle are less likely to consume everything that has been paid for because the price of a single item is ambiguous.

Although consumers feel less pain when payment and consumption are decoupled, the purchases may not be welfare-enhancing. For instance, DellaVigna and Malmendier (2006) demonstrate that consumers who signed up for monthly gym membership paid more per visit either due to over-optimism regarding their gym attendance or due to their wish to commit to more gym visits which regrettably did not materialize.

Buffering is also influenced by temporal considerations. Paying for a used-up good is more painful than paying for a good to be consumed in the future, for example, a vacation.

1.3 Payment Transparency Hypothesis

The payment transparency hypothesis states that the more transparent the payment, the greater the perceived pain and therefore the greater the aversion to spending (Prelec and Loewenstein 1998; Soman 2003).

Soman (2003) broadly categorizes payment transparency into (1) the physical form which relates to the salient act of spending and (2) the amount which refers to the quantum of outflow.

In terms of physical form, Thomas et al. (2011) find that an expected payment by cash is more painful than an expected payment by credit card. When executing these payments, consumers who pay by check or credit card are more likely to commit to unplanned purchases than those who pay by cash (Inman et al. 2009). The lower aversion to spending using check and credit card may be attributed to the lack of association between spending and payment due to the time gap (Feinberg 1986), while cash involves an immediate depletion of wealth (Soman 2003).

With regard to the amount, Yeung (2014) notes that payment transparency is influenced by the act of counting and paying. He finds that the pain of paying is not reduced by getting subjects to memorize different things before and after the payment. He concludes that payment transparency is not affected by the payment method but by the mental counting, tracking and handing out of the money.

Contrary to the payment transparency hypothesis, Van der Horst and Matthijsen (2013) observe more positive emotions associated with cash payments than with debit card payments. In theory, debit card which has a lower payment transparency (Soman 2003) should induce less pain of paying. Van der Horst and Matthijsen (2013) attribute the discrepancy to the habitual inclination of subjects in the cash-oriented country of the Netherlands.

1.4 *Sunk Cost Fallacy*

Another psychological response to spending is the sunk cost fallacy where consumers persist with a behavior or endeavor because of previously invested time, money or effort (Arkes and Blumer 1985). They choose to remain in a relationship although they are really unhappy because they have invested much time and effort into it. They brave a snowstorm and spend hours to get to a concert because they had pre-purchased the tickets. They overeat and stuff themselves to get their money's worth because they have paid for an all-you-can-eat buffet.

Instead of dwelling on expenses and cost already incurred, decisions should be made based on incremental costs and benefits. Explanations for the sunk cost fallacy include the desire to recover prior losses (Garland and Newport 1991; Kahneman and Tversky 1979; Whyte 1986), the desire not to be wasteful (Arkes 1996) and the desire to justify a prior course of action (Brockner 1992; Teger 1980).

2 Modes of Payment

Research shows that the pain of paying also depends on the mode of payment. According to Soman (2001), the mode of payment affects spending behavior through two mechanisms: (1) a memory process which causes consumers to recall past expenses and (2) an immediacy effect which makes consumers more averse to spending.

Results from a laboratory experiment show that consumers tend to underestimate or forget credit card purchases because the act of paying by credit card is less memorable. In addition, payments made via credit card do not result in an immediate negative impact on wealth so it is a relatively painless way of spending.

Angrisani et al. (2015) find that the number of transactions and payment amounts made on different payment instruments vary. The most common methods of payment, in descending order, are debit card, cash, credit card and personal check. Personal check and credit card tend to be used for larger expenses, while debit card and cash are associated with smaller payments.

Using data from the Federal Reserve Bank of Boston, Koulayev et al. (2016) observe that cash and debit card are most commonly used for payments at brick-and-mortar stores, checks are most popular for paying bills through the mail, while bank account deductions are used mainly for automatic bill payments.

Koulayev et al. (2016) also find that not all the payment instruments are ranked equally along the eight dimensions of security, setup (cost of setting up the payment instrument), acceptance (level of merchant's acceptance), cost (cost of use), control, records (ease of tracking use), speed and ease. Cash is best for setup and acceptance but the worst for security. Credit card is favored for its ability to track and record usage but is most costly to use. Bank account deduction is most secure but has the highest barriers when it comes to setup. Payment through checks is slowest relative to other methods but probably the best for delaying payment with the words "The check is in the mail".

Of the eight dimensions, Koulayev et al. (2016) note that ease is the most important determinant of use, followed by control and cost. These results are generally consistent with Schuh and Stavins (2010).

In terms of demographics, Koulayev et al. (2016) find that wealthier households prefer credit cards, while less wealthy households prefer cash and prepaid cards. Education has a large positive effect on credit card use and a negative effect on cash, check and debit card perhaps because educated households are better able to manage a credit line (Klee 2008). Age is positively correlated with the use of cash and check (Klee 2008).

The decision of what payment instrument to use is also affected by characteristics such as reward and loyalty programs, discounts, surcharges and social status.

2.1 *Cash as a Payment Instrument*

Cash is the most transparent form of payment. When using cash to pay, consumers are less inclined to part with currency in whole denominations compared to equivalent amounts in smaller denominations (Mishra et al. 2006). This phenomenon is known as "bias for the whole" where money in the form of a whole is preferred because it is processed more fluently than the constituent parts.

A possible explanation for spending money in smaller denominations is to get rid of clutter. Mishra et al. (2006) find that people who have smaller denominations are more willing to spend.

In terms of demographics, Koulayev et al. (2016) find that (1) older consumers do not have a higher preference for cash relative to credit and debit, (2) older consumers have a higher preference for paying with checks than the young and (3) the less wealthy consumers use cash more often.

2.2 *Debit Card as a Payment Instrument*

Debit cards provide consumers with direct access to money in their bank account when going about their daily purchases. Debit cards are a convenient way to spend and are used in 28% of payments in the US (Kumar and O'Brien 2019).

It was found that, in countries where trust in financial institutions is weak, debit cards can help the poor to save. Using household survey results from Mexico, Bachas et al. (2017) conclude that debit cards provide a platform for the poor to monitor their account balances while building their trust in the bank in the first 9 to 12 months. These account holders start with small amounts of money in their accounts. Many are worried that the banks will steal their money through hidden fees. After trust has been established, debit cards tied to saving accounts facilitate formal saving, increasing the saving rate by 3% to 5% of income.

However, even within developed countries like the US, debit cards are not accessible to all (Beshears et al. 2018). According to the 2015 FDIC (Federal Deposit Insurance Corporation) National Survey of Unbanked and Underbanked Households, 7% of US households do not hold a check or saving account. These households are unbanked because of various reasons including the lack of funds (57%), desire for privacy (29%), mistrust of banks (28%), high account fees (28%) and unpredictable account fees (24%) (Beshears et al. 2018).

2.3 *Check as a Payment Instrument*

The US payment system experienced a huge decline in the use of checks in the mid-1990s. Schuh and Stavins (2010) attribute this to (1) changes in important payment characteristics such as convenience, cost, record keeping and timing, (2) the availability and acceptance of alternative instruments which are more appealing and (3) the change in demographics such as more young consumers and more poor consumers. Slower processing time and security concerns are also identified as possible reasons in a subsequent study (Schuh and Stavins 2013).

This trend is similarly observed in Australia (Tellez 2017) and the European Union. Silva et al. (2016) find that the charging of fees reduces check usage, while the criminalizing of unfunded checks encourage check usage because of perceived enhanced security.

2.4 *Credit Card as a Payment Instrument*

2.4.1 *Facilitates Spending*

The "buy now, pay later" mentality has permeated our way of life (Borgen 1976; Hirschman 1979) and gained social acceptance (Eastwood 1975). It is a vital part of business, banking and household financial management (Savage 1970).

Studies have shown that the use of credit cards instead of cash as a payment mechanism increases the propensity to spend and enhances the speed and magnitude of spending (Hirschman 1979; Feinberg 1986; Prelec and Simester 2001).

Prelec and Simester (2001) note that participants in an experiment who were told that they will be paying by credit card bid significantly more for a pair of tickets to a sporting event than those who pay in cash.

In a field study where receipts were collected from shoppers at the exit of a large supermarket store, Soman (2003) finds that shoppers who use less transparent modes of payment tend to purchase more non-essential items. However, the transparency of the mode of payment does not have any effect on the purchase of essential items.

In another study where participants were asked to estimate the budget for a hypothetical thanksgiving party where the specified payment mode is either cash or credit card, the estimated cost of the party is significantly higher when credit card is the payment mode (Raghubir and Srivastava 2008). This suggests that the expectation of paying by credit card induces more spending.

2.4.2 Status Symbol

Some credit cards are associated with prestige. A desire to signal high income or wealth may cause consumers to demand such conspicuous status goods.

Bursztyn et al. (2017) conduct a field experiment via an Indonesian bank which markets platinum credit cards meant for high-income consumers. The card has a higher credit limit and offers discounts on luxury goods. The study finds that demand for the card greatly exceeds other cards with identical benefits, suggesting that the demand was driven by the status symbol. The card is mainly used in social settings such as restaurants, bars and clubs where it is likely to be seen by others. However, the demand for the status aspect decreases with income probably because the wealthy have other ways to flaunt their wealth.

2.4.3 Debt Management

Credit cards often require a minimum payment on monthly balances to avoid certain charges and to maintain account status. Minimum payments are helpful when consumers are tight on liquidity but they may result in sub-optimal high-debt levels.

Such concerns are justified as 29% of credit cardholders in the US across credit score spectrum, income and age regularly make minimum or near minimum payments on their cards, incurring an estimated $2.7 billion to $4.7 billion in interest cost (Keys and Wang 2019). Keys and Wang (2019) attribute this to the anchoring effect theorized by Kahneman and Tversky (1974) where consumers use the minimum payment amount as the starting point and adjust upward.

To minimize cost, standard theory holds that consumers should pay toward the credit card with the highest interest rate first. However, Dave Ramsey (2003) who has co-authored many bestselling books on money management believes that the strategy of paying off the lowest balance first will yield some psychological benefit to cardholders when the number of cards with outstanding balances quickly reduce, providing them with momentum to clear all debt.

Using a sample of consumers who are relatively financially sophisticated, younger, educated and creditworthy, Stango and Zinman (2009) examine the penalty fees incurred in their checking and credit card accounts. They find that most penalty fees such as late and over-limit fees, bounced check fees, cash advance fees and balance transfer fees are avoidable, while most interest charges are not avoidable.

Agarwal et al. (2009a) observe that individuals who took high cost payday loans have the alternative of tapping on lower-cost options because they still possess substantial credit card liquidity. This points to an apparent mistake in choosing lower-cost credit options. However, on closer examination, the action is indicative of underlying financial distress because these borrowers are also more likely to suffer credit card delinquency in the following year.

There are also consumers who hold credit card debt while also maintaining high balances in their checking or saving account (Gross and Souleles 2002a). Bertaut and Haliassos (2002) explain the co-existence of credit card debt and liquid assets using the "accountant-shopper" model, where the credit limit serves as a self-control mechanism. This is consistent with Thaler's (1999) mental accounting budgeting system where consumers group money into expenditure, income and wealth and do not treat them as perfectly fungible.

Using Mexican data, Ponce et al. (2008) study the allocation of debt, payments and purchases among the credit cards that consumers already hold. They find that consumers pay more toward the card that they use the most for purchases in the previous month regardless of the interest rate, which is attributable to mental accounting and the lack of financial sophistication.

In a later study, Ponce et al. (2017) find that Mexican consumers borrow on the more expensive card. Instead of repaying credit cards which charge the highest interest rates after making the minimum required payment on all cards, consumers misallocate on average 50% of their payments to lower interest cards. Possible behavioral explanations include limited attention and mental accounting. The mistakes could also be due to relative inexperience with credit cards and lower financial sophistication in a less developed country.

Gathergood et al. (2019) note that the difference in cultural and financial setting in a less developed country is unlikely to be the reason as they find a similar misallocation of 46% among UK consumers. The misallocation is unresponsive to interest rate differentials and repayment amounts. Instead, the repayment behavior follows a balance-matching heuristic where the repayment on each card is matched to the relative balance on each card.

Using an experiment conducted by a large US bank that offered consumers a choice between two credit card contracts, Agarwal et al. (2015) find that, on average, most consumers chose the optimal credit contract but 40% chose the ex post sub-optimal contract, with the probability of choosing the sub-optimal contract declining with the dollar magnitude of the potential error. Those who made larger errors on their initial contract choice are more likely to subsequently switch to the optimal contract. The probability of switching increases with the number of times that the consumers had erred in the past, which is consistent with learning.

2.4.4 Defaults and Unemployment

There are conflicting results on the relationship between unemployment, credit card delinquencies and bankruptcies.

Some find that unemployment leads to a rise in credit card defaults and personal bankruptcy filings (Deng et al. 2000; Grieb et al. 2001). Agarwal and Liu (2003), using data on 700,000 consumers from 1995 to 2001, conclude that unemployment is critical in determining credit card delinquency and bankruptcy.

On the other hand, Gross and Souleles (2002b) find that risk, age, macro and social factors are important in determining default, but not unemployment.

Fay et al. (2002) find that households are more likely to file for bankruptcy when the financial benefit from filing increases. They find little support for the hypothesis that households file for bankruptcy when adverse events occur.

2.4.5 Defaults and Forbearance

Lenders try to reduce losses arising from credit card delinquencies by employing forbearance actions such as lengthening repayment terms, lowering interest rates and re-aging (allow credit card holders to reinstate their 90-day delinquent status by making a minimum payment).

In the context of mortgage, Ambrose and Capone (2000) find that subsequent default risk is higher than the risk of defaulting the first time, especially during the first two years after the initial default. Economic factors that predict the first mortgage default are not helpful in predicting subsequent defaults.

On the contrary, Fuster and Willen (2012) show that allowing borrowers to refinance their mortgage at a lower rate can substantially reduce the likelihood of default.

In the credit card market, Agarwal et al. (2008) find that the risk factors predicting a first default are different from those predicting a second default. Private information is a better predictor of a first default, while FICO (Fair Isaac Corporation) score is a better predictor of a second default. However, the default risk is not higher. Of the re-aged consumers, 78% do not default a second time. The results suggest that the re-aging program provides significant saving to the lender and is successful in rehabilitating liquidity-constrained consumers.

2.4.6 *Adverse Selection*

Agarwal et al. (2010a) find that consumers who respond to credit card solicitations exhibit higher credit risk characteristics than those who do not respond. Those who respond to inferior solicitation offers (higher annual percentage rates) exhibit higher credit risk than those who respond to superior offers. There is strong evidence of adverse selection (Akerlof 1970). Specifically, consumers who respond to inferior offer types are more likely to default and suffer a more severe deterioration of credit quality.

2.4.7 *Cloaked Corruption*

As the Chinese government embarks on its campaign to eliminate corruption, people search for less obvious and less blatant ways of offering bribes. The lack of transparency and proper supervision in China's credit card system makes credit cards a tool for disguised corruption. Agarwal et al. (2016) observe that bureaucrats in regions with high expenses receive 14% to 30% more in credit lines, are more likely to be delinquent and are more likely to be reinstated. In addition, banks that grant more credit lines to bureaucrats have higher government deposits, which is consistent with banks receiving benefits in return.

The corruption crackdown is successful to the extent that the credit line premiums of new bureaucrat accounts (originated in the first year after the crackdown) over non-bureaucrats are smaller than before, and the delinquency rate and reinstatement rate of new and existing bureaucrats have fallen to the same level as non-bureaucrat customers.

2.5 Role of Price Incentives and Fees on Payment Mode

When consumers use credit cards for their transactions, merchants have to pay higher fees. In July 2012, the Eastern District Court of New York approved a class settlement between Visa and MasterCard which allows merchants to impose surcharges on card transactions. Previously, merchants were prohibited from steering consumers among card products. Steering consumers can be attempted by (1) flatly refusing to accept credit card, (2) providing price incentives such as discounts for cash payment, and (3) imposing disincentives such as surcharges for credit card payment (Shy and Stavins 2015).

Existing literature focuses on three mechanisms of incentivizing consumers to use certain payment modes, namely, reward or loyalty programs, bank-imposed fees and merchant-imposed surcharges and discounts.

Agarwal et al. (2010b) study the impact of a 1% cash-back reward by a large US financial institution. They find that (1) cash-back rewards positively and significantly affect spending and debt accumulation, (2) consumers offset their increased spending and debt on their reward card by lowering their spending and debt on other credit cards, that is, rewards are effective in stealing consumers from competitors, (3) only a small financial incentive is required to change consumer behavior and (4) cash-back rewards can effectively spur inactive cardholders to use their card. Cardholders who do not use their card prior to the cash-back program increase their spending and debt more than cardholders with debt prior to the program. In terms of demographics, cash-back programs impact married cardholders more than singles, impact males and females the same way, impact higher-income cardholders more than lower-income and impact those with higher credit limit more. Cardholders who were offered an APR (Annual Percentage Rate) reduction of 10% increase their card spending and debt by substituting some spending and debt from higher interest rate cards to the one with the lower interest rate. The results suggest that rewards and lower interest rates can be used to poach consumers.

Simon et al. (2010) find that when there is a financial cost to accessing credit, consumers tend to use debit card but when there is an interest-free period, they switch to credit card. In addition, introduction of a loyalty program tends to increase credit card use. The direction of substitution is from cash to credit card.

Ching and Hayashi (2010) analyze the impact of abolishing a credit card loyalty program. They find that consumers increase the use of debit cards and decrease the use of credit cards while a small fraction switch from electronic to paper-based payment methods.

Borzekowski et al. (2008) examine the responses of bank consumers who are charged for debit transactions at the point of sale. The bank-imposed fees negatively affect the use of debit cards. A 1.8% fee on debit card transactions is associated with a 12% decline in its use. This suggests that surcharging will likely cause a decrease in the use of the instrument.

In many countries, merchants are prohibited from charging consumers extra for card payments. In the Netherlands where retailers are allowed to surcharge for debit card payments, consumers switch from debit cards to cash (Bolt et al. 2010a).

Another example is the case of IKEA which saw a 15% decline in credit card usage when it imposed a 70-pence surcharge on credit card transactions in its UK stores (Bolt et al. 2010b). A small financial disincentive is enough to change consumer behavior.

When surcharges were imposed on cash payment at tolls, consumers switched to electronic toll payments (Amromin et al. 2006).

Stavins (2018) finds that the occurrence of price incentives based on payment method is infrequent and, when offered cash discounts which are typically small, the probability of a cash transaction increase by 19.2%. The study concludes that merchants' reluctance to offer price discounts and the limited response of consumers explain the low occurrences of such incentives.

3 Consumer Adoption of New Payment Technology

The common assumption is that new payment technologies are cheaper and better for consumers. However, the adoption process is usually slow and uneven across consumers (Hayashi and Klee 2003; Kolodinsky et al. 2004). This raises the question of whether the efficiency accrues only to firms and not to consumers or whether there are other reasons that prevent consumers from switching to the most optimal payment method.

3.1 Demand-Side Factors

The question was partly answered by Schuh and Stavins (2015) who find that (1) the faster speed of payment deduction for Automated Clearing House (ACH) transactions such as online banking bill payments slightly increase consumers' adoption of ACH-based payment methods and (2) the provision of enhanced security features slightly increase the use of credit and debit cards. They conclude that "despite speed and security being statistically significant determinants of consumer payment choice, neither improvement is likely to increase consumer welfare in an economically significant way" because consumer demand for payment methods is inelastic with respect to speed and security. It will require very large improvements to make any significant difference to the adoption or use of these payment methods. Their findings confirm that other attributes such as convenience, cost and record keeping have greater influence on consumer payment choice.

Greene et al. (2014) examine the implementation of a new payment system promising same-day clearing in the UK in 2008. Five years after its implementation, the new system facilitates about 5.2% of non-cash payments in the UK. This achievement is attributed to the enhanced attractiveness of the new system in terms of speed, enabling authorization online or by phone, enhancing fraud protection and detection as well as greater consistency with international transaction standards. Although the system does not offer real-time payment, consumers are open to adopting new innovations as long as they deem the new features useful (Rysman and Schuh 2017).

Demographics also help to provide some answers. There is evidence that younger consumers are more likely to adopt new payment technologies such as mobile payments, debit cards, online banking and digital currencies. The rate of technology adoption is slower for older consumers. Some think that older consumers shy away from technology because their learning cost is high (Mattila et al. 2003). Others believe that it is because the present value of the benefits from adopting a new technology is lower for older consumers who have less time to reap the benefits (Yang and Ching 2014).

3.2 *Supply-Side Factors*

On the supply side, banks with higher market power may encourage technology adoption more aggressively by manipulating the relative quality of their service to encourage consumers to switch to cheaper online payment technologies (Allen et al. 2008). However, in competitive markets, reducing the attractiveness of the offline products may cause consumers to switch over to competitors. Therefore, differences in market structure can help explain the varying rate of technology adoption. Market power will allow a bank to lower its branch service quality and drive its consumers to use electronic banking.

Gowrisankaran and Stavins (2004) find evidence that is consistent with network externalities where a bank's adoption of electronic payment technology benefits other banks that already use the technology because they can then directly exchange payments with one more institution. That is, an increase in the number of users of the technology increases the value of the technology to other users. The implication is that technology adoption decisions are strategic complements and will lead to positive clustering.

Apart from banks, merchants and the telecommunication industry also have a role to play in the speed of adoption of new payment technology. Crowe et al. (2010) confirm the importance of the network effect where the decision of merchants to invest in the infrastructure to facilitate mobile payments is dependent on whether the critical mass of consumers can justify the investment. In analyzing the prospects of a single national mobile payment mechanism in the US, Crowe et al. (2010) point out that commercial agreements between mobile carriers and banks must first be established. However, the non-concentrated banking and telecommunication industries in the US make it unprofitable to engage in such agreements, which contributed to the delay in the adoption of mobile payments in the US.

The development of virtual currencies is another example of how merchants play a part in the adoption of new payment technology. Although only 1% of US consumers own virtual currencies, usage of virtual currencies have jumped almost 30 percentage points from 46% in 2014 to 75% in 2015 (Schuh and Shy 2016). This is driven by payments to merchants, suggesting that the acceptance of merchants facilitated the growth of the new payment technology. However, this may not be an accurate picture as many merchants employ a payment processor to convert virtual currencies to dollars immediately. Industry players are similarly skeptical of its suitability at the point of sale due to its long processing time. The future of virtual currencies as a new payment mechanism remains unclear.

4 Consumer Inattentiveness to Bank Fees

Certain fees such as overdraft fee, credit card late payment fee, over-limit fee and cash advance fee paid by households can be substantial. According to Agarwal et al. (2009b), these fees follow a U-shape pattern over the life cycle of a consumer. They are lowest from age 50 to 60 as households become more experienced but increase with age as cognitive abilities decline (see Fig. 6.1).

4.1 Overdraft Fee

Overdraft occurs when a withdrawal causes the bank account balance to drop below zero. When that occurs, the bank can decline to pay depending on the checking account agreement. Typically, however, the bank will pay overdraft transactions up to a limit and charge an overdraft fee ranging from \$20 to \$35 in addition to the interest on the overdraft amount. If the bank declines to pay, there will be a non-sufficient fund (NSF) fee or

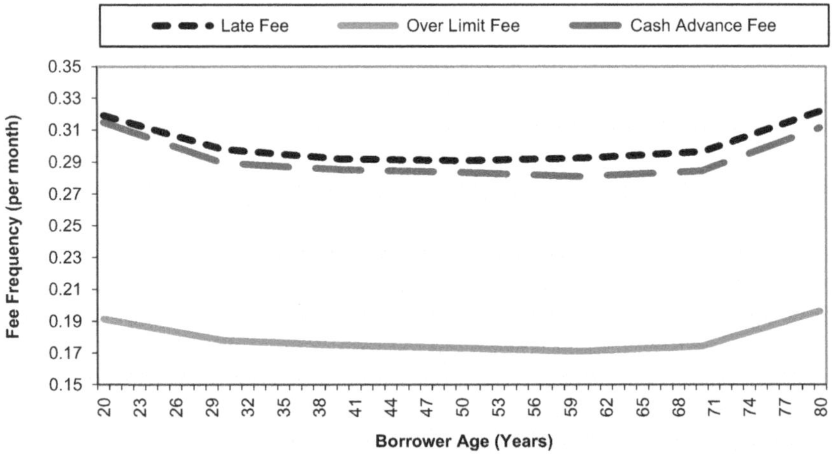

Fig. 6.1 Frequency of fee payment by borrower age. (Source: Agarwal et al. (2009b))

"return item fee" charged, the quantum of which is comparable to an overdraft fee.

According to the Consumer Financial Protection Bureau, these fees total $17 billion each year, with 74% charged to 8% of account holders who overdraft at least ten times in a year (Beshears et al. 2018). These fees can potentially impose substantial financial burden on account holders.

Stango and Zinman (2014) attribute the payment of checking account overdraft fee to limited consumer attention, which they broadly define as incomplete consideration of information concerning account terms or available balances that would inform choices.

Grubb (2015) defines inattention as the consumer being unaware of his own past account usage resulting in crossing usage thresholds and incurring unnecessary fees.

4.2 *Credit Card Late Payment Fee, Over-Limit Fee and Cash Advance Fee*

Agarwal et al. (2008) study how the amount of fee payment change as consumers learn about their existence when they incur them. With the experience gained, they seek to avoid fee payment. The frequency and value of fee payments decline rapidly with account tenure (see Figs. 6.2

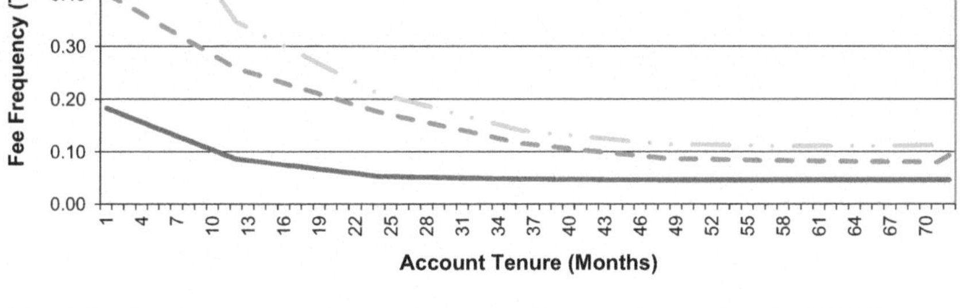

Fig. 6.2 Fee frequency and account tenure. (Source: Agarwal et al. (2008))

and 6.3). The speed of learning varies. Singles learn more than twice as fast as couples. High-income borrowers learn more than twice as fast as low-income borrowers.

When the memory of the costly mistakes fades, consumers forget to be vigilant. They backslide, commit the same offence and pay for their inattention again. The speed of forgetting varies. Older consumers forget faster than middle-aged consumers. Low-income borrowers forget faster than high-income borrowers. Although consumers forget, the knowledge gained is more than the knowledge lost. Over time, fee payments drastically fall (Agarwal et al. 2008).

Papers that have documented forgetting effects include Malmendier and Nagel (2011) who note that investors in stock markets tend to weight their own recent experience of returns more heavily than older historical returns, and Haselhuhn et al. (2012) who find that paying a fine for returning a video late reduces the probability of a late fee in the next visit but the effect declines with time.

Studies have shown that households improve their decisions as they acquire more experience. Miravete (2003) shows that consumers learn from their mistakes and switch telephone calling plans in order to minimize monthly bills in response to very small differences in cost. Agarwal et al. (2015) observe that consumers who choose sub-optimal credit card

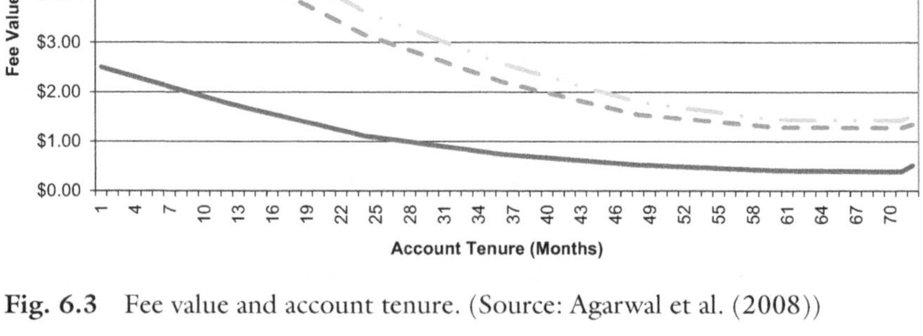

Fig. 6.3 Fee value and account tenure. (Source: Agarwal et al. (2008))

contracts subsequently switch to the optimal contract to minimize their costs.

4.3 *Improving Consumer Attention Using Technology*

In view of the inattention and learning behavior of consumers, technology can be leveraged to provide consumers with timely reminders so that they can avoid these fees.

Medina (2017) finds that smartphone push notifications at different stages of the credit card billing cycle help reduce credit card late payment fees by 13%, although attention to other less salient but similarly important tasks may be crowded out.

Fernandes et al. (2014) propose "just-in-time" intervention in response to the decay in the effects of financial education.

Riding on the increasing popularity of online educational content and video services, Carlin et al. (2018) propose using online videos with clear actionable content to help households make better financial decisions such as choosing the best credit card given multiple offerings.

The growing use of new financial technology in daily payments also presents opportunities to help consumers overcome their inattention.

Using the login and credit data of a new smartphone application for personal financial management launched in Iceland, Carlin et al. (2017) observe that the mere improvement in access to information helps to reduce financial fees. Each login is associated with US$1.73 saved on monthly bank fees, which is economically meaningful especially for low-income households. With respect to different demographic groups, FinTech adoption results in fewer financial fees and penalties on the part of Millennials and Generation X. Baby Boomers, however, do not benefit from the new technology. Between genders, men's login frequency is twice that of women across all age groups but the economic impact of access is higher for women.

5 Conclusion

The act of paying evokes positive and negative feelings. Theories that attempt to explain the psychology of consumer payment behavior include acquisition and transaction utility, buffering hypothesis, payment transparency hypothesis and sunk cost fallacy.

The pain of paying also depends on the payment mode. Popular payment modes include cash, debit card, check and credit card. The choice of the payment mode depends on the characteristics of the instrument such as social status, reward program, credit limit, speed, convenience and security.

The rate of adoption of new payment technologies is slow and uneven across consumers because of demand factors (e.g., characteristics of the payment instruments, demographics) and supply factors (e.g., market power, network effect).

Finally, the chapter wraps up with the topics of consumer inattention resulting in unnecessary fee payment, consumer learning when such bad experiences occur and consumer forgetfulness where the same costly mistakes are made again.

References

Agarwal, Sumit, and Chunlin Liu. 2003. Determinants of Credit Card Delinquency and Bankruptcy: Macroeconomic Factors. *Journal of Economics and Finance* 27 (1): 75–84.

Agarwal, Sumit, John C. Driscoll, Xavier Gabaix, and David Laibson. 2008. Learning in the Credit Card Market. NBER Working Paper #13822.

Agarwal, Sumit, Paige M. Skiba, and Jeremy Tobacman. 2009a. Payday Loans and Credit Cards: New Liquidity and Credit Scoring Puzzles? *American Economic Review: Papers and Proceeding* 99 (2): 412–417.

Agarwal, Sumit, John C. Driscoll, Xavier Gabaix, and David Laibson. 2009b. The Age of Reason: Financial Decisions over the Life Cycle and Implications for Regulation. *Brookings Papers on Economic Activity* 2009 (2): 51–117.

Agarwal, Sumit, Souphala Chomsisengphet, and Chunlin Liu. 2010a. The Importance of Adverse Selection in the Credit Card Market: Evidence from Randomized Trials of Credit Card Solicitations. *Journal of Money, Credit and Banking* 42 (4): 743–754.

Agarwal, Sumit, Chakravorti Sujit, and Lunn Anna. 2010b. Why Do Banks Reward Their Customers to Use Their Credit Cards? Federal Reserve Bank of Chicago Working Paper 2010-19.

Agarwal, Sumit, Souphala Chomsisengphet, Chunlin Liu, and Nicholas S. Souleles. 2015. Do Consumers Choose the Right Credit Contracts? *The Review of Corporate Finance Studies* 4 (2): 239–247.

Agarwal, Sumit, Qian Wenlan, and Zhang Jian. 2016. Pick a Card, Any Card: Cloaked Corruption in China. *The Straits Times*.

Akerlof, George A. 1970. The Market for 'Lemons': Quality Uncertainty and the Market Mechanism. *Quarterly Journal of Economics* 84: 488–500.

Allen, Jason, Robert C. Clark, and Jean-Francois Houde. 2008. Market Structure and the Diffusion of E-Commerce: Evidence from the Retail Banking Industry. Bank of Canada Working Paper 1701-93972008-32.

Ambrose, Brent W., and Charles A. Capone. 2000. The Hazard Rates of First and Second Defaults. *Journal of Real Estate Finance and Economics* 20: 275–293.

Amromin, Gene, Carrie Jankowski, and Richard D. Porter. 2006. Transforming Payment Choices by Doubling Fees on the Illinois Tollway. *Economic Perspectives* 31 (2): 22–47.

Angrisani, Marco, Arie Kapteyn, and Scott Schuh. 2015. Measuring Household Spending and Payment Habits: The Role of "Typical" and "Specific" Time Frames in Survey Questions. In *Improving the Measurement of Consumer Expenditures,* ed. Christopher D. Carroll, Thomas F. Crossley and John Sabelhaus, 414–40. The University of Chicago Press.

Arkes, Hal R. 1996. The Psychology of Waste. *Journal of Behavioral Decision Making* 9 (3): 213–224.

Arkes, Hal R., and Catherine Blumer. 1985. The Psychology of Sunk Cost. *Organizational Behavior and Human Decision Processes* 35: 124–140.

Bachas, Pierre, Paul Gertler, Sean Higgins, and Enrique Seira. 2017. Banking on Trust: How Debit Cards Enable the Poor to Save More. NBER Working Paper #23252.

Bertaut, Carol C., and Michael Haliassos. 2002. Debt Revolvers for Self-Control. HERMES Center Working Paper 01-11: 1–39.

Beshears, John, James J. Choi, David Laibson, and Brigitte C. Madrian. 2018. Behavioral Household Finance. NBER Working Paper #24854.

Bolt, Wilko, Nicole Jonker, and Corry van Renselaar. 2010a. Incentives at the Counter: An Empirical Analysis of Surcharging Card Payments and Payment Behavior in the Netherlands. *Journal of Banking and Finance* 34 (8): 1738–1744.

Bolt, Wilko, Santiago Carbo-Valverde, Sujit Chakravorti, Sergio Gorjon, and Francisco Roiguez Fernandez. 2010b. What is the Role of Public Authorities in Retail Payment Systems? Federal Reserve Bank of Chicago Fed Letter, 280a.

Borgen, Winston C. 1976. *Learning Experiences in Retailing: Text and Cases.* New York: Goodyear.

Borzekowski, Ron, Kiser Elizabeth, and Ahmed Shiaster. 2008. Consumers' Use of Debit Cards: Patterns, Preferences and Price Response. *Journal of Money, Credit and Banking* 40 (1): 149–172.

Brockner, Joel. 1992. The Escalation of Commitment to a Failing Course of Action: Toward Theoretical Progress. *Academy of Management Review* 17 (1): 39–61.

Bursztyn, Leonard, Bruno Ferman, Stefano Fiorin, Martin Kanz, and Gautum Rao. 2017. Status Goods: Experimental Evidence from Platinum Credit Cards. *The Quarterly Journal of Economics* 133 (3): 1561–1595.

Carlin, Bruce I., Li Jiang, and Stephen A. Spiller. 2018. Millennial-Style Learning: Search Intensity, Decision Making and Information Sharing. *Management Science* 64 (7): 3313–3330.

Carlin, Bruce I., Arna Olafsson, and Michaela Pagel. 2017. Fintech Adoption across Generations: Financial Fitness in the Information Age. NBER Working Paper #23798.

Ching, Andrew, and Fumiko Hayashi. 2010. Payment Card Rewards Programs and Consumer Payment Choice. *Journal of Banking and Finance* 34 (8): 1773–1787.

Crowe, Marianne, Marc Rysman, and Joanna Stavins. 2010. Mobile Payments in the United States at Retail Point of Sale: Current Market and Future Prospects. Federal Reserve Bank of Boston Public Policy Discussion Paper 10-2.

Dalton, Amy N., and Huang Li. 2014. Motivated Forgetting in Response to Social Identity Threat. *Journal of Consumer Research* 40 (6): 1017–1038.

DellaVigna, Stefano, and Ulrike Malmendier. 2006. Paying Not to Go to the Gym. *The American Economic Review* 96 (3): 694–719.

Deng, Yongheng, John M. Quigley, and Robert V. Order. 2000. Mortgage Termination, Heterogeneity and the Exercise of Mortgage Options. *Econometrica* 68: 275–307.

Eastwood, David. 1975. Consumer Credit and the Theory of Consumer Behavior. *Journal of Behavioral Economics* 4: 39–105.

Fay, Scott, Erik Hurst, and Michelle J. White. 2002. The Household Bankruptcy Decision. *American Economic Review* 92: 706–718.

Feinberg, Richard A. 1986. Credit Cards as Spending Facilitating Stimuli: A Conditioning Interpretation. *Journal of Consumer Research* 13 (3): 348–356.

Fernandes, Daniel, John G. Lynch, and Richard G. Netemeyer. 2014. Financial Literacy, Financial Education and Downstream Financial Behaviors. *Management Science* 60 (8): 1861–1883.

Fuster, Andreas, and Paul S. Willen. 2012. Payment Size, Negative Equity and Mortgage Default. Federal Reserve Bank of New York Staff Reports No. 582.

Garland, Howard, and Stephanie Newport. 1991. Effects of Absolute and Relative Sunk Costs on the Decision to Persist with a Course of Action. *Organizational Behavior and Human Decision Processes* 48: 55–69.

Gathergood, John, Neale Mahoney, Neil Stewart, and Joerg Weber. 2019. How do Individuals Repay their Debt? The Balance-Matching Heuristic. *American Economic Review* 109 (3): 844–875.

Gowrisankaran, Gautam, and Joanna Stavins. 2004. Network Externalities and Technology Adoption: Lessons from Electronic Payments. *The RAND Journal of Economics* 35 (2): 260–276.

Greene, Claire, Marc Rysman, Scott Schuh, and Oz Shy. 2014. Costs and Benefits of Building Faster Payment Systems: The U.K. Experience and Implications for the United States. Federal Reserve Bank of Boston Research Paper Series Current Policy Perspectives 14-5.

Grieb, Terrance, Charles Hegji, and Steven T. Jones. 2001. Macroeconomic Factors, Consumer Behavior and Bankcard Default Rates. *Journal of Economic and Finance* 25: 316–327.

Gross, David B., and Nicholas S. Souleles. 2002a. Do Liquidity Constraints and Interest Rates Matter for Consumer Behavior? Evidence from Credit Card Data. *Quarterly Journal of Economics* 117 (1): 149–185.

———. 2002b. An Empirical Analysis of Personal Bankruptcy and Delinquency. *Review of Financial Studies* 15: 319–347.

Grubb, Michael D. 2015. Consumer Inattention and Bill-Shock Regulation. *The Review of Economic Studies* 82 (1): 219–257.

Haselhuhn, Michael, Devin Pope, Maurice Schweitzer, and Peter Fishman. 2012. How Personal Experience with a Fine Influences Behavior. *Management Science* 58 (1): 35–51.

Hayashi, Fumiko, and Elizabeth Klee. 2003. Technology Adoption and Consumer Payments: Evidence from Survey Data. *Review of Network Economics* 2 (2): 175–190.

Hirschman, Elizabeth. 1979. Differences in Consumer Purchase Behavior of Credit Card Payment System. *Journal of Consumer Research* 6: 58–66.

Inman, Jeffrey, Russell S. Winer, and Rosellina Ferraro. 2009. The Interplay among Category Characteristics, Customer Characteristics and Customer Activities on In-Store Decision Making. *Journal of Marketing* 73 (5): 19–29.

Kahneman, Daniel, and Amos Tversky. 1974. Judgment under Uncertainty: Heuristics and Biases. *Science* 185: 1124–1131.

———. 1979. Prospect Theory: An Analysis of Decision under Risk. *Econometrica* 47 (2): 363–391.

Keys, Benjamin J., and Jialan Wang. 2019. Minimum Payments and Debt Paydown in Consumer Credit Cards. *Journal of Financial Economics* 131 (3): 528–548.

Klee, Elizabeth. 2008. How People Pay: Evidence from Grocery Store Data. *Journal of Monetary Economics* 55: 526–541.

Kolodinsky, Jane M., Jeanne M. Hogarth, and Marianne A. Hilgert. 2004. The Adoption of Electronic Banking Technologies by US Consumers. *International Journal of Bank Management* 22 (4): 238–259.

Koulayev, Sergei, Marc Rysman, Scott Schuh, and Joanna Stavins. 2016. Explaining Adoption and Use of Payment Instruments by US Consumers. *The RAND Journal of Economics* 47 (2): 293–325.

Kumar, Raynil, and Shaun O'Brien. 2019. 2019 Findings from the Diary of Consumer Payment Choice. Federal Bank of San Francisco.

Lee, Leonard, and Claire I. Tsai. 2013. How Price Promotions Influence Postpurchase Consumption Experience over Time. *Journal of Consumer Research* 40: 943–959.

Malmendier, Ulrike, and Stefan Nagel. 2011. Depression Babies: Do Macroeconomic Experiences Affect Risk-Taking? *Quarterly Journal of Economics* 126 (1): 373–416.

Mattila, Minna, Heikki Karjaluoto, and Tapio Pento. 2003. Internet Banking Adoption among Mature Customers: Early Majority or Laggards? *Journal of Services Marketing* 17 (5): 514–528.

Medina, Paolina C. 2017. Selective Attention in Consumer Finance: Evidence from a Randomized Intervention in the Credit Card Market. Texas A&M University, Working Paper

Miravete, Eugenio J. 2003. Choosing the Wrong Calling Plan? Ignorance and Learning. *American Economic Review* 93 (2): 297–310.

Mishra, Himanshu, Arul Mishra, and Dhananjay Nayakankuppam. 2006. Money: A Bias for the Whole. *Journal of Consumer Research* 32: 541–549.

Ponce, Alejandro, Enrique Seira, and Guillermo Zamarripa. 2008. Do Consumers Borrow on their Cheapest Credit Card? Evidence from Mexico. Banco De Mexico Working Papers 2014-03.

———. 2017. Borrowing on the Wrong Credit Card? Evidence from Mexico. *American Economic Review* 107 (4): 1335–1361.

Prelec, Drazen, and Duncan Simester. 2001. Always Leave Home Without It: A Further Investigation of the Credit Card Effect on Willingness to Pay. *Marketing Letters* 12 (1): 5–12.

Prelec, Drazen, and George Loewenstein. 1998. The Red and the Black: Mental Accounting of Savings and Debt. *Marketing Science* 17 (1): 4–28.

Raghubir, Priya, and Joydeen Srivastava. 2008. Monopoly Money: The Effect of Payment Coupling and Form on Spending Behavior. *Journal of Experimental Psychology: Applied* 14 (3): 213–225.

Ramsey, Dave. 2003. *The Total Money Makeover: A Proven Plan for Financial Fitness.* Nashville: Thomas Nelson.

Rysman, Marc, and Scott Schuh. 2017. New Innovations in Payments. National Bureau of Economic Research Working Paper #22358

Savage, John. 1970. Bank Credit Cards: Their Impact on Retailers. *Banking* 63 (1): 39–92.

Schuh, Scott, and Oz Shy. 2016. U.S. Consumers' Adoption and Use of Bitcoin and other Virtual Currencies. Unpublished Working Paper. dnb.nl/en/binaries/Consumer%20VC%20paper_DNB_FINAL_corrected_tcm47-344530.pdf

Schuh, Scott, and Joanna Stavins. 2010. Why are (Some) Consumers (Finally) Writing Fewer Checks? The Role of Payment Characteristics. *Journal of Banking and Finance* 34: 1745–1758.

———. 2013. How Consumers Pay: Adoption and Use of Payments. *Accounting and Finance Research* 2 (2): 1–21.

———. 2015. How Do Speed and Security Influence Consumers' Payment Behavior? European Central Bank Working Paper Series No 1871: 1–40.

Shy, Oz, and Joanna Stavins. 2015. Merchant Steering of Consumer Payment Choice: Evidence from a 2012 Diary Survey. *Journal of Behavioral and Experimental Economics* 55: 1–9.

Silva, Vania G., Esmeralda A. Ramalho, and Carlos R. Vieira. 2016. The Use of Cheques in the European Union: A Cross-Country Analysis. *Open Economies Review* 28 (3): 581–602.

Simon, John, Smith Kylie, and West Tim. 2010. Price Incentives and Consumer Payment Behavior. *Journal of Banking and Finance* 34 (8): 1759–1772.

Soman, Dilip. 2001. Effects of Payment Mechanism on Spending Behavior: The Role of Rehearsal and Immediacy of Payments. *Journal of Consumer Research* 27: 460–474.

———. 2003. The Effect of Payment Transparency on Consumption: Quasi-Experiments from the Field. *Marketing Letters* 14 (3): 173–183.

Soman, Dilip, and John T. Gourville. 2018. Transaction Decoupling: How Price Bundling Affects the Decision to Consume. *Journal of Marketing Research* 38 (1): 30–44.

Stango, Victor, and Jonathan Zinman. 2009. What do Consumers Really Pay on Their Checking and Credit Card Accounts? Explicit, Implicit, and Avoidable Costs. *American Economic Review Papers and Proceedings* 99 (2): 424–429.

———. 2014. Limited and Varying Consumer Attention: Evidence from Shocks to the Salience of Bank Overdraft Fees. *The Review of Financial Studies* 27 (4): 990–1030.

Stavins, Joanna. 2018. Consumer Preferences for Payment Methods: Role of Discounts and Surcharges. *Journal of Banking and Finance* 94: 35–53.

Teger, Allan I. 1980. *Too Much Invested to Quit: The Psychology of the Escalation of Conflict*. New York: Pergamon Press.

Tellez, Ed. 2017. The Ongoing Decline of the Cheque System. Reserve Bank of Australia, June Quarter 2017.

Thaler, Richard. 1985. Mental Accounting and Consumer Choice. *Marketing Science* 4 (3): 199–214.

Thaler, Richard H. 1999. Mental Accounting Matters. *Journal of Behavioral Decision Making* 12 (3): 183–206.

Thomas, Manoj, Kalpesh K. Desai, and Satheeshkumar Seenivasan. 2011. How Credit Card Payments Increase Unhealthy Food Purchases: Visceral Regulation of Vices. *Journal of Consumer Research* 38 (1): 126–139.

Van der Horst, Frank, and Ester Matthijsen. 2013. The Irrationality of Payment Behaviour. *De Nederlandsche Bank Occasional Studies* 11(4).

Whyte, Glen. 1986. Escalating Commitment to a Course of Action: A Reinterpretation. *Academy of Management Review* 11: 311–321.

Yang, Botao, and Andrew T. Ching. 2014. Dynamics of Consumer Adoption of Financial Innovation: The Case of ATM Cards. *Management Science* 60 (4): 805–1081.

Yang, Haiyang, Ziv Carmon, and Ravi Dhar. 2012. More Possessions Can Make You Less Happy. *Advances in Consumer Research* 40: 106–111.
Yeung, Kam L. 2014. Exploring the Origin of Pain of Payment in Cash and its Relevance to Computer Payment Interface. PhD diss., Iowa State University.
Zellermayer, Ofer. 1996. The Pain of Paying. ProQuest Dessertations Publishing. Carnegie Mellon University.

CHAPTER 7

Borrowing

1 Introduction

More households participate in the debt market than the stock market. In fact, most households, including poor ones, have a stake in the debt market.

Household debt comprises all the money borrowed by individuals in the form of loans that are to be repaid later. These loans can be secured or unsecured. Secured loans are those where the lender has the right to repossess the collateral if the borrower is unable to repay, such as mortgages and vehicle loans. Unsecured loans are those without collaterals, such as personal loans, student loans, credit card balances, overdrafts and payday loans. Household credit participation increases with economic development (Valckx et al. 2017).

As of the third quarter of 2019, household debt in the US totaled US$13.95 trillion (Federal Reserve Bank of New York 2019). The top four debt markets are mortgages (US$9.4 trillion), student loans (US$1.5 trillion), vehicle loans (US$1.3 trillion) and credit card loans (US$0.88 trillion).

Growth in household debt is generally viewed as beneficial as debt improves the standard of living of individuals and enhances economic growth (Levine 1998; Beck and Levine 2004). The growth benefits start to decline when leverage becomes too high (Gourinchas and Obstfeld 2012; Arcand et al. 2015; Sahay et al. 2015).

Household indebtedness is a source of financial vulnerability. In the event of macroeconomic shocks, collateral value will reduce, triggering

S. Agarwal et al., *Household Finance*,
https://doi.org/10.1007/978-981-15-5526-8_7

borrowing constraints and deleveraging for households. If these shocks are sufficiently large, they can cause debt defaults. If these are mortgage defaults, they will put downward pressure on house prices resulting in a vicious cycle. Negative spillovers may affect aggregate demand, employment and macro-financial stability (Eggertsson and Krugman 2012; Korinek and Simsek 2016).

The adverse effects are more pronounced in markets with higher average household debt and credit market participation, and countries with more open capital accounts, fixed exchange rates, less developed financial systems, lower transparency, lower consumer financial protection, lower quality of supervision and higher income inequality.

1.1 Role of Household Debt in the 2008 Financial Crisis

It is widely argued that the rapid rise in household debt from 2002 to 2006 set the stage for the increase in defaults from 2006 to 2008 (Mian and Sufi 2011). The US banking deregulation in 2004 altered the capital requirements for banks, increased their willingness to lend and made credit available to households previously denied access (Mian and Sufi 2018). This credit-driven household channel boosted demand resulting in an enormous accumulation of mortgages, home equity loans, automotive loans and consumer durable loans (Di Maggio and Kermani 2017). When the increase in household debt could not be sustained, the rapid decline in household demand had severe repercussions.

Empirical evidence points to a group of borrowers whose defaults eventually led to the 2008 financial crisis (Albanesi et al. 2017). They belong to the middle of the credit score distribution which traditionally had low default rates. Further investigation shows that these defaulters are real estate investors who used riskier non-standard mortgages with higher interest rates. They have an incentive to maximize leverage and invest in properties regardless of their quality as their losses are limited (Haughwout et al. 2011).

After the housing bust, financial institutions left thinly capitalized responded with tightened lending standards and higher interest rates (Hall 2011).

1.2 *In the Aftermath of the Crisis*

Hall (2011) highlights three related sources of declines in demand that retard the recovery of the US economy in the aftermath. They are (1) the debt overhang from the buying frenzy before the crisis, (2) the buildup of excess housing stock and consumer durables and (3) the financial friction from the decline in house prices.

US counties with higher household debt experience larger house price declines and face consumption declines of automobiles, groceries and durables (Mian and Sufi 2012). These had macro repercussions in the form of high unemployment, lackluster recovery and the subsequent slump (Mian et al. 2013).

The level of household debt to GDP ratio fell in the US, UK and various European countries such as Iceland, Ireland, Portugal, Spain and German, but in other advanced economies such as Australia and Canada, the ratio rose. The rise in the ratio turned out to be driven by the drop in GDP growth (Valckx et al. 2017).

In emerging economies such as Chile, China, Malaysia, Thailand, Paraguay, the growth of household debt, fuelled by the decline in interest rate, also exceeds GDP growth (Valckx et al. 2017).

2 Why Do Households Borrow?

Households borrow for five main reasons: (1) temporary fluctuations in income (Guerrieri and Lorenzoni 2017), (2) investment in closely held businesses (Robb and Robinson 2014), (3) to smooth consumption (Eggertsson and Krugman 2012), (4) behavioral biases and (5) investment in illiquid assets.

2.1 *Temporary Fluctuations in Income*

In the life cycle and permanent income hypothesis (PIH), a temporary fluctuation in income should not change consumption. The temporary fluctuation may be due to a bad harvest, an unexpected medical bill or a short-term business closure for renovation works to be done.

For example, a 40% paycheck cut during the 2013 US federal government shutdown is a temporary shock which only affects the timing of the payments and therefore should not affect consumption. Gelman et al. (2018) find that households smoothed their consumption by rescheduling their mortgage and credit card payments. This suggests that individuals smooth consumption by borrowing, which is consistent with the life cycle model.

Baugh et al. (2017) find that variation in income timing leads to substitution from bank-based transactions (such as checks, debit card transactions, ATM withdrawals) to credit card transactions. The study suggests that policies and technologies that help households align the timing of their income and expenditure streams will improve financial health.

2.2 Investment in Closely Held Businesses

In the initial years of operation, many small businesses rely on lines of credit backed by personal guarantee and personal assets of the owner. Like credit cards for individuals, lines of credit augment the working capital of businesses and help in managing the mismatch in the timing of revenues and expenses.

While pledging of personal assets help to mitigate the risks of lenders, owners have limited collateral especially during hard times (Moon 2010; Avery et al. 1998). The reliance on bank debt backed by personal collateral underscores the importance of a liquid credit market for the success of small businesses.

2.3 Smooth Consumption

Both the PIH and life cycle hypothesis embrace the view that households smooth their consumption. Consumption will not vary unless long-term expectations of income change. Households seek to smooth their consumption by borrowing or saving.

In practice, households often face liquidity constraints. Liquidity-constrained households take precautionary measures by saving in good times to meet consumption needs during bad times (Deaton 1991; Carroll 1992).

The level of household debt varies with demographics. Younger households that anticipate future income growth tend to borrow more (Blundell et al. 1994).

2.4 *Behavioral Biases*

Some households have a preference for current consumption. Meier and Sprenger (2010) find that present-biased individuals, defined as those who have a desire for immediate consumption, have higher revolving credit card balances.

Using a randomized campaign of six different credit cards with varying introductory interest rates and durations, Shui and Ausubel (2004) find evidence of time inconsistency in consumer behavior which can be explained by hyperbolic preferences. Respondents do not take advantage of opportunities to reduce interest payments on existing debt. They prefer an introductory offer with a lower interest rate and shorter duration to one with a higher interest rate and a longer duration, even though they would benefit more from choosing the latter. In addition, they are reluctant to switch their credit cards and many who have switched before fail to switch again. The results suggest that the respondents have a self-control problem with some present bias.

Another form of behavioral bias is optimism (Geanakoplos 2010). Some buyers think that prices for their preferred assets (such as houses) will keep growing. They overreact to news and choose to borrow against future consumption to purchase these assets, sometimes beyond what they can afford (Fuster et al. 2010).

Cultural biases may affect the level of household debt. Almenberg et al. (2018) find that Swedish consumers have similar debt attitudes as their parents, suggesting a cultural element that is passed down along family lines.

2.5 *Investment in Illiquid Assets*

An overwhelming majority of assets held by households are illiquid. The largest illiquid asset for most household is their residential property. Many of these illiquid assets have the same property as the goose that lays the golden egg (Laibson 1997). Examples include pension, insurance, home, land and consumer durable. They promise high gains but are difficult to realize at short notice.

When households borrow to purchase illiquid assets, there are macro implications. House prices, for example, affect the economy through the wealth effect. House price appreciation leads to (1) wealthier households who are more confident about spending, (2) more valuable collateral and better access to credit, (3) less consumption volatility and (4) better investment opportunities.

3 Effect of Debt on Borrowers

3.1 Psychological Stress

Debt can affect the mental well-being of consumers. Dunn and Mirzaie (2015) observe that borrowers during the 2008 financial crisis reported higher psychological stress as bank foreclosures and repossessions increased. This is similarly observed by Drentea (2000) who finds a correlation between debt level and anxiety level.

The positive correlation between debt and psychological stress can manifest physically (Kim and Lyons 2008) with problems such as obesity (Keese and Schmitz 2012), ulcer, heart attack and migraine headache (Lavrakas and Tompson 2009).

The stress can also affect career choice. Higher student loans reduce the probability of enrolling in graduate school to pursue higher education (Chakrabarti et al. 2020). Students with more loans end up in jobs with higher wages but lower job satisfaction. To satisfy their budget constraint, these students substitute intangible job satisfaction for a higher wage (Lise 2013).

Student loans can also affect relationships, marriage and child rearing outcomes. Sieg and Wang (2017) find that female lawyers with higher student loans tend to delay marriage, marry men with lower earnings and delay child rearing. The intuition is that with larger negative wealth, they have fewer opportunities in the marriage market, have poorer marriage outcomes and experience a delay in meeting an acceptable spouse to have children. Newlywed couples who assume debt become less happy in their marriage but there are less instances of divorce arising from these financial conflicts (Dew 2008, 2011).

Borrowers can also find themselves in a perpetual debt spiral (debt trap) where they are unable to service high-interest loans. This is most common in poorer or developing countries (Banerjee 2004) with interest rates varying from 11% to 93% (Banerjee and Duflo 2007). Karlan et al. (2019) contextualize the debt trap through their study of Indian and Filipino small-scale entrepreneurs. They observe that most borrowers return to debt within six weeks and, even with a windfall, go back into the debt trap again. They attribute the findings to (1) present bias, (2) lack of saving channels to accumulate capital, (3) lack of understanding of long-term costs of borrowing at high rates and (4) business shocks.

3.2 *Debt Repayment*

Traditionally, debt is repaid based on a pre-agreed rate for a fixed period of time. For borrowers who experience job loss or income fluctuation, the commitment to pay may affect their consumption ability. They may even be delinquent in their payment or default.

As of 2014, one-quarter of student loan recipients have defaulted (Cox et al. 2018). This will affect their credit scores and limit their access to future credit. The poor credit record may also adversely affect their job prospects and lead to more debt at higher interest rates.

Fixed repayment plans put student loan recipients at the risk of default during periods of low income. The desire to avoid this risk may lead them to avoid risky but high return career paths.

To reduce the pressure on students, an income-based repayment (IBR) "Pay-As-You-Earn" scheme was introduced in 2010. The IBR scheme allows students to pay income-contingent amounts, providing insurance against unaffordable loan payments. A similar program, "Repayment Assistance Plan", was introduced in Canada.

Abraham et al. (2018a) find that student loan recipients under the IBR scheme choose higher-paying but riskier jobs to raise their expected net income.

Luo and Mongey (2019) find that under the less pressing IBR repayment scheme, students who used to take jobs with higher wages but lower satisfaction are now able to enjoy greater welfare from the higher consumption they can afford and the higher job satisfaction they experience.

3.3 *Credit Scores*

Credit checks by companies prior to a hire allow for efficient matches of labor but can negatively affect borrowers. Employers may discriminate based on the credit scores of the applicant (Corbae et al. 2013). These practices depress the potential wages of affected employees and can potentially lead to a poverty trap. Using data from Sweden, Bos et al. (2018) observe that each additional year of negative credit information reduces employment by 3 percentage points and earnings by US$1000.

Herkenhoff et al. (2016) find that increases in borrowing capacity, following a mandatory ten-year bankruptcy flag removal, encourage workers to move into self-employment, to borrow significantly and to become entrepreneurs. These startups tend to be in capital-intensive and external finance-intensive industries.

4 Reasons for the Growth in Household Debt

Dynan and Kohn (2007) argue that the following competing explanations cannot explain the growth in household indebtedness: (1) impatience or risk aversion, (2) expectation of future income, (3) change in interest rates and (4) reduced precautionary saving.

Instead, Dynan and Kohn (2007) attribute the growth in household indebtedness to (1) change in the demographics of the US population as baby boomers move into their borrowing years, (2) the high cost of education resulting in more student loans, (3) high house prices resulting in higher mortgages (Christelis et al. 2017), (4) the wealth effect of high house prices which lead to more consumption and more borrowing against home equity, (5) financial technology which facilitate the evaluation of credit risk of prospective borrowers, (6) new techniques that allow lenders to underwrite and manage risk and (7) financial innovation that leads to the democratization of credit.

Dynan (2009) believes that the growth in household indebtedness is due to the expansion of financial opportunities and new lending approaches, which arise from risk-based pricing, securitization and lower distribution costs.

Others trace the growth in debt to changes in the income distribution. The growing income inequality creates political pressure to encourage easy lending to the poor and middle class (Rajan 2010; Reich 2010; Kumhof et al. 2015). It is argued that this helps maintain their consumption, keeping demand and job creation robust within the economy despite stagnating incomes.

Other factors that have contributed to the growth in household debt include (1) subprime mortgages made to borrowers with poor credit profiles who would otherwise not have obtained credit (Mayer et al. 2009), (2) mortgage securitization which lowered the cost of home loans (Kolari et al. 1998), (3) rise in short-term high-cost payday loans (Skiba and Tobacman 2009) and (4) enhanced screening technology resulting in an expansion of credit card lending (Dick and Lehnert 2010).

5 Household Debt Efficiency

This section applies the four matrix from Zinman (2015) to assess household debt efficiency by examining whether households are better off with debt, whether they minimize costs among loans they already have, whether they choose optimal debt contracts in the market and whether they default optimally.

5.1 Do Financial Condition and Subjective Well-Being of Borrowers Improve?

5.1.1 Permanent Income Hypothesis Model on Borrower Welfare

Under the Permanent Income Hypothesis where consumers do not face any liquidity constraints and can borrow without restriction, a change in income that is anticipated will not lead to a change in consumption. The marginal propensity to consume (MPC) out of predictable income or liquidity is zero.

In the alternative view of the world where liquidity constraints are prevalent and precautionary motives exist, the MPC out of liquidity can approach one where consumers use the marginal increase in income almost entirely on consumption (Deaton 1991; Carroll 1992; Ludvigson 1999).

Gross and Souleles (2002a) provide evidence on this alternative view by analyzing the MPC out of increase in credit card limit. They find that MPC is larger for people who are near their credit limit, an observation which is consistent with binding liquidity constraints. The MPC is also significant for people who are well below their credit limit, a finding which is consistent with the precautionary motive model. The study shows that an increase in credit limit generates an immediate and significant rise in debt, counter to the Permanent Income Hypothesis.

5.1.2 Neoclassical Model on Borrower Welfare

Even if the cost of borrowing is high, households may still be better off with debt. The high cost of borrowing can happen under a purely neoclassical full information model where borrowers pay a high fee on a small transaction, the marginal utility of the transaction is high and cheaper sources of liquidity are not available. The neoclassical model predicts that consumers are better off with the credit as their actions reveal their preferences.

In the event of sudden personal emergencies, for example, illness or job loss, or the event of market-wide temporary negative shocks, such as hurricanes and blizzards, households with no access to other cheaper forms of financing take out payday loans. They are fully informed about the high interest rates associated with payday loans and are not being preyed upon. Neither do they have any self-control problem.

Many of the borrowers who fall under this category are less well-to-do. They may be racial minorities with limited liquid assets (Graves 2003; Elliehausen 2009). They may have been denied credit in the past year, have exhausted their credit card limit, have difficulty accessing credit or have little access to home equity (Lawrence and Elliehausen 2008; Lusardi and Tufano 2015). For such financially constrained households, short-term unsecured payday loans may be welfare improving, even at cost as high as 400% APR (Morse 2011).

If access to payday loans is restricted, these consumers may not have sufficient funds to meet the basics of food consumption, mortgage payments and home repairs (Dobridge 2014). They may experience a general deterioration of financial condition and face returned checks, late fees, disconnected phone lines, utility suspensions, repossessions and, in some cases, foreclosures and evictions (Zinman 2010). They may have to incur high fees to restart electricity or telephone services (Community Financial Services Association of America 2006). These anecdotes suggest that high-cost loans such as payday loans benefit responsible users who do not have access to lower-cost alternatives.

Some studies on these high-cost borrowers find evidence that contradict the rationality assumption made. They find that payday loan customers are associated with arrears in mortgage, rent and utilities, delayed medical and dental care (Melzer 2011), declines in job performance (Carrell and Zinman 2014), low levels of financial literacy (Lusardi and Tufano 2015; Bertrand and Morse 2011) and probable bankruptcy (Skiba and Tobacman 2009).

To enhance the decision making process of borrowers, Bertrand and Morse (2011) conduct an experiment that highlight the fees paid, the cost of comparable products and the repayment profile of payday loans. The experiment saw a reduction in the frequency and amount of payday borrowing. It shows that information disclosures targeting specific cognitive biases can improve decision making.

5.2 *Do Borrowers Choose Deals That Minimize Their Costs?*

5.2.1 *Peer Effect*

Debt choice can be influenced by one's neighborhood. Miller and Soo (2018) track participants of the "Moving to Opportunity" experiment which offered vouchers to low-income families to move to better neighborhood via randomized lotteries. Despite better neighborhoods possibly having a higher cost of living, they find an improvement in the financial health of families who move to these areas. Younger children have higher credit scores, higher credit limit and use more credit in their lifetime, while older children and adults exhibit an improvement in debt delinquency behaviors and smaller overdue debts. Their results are similar to studies which find that neighborhoods can influence financial health and decisions through the peer effect (Gross and Souleles 2002a, b; Duflo and Saez 2012; Bursztyn et al. 2014).

5.2.2 *Costly Mistakes*

There are evidences which suggest that borrowers do not choose deals that minimize their costs. Even with a mortgage counselor, borrowers do not choose optimal mortgage products (Agarwal et al. 2010).

Borrowers face price dispersion where the cost of a loan can vary across lenders. The search costs and time needed to understand the terms and conditions behind many financial products affect the ability of borrowers to choose an optimal loan (Hortacsu and Syverson 2004). Campbell et al. (2011a) find that mark-ups charged by retailers, who have market power, can be avoided with some modest shopping effort.

Some borrowers suffer from present biases and seek to extract equity for consumption (Ausubel 1991; Meier and Sprenger 2010). Some are overly impatient in the short run and borrow excessively. This bias also manifests in borrowers failing to keep to their debt pay down plan (Kuchler and Pagel 2018) and incurring unnecessary overdue costs.

Some assume loans with high interest rate, such as payday loans, even though they have access to lower-cost credit, such as unused balances in credit card (Agarwal et al. 2009).

Some mistakes on the part of borrowers are due to loan product steering where they are led to more expensive mortgage products (Agarwal et al. 2016a). There are also mistakes due to uninformative sales tactics where the advertising contents highlight low initial mortgage rates but do not reveal the higher reset rates (Gurun et al. 2016; Agarwal et al. 2017a).

Some lenders use junk mail to influence consumer choices (Agarwal and Ambrose 2018). Evidence shows that naïve borrowers are persuaded by these advertising efforts.

Gabaix and Laibson (2006) highlight technologies of persuasion via uninformative sales tactics and shrouding of the product's negative attributes, such as ATM usage fees, bounced check fees and minimum balance fees.

Stango and Zinman (2011) show that consumers underestimate the cost of debt when lenders market "low monthly payments" shrouding interest rates.

Other examples include teaser pricing for bank checking account overdraft (Stango and Zinman 2014) and credit card introductory rates (Agarwal et al. 2015) which hinder efficient cost minimization.

Personal experiences from such financial mistakes are slow to accumulate as the outcomes may be delayed or are due to random shocks. Agarwal et al. (2013) measure the learning dynamics in the credit card market. They find that even though last month's fee payment is associated with a 40% reduction in current month fee payment, over time the negative association diminishes (See Fig. 7.1), exhibiting a recency effect that hampers learning.

5.2.3 *Debt Refinancing*

One common form of mortgage is long-term amortizing mortgage with fixed nominal interest rate that protects borrowers from rising inflation. This form of mortgage typically has an option for borrowers to refinance when inflation declines. However, the decision to refinance is complex (Agarwal and Mazumder 2013) with 50% of borrowers refinancing at the optimal range. To refinance optimally, a borrower must choose the correct interest rate difference and must also refinance at the correct time.

Agarwal et al. (2016b) find that homeowners commit the mistake of waiting too long to refinance (error of omission) or refinancing at a rate which could have been lower (error of commission). They also observe that borrower characteristics such as the sophistication of the decision matrix can affect the frequency of these errors. This explains why sophisticated households benefit from cross-subsidies of naïve households who fail to refinance (Campbell et al. 2011a).

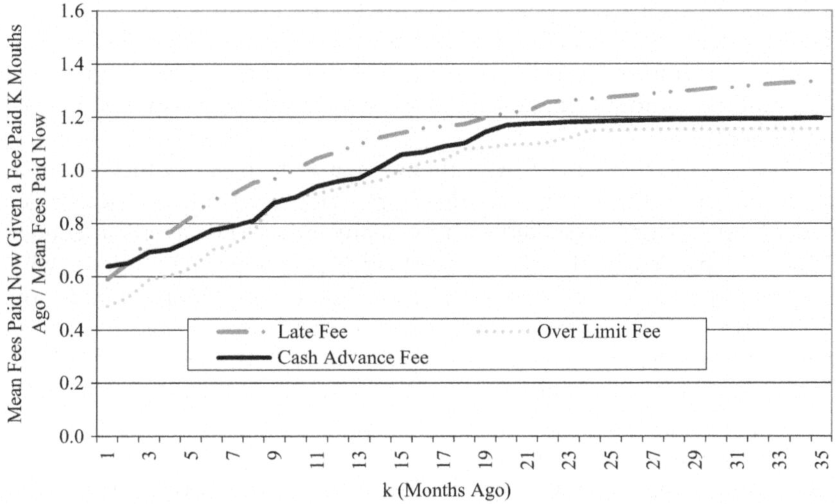

Fig. 7.1 Impact of Fees paid k months ago on Fees paid now. (Source: Agarwal et al. 2013)

Even for adjustable-rate mortgages, there are areas of inefficiency. In theory, homeowners will benefit by shifting to an adjustable-rate mortgage that moves with variations in market rates. However, changes in monthly payments can have serious consequences for homeowners who are liquidity constrained (Campbell and Cocco 2003). Furthermore, some banks offer low "teaser rates" for the initial few years before charging much higher rates thereafter, making it difficult for households to manage them properly. Miles (2004) shows that in UK where adjustable teaser rates are a standard practice, households end up paying more.

5.2.4 *Student Loans*

There is a growing concern that students are making uninformed borrowing decisions. A nationally representative survey reflects that most student loan recipients do not calculate the size of their future monthly payments before deciding whether and how much to borrow (Lusardi et al. 2016).

Currently, most policies tackling this assume the lack of financial information is a major cause of such inefficiency. The 2018 "PROSPER Act" makes student counseling a requirement for federal loan programs. The "Know Before You Owe Act" follows suit in 2019 where students must be informed of their likely loan repayments before taking a loan. Marx and Turner (2019) find that students are nonetheless inattentive and stay stuck to a pre-determined loan size even when reminded that they can choose a different loan amount, suggesting that the intervention has limited impact on students.

Marx and Turner (2019) hypothesize that instead of insufficient information, there is information overload or choice overload. Individuals get overwhelmed when presented with too many options (Iyengar and Lepper 2000). In particular, the choice overload happens among students who (1) are unfamiliar or unsupported in making a loan decision (Anderson et al. 2018), (2) are prone to nudges and heuristics or (3) have lower cognitive ability (Dynarski and Scott-Clayton 2006; Bettinger et al. 2012).

Students suffer from choice overload in terms of repayment method. Although many are eligible for the income-based repayment (IBR) scheme, less than one-quarter opt for it. Cox et al. (2018) attribute this lukewarm response toward the IBR scheme to borrower preference for the default repayment option, even if it is a sub-optimal choice. This suggests that an easy intervention to lower the default rate is to build on this default bias by changing the amount of loan aid listed in the financial aid award letter, without changing the cost to the college or the choices available to the students (Marx and Turner 2018).

Lochner et al. (2018) suggest that the non-monetary costs associated with income verification to determine those most in need may be a hidden cost that pushes eligible students away from the IBR scheme.

Biases also plague students such as an aversion toward debt (Field 2009). This fear of debt creates an additional psychic cost which discourages them from making an optimal loan decision for their education and careers (Caetano et al. 2011).

Another bias is self-control. Cadena and Keys (2013) find that one in six undergraduate students turn down interest-free loans because they wish to limit their own liquidity to control their own impulses and prevent excessive consumption during school.

The way that the application is designed can also influence their decision. Framing bias in the contract description and the choice of words are important (Pallais 2015; Evans et al. 2018; Abraham et al. 2018a, b).

Past interventions have produced mixed results. Schmeiser et al. (2017) examine a comprehensive intervention aimed at reducing borrowing among students carrying high loan balances. They find only a 2% reduction in the amount borrowed and no effect on the probability of borrowing. In contrast, Marx and Turner (2019) find that sending students an email showing average borrowing of past graduates reduces the amount borrowed by 13%.

5.2.5 *Factors Not Within Control of Borrowers*

Carvalho et al. (2019) suggest that credit inefficiency where borrowers pay a higher-than-market rate may be due to financial misfortunes including income shocks, liquidity shocks and expenditure shocks.

Credit inefficiency may also be driven by demography such as differential racial treatments. Charles and Hurst (2002) find that Black applicants are twice as likely to be rejected credit even after accounting for credit history and household wealth. Cohen (2012) notes that, at finance companies, a higher percentage of Blacks are charged interest rate mark-ups than Whites when they take loans to purchase vehicles.

However, Charles et al. (2008) find that for persons whose credit ratings enable them to quality for very low rates, differential racial treatment is not a concern for vehicle loans at traditional banking institutions. It is therefore a puzzle why Blacks choose to go to finance companies instead of traditional banking institutions. Possible explanations include racial differences in financial literacy and racial differences in rejection probabilities at traditional banking institutions.

5.3 *Do Borrowers Minimize Cost Across Their Existing Debt Contracts and Assets?*

5.3.1 *Credit Card Debt*

For credit cards, the optimal behavior is to make the minimum required payments on all cards, repaying cards that charge higher interest rates first before allocating payments to lower interest rate cards.

Stango and Zinman (2016) find that households who have higher education and income are remarkably efficient at minimizing financing costs when allocating their credit card debt across multiple credit cards.

In contrast, Gathergood et al. (2019) notice that of the 85% of their study targets who should have put all of their payments on the high interest rate card, only 10% do so.

Ponce et al. (2017) find that Mexican households similarly do not follow a strictly cost-minimizing strategy. They borrow a large fraction of their debt from the higher interest credit card that they possess, are unaware of the contractual interest rate and rely on mental accounts to organize credit card purchases and payments.

Households appear to be inattentive. They exhibit an incomplete consideration of information in making choices and a lack of awareness of past account usage and available balances (Grubb 2014). Anecdotes include consumers paying hefty overdraft fees when they have available sources of liquidity in another bank account or unused balances on their credit cards (Stango and Zinman 2014).

Gathergood et al. (2019) suggest the balance-matching heuristic of households as an alternative explanation to inattentiveness. Under "balance-matching", households allocate repayments across credit cards in the same ratio of an anchor, where the anchor is the balance remaining on the card. In other words, in a given month, the households repay a constant percentage of the balance on each card.

5.3.2 Revolving Credit Card Debt and Liquid Assets

Gross and Souleles (2002a, b) document a phenomenon where households who revolve credit card debt also hold liquid assets that can be, but are not, used for credit card debt repayment. This is coined as the credit card debt puzzle. Gross and Souleles (2002a, b) suggest that this can be explained by behavioral models.

The puzzle may be explained by the self-control model which describes a household made up of a worker and a shopper where the worker undertakes costly actions to limit the compulsive spending of the shopper (Bertaut et al. 2008). This seems drastic given that there are less expensive control options available such as lowering the credit limit or holding fewer credit cards.

The puzzle may also be driven by bankruptcy laws where individuals have to forfeit assets above a certain exemption level. They will be better off if they hold assets right up to the exemption level to take with them into their post-bankruptcy life, while their debts disappear. This explains why they strategically hold low-return liquid assets even while they have a significant amount of high-interest debt before they file for bankruptcy (Lehnert and Maki 2002).

Some do not think that "borrowing high and lending low" is a puzzle. Zinman (2007) argues that credit card and demand deposit are different assets. Demand deposit can be converted to cash more easily. Thus, it is more liquid and hence has implicit value.

Telyukova (2013) describes it as transaction friction. She points out that certain expenditures, both predictable and unpredictable, cannot be paid for by credit card. Predictable expenditures that cannot be paid for by credit cards include mortgage payments, rent payments, utilities, babysitting and daycare services, while unpredictable expenditures that cannot be paid for by credit cards include household repairs, small auto repairs and dental services.

5.3.3 Credit Card Debt and Retirement Saving

The coexistence of frequent card borrowing and voluntary retirement saving for the same individual is also labeled a paradox/puzzle (Laibson et al. 2003).

A resolution is to assume that individuals have hyperbolic discount functions (Phelps and Pollak 1968), where they act both patiently and impatiently. The hyperbolic individual saves aggressively for retirement, primarily in illiquid form where he will incur a significant penalty for early withdrawal and borrow frequently in the credit card market.

5.4 Are Defaults Optimal?

5.4.1 What Happens During a Default?

Consumers face the choice of not just whether to default but also how, either informally or filing for bankruptcy protection (Zinman 2015).

Foreclosures in the mortgage market are costly. From a social perspective, they can negatively affect prices of surrounding properties (Campbell et al. 2011b).

For the borrower, the foreclosure will have a severe impact on future access to mortgage and non-mortgage credit. For the lender, the foreclosure involves time costs and monetary costs such as maintenance, depreciation and real estate agent fees to resell the property usually at less than the outstanding balance on the mortgage. In this light, lender will be better off taking a small loss to modify the loan than to initiate a costly foreclosure (Gerardi and Li 2010).

Some of the tools devised to combat foreclosures allow the borrower to remain in his home. A borrower facing short-term difficulties is allowed to resume regular monthly payments plus some past-due amount. A borrower with short-term but slightly larger financial problems is provided forbearance for a given period for him to catch up with the payments. A borrower facing more permanent shocks may have loan modifications which will help the lender recover far more than from foreclosures. A loan modification involves changing the terms of the mortgage contract to lower the borrower's monthly mortgage payment and, in some cases, also to lower the amount of principal owed.

On the other hand, there are tools that force the borrower to move out of his home. In a pre-foreclosure sale, the lender allows the house to be sold for less than the amount owing with the remaining debt to be repaid later or simply forgiven (Cutts and Green 2005). In a deed in lieu, the borrower hands over the collateral property to the lender voluntarily and is absolved of all obligations. These two alternatives are, however, not so common because the financially distressed borrower is unlikely to give up his home willingly and forgiveness of debt may result in tax obligations.

5.4.2 Loan Renegotiation

As foreclosures tend to depress the housing market, policy makers have responded with loss mitigation tools aimed at encouraging lenders to renegotiate. An example is the Making Home Affordable (MHA) initiative launched by the Obama Administration in March 2009 that encourages loan modifications through the Home Affordable Modification Program (HAMP). The program relies on voluntary participation of lenders by providing them sizeable financial incentives to renegotiate distressed residential loans. The primary aim is to lower the number of foreclosures, but these efforts have limited effect, reaching only one-third of the targeted borrowers (Agarwal et al. 2017b).

One reason is the presence of mortgage-backed securities (MBS) in the US where banks bundle the loans they give to homeowners into tranches and sell them to investors. Given the dispersed ownership of these loans, there is an agency problem between the mortgage servicer and the investors which makes the renegotiation and modification of the loans prohibitively costly (Korgaonkar 2019). Piskorski et al. (2010) similarly conclude that securitized mortgages create a bias toward foreclosure. The contract frictions prevent borrowers from renegotiating loan terms (Maturana 2017).

However, Adelino et al. (2013) argue that securitization does not impede renegotiation of mortgages. Instead, they find that asymmetric information stemming from self-cure risk (where borrowers recover and become current) and re-default risk (where modified mortgages become delinquent again) limit the willingness of lenders to renegotiate or provide loan modification to borrowers since they cannot differentiate between borrowers who are truly distressed from those who are not.

Self-cure risk is supported by Capone (1996) who finds that 70–80% of borrowers at 90-day delinquency were able to "self-cure", that is, overcome their financial problems and repay the entire amount of the loan without assistance from lenders. Therefore, lenders will not want to be over-generous in their loan modification to avoid adverse selection situations where borrowers strategically default to gain concessions on their loans (Riddiough and Wyatt 1994).

Adelino et al. (2013) provide evidence of re-default risk. They observe that 40–60% of borrowers who receive modification end up back in serious delinquency within six months. Given the large re-default risk, lenders will have less incentive to renegotiate loans.

If lenders expect house prices to fall and re-default rates to be high, they may prefer to forgo renegotiation and foreclose immediately (Foote et al. 2009). If borrowers expect house prices to appreciate, they may choose to stay in the house and not default so loan modification may not be necessary (Foote et al. 2009).

Another factor is the extent of willingness of financial intermediaries to renegotiate the loans. Anecdotes such as understaffed call centers and limited pre-existing organizational capabilities on the part of financial intermediaries reflect negatively on the will to avoid foreclosures (Agarwal et al. 2017b).

5.4.3 Default

When borrowers default and file for bankruptcy under Chap. 13 bankruptcy protection, they are allowed to keep their primary property and catch up on the payments. Dobbie and Song (2015) find that Chap. 13 decreases foreclosure rates by 19.1%, which suggests that the protection enables borrowers to default in an efficient manner.

6 Do the Markets Supply an Efficient Quantity of Credit?

This section reviews the key theories behind the perception of credit undersupply versus credit oversupply (Zinman 2014).

Theories supporting the view of credit undersupply include (1) evidence of price dispersion in consumer credit, (2) missing "rungs" in the lending ladder and (3) asymmetric information.

Substantial price dispersion in consumer credit is consistent with lenders enjoying market power due to search and switch costs (Woodward and Hall 2012; Stango and Zinman 2013; Zinman 2014).

Missing "rungs" in the lending ladder is found between credit cards at 30% APR and payday loans at more than 100% APR (Zinman 2014). The gap suggests that there are borrowers whose needs are not fully met so they either underpay or overpay. Zinman (2014) postulates that this could be due to regulations restricting high-cost consumer loans (Carrell and Zinman 2014) or to asymmetric information including problems in screening borrowers (Einav et al. 2013).

The asymmetric information typically considers one of three situations. First, "hidden information" such as repayment likelihood of borrowers or profitability of lenders can lead to adverse selection on project risks and borrower types (Dobbie and Skiba 2013). Second, "hidden actions" such as reduced repayment effort of the borrower after the disbursement of the loans are hard to predict. Third, hidden information and hidden action interact, for example, missing information in the contract induce borrowers to commit moral hazard leading to credit rationing and an undersupply of credit (Zinman 2014).

Theories in support of the view that there is credit oversupply include (1) advantageous selection, (2) fire sales of collateral, (3) a slow recovery from shock, (4) cash-out refinancing of mortgage and (5) behavioral consumers who borrow excessively.

Advantageous selection in the credit market can happen when less risky borrowers borrow at unfavorable terms and choose a credit supply beyond what they require (De Meza and Webb 2000).

Fire sales of collateral can happen in the event of a bad shock. Lenders become concerned about collateral values and force borrowers to repay their loan by selling the collateral. The mass selling of collaterals can cause the value of other collaterals to fall giving rise to the perception that there is too much debt (Mian and Sufi 2015).

An area entering a downturn with high leverage will face a higher drop in demand for credit. This slow recovery from the shock in the presence of high leverage will give the impression of credit oversupply (Hall 2011; Mian and Sufi 2011).

Borrowers can refinance and cash out when house prices appreciate. However, it is difficult to decrease leverage when house prices decline due to the lumpy nature of properties, creating a situation of oversupply of credit (Khandani et al. 2013).

There are consumers who are psychologically predisposed to borrow too much (Skiba and Tobacman 2008). They may be described as seeking immediate gratification, being overconfident in their repayment ability or suffering from inattention (Mann 2013). Some behavioral households feel that they have more control over outcomes (Perry and Morris 2005), while others have the propensity to gamble (Kumar 2009).

There are mixed empirical evidences on whether markets oversupply or undersupply credit depending on the different conditions studied, such as a market heading into a downturn versus a market during a downturn; rational borrowers versus behavioral borrowers; shrouded versus transparent pricing and collateralized versus uncollateralized loans.

7 High Cost of Credit

There is no one unifying theory that can explain the high cost of credit. Some attribute it to (1) the undersupply of credit where lenders enjoy market power due to search or switch cost (Knittel and Stango 2003); (2) the regulatory failure to approve the very products that borrowers want (Kaufman 2013); (3) asymmetric information leading to capital rationing (Dobbie and Skiba 2013); (4) lenders that seek to exploit behavioral households (DellaVigna 2009) and (5) the unwillingness of households to pay for advice (Malkiel 2013).

In the wake of the 2008 financial crisis, interventions that may improve the provision of lending services have proliferated. These interventions include those that seek to (1) directly affect prices and quantities by controlling access and providing interest rate subsidies; (2) mandate point-of-sale disclosure to mitigate behavioral biases (Bertrand and Morse 2011) and (3) promote financial literacy to reduce psychological biases (Lusardi and Mitchell 2014; Korniotis and Kumar 2013).

8 Conclusion

Most households borrow. In fact, some over borrow. The most popular forms of household debt are mortgages, student loans, vehicle loans and credit card loans.

Households borrow to tie over temporary fluctuations in income, smooth consumption, invest in private businesses, buy illiquid assets or satisfy behavioral biases like present bias, optimism and cultural bias.

Over-leveraging can lead to psychological stress, affect relationships, influence career choices, result in negative credit scores and impact job prospects.

Many studies have explored household debt efficiency with various conclusions regarding welfare improvement, cost minimization, debt optimization and default optimization.

There are opposing views of whether the market supplies an efficient quantity of credit. Evidences of credit undersupply include price dispersion in consumer credit and missing "rungs" in the lending ladder. On the other hand, signs of credit oversupply include advantageous selection, fire sales of collateral, cash-out refinancing of mortgage and excessive borrowing.

References

Abraham, Katharine G., Emel Filiz-Ozbay, Erkut Y. Ozbay, and Lesley J. Turner. 2018a. Behavioral Effects of Student Loan Repayment Plan Options on Borrowers' Career Decisions: Theory and Experimental Evidence. NBER Working Paper #248043.

———. 2018b. Framing Effects, Earnings Expectations, and the Design of Student Loan Repayment Schemes. NBER Working Paper #24484.

Adelino, Manuel, Kristopher Gerardi, and Paul S. Willen. 2013. Why Don't Lenders Renegotiate More Home Mortgages? Redefaults, Self-Cures and Securitization. *Journal of Monetary Economics* 60 (7): 835–853.

Agarwal, Sumit, and Brent W. Ambrose. 2018. The Effect of Advertising on Home Equity Credit Choices. In *Research Handbook on Behavioral Law and Economics*, ed. Joshua C. Teitelbaum and Kathryn Zeiler, 122–152. Edward Elgar Publishing.

Agarwal, Sumit, and Bhashkar Mazumder. 2013. Cognitive Abilities and Household Financial Decision Making. *American Economic Journal: Applied Economics* 5 (1): 193–207.

Agarwal, Sumit, Paige Marta Skiba, and Jeremy Tobacman. 2009. Payday Loans and Credit Cards: New Liquidity and Credit Scoring Puzzles? *American Economic Review: Papers and Proceeding* 99 (2): 412–417.

Agarwal, Sumit, Gene Amromin, Itzhak Ben-David, Souphala Chomsisengphet, and Douglas D. Evanoff. 2010. Learning to Cope: Voluntary Financial

Education and Loan Performance during a Housing Crisis. *The American Economic Review* 100 (2): 495–500.

Agarwal, Sumit, John C. Driscoll, Xavier Gabaix, and David Laibson. 2013. Learning in the Credit Card Market. *SSRN*. Accessed March 18, 2020. https://papers.ssrn.com/sol3/papers.cfm?abstract_id=1091623.

Agarwal, Sumit, Souphala Chomsisengphet, Liu Chunlin, and Nicholas S. Souleles. 2015. Do Consumers Choose the Right Credit Contracts? *The Review of Corporate Finance Studies* 4 (2): 239–247.

Agarwal, Sumit, Gene Amromin, Itzhak Ben-David, and Dougals D. Evanoff. 2016a. Loan Product Steering in Mortgage Markets. NBER Working Paper #22696.

Agarwal, Sumit, Richard J. Rosen, and Vincent Yao. 2016b. Why Do Borrowers Make Mortgage Refinancing Mistakes? *Management Science* 62 (12): 3494–3509.

Agarwal, Sumit, Changcheng Song, and Vincent W. Yao. 2017a. Banking Competition and Shrouded Attributes: Evidence from the US Mortgage Market. Georgetown McDonough School of Business Research Working Paper No. 2900287.

Agarwal, Sumit, Gene Amromin, Itzhak Ben-David, Souphala Chomsisengphet, Tomasz Piskorski, and Amit Seru. 2017b. Policy Intervention in Debt Renegotiation: Evidence from the Home Affordable Modification Program. *Journal of Political Economy* 125 (3): 654–712.

Albanesi, Stefania, Giacomo De Giorgi, and Jaromir Nosal. 2017. Credit Growth and the Financial Crisis: A New Narrative. NBER Working Paper #23740.

Almenberg, Johan, Annamaria Lusardi, Jenny Säve-Söderbergh, and Roine Vestman. 2018. Attitudes Toward Debt and Debt Behavior. NBER Working Paper #24935.

Anderson, Drew M., Johnathan G. Conzelmann, and Austin T. Lacy. 2018. The State of Financial Knowledge in College: New Evidence from a National Survey. RAND Working Paper WR-1256.

Arcand, Jean Louis, Enrico Berkes, and Ugo Panizza. 2015. Too Much Finance? *Journal of Economic Growth* 20 (2): 105–148.

Ausubel, Lawrence M. 1991. The Failure of Competition in the Credit Card Market. *American Economic Review* 81 (1): 50–81.

Avery, Robert B., Raphael W. Bostic, and Katherine A. Samolyk. 1998. The Role of Personal Wealth in Small Business Finance. *Journal of Banking and Finance* 22: 1019–1061.

Banerjee, Abhijit V. 2004. Inequality and Investment. Unpublished Working Paper. Accessed March 20, 2020. https://economics.mit.edu/files/514.

Banerjee, Abhijit V., and Esther Duflo. 2007. The Economic Lives of the Poor. *Journal of Economic Perspectives* 21 (1): 141–168.

Baugh, Brian, Jesse B. Leary, and Jialan Wang. 2017. When Is It Hard to Make Ends Meet? Paper presented at the 2018 NBER Summer Institute—Household Finance, Cambridge, July 28.

Beck, Thorsten, and Ross Levine. 2004. Stock Markets, Banks, and Growth: Panel Evidence. *Journal of Banking and Finance* 28 (3): 423–442.

Bertaut, Carol C., Haliassos Michael, and Michael Reitter. 2008. Credit Card Debt Puzzles and Debt Revolvers for Self-Control. *Review of Finance* 13: 657–692.

Bertrand, Marriane, and Adair Morse. 2011. Information Disclosure, Cognitive Biases, and Payday Borrowing. *Journal of Finance* 66 (6): 1865–1893.

Bettinger, Eric, Lisa Sanbonmatsu, Bridget T. Long, and Philip Oreopoulos. 2012. The Role of Simplification and Information in College Decisions: Results from the H&R Block FAFSA Experiment. *Quarterly Journal of Economics* 127 (3): 1205–1242.

Blundell, Richard, Martin Browning, and Costas Meghir. 1994. Consumer Demand and the Life-Cycle Allocation of Household Expenditures. *Review of Economic Studies* 61 (1): 57–80.

Bos, Marieke, Emily Breza, and Andres Liberman. 2018. The Labor Market Effects of Credit Market Information. *The Review of Financial Studies* 31 (6): 2005–2037.

Bursztyn, Leonardo, Florian Ederer, Bruno Ferman, and Noah Yuchtman. 2014. Understanding Mechanisms Underlying Peer Effects: Evidence from a Field Experiment in Financial Decisions. *Econometrica* 82: 1273–1301.

Cadena, Brian C., and Benjamin J. Keys. 2013. Can Self-Control Explain Avoiding Free Money? Evidence from Interest-Free Student Loans. *Review of Economics and Statistics.* 95 (4): 1117–1129.

Caetano, Gregorio, Miguel Palacios, and Harry Anthony Patrinos. 2011. Measuring Aversion to Debt: An Experiment among Student Loan Candidates. World Bank Policy Research Working Paper No. 5737.

Campbell, John Y., and Joao F. Cocco. 2003. Household Risk Management and Optimal Mortgage Choice. *Quarterly Journal of Economics* 118 (4): 1449–1494.

Campbell, John Y., Howell E. Jackson, Brigitte C. Madrian, and Peter Tufano. 2011a. Consumer Financial Protection. *Journal of Economic Perspectives* 25 (1): 91–114.

Campbell, John Y., Stefano Giglio, and Parag Pathak. 2011b. Forced Sales and House Prices. *American Economic Review* 101 (5): 2108–2131.

Capone, Charles A. 1996. Providing Alternatives to Mortgage Foreclosure: A Report to Congress. *Office of Policy Department and Research*. Accessed March 24, 2020. https://www.huduser.gov/portal/publications/hsgfin/mortgage.html.

Carrell, Scott, and Jonathan Zinman. 2014. In Harm's Way? Payday Loan Access and Military Personnel Performance. *The Review of Financial Studies* 27 (9): 2805–2840.

Carroll, Christopher D. 1992. The Buffer-Stock Theory of Saving: Some Macroeconomic Evidence. *Brookings Papers on Economic Activity* 23: 61–156.

Carvalho, Leandro, Arna Olafsson, and Dan Silverman. 2019. Misfortune and Mistake: The Financial Conditions and Decision-Making Ability of High-Cost Loan Borrowers. NBER Working Paper #26328.

Chakrabarti, Rajashri, Vyacheslav Fos, Andres Liberman, and Constantine Yannelis. 2020. Tuition Debt and Human Capital. *Federal Reserve Bank of New York Staff Report* 912.

Charles, Kerwin K., and Erik Hurst. 2002. The Transition to Home Ownership and the Black-White Wealth Gap. *Review of Economics and Statistics* 84 (2): 281–297.

Charles, Kerwin K., Erik Hurst, and Melvin Stephens. 2008. Rates for Vehicle Loans: Race and Loan Source. *American Economic Review Papers and Proceedings* 98 (2): 315–320.

Christelis, Dimitris, Michael Ehrmann, and Dimitris Georgarakos. 2017. Exploring Differences in Household Debt across the United States and Euro Area Countries. Centre for Studies in Economics and Finance Working Paper 465. University of Naples, Italy.

Cohen, Mark A. 2012. Imperfect Competition in Auto Lending: Subjective Markup, Racial Disparity, and Class Action Litigation. *Review of Law & Economics* 8 (1): 21–58.

Community Financial Services Association of America. 2006. National Data on Short-Term Credit Alternatives. *Community Financial Services Association of America*. Accessed March 21, 2020. http://www.cfsa.net/downloads/National_Data_on_Short_Term_Credit_Alternatives.pdf.

Corbae, Dean, Andrew Glover, and Daphne Chen. 2013. Can Employer Credit Checks Create Poverty Traps? Paper presented for Meeting for the Society for Economic Dynamics.

Cox, James C., Daniel Kreisman, and Susan Dynarski. 2018. Designed to Fail: Effects of the Default Option and Information Complexity on Student Loan Repayment. NBER Working Paper #25258.

Cutts, Amy, and Richard Green. 2005. Innovative Servicing Technology: Smart Enough to Keep People in their Houses? In *Building Assets, Building Credit: Creating Wealth in Low-Income Communities*, 348–377. Washington, DC: Brookings Institution Press.

De Meza, David, and David Webb. 2000. Does Credit Rationing Imply Insufficient Lending? *Journal of Public Economics* 78 (3): 215–234.

Deaton, Angus. 1991. Saving and Liquidity Constraints. *Econometrica* 59 (5): 1221–1248.

DellaVigna, Stefano. 2009. Psychology and Economics: Evidence from the Field. *Journal of Economic Literature* 47: 315–372.
Dew, Jeffery. 2008. The Relationship Between Debt Change and Marital Satisfaction Change in Recently Married Couples. *Family Relations* 57: 60–71.
———. 2011. The Association between Consumer Debt and the Likelihood of Divorce. *Journal of Family Economics* 32: 554–565.
Di Maggio, Marco, and Amir Kermani. 2017. Credit-Induced Boom and Bust. *Review of Financial Studies* 30 (11): 3711–3758.
Dick, Astrid, and Andreas Lehnert. 2010. Personal Bankruptcy and Credit Market Competition. *The Journal of Finance* 65 (2): 655–686.
Dobbie, Will, and Paige Marta Skiba. 2013. Information Asymmetries in Consumer Credit Markets: Evidence from Payday Lending. *American Economic Journal: Applied Economics* 5 (4): 256–282.
Dobbie, Will, and Jae Song. 2015. Debt Relief and Debtor Outcomes: Measuring the Effects of Consumer Bankruptcy Protection. *American Economic Review* 105 (3): 1272–1311.
Dobridge, Christine. 2014. Heterogeneous Effects of Household Credit: The Payday Lending Case. Working Paper. The Wharton School.
Drentea, Patricia. 2000. Age, Debt, and Anxiety. *Journal of Health and Social Behavior* 41 (4): 437–450.
Duflo, Esther, and Emmanuel Saez. 2012. The Role of Information and Social Interactions in Retirement Plan Decisions: Evidence from a Randomized Experiment. *Quarterly Journal of Economics* 118: 815–842.
Dunn, Lucia F., and Ida A. Mirzaie. 2015. Consumer Debt Stress, Changes in Household debt and the great recession. *Western Economic Association International* 54 (1): 201–214.
Dynan, Karen E. 2009. Changing Household Financial Opportunities and Economic Security. *Journal of Economic Perspectives* 23 (4): 49–68.
Dynan, Karen E., and Donald L. Kohn. 2007. The Rise in U.S. Household Indebtedness: Causes and Consequences. In *The Structure and the Resilience of the Financial System: Proceedings of a Conference*, ed. Christopher Kent and Jeremy Lawson, 84–113. Reserve Bank of Australia #2007–37.
Dynarski, Susan M., and Judith E. Scott-Clayton. 2006. The Cost of Complexity in Federal Student Aid: Lessons From Optimal Tax Theory And Behavioral Economics. *National Tax Journal* 59 (2): 319–356.
Eggertsson, Gauti Bergþóruson, and Paul Krugman. 2012. Debt, Deleveraging, and the Liquidity Trap: A Fisher-Minsky-Koo Approach. *The Quarterly Journal of Economics* 127 (3): 1469–1513.
Einav, Liran, Mark Jenkins, and Jonathan Levin. 2013. The Impact of Credit Scoring on Consumer Lending. *The RAND Journal of Economics* 44 (2): 249–274.

Elliehausen, Gregory. 2009. An Analysis of Consumers' Use of Payday Loans. *Financial Services Research Program, Monograph No. 41.*

Evans, Brent J., Angela Boatman, and Adela Soliz. 2018. Framing and Labeling Effects in Preferences for Borrowing for College: An Experimental Analysis. *Research in Higher Education* 60 (4): 438–457.

Federal Reserve Bank of New York. 2019. Household Debt and Credit. *Federal Reserve Bank of New York Research and Statistics Group*, 3.

Field, Erica. 2009. Educational Debt Burden and Career Choice: Evidence from a Financial Aid Experiment at NYU Law School. *American Economic Journal: Applied Economics* 1 (1): 1–21.

Foote, Christopher, Kristopher Gerardi, Lorenz Goette, and Paul Willen. 2009. Reducing Foreclosures: No Easy Answers. NBER Working Paper #15063.

Fuster, Andreas, David Laibson, and Brock Mendel. 2010. Natural Expectations and Macroeconomic Fluctuations. *Journal of Economic Perspectives* 24 (4): 67–84.

Gabaix, Xavier, and David Laibson. 2006. Shrouded Attributes, Consumer Myopia, and Information Suppression in Competitive Markets. *Quarterly Journal of Economics* 121 (2): 505–540.

Gathergood, John, Neale Mahoney, Neil Stewart, and Joerg Weber. 2019. How Do Individuals Repay Their Debt? The Balance-Matching Heuristic. *American Economic Review* 109 (3): 844–875.

Geanakoplos, John. 2010. The Leverage Cycle. In *NBER Macroeconomics Annual 2009, vol. 24*, ed. Darron Acemoglu, Kenneth Rogof, and Michael Woodford, 1–65. Cambridge, MA: National Bureau of Economic Research.

Gelman, Michael, Shachar Kariv, Matthew D. Shapiro, Dan Silverman, and Steven Tadelis. 2018. How Individuals Respond to a Liquidity Shock: Evidence from the 2013 Government Shutdown. NBER Working Paper #21025.

Gerardi, Kristopher, and Wenli Li. 2010. Mortgage Foreclosure Preventions Efforts. *Economic Review* 95 (2): 1–13.

Gourinchas, Pierre-Olivier, and Maurice Obstfeld. 2012. Stories of the Twentieth Century for the Twenty-First. *American Economic Journal: Macroeconomics* 4 (1): 226–265.

Graves, Stephen M. 2003. Landscapes of Predation, Landscapes of Neglect: A Locational Analysis of Payday Lenders and Banks. *The Professional Geographer* 55 (3): 303–317.

Gross, David, and Nicholas S. Souleles. 2002a. Do Liquidity Constraints and Interest Rates Matter for Consumer Behavior? Evidence from Credit Card Data. *Quarterly Journal of Economics* 117: 149–185.

———. 2002b. Explaining the Increase in Bankruptcy and Delinquency: Stigma Versus Risk-Composition. *Review of Financial Studies* 15: 319–347.

Grubb, Michael. 2014. Consumer Inattention and Bill-Shock Regulation. *The Review of Economic Studies* 82 (1): 219–257.

Guerrieri, Veronica, and Guido Lorenzoni. 2017. Credit Crises, Precautionary Savings, and the Liquidity Trap. *The Quarterly Journal of Economics* 132 (3): 1427–1467.

Gurun, Umit G., Gregor Matvos, and Amit Seru. 2016. Advertising Expensive Mortgages. *Journal of Finance* 71 (5): 2371–2416.

Hall, Robert E. 2011. The Long Slump. *American Economic Review* 101: 431–460.

Haughwout, Andrew, Donghoon Lee, Joseph S. Tracy, and Wilbert Van der Klaauw. 2011. Real Estate Investors, the Leverage Cycle, and the Housing Market Crisis. *Federal Reserve Bank of New York Staff Report* #514.

Herkenhoff, Kyle, Gordon Phillips, and Ethan Cohen-Cole. 2016. The Impact of Consumer Credit Access on Employment, Earnings and Entrepreneurship. NBER Working Paper #22846.

Hortacsu, Ali, and Chad Syverson. 2004. Product Differentiation, Search Costs, and Competition in the Mutual Fund Industry: A Case Study of S&P 500 Index Funds. *Quarterly Journal of Economics* 119 (2): 403–456.

Iyengar, Sheena S., and Mark R. Lepper. 2000. When Choice is Demotivating: Can One Desire Too Much of a Good Thing? *Journal of Personality and Social Psychology* 79 (6): 995–1006.

Karlan, Dean, Sendhil Mullainathan, and Benjamin N. Roth. 2019. Debt Traps? Market Vendors and Moneylender Debt in India and the Philippines. *American Economic Review* 1 (1): 27–42.

Kaufman, Alex. 2013. Payday Lending Regulation. Finance and Economics Discussion Series Working Paper No. 2013-62.

Keese, Matthias, and Hendrik Schmitz. 2012. Broke, Ill, and Obese: Is There an Effect of Household Debt on Health? *The Review of Income and Wealth* 60 (3): 525–541.

Khandani, Amir E., Andrew W. Lo, and Robert C. Merton. 2013. Systemic Risk and the Refinancing Ratchet Effect. *Journal of Financial Economics* 108 (1): 29–45.

Kim, Hyungsoo, and Angela Christine Lyons. 2008. No Pain, No Strain: Impact of Health on the Financial Security of Older Americans. *Journal of Consumer Affairs* 42 (1): 9–36.

Knittel, Chris, and Victor Stango. 2003. Price Ceilings, Focal Points and Tacit Collusion: Evidence from Credit Cards. *American Economic Review* 93 (5): 1703–1729.

Kolari, James W., Donald R. Fraser, and Ali Anari. 1998. The Effects of Securitization on Mortgage Market Yields: A Cointegration Analysis. *Real Estate Economics* 26 (4): 677–693.

Korgaonkar, Sanket. 2019. Multiple Tranches, Information Asymmetry and the Impediments to Mortgage Renegotiation. *SSRN*. Accessed March 24, 2020. https://papers.ssrn.com/sol3/papers.cfm?abstract_id=3040447.

Korinek, Anton, and Alp Simsek. 2016. Liquidity Trap and Excessive Leverage. *American Economic Review* 106 (3): 699–738.

Korniotis, George M., and Alok Kumar. 2013. Do Portfolio Distortions Reflect Superior Information or Psychological Biases? *Journal of Financial and Quantitative Analysis* 48 (1): 1–45.

Kuchler, Theresa, and Michaela Pagel. 2018. Sticking to Your Plan: The Role of Present Bias for Credit Card Paydown. NBER Working Paper #24881.

Kumar, Alok. 2009. Who Gambles in the Stock Market? *Journal of Finance* 64 (4): 1889–1933.

Kumhof, Michael, Romain Rancière, and Pablo Winant. 2015. Inequality, Leverage, and Crises. *American Economic Review* 105 (3): 1217–1245.

Laibson, David. 1997. Golden Eggs and Hyperbolic Discounting. *Quarterly Journal of Economics* 112 (2): 443–477.

Laibson, David, Andrea Repetto, and Jeremy Tobacman. 2003. A Debt Puzzle. In *Knowledge, Information, and Expectations in Modern Economics: In Honor of Edmund S. Phelps*, ed. Aghion Phillippe, Roman Frydman, Joseph Stiglitz, and M. Woodford, 228–266. Princeton, NJ: Princeton University Press.

Lavrakas, Paul, and Trever N. Tompson. 2009. New Research on the Measurement of Debt Stress and Related Health Problems. American Association for Public Opinion Research, Florida.

Lawrence, Edward C., and Gregory Elliehausen. 2008. A Comparative Analysis of Payday Loan Customers. *Contemporary Economic Policy* 26 (2): 299–316.

Lehnert, Andreas, and Dean M. Maki. 2002. Consumption, Debt, and Portfolio Choice: Testing the Effect of Bankruptcy Law. *The Federal Reserve Board* 02/2002.

Levine, Ross. 1998. The Legal Environment, Banks, and Long-Run Economic Growth. *Journal of Money, Credit and Banking* 30 (3): 596–613.

Lise, Jeremy. 2013. On-the-Job Search and Precautionary Savings. *Review of Economic Studies* 80 (3): 1086–1113.

Lochner, Lance, Todd Stinebrickner, and Utku Suleymanoglu. 2018. Parental Support, Savings and Student Loan Repayment. NBER Working Paper #24863.

Ludvigson, Sydney C. 1999. Consumption and Credit: A Model of Time-Varying Liquidity Constraints. *Review of Economics and Statistics* 81 (3): 434–447.

Luo, Mi, and Simon Mongey. 2019. Assets and Job Choice: Student Debt, Wages and Amenities. NBER Working Paper# 25801.

Lusardi, Annamaria, and Peter Tufano. 2015. Debt Literacy, Financial Experiences, and Overindebtedness. *Journal of Pension Economics and Finance* 14 (4): 332–368.

Lusardi, Annamaria, and Olivia S. Mitchell. 2014. The Economic Importance of Financial Literacy: Theory and Evidence. *Journal of Economic Literature* 52 (1): 5–44.

Lusardi, Annamaria, Carlo de Bassa Scheresberg, and Noemi Oggero. 2016. Student Loan Debt in the US: An Analysis of the 2015 NFCS Data. *Global Financial Literacy Excellence Center Policy Brief.* Accessed March 21, 2020. https://pensionresearchcouncil.wharton.upenn.edu/wp-content/uploads/2017/09/WP-2017-15-Lusardi-et-al.pdf.

Malkiel, Burton G. 2013. Asset Management Fees and the Growth of Finance. *Journal of Economic Perspectives* 27 (2): 97–108.

Mann, Ronald. 2013. Assessing the Optimism of Payday Loan Borrowers. *Supreme Court Economic Review* 21.

Marx, Benjamin M., and Lesley J. Turner. 2018. Borrowing Trouble? Student Loans, the Cost of Borrowing, and Implications for the Effectiveness of Need-Based Grant Aid. *American Economic Journal: Applied Economics* 10 (2): 163–201.

———. 2019. Student Loan Choice Overload. NBER Working Paper #25905.

Maturana, Gonzalo. 2017. When Are Modifications of Securitized Loans Beneficial to Investors? *The Review of Financial Studies* 30 (11): 3824–3857.

Mayer, Christopher, Karen Pence, and Shane M. Sherlund. 2009. The Rise in Mortgage Defaults. *The Journal of Economic Perspectives* 23 (1): 27–50.

Meier, Stephan, and Charles Sprenger. 2010. Present-Biased Preferences and Credit Card Borrowing. *American Economic Journal: Applied Economics* 2 (1): 193–210.

Melzer, Brian T. 2011. The Real Costs of Credit Access: Evidence from the Payday Lending Market. *Quarterly Journal of Economics* 126 (1): 517–555.

Mian, Atif, and Amir Sufi. 2011. House Prices, Home Equity Based Borrowing, and the U.S. Household Leverage Crisis. *American Economic Review* 101: 2132–2156.

———. 2012. What Explains High Unemployment? The Aggregate Demand Channel. NBER Working Paper #17830.

———. 2015. Foreclosures, House Prices and the Real Economy. *Journal of Finance* 70 (6): 2587–2634.

———. 2018. Finance and Business Cycles: The Credit-Driven Household Demand Channel. *The Journal of Economic Perspectives* 32 (3): 31–58.

Mian, Atif, Kamalesh Rao, and Amir Sufi. 2013. Household Balance Sheets, Consumption, and the Economic Slump. *The Quarterly Journal of Economics* 128 (4): 1687–1726.

Miles, David. 2004. *The UK Mortgage Market: Taking a Longer-Term View.* London: HM Treasury.

Miller, Sarah, and Cindy K. Soo. 2018. Do Neighborhoods Affect Credit Market Decisions of Low-Income Borrowers? Evidence from the Moving to Opportunity Experiment. NBER Working Paper #25023.

Moon, John. 2010. Small Business Finance and Personal Assets. *Federal Reserve Board of Governors* 21(3).

Morse, Adair. 2011. Payday Lenders: Heroes or Villains? *Journal of Financial Economics* 102 (1): 28–44.

Pallais, Amanda. 2015. Small Differences that Matter: Mistakes in Applying to College. *Journal of Labor Economics* 33 (2): 493–520.

Perry, Vanessa G., and Marlene D. Morris. 2005. Who Is in Control? The Role of Self-Perception, Knowledge, and Income in Explaining Consumer Financial Behavior. *Journal of Consumer Affairs 39* (2): 299–313.

Phelps, Edmund S., and Robert A. Pollak. 1968. On Second-best National Saving and Game-equilibrium Growth. *Review of Economic Studies* 35 (2): 185–199.

Piskorski, Tomasz, Amit Seru, and Vikrant Vig. 2010. Securitization and Distressed Loan Renegotiation: Evidence from the Subprime Mortgage Crisis. *Journal of Financial Economics* 97 (3): 369–397.

Ponce, Alejandro, Enrique Seira, and Guillermo Zamarripa. 2017. Borrowing on the Wrong Credit Card?: Evidence from Mexico. *The American Economic Review* 107 (4): 1335–1361.

Rajan, Raghuram G. 2010. *Fault Lines: How Hidden Fractures Still Threaten the World Economy.* Princeton, NJ: Princeton University Press.

Reich, Robert. 2010. *Aftershock: The Next Economy and America's Future.* New York: Random House.

Riddiough, Timothy J., and Steve B. Wyatt. 1994. Wimp or Tough Guy: Sequential Default Risk and Signaling with Mortgages. *Journal of Real Estate Finance and Economics* 9 (3): 299–321.

Robb, Alicia M., and David T. Robinson. 2014. The Capital Structure Decisions of New Firms. *The Review of Financial Studies* 27 (1): 153–179.

Sahay, Ratna, Martin Čihák, Papa N'Diaye, Adolfo Barajas, Ran Bi, Diana Ayala, Yuan Gao, et al. 2015. Rethinking Financial Deepening: Stability and Growth in Emerging Markets. Paper presented for International Monetary Fund Staff Discussion Note, International Monetary Fund, Washington DC, May.

Schmeiser, Maximilian, Christina Stoddard, and Carly Urban. 2017. Does Salient Financial Information Affect Academic Performance and Borrowing Behavior Among College Students? *Economics of Education Review* 56: 95–109.

Shui, Haiyan, and Lawrence M. Ausubel. 2004. Time Inconsistency in the Credit Card Market. SSRN. Accessed March 24, 2020. https://papers.ssrn.com/sol3/papers.cfm?abstract_id=586622.

Sieg, Holger, and Yu Wang. 2017. The Impact of Student Debt on Education, Career, and Marriage Choices of Female Lawyers. *European Economic Review* 109 (2018): 124–147.

Skiba, Paige Marta, and Jeremy Tobacman. 2008. Payday Loans, Uncertainty and Discounting: Explaining Patterns of Borrowing, Repayment, and Default. Vanderbilt Law and Economics Research Paper No. 08-33.

———. 2009. Do Payday Loans Cause Bankruptcy? *The Journal of Law and Economics* 62: 485–519.

Stango, Victor, and Jonathan Zinman. 2011. Fuzzy Math, Disclosure Regulation and Credit Market Outcomes: Evidence from Truth in Lending Reform. *Review of Financial Studies* 24 (2): 506–534.

———. 2013. Borrowing High vs. Borrowing Higher: Sources and Consequences of Dispersion in Individual Borrowing Costs. Working paper. University of California-Davis, Davis, CA.

———. 2014. Limited and Varying Consumer Attention: Evidence from Shocks to the Salience of Bank Overdraft Fees. *The Review of Financial Studies* 27 (4): 990–1030.

———. 2016. Borrowing High versus Borrowing Higher: Price Dispersion, Shopping Behavior, and Debt Allocation in the US Credit Card Market. *The Review of Financial Studies* 29 (4): 979–1006.

Telyukova, Irina A. 2013. Household Need for Liquidity and the Credit Card Debt Puzzle. *The Review of Financial Studies* 80 (3): 1148–1177.

Valckx, Nico, Adrian Alter, Alan Xiaochen Feng, Xinze Yao, Machiko Narita, Feng Li, and Xiaomeng Lu. 2017. Household Debt and Financial Stability. In *Global Financial Stability Report: Is Growth at Risk?* ed. Dong He and Claudio Raddatz, 53–90. International Monetary Fund.

Woodward, Susan E., and Robert E. Hall. 2012. Diagnosing Consumer Confusion and Sub-Optimal Shopping Effort: Theory and Mortgage-Market Evidence. *The American Economic Review* 102 (7): 3249–3276.

Zinman, Jonathan. 2007. Household Borrowing High and Lending Low under No-Arbitrage. Unpublished Working Paper.

———. 2010. Restricting Consumer Credit Access: Household Survey Evidence on Effects around the Oregon Rate Cap. *Journal of Banking and Finance* 34 (3): 546–556.

———. 2014. Consumer Credit: Too Much or Too Little (or Just Right)? *Journal of Legal Studies* 43 (S2): 209–237.

———. 2015. Household Debt: Facts, Puzzles, Theories and Policies. *Annual Review of Economics* 7: 251–276.

CHAPTER 8

Risk Management

1 Introduction

Despite remarkable reduction in extreme poverty in many parts of the world, risks that threaten people's health and financial well-being still abound. These risks may be due to systemic shocks such as natural disasters and economic crisis or idiosyncratic shocks such as job losses, accidents, disabilities, illnesses and thefts.

Measures to address systemic shocks include better macroeconomic management, disaster risk management, flood insurance, rainfall insurance and social protection, while steps to counter idiosyncratic shocks focus mainly on life and health insurance.

1.1 Personal Risk Management Strategies

Some of the common ways that households use to cope with financial risks include precautionary saving for unexpected events, purchasing in bulk, buying cheaper substitutes and consuming prudently (Banks and Bowman 2017).

In classical economics, households use insurance products to smooth consumption in the presence of shocks.

S. Agarwal et al., *Household Finance*,
https://doi.org/10.1007/978-981-15-5526-8_8

1.2 What Is Insurance?

Insurance is a formalized system of cooperative help and risk sharing, where individuals contribute premiums to a fund from which benefits are paid. It is a financial safeguard or safety net to help ensure that when things go wrong, the impact will be financially manageable.

To price premiums, customers are assigned a risk profile. Insurance companies that most accurately profile customers have a strong competitive advantage (Swedloff 2014). The use of big data (such as phone data, social media, health records, shopping habits, utilities and water use patterns) and sophisticated algorithms have taken risk rating to a whole new level. Detailed analysis of granular data ensures that low-risk customers get to enjoy lower premiums. However, the Actuaries Institute of Australia (2016) observes that:

> *At the extreme, some policyholders will have their risks assessed as so high that the price will be prohibitive or insurers will decline to provide cover... Unaffordability or unavailability of insurance may marginalize high risk individuals, preventing them from participating in all of life's activities. Examples of how this already occurs today are a breast cancer patient who cannot fly because travel insurance is not accessible, or a mortgage application is denied.*

1.3 How Do the Poor Manage Risk?

Evidence suggests that poorer or lower income households are less well insured against many types of risks than richer households (Rampini and Viswanathan 2017). Low-income households are the most exposed to the risk of financially harmful events but they are also the most likely to lack insurance coverage. This is usually framed as a problem of affordability and access (Quantum Market Research 2013). Households with below-median income have less home and contents insurance, life insurance and car insurance.

However, beyond affordability and access, low-income households also face insecure employment and unstable income which make paying for insurance an added financial risk (Banks and Bowman 2017). Some stay in high-risk areas that are prone to flood, storm or fire, which attract higher premiums (Banks and Bowman 2017). For some of these households, not insuring may be a rational decision.

In situations where formal risk management tools are not available, the first source of defence is usually asset holdings which help to smooth the impact of shocks on consumption (De Vreyer and Lambert 2020). Farmers in Nigeria, for example, smooth consumption by depleting wealth after unexpected income shocks (Udry 1995). Unfortunately, there is a high proportion of poor households that have little accumulated wealth and limited access to loans (Zeller et al. 1997; Robinson 2002; Rogg 2006).

Sugiyanto et al. (2012) examine possible consumption smoothing strategies among the poorest households in Yogyakarta, Indonesia. The major causes of income fluctuations are seasonal factors, low demand, project completion, contract completion and natural disasters. The consumption smoothing strategies can be broadly divided into two categories: ex ante and ex post. Ex ante strategies comprise financial saving, asset accumulation and insurance but there is hardly any insurance among the poorest. For most households, saving is the most obvious response with 56% saving at home, 29% at formal financial institutions and others at informal institutions. Ex post strategies include income-generating activities, home production, loans and transfers. Most households choose to borrow money, sell assets and apply for government subsidies.

In communities that are more tightly knitted, households share risks using informal credit and reciprocity-based networks to smooth consumption (Townsend 1994).

2 Life Cycle Risks

There are three major classes of risks related to the life cycle. They are (1) mortality risk which is associated with premature death, (2) longevity risk which is associated with long life and (3) health and disability risk which is associated with physical and mental well-being.

Due to increases in life expectancy, longevity risk has become a dominant focus. Longer life spans create a significant burden for the government particularly where falling birth rates funneled fewer people into the workforce. As the working population shrinks relative to retirees, there are social, cultural and economic consequences.

The longevity trend and changing demographics require a system that encourages individuals to save appropriately. Studies have shown that most people underestimate how long they can live, which have important implications for retirement planning. People may outlive their saving or have a lower than expected standard of living.

Quality of life is another issue. People may live longer but they also tend to have more health issues. The other important financial risk that the elderly face is health cost risk.

In designing a system to provide financial security to the elderly, both longevity risk and health cost risk should be taken into consideration.

3 Types of Life Insurance Policies

Broadly, insurance can be divided into two categories: life insurance and general insurance.

Life insurance policies are where premiums are paid regularly to ensure payment of an agreed sum upon death of the policy holder or when he reaches a certain age. As the event will definitely happen, this type of insurance is also known as assurance.

In all contracts of life insurance, insurable interest is compulsory at the time the policy is taken. In other words, the relationship between the buyer and the insured must be legal and the death of the insured must result in financial loss to the buyer. Examples of insurable interest include husband and wife, parent and child, creditor and debtor and employer and employee.

Apart from the obvious advantage of protection for the family and dependents, life insurance policies may be used as security for loans (policy holder may borrow against the insurance policy from the insurance company), may provide tax relief (premiums may be tax deductible), may help in estate planning (proceeds from the life insurance policy can form a separate estate) and may qualify as part of a family trust (protection against creditors).

3.1 Empirical Evidences on Life Insurance Policies

The theory that life insurance policies protect against the possible death of household members so that the surviving members can continue to consume as before is backed by Hurd and Wise (1989), who observe sharp declines in living standards among women upon the death of their spouse. This is supported by Auerbach and Kotlikoff (1991) who find that 25% to 30% of women will suffer a loss in consumption if widowed.

On the contrary, Bernheim et al. (2003) find that the average change in living standards resulting from a spouse's death is small, both in absolute terms and relative to the decline that would occur without insurance. On further analysis, however, the study highlights that the average concealed a mismatch between life insurance holdings and financial vulnerabilities. The most vulnerable households do not purchase more insurance coverage, while the least vulnerable have large insurance holdings. There are substantial uninsured financial vulnerabilities, particularly among low-income households, couples with very different earnings, relatively young households, couples with dependent children and non-whites. Households are more inclined to protect wives than husbands and secondary earners than primary earners.

He (2011) observes that individuals with lower mortality risk (risk of premature death or death before retirement) are more likely to lapse or cancel a policy and to cancel one of greater value than individuals with higher mortality risk.

Fang and Kung (2012) note that richer, younger, healthier, married and higher income individuals are more likely to own life insurance policies than poorer, older, unhealthier, widowed and lower income individuals and that changes in marital status and other variables related to bequest motives lead policyholders to adjust their life insurances by either lapsing with no coverage or lapsing by re-optimizing coverages. In addition, individuals who have experienced negative health shocks are more likely to keep their existing policies. The study concludes that income and health shocks are relatively more important than bequest motive shocks in explaining life insurance lapsations when the policyholders are young. However, as the policyholders age, bequest motive shocks become more important in explaining lapsations than income and health shocks.

Life insurance policies take three basic forms, namely, term or temporary insurance, whole life or permanent insurance and endowment. Of these, term policies are the cheapest, while endowments are the dearest. Life insurance policies may have attached riders, which are extras that can be added to give increased protection for an extra premium. Popular riders include critical illnesses, total and permanent disability benefits, personal accident benefits and hospitalization benefits.

3.2 Whole Life Policies

A whole life insurance policy covers a person's entire life usually at a fixed premium. If a policyholder surrenders the policy to the insurance company before the end of the coverage period, there is usually some cash surrender value. The cash surrender value does not depend on the health status of the policyholder at the time of surrender.

Some whole life policies participate in the profits of the insurer. The policyholder's share of the profits is called a bonus. It may be in the form of cash. If it adds to the sum assured, it is known as simple reversionary bonus. If the bonus is computed based on the sum assured plus the reversionary bonus previously declared, it is known as compound reversionary bonus. If an additional bonus is paid at maturity, it is known as maturity or terminal bonus. Over time, a whole life policy builds up cash surrender value which can be used in several ways: (1) it can be paid to the policy holder should he decide to terminate the policy, (2) it can be used to pay future premiums should the policy holder decide to convert to a paid-up insurance policy and (3) it can be borrowed by the policyholder at an appropriate interest rate.

3.3 Term Policies

A term life insurance policy covers a person for a specified duration at a fixed or variable premium for each year. If the insured dies during the coverage period, the life insurance company pays the face amount of the policy provided the premium payment did not lapse.

If the insured survives the period, there is no payout. As a term policy does not accumulate cash surrender value, it is cheaper and is particularly useful if maximum coverage is needed for a short period of time. If continued coverage after the said period is desirable, a non-cancellable guaranteed renewable policy is advisable.

3.3.1 Empirical Evidences on Term Policies

Inkmann and Michaelides (2012) use term insurance data to make a case for the presence of the bequest motive. They focus on retired households in order to eliminate the possibility of employer-provided life insurance and exclude households with outstanding mortgages in order to rule out life insurance required by mortgage contracts. They find that the demand for term insurance is associated with variables related to bequest motives such as marriage, parenthood and a stated preference to leave bequests.

3.4 Endowment Policies

For many households, saving a portion of their earnings is too difficult because of its non-compulsory nature. For these households, buying insurance policies packaged as saving plans make sense. Once the insurance policy is bought, the insured must pay the premiums or lose the policy, that is, he will be forced to save. All insurance saving plans are based on endowment insurance policies.

An endowment insurance policy pays on death or maturity, whichever comes first. Premiums are paid during the life of the insured or until maturity, whichever is shorter. The policy combines saving and protection against risk. It provides a lump sum for dependents in case of premature death or a lump sum on maturity for the insured's own use.

An education insurance policy is an endowment insurance policy taken on the life of the parent with the child as the named beneficiary. The purpose is a forced saving plan toward a targeted amount. If the parent dies and the premiums stop, the child will still get the full amount at maturity. If the child dies before maturity, the policy pays the sum insured to the parent.

A variation of the endowment insurance policy is the growth insurance policy where the premium is paid in the form of a single lump sum upfront.

3.4.1 Empirical Evidences on Endowment Policies

Inkmann and Michaelides (2012) separate their sample into stockholders and non-stockholders to make a distinction between the wealthier and more educated households who can better afford financial products and understand financial markets. They find that stockholders, who are wealthier and better educated than non-stockholders, are more likely to invest in endowment plans.

3.5 Annuities

An annuity is a life insurance policy in reverse. It protects the annuitant against the event of living longer than expected—a possibility which the annuitant wishes to occur. This situation is in sharp contrast to life assurance which insures a person against his unwanted death. In this respect, an annuity is a unique insurance product because it sets up a clear conflict of interest in which the annuitant effectively desires the insured event (longevity) to happen.

The annuitant pays (1) a lump sum single premium or (2) a fixed annual premium or (3) a flexible premium to an insurance company who guarantees a regular income for an agreed period of time. The premium varies depending on the age at which the annuity is purchased, the age at which annuity payments begin and extra benefits such as medical consultations.

The length of the annuity can be (1) for the life of the annuitant without refund, (2) for an agreed term with the balance returned to beneficiaries if the annuitant dies before the end of the term or (3) for a guaranteed fixed period during which if the annuitant dies, his beneficiaries get the balance but if the annuitant lives beyond the fixed period, the receipts will continue until his death.

It can cover one life (a simple life annuity where the annuity receipts end when the annuitant dies) or more than one life (a joint life survivorship annuity where the annuity receipts end when both the annuitant and co-annuitant die).

The annuity receipt interval can be monthly, quarterly, semi-annually or yearly. The receipts can start immediately or after an agreed time lapse. Generally, annuity receipts receive favorable tax treatment.

The primary advantage of an annuity is the implied insurance against outliving one's assets (Shu et al. 2018). People who expect to live longer or those who are more risk averse will find annuities attractive.

The primary disadvantage is the transfer of the assets to the insurance company, which means they are not available for transfer to beneficiaries or for use during emergencies.

3.5.1 Empirical Evidences on Annuities

In the US, annuities are not important until the 1930s when its popularity suddenly grew for two main reasons (Poterba 1997). First, the group annuity market for corporate pension plans began to develop in the 1930s. Second, the 1929 stock market crash saw the flight toward safe haven investments such as annuities.

However, things changed in the late 1930s when the mortality tables for pricing annuities were revised to incorporate the increase in life expectancies, resulting in higher premiums. In addition, the US Congress established the Old Age and Survivors insurance program in 1935 as a mandatory retirement income system under Social Security. The key characteristic of Social Security as a pay-as-you-go payroll tax financing and a redistributive defined benefit plan addressed many policy concerns in the aftermath of the Great Depression.

What is the rationale of providing old age annuities through Social Security, a forced saving program, instead of allowing individuals to save and provide for themselves via the private market for annuities?

Several arguments were put forward (Diamond 1977). First, the pay-as-you-go program serves the function of income redistribution. Second, individuals may underestimate their life expectancies and may not have the discipline to plan for their own retirement. Third, individuals may not be able to purchase annuities if they have higher than average mortality risk or may not have a long enough working life to accumulate sufficient funds. Fourth, Social Security would eliminate unnecessary and wasteful marketing and advertising costs by insurance companies which would ultimately have to be shouldered by the annuitants. Finally, there is the possibility that the insurance companies may become insolvent.

Studies have shown that, apart from public social security, households spend very little on private annuities (Warshawsky 1988, 1997). Below are some possible explanations.

The standard explanation for the low demand is the high premiums to compensate insurers for adverse selection. Those who buy annuities tend to be in good health and may live longer than the average person. Therefore, insurance companies will charge high premiums to protect themselves. The high premiums will naturally reduce the attractiveness of annuities (Mitchell et al. 1999). Evidences show that an average annuity policy available to a 65-year-old man in 1995 delivers annuity receipts of between 80 cents and 85 cents per dollar of premium paid, with substantial heterogeneity across providers (Mitchell et al. 1999).

Next is the presence of pre-existing annuitized resources such as annuity income streams from public retirement programs, an example of which is Social Security. Brown and Poterba (2000) confirm that single individuals who have pre-existing annuity wealth demand less additional annuities. For the median retired couple, Dushi and Webb (2004) find that a high proportion of pre-annuitized wealth explains why they fail to voluntarily annuitize. Inkmann et al. (2011) confirm that the annuity market participation is decreasing in pension income.

Intergenerational altruism has been explored as a potential explanation for limited annuity demand (Laitner 1997). The idea is that a parent household may transfer resources to a child household and vice versa. The reason is presumably because people care for their close ones and seek to maximize a combination of lifetime well-being not only for themselves but also for their close relations.

People who wish to bequest some wealth will annuitize less. Bernheim (1991) concludes that households have strong bequest motives and that a significant fraction of their saving is for that purpose. Inkmann et al. (2011) find that a possible bequest motive for the surviving spouse leads to lower annuity participation.

Hurd (1987), on the other hand, presents evidence contrary to the bequest motive because he finds no difference in the wealth decumulation of households with and without children.

However, Bernheim (1991) argues that the seemingly contrasting results can be reconciled. First, childless households may still wish to leave bequests to relatives. Second, those with children may not need as much precautionary saving as they have altruistic children to take care of them.

There is also evidence that consumption and bequest sharing arrangements within marriage and larger families may be a substitute for risk sharing via annuities. For example, a couple can pool their resources with one inheriting everything when the other dies so that the one who lives longest is aided by the other's estate. This can explain why married couples place lower value on purchasing annuities. Adding a third adult such as a grown child broadens the risk sharing. For example, the two parents and the adult child can come to an agreement that if the parents die young, the child will inherit the sum but if either or both parents live to a ripe old age and the sum is exhausted, the child will step forward with financial support (Kotlikoff and Spivak 1981).

In addition, the trust and information sharing within the family alleviate the moral hazard problem, adverse selection problem, transaction cost and deception commonly encountered in the insurance market (Kotlikoff and Spivak 1981).

Brown and Poterba (2000) find that married couples value joint and survivor annuity products even less than single individuals value single life annuities. Given the significant fraction of married couples in the population, the study can help explain the limited size of the private annuity market.

Another possible reason is the uncertainty surrounding medical payments and long-term nursing care. Peijnenburg et al. (2017) find that medical expense risk increases the need for liquidity so households may choose to hold liquid wealth and annuitize less. This is especially so if the medical expense risk is high in the early years of retirement.

Yet another reason is the lack of cognitive ability or financial literacy to make the right decision (Inkmann et al. 2011). Simon et al. (2015) measure the personal discount rates (PDR) of military personnel by giving them a choice of accepting an immediate cash payment of US$30,000 versus a more generous retirement pension. Military personnel with higher PDR tend to save less, face more financial difficulties and pay higher interest rates on credit cards and car loans. The study confirms that individuals with higher cognitive ability are better informed about their retirement choices.

Aversion of annuity may be due to behavioral biasness. Survey evidence shows that the manner in which an annuity is presented to customers plays a primary role in its receptiveness. Respondents will prefer an annuity over alternative products when presented in a consumption frame that considers consequences for lifelong consumption. When presented in an investment frame, annuities are unattractive as they exhibit high risk without high returns. This shows the importance of framing for annuities (Brown et al. 2008).

Finally, the lack of actuarially fair annuities can be a possible explanation for the low participation rate (Mitchell et al. 1999; Finkelstein and Poterba 2002, 2004).

4 Types of General Insurance Policies

Unlike life insurance policies which protect against events that will definitely happen, general insurance policies protect (1) the insured against events that may or may not happen such as critical illnesses, accidents or unfortunate incidents during travels and (2) the insured's personal possessions such as crops, motor vehicles, property and home contents against events that may or may not happen such as accidents, robberies, droughts and floods.

4.1 Disability Income Protection

Disability income protection (DIP) offers financial support while individuals adjust or adapt to their disabilities. It pays a guaranteed monthly income should the insured be too sick or injured to work. The premiums paid will depend on the occupational categories whether professional, white collared, qualified or unskilled, as well as the benefit (between two-thirds to three-quarters of the normal income), the term (one to five years up to a specified age) and the waiting period (two weeks to three months before benefits are paid). DIP is one of the most complex policies because (1) the definition of personal income may be an area of contention, (2) the policy may be worded to offset other income received such as worker's compensation and (3) the disability may be defined based on the effect on earning capacity or the ability to perform the insured's usual occupation or just any gainful work.

4.1.1 Empirical Evidences on DIP

Börsch-Supran et al. (2017) study the effect of disability income (DI) benefits on health. They find a higher rate of the patient's recovery from the disability in countries with generous DI. The results are similar for both work disabled persons who received DI and those who did not. They conclude that the interrelationship between the generosity of the DI system and the effect of DI receipt on health is unclear.

4.2 Medical Insurance

The soaring cost of medical care is a concern to many. It is estimated that 80% of a person's lifetime medical expenses are spent in the last two years of his life. Room costs, charges for operating theaters, medications, dressings when added to the bills of the surgeon and anesthetist for a simple operation can be a sizable sum. Long-term illnesses like AIDS, cancer, heart disease, stroke and kidney disease are even more draining.

Medical insurance can be divided into two broad categories: (1) hospital and surgical and (2) hospital benefits.

Hospital and surgical cover expenses incurred when an individual is admitted which include operating theatre, surgery, X-rays and other fees. These expenses are claimable with detailed hospital receipts. An individual can only claim against one hospital and surgical insurance policy for each hospital stay. Most hospital and surgical insurance policies have a deductible, that is, they do not cover the full cost of the stay.

Hospital benefits refer to hospital cash amounts per day up to a maximum number of days per year. These benefits may include long-term care in nursing homes and rehabilitation costs. It is possible to claim against multiple hospital benefit insurance policies.

4.2.1 Empirical Evidences on Health Insurance

The fraction of people with health insurance increases with income and age (DeNavas-Walt et al. 2008).

Unlike standard health insurance policies that primarily pay for the diagnosis and treatment of medical conditions, long-term care insurance policies are designed to help pay for assistance with basic functions of daily living, whether at home or at an institution, and for individuals who have physical or cognitive impairments. Theory suggests that individuals should value such policies which insure against highly uncertain but potentially costly events, but many are not covered.

Brown and Finkelstein (2007) suggest that supply-side factors have an impact on the pricing of long-term care insurance policies but high premiums cannot fully explain the limited size of the market. Other plausible explanations include lack of understanding, role of substitutes such as families in providing care and the role of public insurance programs (Brown and Finkelstein 2007).

Brown and Finkelstein (2009) observe that long-term care insurance of elderly individuals aged 60 and above is increasing in wealth, with 3%, 6%, 11% and 20% for the bottom, second, third and top quartiles, respectively. Thus, one factor affecting demand is wealth.

4.3 Critical Illness, Dread Disease and Trauma Insurance Policies

Critical illness, dread disease and trauma insurance policies are meant for major illnesses which require long-term treatment and significant lifestyle changes. Such policies are designed to pay a lump sum on diagnosis so that the insured has the opportunity to seek specialist treatment and maintain his lifestyle.

Critical illness insurance policies can be stand-alone policies or riders attached to other policies. Claims under critical illness policies do not affect benefits under disability policy and income protection policy so an individual can buy multiple critical illness policies, if they wish to have additional protection.

4.3.1 Empirical Evidence on Critical Illness Insurance

Eling et al. (2017) find adverse selection in the group insurance market for critical illnesses. Adverse selection refers to the tendency for individuals with higher risk to purchase the insurance than those with lower risk. The paper documents that adverse selection diminishes if the group renews its critical illness insurance with the same insurer. They attribute this to the insurer learning about the group, which enables the insurer to charge fair premiums accordingly.

4.4 Travel Insurance

When on holiday abroad, coverage from life insurance policies, worldwide accident insurance policies, disability income insurance policies and critical illness insurance policies continue to apply.

However, the same cannot be said for hospital and surgical, and hospital benefits insurance policies. Travel insurance policies are required to cover these gaps and other inconveniences such as lost baggages, damaged baggages, baggage delays, loss of hand phones, trip cancelations due to illnesses, bushfires or earthquakes, travel delays due to weather, strike or mechanical breakdown, evacuation due to injury or illness, repatriation of remains, and personal liability to a third party for injury, loss or damage to property. Travel insurance policies are priced according to the type of events covered, the amount of coverage, the length of travel and the destination countries. As claims can only be made against only one policy per trip, it is unnecessary to buy multiple travel insurance policies. However, when renting a vehicle, it is advisable to buy the insurance offered as many travel insurance policies do not cover injuries or damages caused to third parties when a rented vehicle is used.

4.4.1 Empirical Evidences on Travel Insurance

Johnson et al. (1993) examine how much a group of US university students would pay for terrorism travel insurance to Thailand. Respondents were split into two groups. The first group provided estimates for a half trip, while the second group reported the price for a round trip. The results show that the flight back and ground coverage were judged to be more valuable. The paper concludes that the insurance decisions are based on distorted beliefs concerning the probability and size of losses.

Lo et al. (2011) study the uptake of travel risk-reduction strategies by Hong Kong residents. They find that female travelers with higher income and education, more experienced travelers and those traveling to long-haul destinations are more likely to buy travel insurance.

Sarman et al. (2019) survey international travelers from Australia, Canada, the UK and the US. They find that personality traits of conscientiousness and neuroticism are positively related to travel insurance purchase behavior. They conclude that travel insurance is a normal good. Older travelers and those who seek advice from a commercial operator in the process of travel booking are more likely to purchase travel insurance.

4.5 *Car Insurance*

It is compulsory for all road vehicles to have third-party insurance against unlimited liability for deaths or injuries to third parties and passengers. The insurance covers the people in the other vehicle and passengers in the driver's vehicle, but not the driver or the vehicles involved.

A more comprehensive insurance policy will cover unlimited liability for deaths or injuries to third parties and passengers, as well as the vehicles involved in the accident. It will also pay for market value of the car if it is stolen. However, it does not cover the driver himself.

The driver may choose to have extra protection such as personal accident insurance to guard against injuries and death, to cover accommodation and the cost of hiring a car when stranded because of accident or theft.

The premium charged by the insurance company depends on the sum insured, the make of the car (rare cars with expensive replacement parts require higher premiums), style of the car (sports cars attract thieves and therefore require higher premiums), engine capacity of the car (higher engine capacity are capable of greater speed and therefore require higher premiums), driver's claim record (clean records enjoy premium discounts) and age of driver (younger inexperienced drivers require higher premiums).

There are certain oversights to avoid. Before young family members with new licenses are allowed to drive the family car, they will have to be added to the insurance policy first with premiums adjusted accordingly. Car enthusiasts who modify their suspensions, add turbochargers or special carburettors may get into trouble if they do not inform the insurance companies. Certain modification may invalidate the insurance policy or may result in higher premiums.

4.5.1 Empirical Evidences on Car Insurance

There is a general consensus that adverse selection is absent in the automotive insurance market. Chiappori and Salanie (2000), Dionne et al. (2001), Saito (2006) and Zavadil (2015) find no evidence of a systematic relationship between risk and coverage in the French, Quebec, the Netherlands and Japanese automobile insurance markets, respectively.

Spindler et al. (2014) leverage on the unique institutional setting in Germany where there are two tiers of automotive insurance, namely, basic and complete coverages. They find evidence of adverse selection only for the automotive insurance with basic coverage. They attribute the results to the experience rating system in Germany that is required for automotive insurance with complete coverage.

Some studies go further to make a distinction between adverse selection and moral hazard. The former argues that riskier drivers seek more insurance. The latter proposes that drivers become riskier because they have insurance. However, to test this would require access to information about risk preferences before and after the drivers sign up for automotive insurance.

Li et al. (2007) and Wang et al. (2008) find evidence of moral hazard among automotive drivers in Taiwan. Gao et al. (2017) conduct a similar study in China but did not find evidence of ex ante moral hazard.

4.6 Property and Home Content Insurance

It is in the interests of the household and that of the lender to protect the home and loan collateral, respectively. In fact, home insurance against loss or damage caused by fire and other perils (such as explosion, storm, earthquake, theft and flood) is often a requirement of a mortgage. Standard home insurance policies cover the residential buildings, garages, fences, in-ground pool and permanent fixtures like light fittings, air conditioners, shower screens, toilets, baths, pipes, cables and wires. Common exclusions include damages caused by termites, pets, war, terrorism and residents.

An accidental damage insurance policy, as opposed to a defined events insurance policy, covers everything except exclusions. As the exclusions in both a defined events insurance policy and an accidental damage insurance policy are generally the same, the coverage under an accidental damage policy is much wider.

Some homeowners also purchase mortgage insurance to cover the outstanding loan on the home. This is to protect dependents in the event of an untimely end.

Some buy a separate home content insurance to protect their household goods and valuables such as furniture, household appliances, jewelry, antiques and collectibles. The premiums will vary depending on the choice of coverage, whether replacement/reinstatement or indemnity.

Under a replacement policy, the insured gets new for old, while under an indemnity policy, the insured gets the depreciated value. The premiums also vary depending on geographical coverage (e.g., protecting a watch against risk of physical loss and damage anywhere in the world).

Some homeowners buy a personal legal liability insurance policy to protect against legal claims and expenses for accidents resulting in death or injury within their properties, for example, a guest slipping and breaking his leg.

4.6.1 Empirical Evidences on Property and Casualty Insurance Policies

Homeowners underestimate the probability of a disaster (McClelland et al. 1993). Some are myopic in their focus on the upfront costs instead of the delayed benefits of claim payments (Meyer and Hutchinson 2001). Some have separate mental accounts for different expenditures and a fixed budget for different categories (Thaler 1999). Some are influenced by actions of neighbors (Heal and Kunreuther 2005). Some do not know the probability of these events and the prevailing premiums (Kunreuther and Pauly 2004). Better information about the probabilities and the level of insurer loading charges may help to simplify the purchase decision and motivate better insurance coverage.

Browne and Hoyt (2000) observe that flood insurance purchase is affected by price and income, with the take-up being positively related to prior year disaster losses. Dixon et al. (2006) show that demand of flood insurance is affected by price and that people subject to coastal flooding are more likely to demand for insurance.

Zahran et al. (2009) find that prior flood experience, proximity to floodplain and higher education attainment levels are positively correlated with flood insurance take-up rates. Kousky (2010) concludes that the take-up rate for flood insurance increases with high-risk floodplains but decreases with levee protection along major rivers. Atreya et al. (2015) find that flood insurance penetration rates are higher for coastal areas and recent floods temporarily increase insurance purchases but the effect fades after three years.

Studies have found that the purchase of flood insurance increases with education and age (Kunreuther et al. 1978; Baumann and Sims 1978; Atreya et al. 2015). In addition, race seems to matter with African Americans more likely to purchase flood insurance (Atreya et al. 2015).

In addition to the risk of flood, there is the risk of drought. Gine et al. (2008) examine rainfall insurance policies offered to small farmers in the Andhra Pradesh region of southern India. These policies, sold in small unit sizes, are available before the start of a monsoon season and pay when rainfall is below a threshold. The study finds that purchase of rainfall insurance increases with wealth, land and understanding but decreases with borrowing constraints.

A follow-up study finds that farmers who receive a positive liquidity shock are more likely to buy rainfall insurance (Cole et al. 2013). The effect is stronger among less wealthy farmers.

However, while the demand for rainfall insurance is price sensitive, lower prices (generated by subsidies, greater efficiencies or competitions) are insufficient to induce widespread adoption. Other factors such as lack of trust or understanding of the insurance product, liquidity constraints due to competing uses for limited funds and limited attention present important barriers to adoption (Cole et al. 2013).

Although liberal aid is forthcoming from the government if the magnitude of the destruction is massive, there is little empirical evidence to suggest that the expectation of disaster relief discourages individuals from investing in risk mitigation measures and purchasing insurance to manage risk ex ante (Kunreuther 2006). Atreya et al. (2015) do not find that government investment in mitigation and the demand for flood insurance are substitutes. Similarly, Zahran et al. (2009) and Botzen et al. (2009) show that government mitigation efforts (which translate to flood premium discounts) lead to more people buying flood insurance.

5 Reasons for Underinsurance

Underinsurance refers to not having a policy or having a policy without sufficient coverage. This can arise due to economic features that make insurance unattainable, limitations of insurance benefit design or barriers to accessing healthcare (Lavarreda et al. 2011).

Regarding economic features that make insurance unattainable, Bernheim et al. (2003) find that underinsurance is more common among couples with asymmetric earnings, couples with dependent children, low-income households and younger households. These households will have to make a tradeoff between insurance and other goods. The economics of these tradeoffs are governed by price, income distribution and preferences.

With regard to price, some do not buy insurance because of information asymmetries which lead them to believe that the premiums are actuarially unfair (Mitchel 2011). With regard to income distribution, some households put other financial priorities and spending needs before a policy purchase (Mitchel 2003). Other reasons for underinsurance include unawareness about the need for insurance (Mitchel 2003).

To increase insurance penetration, it is necessary to take into account the social needs of households and the economic choices that households face (Levy and DeLeire 2008).

Given that some households find insurance planning complex, Caponecchia and Tan (2019) recommend simpler products. Redzuan et al. (2016) propose that governments undertake liberalization measures, provide tax reliefs for life insurance and expand social security coverage.

6 Labor Income Risk and Mortgage Choice

As the home is the largest asset purchase for most, mortgage choice is an important aspect of household risk management and can have large impact on household welfare. The choice between the two conventional mortgages, adjustable-rate mortgages (ARMs) and fixed-rate mortgages (FRMs), depends crucially on labor income characteristics. This is because markets are not complete. Households have problems borrowing against future income and insuring against labor income risk. Labor income risk refers to the uncertainty of future income streams.

ARMs are exposed to the risk of variability in monthly payments if nominal interest rates increase. The variability will not matter if the household can borrow against future income. However, if borrowing constraints coincide with low income and low house prices, households may face unpleasant consequences. This is the income risk. Thus, households with larger mortgages relative to income and volatile income will avoid ARMs. Households with higher probabilities of moving and therefore higher chance of prepayment are more likely to use ARMs (Dhillon et al. 1987).

FRMs are sensitive to inflation. If nominal interest rate rises, the household gains from the cheap fixed rate. If nominal interest rate falls, households can take advantage of the prepayment option by taking out a new mortgage contract at a lower interest rate. The option to prepay comes at a cost of a higher interest rate on the FRM versus ARM. Thus, the FRM is expensive when inflation is stable. This is the wealth risk. FRMs appeal to risk-averse households with large mortgages, risky income, high default cost and low moving probability, but FRMs are risky in an environment with uncertain inflation.

Campbell and Cocco (2003) find large welfare gains from the availability of inflation-indexed FRMs where the interest rates are fixed in real terms. Some of the welfare gains arise from the reduced mortgage payments in the early part of the mortgage contract when borrowing constraints are more severe.

Kim and Ziobrowski (2016) compare how borrowers perceive the risk of ARMs and FRMs over time with the short-term interest rate level and housing market conditions. When short-term interest rates are high, borrowers perceive low risk that short-term rate will rise thus opting for ARM. When the housing market is down, households become more risk averse to fluctuations in rates thus opting for FRM.

7 Credit Risk and Credit Scores

Credit risk refers to the uncertainty that households are able to make timely payments on their loans.

With the substantial rise of credit card debt, there have been attempts to mitigate defaults by accessing information gained through relationship banking and by employing forbearance options such as lengthening repayment terms.

Agarwal et al. (2008) document that approximately 22% of the re-aged credit card accounts default again, mostly in the first 24 months after reinstatement. Figure 8.1 shows that reinstated credit card holders have a higher risk of a second default in the first 24 months after reinstatement than cardholders defaulting for the first time in the first 24 months after origination. Of those who did not default again, 78% saw an improvement in their credit scores. The study shows that the forbearance program helps to cure liquidity-constrained borrowers out of default.

Relationship banking can mitigate credit card risk. Agarwal et al. (2018) find that credit card account holders who have other relationships with the bank have lower default rates. The results are consistent with a monitoring effect where the lender has more information about the borrower.

Debt delinquency hurt households. Credit checks by companies prior to a hire can negatively affect the chances of landing a job if borrowers are delinquent in their credit card payments, mortgage installments or worse still default on a loan (Corbae et al. 2013). Poor credit scores depress wages and can affect one's career trajectory (Bos et al. 2018).

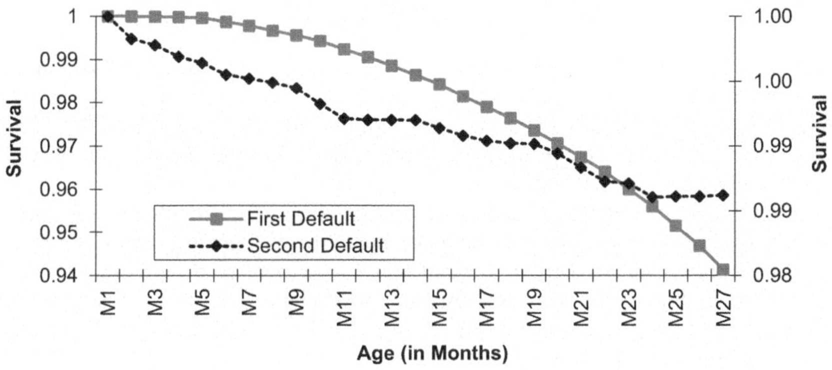

Fig. 8.1 Survival function for the first and second default. (Source: Agarwal et al. 2008)

8 Conclusion

Empirical evidences show that households do not make optimal insurance decisions. There is generally inadequate life insurance coverage and surviving members are less well off. Those who are more vulnerable do not purchase more insurance.

As for annuities to protect against living longer than expected, evidences show that households spend little on private annuities because of adverse selection issues, pre-existing public annuity programs, intergenerational altruism, risk sharing among family members, health cost risk, financial illiteracy and unfairly priced premiums.

There is also insufficient general insurance against low-probability high-loss catastrophic events. The underinsurance is mainly due to underestimation of risk, myopic focus on the upfront costs, lack of information on the probability of occurrence and the premiums to be paid.

General insurance purchases are positively related to wealth, prior experience, proximity to disaster areas, education level and age. There is evidence that race seems to matter. Government investment in mitigation measures and the expectation of government aid relief do not reduce the demand for insurance coverage.

Labor income risk is an important determinant of mortgage choice. If income is volatile and uncertain, households will prefer FRMs.

Proper credit risk management is critical for individuals as a poor credit record can affect their wage and career trajectory.

References

Actuaries Institute. 2016. The Impact of Big Data on the Future of Insurance. *Green Paper.*

Agarwal, Sumit, Souphala Chomsisengphet, and Lawrence Mielnicki. 2008. Do Forbearance Plans Help Mitigate Credit Card Losses? *Journal of Family Economics Issue* 29: 192–195.

Agarwal, Sumit, Souphala Chomsisengphet, Chunlin Liu, Changcheng Song, and Nicholas S. Souleles. 2018. Benefits of Relationship Banking: Evidence from Consumer Credit Markets. *Journal of Monetary Economics* 96: 16–32.

Atreya, Ajita, Susana Ferreira, and Erwann Michel-Kerjan. 2015. What Drives Households to Buy Flood Insurance? New Evidence from Georgia. *Ecological Economics* 117: 153–161.

Auerbach, Alan J., and Laurence J. Kotlikoff. 1991. The Adequacy of Life Insurance Purchases. *Journal of Financial Intermediation* 1 (3): 215–241.

Banks, Marcus, and Dina Bowman. 2017. *Juggling Risks: Insurance in Households Struggling with Financial Insecurity.* Brotherhood of St Laurence: Research and Policy Centre.

Baumann, Duane D., and John H. Sims. 1978. Flood Insurance: Some Determinants of Adoption. *Economic Geography* 54 (3): 189–196.

Bernheim, Douglas B. 1991. How Strong Are the Bequest Motives? Evidence Based on Estimates of the Demand for Life Insurance and Annuities. *Journal of Political Economy* 99 (5): 899–927.

Bernheim, Douglas B., Lorenzo Forni, Jagadeesh Gokhale, and Laurence J. Kotlikoff. 2003. The Mismatch between Life Insurance Holdings and Financial Vulnerabilities: Evidence from the Health and Retirement Study. *The American Economic Review* 93 (1): 354–365.

Börsch-Supran, Axel, Tabea Bucher-Koenen, and Felizia Hanemann. 2017. Does Disability Insurance Improve Health and Well-Being? MEA Discussion Paper Series 09-2017, Munich Center for the Economics of Aging at the Max Planck Institute for Social Law and Social Policy.

Bos, Marieke, Emily Breza, and Andres Liberman. 2018. The Labor Market Effects of Credit Market Information. *The Review of Financial Studies* 31 (6): 2005–2037.

Botzen, Wouter J.W., Jeroen C.J.H. Aerts, and Jeroen Van den Bergh. 2009. Willingness of Homeowners to Mitigate Climate Risk through Insurance. *Ecological Economics* 68 (8): 2265–2277.

Brown, Jeffrey R., and Amy Finkelstein. 2007. Why Is the Market for Long-Term Care Insurance So Small? *Journal of Public Economics* 91 (10): 1967–1991.

———. 2009. The Private Market for Long-Term Care Insurance in the US: A Review of the Evidence. *Journal of Risk and Insurance* 76 (1): 5–29.

Brown, Jeffrey R., and James M. Poterba. 2000. Joint Life Annuities and Annuity Demand by Married Couples. *Journal of Risk and Insurance* 67 (4): 527–553.

Brown, Jeffrey R., Jeffrey R. Kling, Sendhil Mullainathan, and Marian V. Wrobel. 2008. Why Don't People Insure Late-Life Consumption? A Framing Explanation of the Under-Annuitization Puzzle. *American Economic Review* 98 (2): 304–309.

Browne, Mark J., and Robert E. Hoyt. 2000. The Demand for Flood Insurance: Empirical Evidence. *Journal of Risk and Uncertainty* 20 (3): 291–306.

Campbell, John Y., and Joao F. Cocco. 2003. Household Risk Management and Optimal Mortgage Choice. *Quarterly Journal of Economics* 118 (4): 1449–1494.

Caponecchia, Carlo, and David T. Tan. 2019. Exploring the Traveler Underinsurance Problem. *Annals of Tourism Research* 76: 343–345.

Chiappori, Pierre-Andre, and Bernard Salanie. 2000. Testing for Asymmetric Information in Insurance Markets. *Journal of Political Economy* 108 (1): 56–78.

Cole, Shawn, Xavier Gine, Jeremy Tobacman, Petia Topalova, Robert Townsend, and James I. Vickery. 2013. Barriers to Household Risk Management: Evidence from India. *American Economic Journal: Applied Economics* 5 (1): 104–135.

Corbae, Dean, Andrew Glover, and Daphne Chen. 2013. Can Employer Credit Checks Create Poverty Traps? Paper presented at the 2013 meeting for the Society for Economic Dynamics. 2013 Meeting Papers 875, Society for Economic Dynamics.

DeNavas-Walt, Carmen, Bernadette D. Proctor, and Jessica C. Smith. 2008. *Income, Poverty and Health Insurance Coverage in the US: 2007*. United States Census Bureau.

De Vreyer, Philippe, and Sylvie Lambert. 2020. Inequality, Poverty and the Intra-household Allocation of Consumption in Senegal. The World Bank Economic Review: 1–22.

Dhillon, Upinder S., James D. Shilling, and C.F. Sirmans. 1987. Choosing between Fixed and Adjustable Rate Mortgages. *Journal of Money, Credit and Banking* 19: 260–267.

Diamond, Peter. 1977. A Framework for Social Security Analysis. *Journal of Public Economics* 8: 275–298.

Dionne, Georges, Christian Gouriéroux, and Charles Vanasse. 2001. Testing for Evidence of Adverse Selection in the Automobile Insurance Market: A Comment. *Journal of Political Economy* 109 (2): 444–453.

Dixon, Lloyd, Noreen Clancy, Seth A. Seabury, and Adrian Overton. 2006. *The National Flood Insurance Program's Market Penetration Rate: Estimates and Policy Implications*. Santa Monica, CA: Rand Corporation.

Dushi, Irene, and Anthony Webb. 2004. Annuitization: Keeping Your Options Open. Boston College Center for Retirement Research Working Paper No. 2004-04.

Eling, Martin, Ruo Jia, and Yi Yao. 2017. Between-Group Adverse Selection: Evidence from Group Critical Illness Insurance. *Journal of Risk and Insurance* 84 (2): 771–809.

Fang, Hanming, and Edward Kung. 2012. Why Do Life Insurance Policyholders Lapse? The Roles of Income, Health and Bequest Motive Shocks. NBER Working Paper #17899.

Finkelstein, Amy, and James M. Poterba. 2002. Selection Effects in the United Kingdom Individual Annuities Market. *Economic Journal* 112: 28–42.

———. 2004. Adverse Selection in Insurance Markets: Policyholder Evidence from the U.K. Annuity Market. *Journal of Political Economy* 112: 183–208.

Gao, Feng, Michael R. Power, and Jun Wang. 2017. Decomposing Asymmetric Information in China's Automobile Insurance Market. *Journal of Risk and Insurance* 84 (4): 1269–1293.

Gine, Xavier, Robert M. Townsend, and James I. Vickery. 2008. Patterns of Rainfall Insurance Participation in Rural India. *The World Bank Economic Review Advance Access* 22 (3): 539–566.

He, Daifeng. 2011. Is There Dynamic Adverse Selection in the Life Insurance Market? *Economic Letters* 112: 113–115.

Heal, Geoffrey M., and Howard C. Kunreuther. 2005. You Can Only Die Once: Interdependent Security in an Uncertain World. In *The Economic Impacts of Terrorist Attacks*, ed. Harry W. Richardson, Peter Gordan, and James E. Moore II. Cheltenham: Edward Elgar.

Hurd, Michael D. 1987. Savings of the Elderly and Desired Bequests. *American Economic Review* 77 (3): 298–312.

Hurd, Michael D., and David A. Wise. 1989. The Wealth and Poverty of Widows: Assets Before and After the Husband's Death. In *The Economics of Aging*, ed. David A. Wise, 177–199. University of Chicago Press.

Inkmann, Joachim, and Alexander Michaelides. 2012. Can the Life Insurance Market Provide Evidence for a Bequest Motive? *The Journal of Risk and Insurance* 79 (3): 671–695.

Inkmann, Joachim, Paula Lopes, and Alexander Michaelides. 2011. How Deep Is the Annuity Market Participation Puzzle? *Review of Financial Studies* 24 (1): 279–319.

Johnson, Eric J., John Hershey, Jacqueline Meszaros, and Howard Kunreuther. 1993. Framing, Probability Distortions, and Insurance Decisions. *Journal of Risk and Uncertainty* 7 (1): 35–51.

Kim, Dongshin, and Alan J. Ziobrowski. 2016. The Borrower's Perceived Risk in Mortgage Choice. *Real Estate Economics* 44 (3): 606–626.

Kotlikoff, Laurence J., and Avia Spivak. 1981. The Family as an Incomplete Annuities Market. *Journal of Political Economy* 89 (2): 372–391.

Kousky, Carolyn. 2010. Understanding the Demand for Flood Insurance. *Natural Hazards Review* 12 (2): 96–110.

Kunreuther, Howard C. 2006. Disaster Mitigation and Insurance: Learning from Katrina. *The Annals of the American Academy* 604: 208–227.

Kunreuther, Howard C., and Mark Pauly. 2004. Neglecting Disaster: Why Don't People Insure Against Large Losses? *The Journal of Risk and Uncertainty* 28 (1): 5–21.

Kunreuther, Howard C., Ralph Ginsberg, Louis Miller, Philip Sagi, Bradley Borkan, and Katz Norman. 1978. *Disaster Insurance Protection: Public Policy Lessons*. New York: John Wiley and Sons.

Laitner, John A. 1997. Intergenerational and Interhousehold Economic Links. In *Handbook of Population and Family Economics 1(A)*, ed. Mark Rosenzweig and Oded Stark, 190–235. Amsterdam, North Holland: Elsevier.

Lavarreda, Shana A., Richard E. Brown, and Claudie Dandurand Bolduc. 2011. Underinsurance in the United States: An Interaction of Costs to Consumers, Benefit Design, and Access to Care. *Annual Review of Public Health* 32 (1): 471–482.

Levy, Helen, and Thomas DeLeire. 2008. What Do People Buy When They Don't Buy Health Insurance and What Does that Say about Why They Are Uninsured. *Inquiry* 45 (4): 365–379.

Li, Chu-Shiu, Chwen-Chi Liu, and Jia-Hsing Yeh. 2007. The Incentive Effects of Increasing Per-Claim Deductible Contracts in Automobile Insurance. *Journal of Risk and Insurance* 74 (2): 441–459.

Lo, Ada S., Catherine Cheung, and Rob Law. 2011. Hong Kong Residents' Adoption of Risk Reduction Strategies in Leisure Travel. *Journal of Travel & Tourism Marketing* 28 (3): 240–260.

McClelland, Gary, William D. Schulze, and Don L. Coursey. 1993. Insurance for Low Probability Hazards: A Bimodal Response to Unlikely Events. *Journal of Risk and Uncertainty* 7: 95–116.

Meyer, Robert J., and Wesley J. Hutchinson. 2001. Bumbling Geniuses: The Power of Everyday Reasoning in Multi-stage Decision Making. In *Wharton on Making Decisions*, ed. Stephen J. Hoch and Howard C. Kunreuther, 37–61. New York: John Wiley and Sons.

Mitchel, James O. 2003. The Adequacy of Life Insurance Coverage in U.S. Households. *Journal of Financial Service Professionals* 57 (3): 54.

———. 2011. *Insurance Barometer Study*. USA LIFE Foundation and LL Global Inc.

Mitchell, Olivia S., James M. Poterba, Mark J. Warshawsky, and Jeffrey R. Brown. 1999. New Evidence on Money's Worth of Individual Annuities. *American Economic Review* 89 (5): 1299–1318.

Peijnenburg, Kim, Theo Nijman, and Bas J.M. Werker. 2017. Health Cost Risk: A Potential Solution to the Annuity Puzzle. *The Economic Journal* 127: 1598–1625.

Poterba, James M. 1997. The History of Annuities in the United States. NBER Working Paper #6001.

Quantum Market Research. 2013. The Understand Insurance Research Report. Insurance Council of Australia, Sydney.

Rampini, Adriano A., and S. Viswanathan. 2017. Household Risk Management. NBER Working Paper #22293.

Redzuan, Hendon, Rubayah Yakob, and Zaida Isa. 2016. Underinsurance in Malaysia: The Application of the Monte Carlo Simulation. *Journal Pengurusan* 47 (1): 131–142.

Robinson, Marguerite S. 2002. *The Microfinance Revolution: Lessons from Indonesia*. United States: The World Bank Group.

Rogg, Christian. 2006. Asset Portfolios in Africa: Evidence from Rural Ethiopia. WIDER Working Paper Series 145, World Institute for Development Economic Research UNU-WIDER.

Saito, Kazuya. 2006. Testing for Asymmetric Information in the Automobile Insurance Market Under Rate Regulation. *The Journal of Risk and Insurance* 73 (2): 335–356.

Sarman, Igor, Riccardo Curtale, and Homa Hajibaba. 2019. Drivers of Travel Insurance Purchase. *Journal of Travel Research* 59 (3): 545–558.

Shu, Suzanne B., Robert Zeithammer, and John W. Payne. 2018. The Pivotal Role of Fairness: Which Consumers Like Annuities? *Financial Planning Review* 1: 3–4.

Simon, Curtis J., John T. Warner, and Saul Pleeter. 2015. Discounting, Cognition and Financial Awareness: New Evidence from a Change in the Military Retirement System. *Economic Inquiry* 53 (1): 319–334.

Spindler, Martin, Joachim Winter, and Steffen Hagmayer. 2014. Asymmetric Information in the Market for Automobile Insurance: Evidence from Germany: Asymmetric Information in the Market for Automobile Insurance. *Journal of Risk and Insurance* 81 (4): 781–801.

Sugiyanto, Catur, Sri Y. Kusumastuti, and Duddy R. Donna. 2012. Managing Risks: How Do Poor Households Smooth Their Income and Consumption? (An Examination of Poor Households in Yogyakarta, Indonesia). Institute for Money, Technology and Financial Inclusion Working Paper.

Swedloff, Rick. 2014. Risk Classification's Big Data (R)evolution. *Connecticut Insurance Law Journal* 21: 339–373.

Thaler, Richard. 1999. Mental Accounting Matters. *Journal of Behavioral Decision Making* 12: 183–206.

Townsend, Robert M. 1994. Risk and Insurance in Village India. *Econometrica* 62 (3): 539–591.

Udry, Christopher. 1995. Risk and Saving in Northern Nigeria. *The American Economic Review* 85: 1287–1300.

Wang, Jennifer, Ching-Fan Chung, and Larry Y. Tzeng. 2008. An Empirical Analysis of the Effects of Increasing Deductibles on Moral Hazard. *Journal of Risk and Insurance* 75 (3): 551–566.

Warshawsky, Mark. 1988. Private Annuity Markets in the United States: 1919–1984. *Journal of Risk and Insurance* 55 (3): 518–528.
Warshawsky, Mark J. 1997. The Market for Individual Annuities and the Reform of Social Security. *Benefits Quarterly* 13 (3), 3rd Quarter: 66–76.
Zahran, Sammy, Stephan Weiler, Samuel D. Brody, Michael K. Lindell, and Wesley E. Highfield. 2009. Modeling National Flood Insurance Policy Holding at the County Scale in Florida, 1999–2005. *Ecological Economics* 68 (10): 2627–2636.
Zavadil, Tibor. 2015. Do the Better Insured Cause More Damage? Testing for Asymmetric Information in Car Insurance. *Journal of Risk and Insurance* 82 (4): 865–889.
Zeller, Manfred, Gertrud Schrieder, Joachim von Braun, and Franz Heidhues. 1997. Rural Finance for Food Security for the Poor. In *Food Policy Review*. International Food Policy Research Institute.

CHAPTER 9

Financial Inclusion and Financial Technology

1 Introduction

Financial exclusion is a problem prevalent in both emerging and developed economies. Financial exclusion prevents the poor and disadvantaged from accessing formal financial systems (Conroy 2005). As per the 2014 World Bank database, 6% of unbanked adults or 53 million people are from the Organization for Economic Co-operation and Development (OECD) countries (The World Bank Group 2015).

The unbanked and underbanked use alternate channels, such as money transfer services, check cashing services and loan facilities, to meet their financial needs but face exorbitant pricing.

Money transfer services include remittances and prepaid cards. According to the World Bank Group (2016), the global average fee paid on remittances is a high 8%. This is way beyond the 3% goal set as the Sustainable Development Goal (SDG) by the United Nations to reduce inequality within and among countries.

Loan facilities include pawn shops, rent-to-own services, pay-check advances and payday lenders. These are usually at very high rates. A study finds that consumers who rent goods and pay weekly rent end up paying several times the actual cost (Financial Inclusion Center 2016).

S. Agarwal et al., *Household Finance*,
https://doi.org/10.1007/978-981-15-5526-8_9

1.1 Microfinance

Traditional banks had been reluctant to cater to the neglected segment because of their unknown risk profile, low income, limited wealth and geographic dispersion which made them too expensive to serve and the returns too low to bother.

In the 1990s, microfinance initiatives such as the Grameen Bank drew attention to lending through well-organized groups, replacing economic collateral with the discipline of peer pressure to ensure repayment and financial sustainability of these initiatives.

Unfortunately, by 2008, there were concerns of over-indebtedness and skepticism about the development potential of microfinance (Duvendack et al. 2011). The microcredits were directed toward very small one-person businesses of low productivity and low odds of survival (Bateman 2015).

1.2 Financial Inclusion and Financial Stability

The 2008 World Bank Annual Report, titled "Finance for All" (The World Bank 2008), reframed the focus from microcredit to a broader term "financial inclusion" which encompasses a wider range of financial products including saving, payment and lending to households and small businesses (Soederberg 2013). However, the global financial crisis in the same year cast doubt on the wisdom of encouraging market-based financial inclusion in the face of risky subprime loans (French et al. 2009).

To shed light on the murky issue, the World Bank published its 2014 Global Financial Development Report rejecting any correlation between financial inclusion and financial instability across a large set of high- and low-income countries (Cihak et al. 2013). The report supports market-based financial inclusion and pushes for private sector innovation of new products and services to "address market failures, meet consumer needs, and overcome behavioral problems" (The World Bank 2013). It believes that financial inclusion is a remedy for inequality and will promote development.

The Alliance for Financial Inclusion (AFI), a network of policy makers and regulators from 90 developing countries, was created in 2011 with funding from the philanthropic organization Bill and Melinda Gates Foundation. Half of its members signed the Maya Declaration to "reach the world's 2.5 billion unbanked" and work with the private sector to establish national financial inclusion strategies (AFI 2014a). The major

Maya commitments include financial literacy, digital financial services, financial sector regulation and financial inclusion data (AFI 2013b, 2015). The AFI aims to use digital financial services to solve the problems of financial access for the unbanked by tapping on their digital footprint and mobile phone usage.

In 2014, Omidyar Network became the second philanthropic organization after the Gates Foundation to partner with AFI (Gabor and Brooks 2017). Omidyar funds and invests in financial technology (FinTech) companies with the potential to evaluate the credit risk of the poor through digital technologies.

1.3 Financial Inclusion in the Digital Age

The pervasiveness of mobile connectivity and smartphone technology opens up new commercial possibilities. Accumulated digital information allows financial service providers to profile each individual customer. These information go beyond e-payment and receipt records to include other digital footprint such as mobile phone records and social network traffic. The harvesting of these digital data enable lenders to map, know and reach previously excluded groups (Bankable Frontier Associates 2014), ultimately to advise, influence and serve them. FinTech has not only made it possible to stake a claim on the neglected segment but to do so in an economically profitable manner.

The reluctance of banks to respond to the needs of the unbanked and underbanked has made room for internet companies, telecoms and start-ups to exercise their ingenuity to make financial inclusion into a viable business model and develop alternative systems.

Stulz (2019) ascribes this to (1) the stringent regulations of banks which stifle their growth, (2) banks' legacy IT systems that hinder the integration of FinTech innovation and (3) organizational friction inherent in diversified financial conglomerates which reduce their efficiency and value.

Challenger banks in the UK, such as N26, Revolut, Starling, Monese, Monzo and Tandem, offer digital banking where customers can access expert advice online for both saving and lending products. These online-only banks not only compete directly with the more established banks but also reach out to the underserved. In 2015, their total lending increased 31.5%, while the Big Five Lenders (Barclays, HSBC, Lloyds Banking Group, Santander and Royal Bank of Scotland) lost 4.9% (Lu 2017).

New financial intermediaries that do not accept traditional deposits and therefore fall outside the realm of regulatory oversight have also expanded rapidly. Buchak et al. (2018) estimate that the market share in mortgage origination of these shadow banks has grown from 30% in 2007 to 50% in 2015. They find that the legal and regulatory burden can explain 60% of shadow bank growth, while the lending technology can explain another 30%.

Stulz (2019), however, is skeptical that traditional banks can be fully replaced. Traditional banks have a large and established consumer base, offer a broad range of products, are experienced in dealing with regulators and, above all, provide the essential service of deposit accounts guaranteed by deposit insurance.

Nonetheless, recent developments have forced traditional banks to rethink their strategies. Many banks have ventured into internet technology in a big way, investing in digital banking and partnering with FinTech companies (Pizzala and Webster 2015). It is estimated that, in 2019, US banks spent US$67 billion on technology to create a more open and inclusive system (Shevlin 2019).

2 FinTech

While technology has helped to make other industries more functional and efficient, the unit cost of financial intermediation has stayed stagnant at approximately 2% of asset value for the past 130 years (Philippon 2015). This is until the arrival of newer businesses that offer financial services at a lower unit cost bypassing traditional intermediaries such as banks.

Although financial technology is not new and incumbents have never been short of new technologies, the term FinTech encapsulates the feared disruptions that have rocked the financial industry.

According to a World Economic Forum report (2015), innovations in financial services are likely to surface where customer frictions give rise to profit opportunities. They are the most impactful where the business model is platform-based, data intensive, capital light and scalable.

The emergence of FinTech and the attendant disruptions are due to a confluence of several factors.

First, technology has opened new doors for competitors to offer alternative digital payment services such as smartphones with contactless payment technologies at point of sale, integrated billing and next-generation security. These secure and reliable digital payment systems offer convenience and peace of mind to consumers.

Second, technology has changed consumer behavior—from browsing in brick-and-mortar stores to online shopping in the comfort of their homes, from meeting relationship managers to interacting with robo-advisors and from joining the queue at the local branch to conducting a multitude of financial services via digital banking. Consumers have been conditioned to demand for higher levels of responsiveness, immediacy, convenience and customization. Accordingly, businesses have to adapt and adopt an integrated digital approach to engage customers.

Third, the use of digital footprint harvested from online transactions has made it easier to screen borrowers and facilitate lending to the previously unbanked. This has eroded the information competitive advantage that incumbents used to possess (Stulz 2019).

Fourth, heavy regulations post 2008 and the increased compliance costs have hindered the growth of the incumbents. New businesses, not subject to these restrictions, are at an advantage. They can provide the same services at a lower cost (Stulz 2019).

Most importantly, FinTech can thrive because there is an ecosystem that connects financial intermediaries, retailers and consumers through a real-time and secure global network. The infrastructure is ready and the stars are aligned for technology to disrupt and usurp as never before.

Chen et al. (2019) formulate a proposed typology of FinTech comprising seven categories, namely (1) cybersecurity (encryption, tokenization, authentication and biometrics), (2) mobile transactions (smartphone, wallets and near-field communications [NFC]), (3) data analytics (big data, cloud computing, machine learning and artificial intelligence), (4) blockchain (cryptocurrency, proof of work, smart contracts and directed acyclic graphs), (5) peer-to-peer (crowdfunding, peer-to-peer [P2P] lending and customer-to-customer payment), (6) robo-advising (artificial intelligence, big data and machine learning) and (7) internet of things (gather data and communicate via internet, smart devices, NFC, wireless sensor networks and actuators).

Using a valuation method that combines stock price responses and patent filing intensities, Chen et al. (2019) find that the most valuable FinTech innovations are internet of things (IoT), robo-advising and blockchain.

2.1 *Financial Innovations*

2.1.1 *Sustaining Innovations*

Some of the financial innovations in retail banking target existing customers. These sustaining innovations improve processes so that services can be offered at a lower cost and user experiences can be enhanced. They are incremental improvements aimed at existing customers (Christensen and Raynor 2003).

In the 1950s, banks significantly expanded credit payments by offering revolving credit and their own credit cards. The 1960s saw the replacement of bank tellers by automatic teller machines (ATMs). Cross-border payments through Swift were established in the 1970s. In the 1980s, online banking and electronic fund transfers were introduced. In the 1990s, the emergence of e-commerce called for new methods of payments, such as PayPal, to manage the risk of online transactions. In the 2000s, further innovations enable P2P payments between customers that use different banks. By the mid-2010s, customers can manage their own accounts via apps and transact on mobile devices.

Through the years, banks have channeled their efforts toward sustaining innovations. They have grown unhindered supporting the needs of the financial services industry.

The more recent financial innovations are not simple enhancements or sustaining innovations aimed at existing bank customers. They are of a different dimension and can potentially disrupt and replace traditional banking services.

2.1.2 *Disruptive Innovations*

In contrast to sustaining innovations, disruptive innovations target new customers. They typically originate at the low end of the market where profit margins are meager.

Many of the successful FinTech companies are those that managed to identify a real need that can be solved by leveraging on existing infrastructure so that scaling can be accomplished at little cost (Lee and Teo 2015).

In the early 2010s, telecom companies began signing agreements to facilitate mobile payments as smartphone penetration even in emerging markets was almost complete. Unbanked consumers could use their smartphones as a contactless card for payment, an e-commerce platform and a location-based payment service. New innovative business models sprang up to take advantage of the extensive reach of the technology.

As profit margins were thin, incumbents had no incentive to challenge the new entrants. With low overheads and high automation, these FinTech companies could scale quickly. They played the role of banks facilitating payments, loans and providing financial advice. For many of them, profit was not key as there were many interested venture capitalists.

Many of these "new entrants" have since gained a foothold and are a force to be reckoned. They may eventually overwhelm and displace the incumbents (Christensen et al. 2015).

2.2 *Big Data in Finance*

Big data is defined as "the information asset characterized by such a high volume, velocity and variety to require specific technology and analytical methods for its transformation into value" (De Mauro et al. 2016).

The proliferation of machine accessible data from e-commerce, online payment devices and sensors as well as better cloud computing capability and machine learning ability have significantly reduced the costs of gathering, storing and analyzing data. The question is whether these alternative information sources and analytical capability can be used to facilitate decision making and how.

Lin et al. (2013) note that online friendships act as a signal of credit worthiness. They examine loans made on a US peer-to-peer lending platform and observe that borrowers with friends on the platform are more likely to get funding and be funded at lower interest rates. The loans are also associated with lower ex post default rates.

Iyer et al. (2015) find that the accuracy of default prediction is 45% higher when non-standard or soft information is available instead of just the borrower's credit score. Using data from Paipaidai, a large P2P Chinese platform, Agarwal et al. (2015) find that the inclusion of a third-party guarantee, where the guarantee is not strictly built on a relationship, leads to better loan terms for the borrower, larger loans, lower spreads and longer maturities. However, these third-party guaranteed loans are associated with a higher delinquency rate, which is consistent with the moral hazard theory because loans without a pre-existing relationship alter the borrowers' incentive and worsen performance.

Zhu (2019) tests for price informativeness of two alternative datasets (data "not from a financial statement or report") which are big data. The first comprises point-of-sale transactions, while the second provides car counts in parking lots of retailers. She finds that these alternative data contain information not publicly disclosed by managers and can predict earnings announcement returns. The price informativeness is stronger in firms where sophisticated investors have higher incentives to uncover information (e.g., firms with higher book-to-market ratios and firms with lower price-to-earnings ratios). In addition, the study finds that alternative data can help to discipline managers by (1) reducing their opportunistic trading based on their private information about future earnings because these alternative data reflect the future earnings to a greater extent and (2) improving the sensitivity of managers to declining investment opportunities so that they can make better downsizing decisions.

Using data from CASHe, a large FinTech lending firm in India, Agarwal et al. (2020) examine the incremental ability of digital mobile footprint variables to predict loan approval, purpose of loan, loan duration and loan default. They find that the number of applications, number of calls and number of text messages are significant features that can predict loan default far ahead of traditional credit scores provided by India's leading credit information company (see Fig. 9.1).

Berg et al. (2019) analyze the information content of consumer digital footprint and information left online when users access or register on the website of an e-commerce firm in Germany. They find that the information content match the credit bureau scores of these individuals. The digital footprint can be used to assess credit risk and grant credit access to underbanked individuals, fostering financial inclusion while controlling for the default rate at the same time.

2.3 *Blockchain and Cryptocurrencies*

2.3.1 *How Blockchain Works*

Blockchain, also known as distributed ledger technology (DLT), is a digital system that records transactions on identical ledgers across thousands of computer network nodes that are maintained by participants or miners. Transactions are time stamped, grouped into blocks and chained together over time to form a blockchain.

Blockchain is secure because each block is built on the preceding one. To change a past block, one needs to change all blocks that have been created after that block. In addition, hackers will have to obtain private keys to the thousands of network nodes in the blockchain. Thus, blockchain

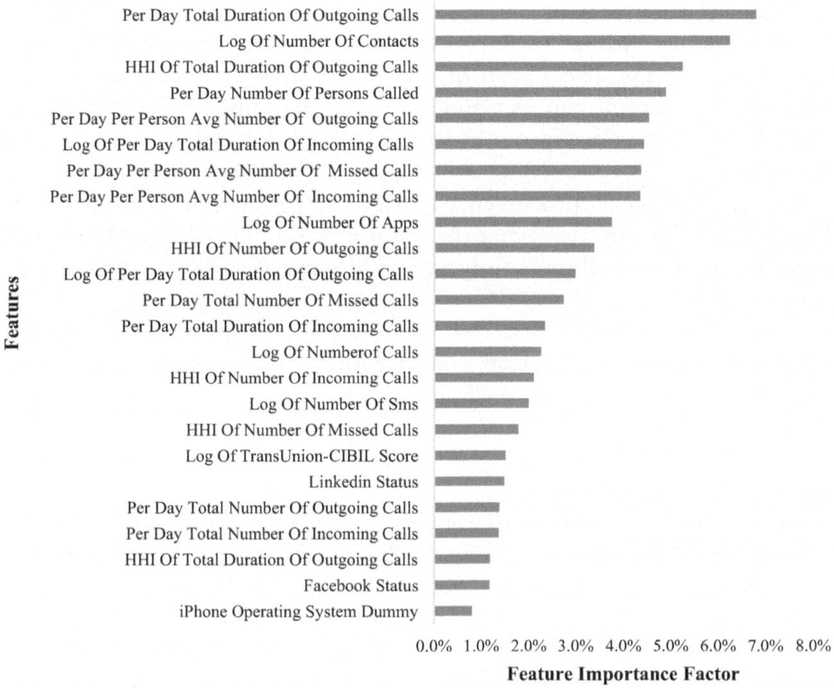

Fig. 9.1 Variable important factors. (Note: Feature Importance Factor refers to probability of predicting loan default. HHI refer to Herfindahl-Hirschman Index which captures whether the calls of an individual are concentrated over a few connections or spread across multiple contacts. Source: Agarwal et al. 2019)

has the potential to displace any business activity that has low transparency and limited traceability.

2.3.2 *Two Versions of Blockchain*

There are two versions of blockchain. The first is the trustless or permissionless blockchain where anyone can access and update the ledger. The second is the blockchain with trust or permissioned blockchain where some institutions or individuals have direct access to the blockchain and are entrusted to update it. The credibility of the permissioned system is preserved through either economic incentives or legal enforcements (Chiu and Koeppl 2019).

Under the trustless or permissionless system, miners solve "proof of work" or computational problems that have nothing to do with the economic transactions. The winner of a "proof of work" competition obtains a reward in the cryptocurrency and has the right to update the blockchain. The miner attaches his "proof of work" to his block before sending it to the network.

The value of the cryptocurrency depends on the credibility of the chain. Thus, miners benefit by playing the longest chain rule. Miners choose the chain by observing all previously solved blocks to maximize their cumulated rewards.

This "proof of work" blockchain protocol was proposed by Nakamoto (2008) to avoid manipulation and collusion. It ensures that no single miner has control over the verification process. The new block becomes the consensus if miners chained their next block to it.

2.3.3 Forks in Blockchain

A fork can happen if miners do not choose the last solved block as the parent. There will then be competing versions of the ledger. The presence of forks reduces the reliability and credibility of the blockchain.

Biais et al. (2019) review some reasons for the existence of forks.

First, delay in transmitting the information that the block has been solved can result in two competing blocks being chained to the same parent, According to Nakamoto (2008), this will not be a problem if miners always choose the longest chain.

Second, "double spending" may happen, where a miner wants to cover a transaction that he himself has made by starting a fork that does not contain the transaction. According to Nakamoto (2008), this is only possible if the miner can solve the "proof of work" faster than the rest of the network.

Third, software upgrades with miners running on two versions can give rise to a soft fork or a hard fork. A soft fork is where the upgraded version remains compatible and is not an issue. A hard fork is where the upgraded version is not compatible and may be rejected by non-upgraded miners. An example of a hard fork that was subsequently resolved was Bitcoin's software upgrade in March 2013 which contained a bug. It required that miners coordinate among themselves to preserve the chain.

Fourth, reward policies, modifications to software and disagreements among miners can also result in hard forks. In 2016, a hack on the venture capital fund, TheDAO, which used the Ethereum blockchain caused money to be diverted (Biais et al. 2019). Some miners on Ethereum decided to erase the "hacked" transaction, while others refused to alter the history of the ledger. As a result, Ethereum split into two hard forks—Ethereum and Ethereum Classic.

In the summer of 2017, disagreement among miners regarding the size of a block led to a compromise solution known as SegWit2x where Bitcoin split into two branches with two different cryptocurrencies, Bitcoin and Bitcoin Cash. In the fall of 2017, a new "proof of work" algorithm resulted in another hard fork, Bitcoin Gold. In December of 2017, different mining software and reward policies in Bitcoin resulted in other hard forks, namely, Bitcoin God, Super Bitcoin, Bitcoin X, Oil Bitcoin, Bitcoin World and Lightning Bitcoin.

2.3.4 Other Uses of Blockchain

Blockchain has given rise to other open-source projects including smart contracts. The ledger provides a decentralized consensus where it can be accepted and acted on by all agents within a system. For example, an agent can verify a transaction and authorize the release of goods remotely, without the need of a centralized arbitrator. This can mitigate information asymmetry and improve welfare and consumer surplus for all parties (Lin and He 2017).

One of the more successful uses of blockchain is a network of banks called the Interbank Information Network (IIN). Started by JPMorgan, Royal Bank of Canada and ANZ in 2017, IIN now comprises more than 70 banks that use a shared-access ledger to verify cross-border transactions.

One of the more prominent uses of blockchain is to act as Bitcoin's ledger and to record all the transactions of Bitcoin (Nakamoto 2008). It is the first cryptocurrency that makes use of the distributed ledger protocol which provides a high degree of anonymity and security. While Bitcoin is not the only widely traded cryptocurrency today, a majority of cryptocurrencies carry a common source of systematic risk correlated with Bitcoin returns (Hu et al. 2019).

2.3.5 Regulatory Concerns of Blockchain and Cryptocurrencies

The blockchain technology and cryptocurrencies, by virtue of the anonymity that they provide, have given rise to regulatory concerns regarding their use in illegal drug and sex trade, pornography, terrorism, money laundering, theft, hacks and murder-for-hire.

Using public Bitcoin blockchain data from January 2009 to July 2017, Foley et al. (2019) find that 26% of Bitcoin users, 46% of Bitcoin transactions, 23% of total dollar value of transactions and 49% of Bitcoin holdings are associated with illegal activities. Illegal users tend to transact more, in smaller-sized transactions, with the same party and use techniques to hide their trades.

Over time, the fraction of illegal Bitcoin activity has declined but the amount remains high. Foley et al. (2019) attribute the decline to the rapid growth of Bitcoin which mechanically reduces the share of illegal activities and the introduction of more opaque cryptocurrencies such as Monero and ZCash.

2.4 *Digital Currencies*

Digital currencies started with the idea of virtual money. DigiCash was born out of a need for anonymity while maintaining control of electronic money flow (Chaum 1998). It was intended to be digitally issued and redeemed by banks without the need for cash. Despite its failure, DigiCash created a framework and laid the foundation for digital cash (Brunton 2019).

This was followed by the emergence of game virtual currencies. These platform-based currencies were originally exchanged "inwardly" where players can exchange in-game virtual dollars for state currency. However, the eventual expansion in activities led to black markets where players trade in-game currency outside of the game (Goldfarb et al. 2015).

The advent of Bitcoin spurred other digital currencies like Ethereum and DogeCoin, eWallet companies like Coin Gecko and digital currency exchange platforms like Zaif and Mt Gox. This revolution of digital currencies presents a radical shift away from the traditional model of monetary exchange.

Raskin et al. (2019) offer a typology of digital currency based on two axes, public versus private and centralization versus decentralized. Private Decentralized Currency like Bitcoin has no central group managing it and no legal protection granted by governments. Private Centralized Currency is run by companies that control not only the issuance but also the maintenance. Public Decentralized Currency like gold is backed but not managed by sovereign states. Public Centralized Currency like state currency is managed by sovereign states that control its usage.

Raskin et al. (2019) conclude that Private Decentralized Currency has huge welfare implications for emerging markets as a form of investment diversification. This is especially so for economies with high volatility and policies based on government interests rather than the welfare of its people (Raskin et al. 2019; Dyhrberg 2016; Chan et al. 2019).

In an Initial Coin Offerings (ICO), cryptocurrencies are sold in the form of tokens which can be traded in the secondary market or be used to exchange for products and services. Adhami et al. (2018) analyze 253 ICOs that occurred from 2014 to 2017. These ICOs originate mainly from the US, Russia, the UK and Canada.

Catalini and Gans (2019) find that entrepreneurs have an incentive to ensure that ICO tokens retain their values even when they do not confer the typical rights associated with equity. However, entrepreneurs may be tempted to issue more tokens post ICO, expropriating early token holders.

Examining 1500 ICOs that raised US$12.9 billion, Howell et al. (2019) conclude that a digital currency with high disclosure, credible commitment and quality signal tends to be better received by consumers. Similarly, Roussou et al. (2018) find that the perceived security and usefulness of a digital currency are the main factors affecting its reception by consumers and firms, while the compatibility with existing values and practices have an indirect effect on the rate of adoption.

A well-designed digital currency requires the establishment of (1) a real-time clearing and settlement system that allows for efficient transaction by consumers and businesses, (2) safe and liquid bank accounts that yield the same rate of return as short-term government securities and (3) a system of transfers between paper and digital cash such that consumers and firms can use paper cash if they so desire (Bordo and Levin 2019).

2.4.1 Regulatory Concerns for Digital Currencies

While digital currencies are relatively safe, transparent and fast, their rapid expansion pose a threat to existing official legal tender, sovereign currencies and the monetary policies of central banks.

Currencies like Ethereum and Libra are created by entities independent of any political authority or commercial sponsor. There is thus an autonomous dimension to these digital currencies relative to central bank-managed fiat currencies which are subject to political or policy goals (Raskin and Yermack 2016). Some argue that this autonomous feature serves as a check on the unilateral monopoly of central banks, preventing the mismanagement of money supply (Raskin and Yermack 2016).

To a central bank, digital currencies are a concern (Hayek 1976). They may result in the de-funding of commercial banks, reinvention of credit creation and relegation of monetary policies.

A 2018 European Central Bank report warns that digital currencies pose issues of fraud, issuer bankruptcy and speculative bubbles (Dabrowski and Janikowski 2018). It recommends that jurisdictions harmonize regulations to reduce such complications. Evidence shows that central banks have differing responses ranging from banning, tolerating to participating in the innovation of digital currencies. Most mature economies have taken the middle ground of allowing their usage and adopting a benign attitude (Raskin 2013).

Some countries have developed their own central bank digital currencies. China recently announced plans to launch pilots for its digital currency as early as 2020 (Palmer 2019). Bordo and Levin (2019) are of the view that state-sponsored digital currency enhances the stability and prudency of a financial system, providing the central bank with an instrument that has an expandable supply and an adjustable interest rate.

2.5 Payments and Financial Inclusion

In the realm of payments, the key disruptive trends are mobile payments or e-wallets, billing platforms, bitcoin wallets, blockchain-based settlement networks, cryptocurrency cross-border payments, accelerated authentication of funds transfer and tracking and cloud-based payroll processing. These offerings make payment processes easier, faster and more straightforward, bypassing currency laws and regulations in different countries.

In contrast to cards, e-wallets do not require point-of-sale (POS) machines or disclosure of bank account information. In 2017, the total transaction value via e-wallets has reached US$350 billion worldwide. This is expected to hit US$1.6 trillion by 2022 (Agarwal et al. 2019).

Of the 11 most valuable FinTech companies in the US (Kauflin 2019), seven are in payments, namely, Stripe (worth US$22.5 billion), Coinbase (worth US$8 billion), Ripple (worth US$5 billion), Circle (worth US$3 billion), Plaid (worth US$2.65 billion), Gusto (worth US$2 billion) and Zenefits (worth US$2 billion). They use fun, social, inexpensive and easy-to-use interfaces to appeal to the young while supporting the unbanked and underbanked.

Launched in 2011, Stripe builds software for businesses to accept payments online.

Coinbase and Ripple, both founded in 2012, apply blockchain technology to facilitate the payment function. Coinbase is a digital currency wallet and platform where consumers can transact with new digital currencies like Bitcoin, Bitcoin Cash, Ethereum and Litecoin. Ripple offers blockchain-based settlement for international transfers and real-time remittances.

Circle was founded in 2013 as a P2P payment technology company but has since become the first regulated crypto exchange in the US.

Plaid started as a simple consumer payment tool in 2012 but has evolved to become a platform that offers developer tools and infrastructure for performing the transfer of data, enabling consumers and businesses to interact with their bank accounts for payments, loan applications and investments.

Gusto was launched in 2012 as a cloud-based platform that simplifies the human resource process of onboarding, payroll, insurance and medical benefit solutions, as well as ensures compliance with tax, labor and immigration laws. Also in the same field is Zenefits which was launched in 2013 to help startups and small businesses manage employee benefits in one place. It has expanded to offer cloud-based software for human resource management with a focus on health insurance coverage.

Giants like Apple and Google are also on the mobile payment bandwagon with Apple Pay and Google Pay. Apple Pay is supported on iPhone, Apple Watch, iPad and Mac, while Google has its Google Wallet app preinstalled on Android phones sold by telecommunications network providers such as Verizon, AT&T and T-Mobile.

2.6 Digital Loans and Financial Inclusion

According to the Expectations and Experiences Consumer Trends Survey, almost two-thirds of US Consumers who applied for loans do so either partially or fully online (Fiserv 2019). In addition, 19% of consumers read loan documents on mobile phones or tablets; 16% upload documents using mobile devices as requested by lenders; 21% receive their loan application decisions via mobile devices and 71% are comfortable with the idea of completing loan applications online.

Digital loans lower the cost of accessing credit for borrowers and reduce the administrative cost for lenders. Some banks evaluate mobile phone usage behavior to predict credit risk and generate alternative credit scores, reducing information asymmetries and potentially reducing the cost of loans (Bjorkegren and Grissen 2018). Increased access and lower cost allow households to escape from the poverty trap (Banerjee et al. 2019).

Bharadwaj et al. (2019) review the effect of digital loans by M-Shwari (an entirely digital bank that provides digital loans through mobiles) in Kenya over a two-year period. They observe an increase in small digital loans especially by those who previously did not qualify. Those who had previously qualified took 37% more loans. The loan access provides households with more resilience to negative shocks and enables them to maintain the same level of consumption despite difficult unforeseen circumstances.

Analyzing the mortgage market in the US, Fuster et al. (2019) observe that FinTech lenders process applications 20% quicker without increasing loan risk. They can also better adapt to demand shocks for mortgage, increasing the likelihood of refinancing and providing borrowers with better access to credit with less market friction (Agarwal et al. 2013).

Jagtiani et al. (2019) find that FinTech lenders have a larger share in areas with higher mortgage denial rates and in areas with lower median credit scores. This suggests that FinTech lenders help to expand credit access to the underserved. Jagtiani and Lemieux (2018) find that consumer lending platforms have penetrated areas that have smaller number of bank branches per capita and areas that are highly competitive. They conclude that Fintech lenders can fill credit gaps in areas where bank offices are lacking and where the local economy is more challenging.

Bartlett et al. (2019) find that traditional lenders discriminate against minorities in the mortgage markets by charging higher interest rate, but FinTech firms are much more willing to lend to them.

Similarly, DiCaprio et al. (2017) document that informal Fintech services can contribute to the financial inclusion of minority groups such as woman-owned firms. Woman-owned firms that experienced bank loan rejections are more likely than male-owned firms to seek informal sources of capital. They argue that the results are of particular relevance to Asia and Africa where uptake of informal finance is high among women and where Fintech is an attractive alternative source of finance.

On the other hand, Parlour et al. (2019) find that the entry of FinTech firms that compete with banks in payment processing can affect the ability of banks to gain information about consumer credit quality. The negative impact involves mainly older and richer consumers who are more reliant on banks. Technologically sophisticated consumers, on the other hand, gain the most from the reduction in cost for payment services. In the case where the FinTech firm is only selling the data instead of lending to consumers, the enhanced data provides banks with better information to assess credit risk, which translates into lower cost for the consumers.

Flögel and Beckamp (2020) highlight that FinTechs may result in deteriorated access to finance for small medium enterprises (SMEs) if FinTechs displace regional banks without preserving the advantages of soft information, superior screening and monitoring technologies.

2.7 Peer-to-Peer Lending and Financial Inclusion

Peer-to-Peer (P2P) refers to consumer-to-consumer financial transactions where an individual can make a payment to another using a smartphone, whether within a country or cross-border. Venmo is one such firm that allows individuals to transfer cash immediately to others. P2P is borne out of a need for alternative services that incumbent financial services do not provide. P2P has since experienced exponential growth and accounts for 30% of the unsecured installment loan sector in 2016 (Blumberg 2017).

Ahmed and Cowan (2019) examine P2P digital lending in Kenya where Mobile Money Transfer Technology (MMT) allows owners to transfer money stored on their mobile phone to their social network. They find that MMT helps fill the need of the unbanked by providing access to cash transfers for healthcare financial needs. Such risk sharing within a community is enabled by FinTech and can potentially alter traditional risk sharing relationships with insurers and banks.

2.7.1 P2P Lending Platforms

Post-global financial crisis, the tightened lending practices made it difficult for those with lower credit rating to obtain traditional loans. This resulted in the emergence of alternative lending mechanisms such as P2P lending platforms (also known as marketplace lending) which allow individuals and small businesses to continue to borrow. Well-known P2P lending platforms in the US include LendingClub, Prosper, Upstart, CircleBack and PeerForm.

These platforms use technology to collect standardized information and pre-screen loan applications into different risk buckets. Investors then further screen the borrowers before directly investing in individual loans, bearing the risk of default. These marketplace lending platforms challenge the traditional role of a bank by facilitating transactions between investors and borrowers directly. They also compete with banks by undercutting the interest rates charged.

Within these P2P marketplaces, there are financial intermediaries that facilitate credit activities. Berger and Gleisner (2009) document that groups on Propser, a US P2P lending platform, act as financial intermediaries and are able to signal credit conditions of borrowers to help reduce information asymmetries, and hence facilitate credit lending. In 2018, the global P2P market is worth US$34 billion and is projected to hit US$589 billion by 2025 (MarketWatch 2019).

Jagtiani and Lemieux (2019) document that non-traditional alternative data on P2P platforms allow borrowers with fewer or inaccurate credit records (based on FICO scores) to have better loan ratings and obtain lower-priced credit. The rating grades based on alternative data have performed well in predicting loan performance.

Wang et al. (2018) find that the soft information shared on a Chinese P2P platform serve as a valuable input for credit appraisal, and together with standard hard measures of credit can be used to improve loan performance.

Ding et al. (2019) study a separate Chinese P2P platform. They find an effective reputation mechanism in P2P lending where lenders factor in borrowers' reputation in their lending decisions with good reputation lowering default probability. Borrowers with better historical performance are more likely to obtain loans and do so at lower cost. Ding et al. (2019) conclude that in P2P lending, the reputation mechanism can discipline borrowers' behavior.

Using German consumer credit data, De Roure et al. (2019) document that when banks face higher regulatory costs, bank lending declines while P2P lending increases. At the same time, they find that P2P lending takes away the riskiest and least profitable customers from banks, and the risk-adjusted interest rates are lower than banks.

On the other hand, Wolfe and Yoo (2017) document that P2P lending in the US are gaining loans from customers of small commercial banks. In other words, P2P lending and bank lending are partial substitutes.

Analyzing data from LendingClub, Tang (2019) documents that P2P platforms are substitutes for banks serving infra-marginal bank borrowers but are complements with respect to small loans. Her results indicate that the credit expansion for US P2P lending platforms likely occur among borrowers who already have access to bank credit.

This is supported by Di Maggio and Yao (2019) who find that FinTech lenders are not after underserved marginal borrowers. Instead, the borrowers tend to have mid-range credit score and are using the relaxation of credit constraints to borrow above their means. Fuster et al. (2018) who examine the US mortgage market find little evidence that FinTech lenders are more effective in reaching out to the underserved. This means that P2P lending platforms in the US are substitutes for banks.

The most prominent feature that distinguishes P2P lending from traditional banking is the heavy reliance on screening and information production by investors (Vallee and Zeng 2019). While P2P lending helps to solve some problems, there is still the issue of information inequality. One such issue is the participation of sophisticated investors, whose adverse selection tends to disadvantage non-sophisticated investors. Vallee and Zeng (2019) study the joint information production of the platform and the investors. They find that if the platform chooses a high pre-screening intensity and low information provision, unsophisticated investors will be willing to invest and sophisticated investors will perform less well.

2.7.2 Equity Crowdfunding

Another alternative online financing platform is equity crowdfunding (such as Kickstarter) which raises capital from the crowd through the sale of company securities. Equity crowdfunding is growing, with a report estimating over 300 successful UK investment campaigns in 2017, making crowdfunders the second largest investor category in the UK, after venture capitalists (Halmari et al. 2017).

Equity crowdfunding has widened access to capital raising activities, allowing new companies to grow at a quicker pace and shorten the average time during the early funding stages.

2.8 Robo-Advising and Financial Inclusion

Financial theory predicts that households benefit from stock market participation as long as equity premium is positive. However, many investors do not diversify or hold appropriately diversified portfolios (Blume and Friend 1975). They are therefore exposed to idiosyncratic risk (Badarinza et al. 2016).

These investors can potentially benefit from having financial advisors but they are costly and financial advisors themselves are prone to behavioral biases. These biases include the disposition effect (more likely to realize gains than losses), trend chasing (tend to purchase stocks after a set of positive returns) and the rank effect (more likely to sell the best-performing and worst-performing stocks) (Foerster et al. 2017).

The automation of advisory functions via robo-advisors helps to improve accessibility to sophisticated wealth management tools often through mobile apps, without the attached behavioral biases of their human counterparts. The disruption to the traditional advisory channel is a response to the needs of an investor segment that is too small to be of interest to incumbent financial advisors.

Robo-advisors deliver and execute financial advice to investors through an automated replicable algorithm, based on financial theory, at a much lower cost (Abraham et al. 2019). Other advantages include speed, transparency, convenience and efficiency in implementing strategies due to inbuilt algorithms.

In 2017, the US had the most number of robo-advisors translating to 57% of the robo-advising market with more than US$400 billion of assets under management (Abraham et al. 2019).

D'Acunto et al. (2019) study the introduction of a wealth management robo-advising technology in a large Indian brokerage house focusing on Indian equities. They find that adopting robo-advising have different effects on investors depending on their level of diversification before adoption. Undiversified investors become more diversified, hold portfolios with less volatility and higher market-adjusted returns. Diversified investors trade more, hold fewer stocks, have lower portfolio volatility but do not perform better. The paper concludes that robo-advisory mitigate behavioral biases, help to bridge the information gap and facilitate financial inclusion through investing.

2.9 Technology and Discrimination

The general perception is that face-to-face interaction and human decision making result in costly discrimination. Morton et al. (2003) find that black and latino car purchasers pay more than white car purchasers in face-to-face sales negotiation compared to internet sales. Bartlett et al. (2019) find that the discrepancy in the rates charged to white and black/latino borrowers is higher for conventional lenders than for algorithmic lenders.

They conclude that FinTech algorithmic decision making discriminate 40% less than face-to-face lenders and do not discriminate against minority borrowers. The belief is that technology can replace human interaction and displace human discretion which is a traditional source of discrimination.

However, it is recognized that technology does not totally remove human involvement. Morse and Pence (2020) argue that algorithms can introduce discrimination from human involvement at the development stage via five gateways. First, algorithms are designed and coded by humans (Caliskan et al. 2017). Second, the setup of the optimization problem and the choice of a training data set, if it is unrepresentative of the population, can bias the output (Barocas and Selbst 2016; Buolomwini and Gebru 2018). Third, customers are scored for creditworthiness through their digital footprint using proxies which may be related to variables that are tied to past or present discrimination such as family resources, education and employment history. Fourth, algorithms can infer with great precision the propensity of customers to shop around and their willingness to pay and may use the inference to apply discriminatory pricing. Fifth, technology allows firms to customize advertisements for their target audience resulting in systemic differences in the advertisements that different groups see. This is known as ad targeting. In addition, firms have to compete with other advertisers to display their ads. They do this by bidding and the algorithm allocates the advertising space. This is known as ad delivery. Ad targeting and ad delivery may lead to discrimination.

Morse and Pence (2020) conclude that even while technology removes discretionary discrimination, it introduces new channels of discrimination through the development of the algorithmic process. The net effect remains ambiguous.

Regulation is also evolving to keep pace with technology. The courts, regulators and policy makers will have to determine the list of variables that are correlated with discrimination, whether the focus should shift to prevention by requiring transparency of codes and training sets, how data protection affect the direct and indirect variables used in profiling customers and how to police discrimination on online platforms (Morse and Pence 2020).

3 From Fintech to Bigtech

FinTech startups usually disrupt only a single vertical of the incumbents' business, for example, money transfer at low fees, wealth management using robo-advisors at a fraction of the fees or loans with shorter duration and lower interest rates.

However, once they have enough customers on their platforms (achieved economies of scale), many of them can begin to offer other products as well (seek economies of scope). Some FinTech startups are immensely successful and are now BigTech companies with an established presence in the market such as Amazon, Alibaba, Tencent and Ping An (Stulz 2019).

BigTech companies can challenge traditional banks across numerous product lines. Unlike FinTech companies, BigTech have large databases collected in real time that will enable them to make better decisions. BigTech also have the customer base to operate their own bank to provide financial services. They are not bogged down by government regulations, legacy IT and organizational frictions (Stulz 2019).

Hornuf et al. (2020) study relationships between banks and Fintechs in Canada, France, Germany and the UK. They find that banks are likely to directly cooperate with FinTech startups that pursue a well-defined digital strategy but tend to build product-related collaboration with larger FinTechs.

4 Factors Affecting the Growth of Financial Technology

The rate of FinTech growth varies widely across countries. A report by KPMG on the FinTech industry finds that, in 2017, FinTech funding was at US$31 billion, of which US$15.2 billion was invested in the US, US$7.4 billion in Europe and US$3.9 billion in Asia (Blackman 2019). Several factors have contributed to the difference in the growth rates.

4.1 Network Externality

Government policies that target the adoption of FinTech by consumers or retailers can affect the degree of financial inclusion through network externality. In developing countries, the government adoption of financial inclusion policies and technological innovation can increase the number of people formally introduced into the financial system (Karlan et al. 2016; Demirguc-Kunt et al. 2017). The network effect may amplify the financial inclusion impact.

Tracking the adoption of debit cards two years after the Mexican government introduced debit cards to cash transfer recipients, Higgins (2019) finds that the policy-driven adoption creates a technological spill-over effect to other consumers and retailers. There are also social externalities where users pass on information to non-users, influencing their technological adoption and eventual financial inclusion (Banerjee et al. 2013).

4.2 *Financial Education*

Financial education empowers consumers and helps improve their financial decisions (Hastings et al. 2013). It is estimated that only one in four newly banked global poor has received financial training (Deb and Kubzansky 2012). This makes them vulnerable to predatory behavior.

Jünger and Mietzner (2019) conduct an online survey of German households to gain insights into the adoption of new technologies and services in the financial industry. They find that 31% of survey respondents are willing to consider moving from a traditional bank to a FinTech. These are mainly households who have financial education, low levels of trust and a preference for transparency.

4.3 *Technological Education*

The technological education of consumers affects their adoption of FinTech.

Carlin et al. (2017) find that even though the new mobile technology was adopted by all generation, the rate of adoption differs cross-sectionally. The increased access to the mobile technology benefits Millennials and members of Generation X by making financial information more prominent and lowering their search costs thereby reducing financial fees and penalties. On the other hand, Baby Boomers who are less tech savvy do not benefit from the technology.

4.4 *General Infrastructure*

General infrastructure is key. Any failure in the electricity or mobile network will undermine the reliability of digital innovation for consumers, especially the unbanked and underbanked.

Yermack (2018) associates the level of infrastructure of a country with its legal system. He observes that FinTech succeeds in countries with common law. He explains that the legal structure enables the country to build its communication infrastructure and provide legal protection for investors. These characteristics make the country attractive to investors, which help to support the growth of FinTech platforms.

Haddad and Hornuf (2019) study the distribution of Fintech startups across 55 countries. They find that countries with supporting infrastructure and flexible market regulations have more FinTech startups.

4.5 *Financial Infrastructure*

The presence of a stable financial infrastructure including an established financial system of cash withdrawal and deposit, a payment system and a well-developed capital market are necessary for FinTech to flourish (Demirguc-Kunt et al. 2018).

Allen et al. (2012) find that stock market development is highly correlated with the financial development of a country, possibly due to the free flow of capital and a favorable ecosystem for financial innovation.

4.6 *Population Density*

The population density affects the frequency of interaction and the volume of transactions among firms, households and investors. Infrequent transactions hinder the formation of a viable banking sector, affecting the financial development of a country.

Allen et al. (2012) examine sub-Saharan Africa's financial development using country- and firm-level data sets. They find an association between the percentage of population living in the largest cities, roads per square kilometer and bank branch penetration with financial development (measured by liquid liabilities relative to GDP). This implies that major cities where population density is higher benefit more from FinTech.

5 The Financial Inclusion Revolution

China and India are two of the biggest success stories in financial inclusion. While financial inclusion in China was mainly driven by the technology companies, the growth in India was driven by the government in partnership with the private sector, namely, the banks. This section also covers lesser known success stories of financial inclusion in Kenya which was facilitated by mobile technology and in Rwanda which was aided by community saving and credit cooperatives.

5.1 Financial Inclusion in China

The FinTech revolution in China was led by its technology giants, primarily Alibaba and TenCent. Their easy-to-use platforms and well-orchestrated expansion under visionary leaderships have enabled the real economy to leapfrog from cash to mobile and digital payment systems, bypassing the traditional retail banking system altogether.

5.1.1 Alibaba and Ant Financial Services Group

Alibaba Group Executive Chairman Jack Ma saw the potential of e-commerce in the rural areas. He believed that e-commerce could help to unlock the countryside's potential, "We're really hoping to bring e-commerce to all of China's villages, so that rural people can get a taste of the city life and sell their own products in the cities" (Wang 2014).

The mass migration of the Chinese rural workforce to the cities had created deserted villages and large population of left-behind children (Ding et al. 2018).

In October 2014, Alibaba Group announced that it would invest RMB10 billion (US$1.48 billion) on logistical support, training and hardware infrastructure to build an e-commerce ecosystem to reach 1000 counties and 100,000 villages (Wang 2014).

In December 2014, Alibaba Group used a multi-faceted approach to encourage rural entrepreneurs by providing financial solutions through its affiliated company Ant Financial Services Group (Ant Financials), e-commerce training through Taobao University and marketing support through Taobao Marketplace (Wang 2014).

Alibaba Group set up many Taobao Rural Service Centers at local convenience stores with well-trained village representatives to help the people (1) get accustomed to purchasing and paying bills online, (2) buy train tickets, buy plane tickets and make hotel bookings through Ali Trip, (3) apply for credit from Alipay and (4) purchase medications by uploading doctors' prescriptions through the mobile app AliJK (Ding et al. 2018; Xiang 2014).

The Taobao Rural Service Centers also helped entrepreneurs to set up business on Taobao where they could reach a multitude of cities and customers. This led to the "Taobao village" phenomenon, where many village merchants adopt Taobao as the key trading platform (Alizila 2014). Soon, traditional farming communities were transformed into e-commerce clusters with internet-related and logistic-related job opportunities.

Jack Ma said, "Let the rural people return to the earth, let the intellectuals return to the farms, and send the products of their agriculture all over the nation" (Wang 2014). Apart from bringing e-commerce to the rural area, Alibaba also facilitated financial inclusion through Alipay.

Alipay was established in 2004 as a mobile payment network and, in nine years, it overtook PayPal as the world's largest mobile payment platform. Consumers pay with their smartphones using Alipay Wallet app. Alipay provides features such as credit card bill payment, internet banking, P2P transfer, location-based payment service for ride hailing, utility bill payment and online payment for e-commerce, property fees, tuition fees and traffic fines. Alibaba spun off Alipay in 2011.

In 2013, Alipay launched a financial product known as Yu'e Bao which, in six years, became the biggest money market fund in the world. In 2014, Ant Financials started Zhaocaibao to complement Yu'e Bao. While Yu'e Bao serves as a cash management tool, Zhaocaibao provides wealth management solutions. It was launched as a third-party financial services platform connecting SMEs and individuals.

Alipay rebranded and changed its name to Ant Financials Services Group in 2014. Ant Financials has a number of subsidiaries. Through Ant Credit, it provides micro online loans to online merchants and Taobao sellers. It received approval to set up a private online bank called MYbank in 2014, which utilizes big data analytics to serve SMEs and individual consumers.

In 2015, it started Ant Fortune which is a wealth management platform that offers financial products from other financial institutions. Yu'e Bao is one of the products available on the platform.

Ant Financials also runs Sesame Credit or Zhima Credit, which is an independent credit rating system that uses profile information of the user and his fulfillment of contractual obligations such as credit repayment history to generate a credit score. It is an opt-in service collected with the user's consent. The service provides an opportunity for underbanked individuals to prove that they are trustworthy.

In 2019, Ant Financials established a joint venture with The Vanguard Group to provide retail investment advisory services to Chinese investors based on individual risk preferences, time horizons and investment objectives.

Alibaba has progressed from being just an e-commerce platform to being a provider of wealth management, investment advisory, credit rating and banking services.

5.1.2 TenCent

TenCent started with an instant messaging platform QQ in 1999. QQ remains popular. In 2005, TenCent launched an auction site PaiPai.com and an online payment system TenPay which is similar to PayPal.

In 2011, it launched Weixin a social media app which has since become one of the most powerful and influential app for messaging, video calls and conferencing, video games, photograph and video sharing, location sharing, digital payment and even insurance services. Weixin has since been rebranded as WeChat.

Users of WeChat can use WeChat Pay, a digital wallet service, to make mobile payments and P2P payments. The main competitor of WeChat Pay is AliPay.

In 2014, TenCent rolled out its online wealth management platform Licaitong which competes directly with Zhaocaibao.

In 2015, Tencent launched WeBank which is China's first online-only bank. In 2017, Tencent has its own credit score system known as Tencent Credit which is similar to Alibaba's Sesame Credit.

5.2 Financial Inclusion in India

5.2.1 JAM

The three key enablers for financial inclusion in India are often referred to as JAM, an acronym which stands for Jan Dhan Yojana, Aadhaar and Mobile phones.

Under the biometric digital program Aadhaar, which was launched in 2010, Indian residents have a unique digital identity number linked to fingerprints and iris scans. As of February 2017, Aadhaar has over 1.123 billion enrolled members (DaijiWorld 2017). The Aadhaar authentication technology allows verification of identity without paper evidence and can be used for mobile phone applications, bank accounts, vehicle purchases, insurance policies and mutual fund schemes. It was described by World Bank Chief Economist Paul Romer as the "most sophisticated ID programme in the world" (DaijiWorld 2017).

In August 2014, the government launched the Pradhan Mantri Jan Dhan Yojana (PMJDY) program, which mandates banks to open accounts for citizens who are financially excluded. To promote account utilization, salaries for government employees, pensions to the elderly, widowed and disabled, as well as social benefits such as scholarships for education and cash assistance for expectant mothers are to be paid directly into the Aadhaar-linked bank accounts. The crediting of subsidies directly into Aadhaar-linked bank accounts (known as the Direct Benefit Transfer program) enhances transparency, eliminates leakages and reduces the costs of distributing the funds to intended beneficiaries through various intermediaries. The Indian government claims that the direct transfer helps to eliminate close to 33 million "ghost" or fake liquefied petroleum gas (LPG) cylinder connections under the LPG subsidy program (Jain et al. 2018).

In August 2016, a new national payment network known as the "Unified Payment Interface" (UPI) was launched by a not-for-profit organization called National Payments Corporation of India (NPCI). The NPCI is championed by the Reserve Bank of India and the Association of Indian Banks. The UPI relies on Aadhaar for the verification of a person's identity in real time to make payments and collect cash via smartphones (ET Commentary 2016).

JAM (Jan Dhan Yojana, Aadhaar and Mobile phones) enables India to leapfrog to digital payments, skipping traditional payment channels like debit cards, credit cards and point-of-sale terminals. Individuals can manage funds held in multiple accounts, at various banks and in mobile wallets, to pay merchants and street vendors, transact online and make remittances.

5.2.2 The Demonetization in India and Financial Inclusion

On 8 November 2016, the Indian government announced the withdrawal of existing large denomination 500-rupee and 1000-rupee notes (equivalent to US$7.50 and US$15, respectively) from circulation, effectively making 85% of all Indian bank notes invalid as legal tender overnight.

The policy known as demonetization is meant to curb the prevalence of untaxed or black money, but it also has the effect of accelerating financial inclusion and the use of digital financial services.

As the demonetized notes could only be exchanged for new valid notes at state-regulated financial institutions, it required all adult Indians to interact with the formal financial system. Banks were overwhelmed by the volume of notes that needed to be exchanged. The lack of cash caused significant economic and social disruption.

Post monetization, Agarwal et al. (2018a) document a significant increase in adoption of both traditional cards and non-traditional digital payment modes.

A survey based on 45,000 adults (Schueth and Moler 2017) finds that the increase in the number of registered account holders exceed any single annual increase observed by the Financial Inclusion program, including the period when PMJDY was introduced. The increase is observed in all demographic groups but greatest among women and rural residents.

This shows that friction in access to physical banking such as closures of automatic teller machines (ATM) can hasten the adoption of digital banking (Choi and Loh 2019).

5.3 *Financial Inclusion in Kenya*

In the Kenyan experience, mobile technology was the gateway to financial inclusion.

In 2007, Safaricom (a telecommunication company) and Vodafone Group with the help of the UK Department for International Development launched a short message service mobile money system known as M-Pesa (The Economist 2013).

The M-Pesa platform is a low-tech FinTech service that can be used by customers with basic mobile phones. It enhances convenience, security and the management of small value accounts.

In the first stage of its development, it was used for payments and for transfers between users. Safaricom recruited agents and provided customer training in the use of mobile phone technology and the M-Pesa service.

The model allows Safaricom to issue electronic money which is stored in the phone SIM card in exchange for cash at par value. The cash is held in a trust account separate from the funds of Safaricom. Users may deposit or withdraw cash via M-Pesa and Safaricom agents (acting as human ATMs) who are well distributed throughout the country. They can transfer money to other users and make payment for goods and services. M-Pesa managed to overcome the main constraints that prevented financial inclusion in Kenya, namely, low income, irregular income and physical distance from a bank branch.

In the second stage, mobile banking was incorporated onto the platform. Users who do not have a bank account can use their mobile phone number as their account number. Those who have a bank account can integrate it with their M-Pesa account and transact using their mobile phones.

This enables Kenyan banks to reach the previously unbanked and underserved. Deposits grew which provided banks with the capacity to grow. Over time, other financial services became available such as receiving wages, paying school fees, paying utility bills and applying for government services (e.g., social protection programs for the poor and physically disadvantaged) (Jones et al. 2016).

In the third stage, the transaction and saving data from the platform allow credit scores to be generated for pricing short-term micro credit facilities and help to overcome the collateral handicap. M-Pesa acts as a complement to the banking system and increases the accessibility of formal financial services (Mbiti and Weil 2011).

5.4 *Financial Inclusion in Rwanda*

As of 2008, 79% of Rwandans aged 18 years and older did not have access to formal financial services, while 52% were completely financially excluded (Alliance for Financial Inclusion). A significant amount of money was held in cash which limited the capacity of financial institutions to issue credit and grow.

5.4.1 *Umurenge SACCOs*

In March 2009, a National Saving Mobilization Strategy was launched to create an extensive network of community saving and credit cooperatives (Umurenge SACCOs) to channel deposits into the financial system and to provide financial services to the previously unbanked at low transaction costs. The government played a key role in the setting up of the premises, capacity building of staff, the financial education of the public, infrastructural upgrades of computers, modems and internet access and the provision of subsidies until the Umurenge SACCOs could breakeven (Alliance for Financial Inclusion 2014a, b, c).

The SACCOs are member-based cooperatives that are regulated and supervised by the National Bank of Rwanda under the Microfinance Law. The Umurenge SACCOs were perceived to be more efficient and more customer friendly. In the rural areas, the Rwandans trust the Umurenge SACCOs more than commercial banks.

Initially, Umurenge SACCOs were not allowed to lend. In January 2012, Umurenge SACCOs obtained the license to issue loans and were able to contribute to the microcredit expansion program. Rwanda has a comprehensive credit register that captures the universe of loans extended by commercial banks, Umurenge SACCOs and other microfinance institutions (MFIs).

The Umurenge SACCOs and other MFIs allow the previously unbanked to borrow. The credit register enables the borrowers to build their credit history and establish their credit worthiness.

By 2012, the percentage of Rwandans 18 years and older who did not have access to formal financial institutions has dropped to 58%. Data show that the program significantly contributed to financial inclusion in Rwanda, with 90% of Rwandans living within a 5-km radius of an Umurenge SACCO (Alliance for Financial Inclusion 2014a, b, c). By 2013, 85% of SACCOs have managed to breakeven and achieve self-sustainability.

5.4.2 Switch from Umurenge SACCOs to Commercial Banks

The Umurenge SACCOs increase the probability of obtaining microcredit for the previously unbanked in rural areas and less financially developed areas (Agarwal et al. 2018b).

The program has a spill-over effect. With their established credit worthiness, a large number of first-time borrowers who need a second loan managed to switch to commercial banks where they can get cheaper, longer term and larger loans (Agarwal et al. 2018b). These borrowers are not riskier than existing borrowers at commercial banks, which suggests that they are low-risk borrowers "cream skimmed" from the Umurenge SACCOs. The cream skimming will over time lead to a riskier pool of borrowers at MFIs (Agarwal et al. 2018b).

6 Conclusion

The inability of banks to respond to the needs of the unbanked and underbanked have created opportunities for FinTech firms to use digital data to make financial inclusion into a viable business model and develop alternative systems.

The traditional banks do not find it worthwhile to bother with the neglected segment because of government regulations, legacy IT systems and inherent organizational friction.

The widespread adoption of mobile phones, the advancement of technology infrastructure, the harvesting of big data, the financial education and technological education of the consumers all play a part in the escalation of financial innovation and financial deepening.

Finally, the chapter explores four financial inclusion revolutions that have taken place in China, India, Kenya and Rwanda.

References

Abraham, Facundo, Sergio L. Schmukler, and Jose Tessada. 2019. Robo-advisors: Investing through Machines. World Bank Policy Research Working Paper 134881.

Adhami, Saman, Giancarlo Giudici, and Stefano Martinazzi. 2018. Why Do Businesses Go Crypto? An Empirical Analysis of Initial Coin Offerings. *Journal of Economics and Business* 100: 64–75.

Agarwal, Sumit, John C. Driscoll, and David I. Laibson. 2013. Optimal Mortgage Refinancing: A Closed Form Solution. *Journal of Money, Credit and Banking* 45 (4): 591–622.

Agarwal, Sumit, Yan Li, Chunlin Liu, and Jian Zhang. 2015. Personal Guarantee and Peer-to-Peer Lending: Evidence from China. *SSRN*. Accessed March 19, 2020. https://papers.ssrn.com/sol3/papers.cfm?abstract_id=2638546.

Agarwal, Sumit, Debarati Basu, Pulak Ghosh, Bhuvanesh Pareek, and Jian Zhang. 2018a. Demonetization and Digitization. *SSRN*. Accessed March 18, 2020. https://papers.ssrn.com/sol3/papers.cfm?abstract_id=3197990.

Agarwal, Sumit, Thomas Kigabo, Camelia Minoiu, Andrea Presbitero, and Andre F. Silva. 2018b. Financial Access under the Microscope. International Monetary Fund Working Paper WP/18/208.

Agarwal, Sumit, Wenlan Qian, Bernard Y. Yeung, and Xin Zou. 2019. Mobile Wallet and Entrepreneurial Growth. *American Economic Association Papers and Proceedings* 109: 48–53.

Agarwal, Sumit, Shashwat Alok, Pulak Ghosh, and Sudip Gupta. 2020. Financial Inclusion and Alternate Credit Scoring for the Millennials: Role of Big Data and Machine Learning in Fintech. *SSRN*. Accessed March 18, 2020. https://papers.ssrn.com/sol3/papers.cfm?abstract_id=3507827.

Ahmed, Haseeb, and Benjamin W. Cowan. 2019. Mobile Money and Healthcare Use: Evidence from East Africa. NBER Working Paper #25669.

Alizila. 2014. Viral Villages: E-commerce is Spreading in China's Agrarian Hinterlands. *Alizilia*. Accessed March 19, 2020. https://www.alizila.com/viral-villages-e-commerce-is-spreading-in-chinas-agrarian-hinterlands/.

Allen, Franklin, Elena Carletti, Robert Cull, Lemma W. Senbet, and Patricio Valenzuela. 2012. Resolving the African Financial Development Gap: Cross-Country Comparisons and a Within-Country Study of Kenya. World Bank Policy Research Working Paper No. 6592.

Alliance for Financial Inclusion. 2013. *The 2013 AFI Global Policy Forum (GPF) Report: Driving Policies for Optimal Impact*. Alliance for Financial Inclusion.

———. 2014a. *2014 Maya Declaration Progress Report: Measurable Goals with Optimal Impact*. Alliance for Financial Inclusion.

———. 2014b. *The 2014 AFI Global Policy Forum (GPF) Report: Global Partnerships, National Goals, Empowering People*. Alliance for Financial Inclusion.

———. 2014c. Rwanda's Financial Inclusion Success Story: Umurenge SACCOs. *Alliance for Financial Inclusion*. Accessed March 18, 2020. https://www.findevgateway.org/case-study/2014/07/rwandas-financial-inclusion-success-story-umurenge-saccos.

———. 2015. *The 2015 AFI Global Policy Forum (GPF) Report: Inspiring Innovation to Advance Inclusion*. Alliance for Financial Inclusion.

Badarinza, Cristian, John Y. Campbell, and Tarun Ramadorai. 2016. International Comparative Household Finance. *Annual Review of Economics* 8: 111–144.

Banerjee, Abhijit V., Arun G. Chandrasekhar, Esther Duflo, and Matthew O. Jackson. 2013. The Diffusion of Microfinance. *Science* 341: 363–341.

Banerjee, Abhijit V., Emily Breza, Esther Duflo, and Cynthia Kinnan. 2019. Can Microfinance Unlock a Poverty Trap for Some Entrepreneurs? NBER Working Paper #26346.

Bankable Frontier Associates. 2014. The Journey towards Cash Lite. *Better than Cash Alliance*.

Barocas, Solon, and Andrew D. Selbst. 2016. Big Data's Disparate Impact. *California Law Review* 104: 671–732.

Bartlett, Robert P., Adair Morse, Richard H. Stanton, and Nancy E. Wallace. 2019. Consumer-Lending Discrimination in the FinTech Era. NBER Working Paper #25943.

Bateman, Milford. 2015. South Africa's Post-Apartheid Microcredit Experiment Moving from State-Enforced to Market-Enforced Exploitation. *Forum for Social Economics* 48 (1): 1–29.

Berg, Tobias, Valentin Burg, Ana Gombavic, and Puri Manju. 2019. On the Rise of FinTechs: Credit Scoring Using Digital Footprints. *The Review of Financial Studies*. Accessed March 19, 2020. https://doi.org/10.1093/rfs/hhz099.

Berger, Sven C., and Fabian Gleisner. 2009. Emergence of Financial Intermediaries in Electronic Markets: The Case of Online P2P Lending. *Business Research* 2 (1): 39–65.

Bharadwaj, Prashant, Jack William, and Tavneet Suri. 2019. FinTech and Household Resilience to Shocks: Evidence from Digital Loans in Kenya. NBER Working Paper #25604.

Biais, Bruno, Christophe Bisiere, Matthieu Bouvard, and Catherine Casamatta. 2019. The Blockchain Folk Theorem. *Review of Financial Studies* 32: 1662–1715.

Bjorkegren, Daniel, and Darrell Grissen. 2018. The Potential of Digital Credit to Bank the Poor. *American Economic Review* 108: 68–71.

Blackman, Phil. 2019. Global Fintech Investment Rockets to a Record $111.8B in 2018, Driven by Mega Deals: KPMG Pulse of Fintech. *KPMG International*. Accessed March 18, 2020. https://home.kpmg/xx/en/home/media/press-releases/2019/02/global-fintech-investment-hits-record-in-2018.html.

Blumberg, Dave. 2017. FinTechs Taking Larger Share of Personal Loan Market While Increasing Portfolio Risk-Return Performance. *TransUnion*. Accessed March 19, 2020. https://newsroom.transunion.com/fintechs-taking-larger-share-of-personal-loan-market-while-increasing-portfolio-risk-return-performance/.

Blume, Marshall, and Irwin Friend. 1975. The Asset Structure of Individual Portfolios and Some Implications for Utility Functions. *Journal of Finance* 30: 585–603.

Bordo, Michael D., and Andrew T. Levin. 2019. Digital Cash: Principles and Practical Steps. NBER Working Paper #25455.

Brunton, Finn. 2019. *Digital Cash: The Unknown History of the Anarchists, Utopians, and Technologists Who Created Cryptocurrency*, 47–61. Princeton University Press.

Buchak, Greg, Gregor Matvos, Tomasz Piskorski, and Amit Seru. 2018. Fintech, regulatory arbitrage, and the rise of shadow banks. *Journal of Financial Economics* 130 (3): 453–483.

Buolomwini, Joy, and Timnit Gebru. 2018. Gender Shades: Intersectional Accuracy Disparities in Commercial Gender Classification. *Proceedings of Machine Learning Research* 81: 1–15.

Caliskan, Aylin, Joanna J. Bryson, and Arvind Narayanan. 2017. Semantics Derived Automatically from Language Corpora Contain Human-like Biases. *Science* 356 (6334): 183–186.

Carlin, Bruce I., Arna Olafsson, and Michaela Pagel. 2017. FinTech Adoption across Generations: Financial Fitness in the Information Age. NBER Working Paper #23798.

Catalini, Christian, and Joshua S. Gans. 2019. Initial Coin Offerings and the Value of Crypto Tokens. Rotman School of Management Working Paper No. 3137213.

Chan, Wing H., Minh Le, and W.Wu. Yan. 2019. Holding Bitcoin Longer: The Dynamic Hedging Abilities of Bitcoin. *The Quarterly Review of Economics and Finance* 71: 107–113.

Chaum, David. 1998. Blind Signature for Untraceable Payment. *Advances in Cryptology Proceedings of Crypto* 82 (3): 199–203.

Chen, Mark, Qinxi Wu, and Baozhong Yang. 2019. How Valuable Is FinTech Innovation? *Review of Financial Studies* 32: 2062–2106.

Chiu, Jonathan, and Thorsten V. Koeppl. 2019. Blockchain-Based Settlement for Asset Trading. *Review of Financial Studies* 32: 1716–1753.

Choi, Hyun-Soo, and Roger Loh. 2019. Physical Frictions and Digital Banking Adoption. *SSRN*. Accessed March 18, 2020. https://papers.ssrn.com/sol3/papers.cfm?abstract_id=3333636.

Christensen, Clayton M., and Michael E. Raynor. 2003. *The Innovator's Solution: Creating and Sustaining Successful Growth*. Boston: Harvard Business School Press.

Christensen, Clayton M., Michael E. Raynor, and Rory McDonald. 2015. Disruptive Innovation. *Harvard Business Review* 93 (12): 44–53.

Cihak, Martin, Asli Demirguc-Kunt, Erik Feyen, and Ross Levine. 2013. Financial Development in 205 Economies, 1960–2010. *Journal of Financial Perspectives* 1 (2): 17–36.

Conroy, John. 2005. APEC and Financial Exclusion: Missed Opportunities for Collective Action? *Asia-Pacific Development Journal* 12 (1): 53–79.

D'Acunto, Francesco, Nagpurnanand Prabhala, and Alberto G. Rossi. 2019. The Promises and Pitfalls of Robo-Advising. *Review of Financial Studies* 32: 1983–2020.

Dabrowski, Marek, and Lukasz Janikowski. 2018. *Virtual Currencies and Central Banks Monetary Policy: Challenges Ahead*. Policy Department for Economic, Scientific and Quality of Life Policies.

DaijiWorld. 2017. 'Aadhaar' Most Sophisticated ID Programme in the World: World Bank. *DaijiWorld*. Accessed March 18, 2020. https://www.daijiworld.com/news/newsDisplay.aspx?newsID=442948.

De Mauro, Andrea, Marco Greco, and Michele Grimaldi. 2016. A Formal Definition of Big Data Based on Its Essential Features. *Library Review* 65: 122–135.

De Roure, Calebe, Loriana Pelizzon, and Anjan V. Thakor. 2019. P2P Lenders versus Banks: Cream Skimming or Bottom Fishing? *SSRN*. Accessed March 18, 2020. https://ssrn.com/abstract=3174632.

Deb, Anamitra, and Mike Kubzansky. 2012. Bridging the Gap: The Business Case for Financial Literacy. Report by the Monitor Group. Commissioned and funded by Citi Foundation.

Demirguc-Kunt, Asli, Leora Klapper, and Dorothe Singer. 2017. Financial Inclusion and Inclusive Growth: A Review of Recent Empirical Evidence. World Bank Policy Research Working Paper Series 8040.

Demirguc-Kunt, Asli, Leora Klapper, Dorothe Singer, Saniya Ansar, Jake Hess. 2018. *Global Findex Database 2017: Measuring Financial Inclusion and the Fintech Revolution*. Washington, DC: World Bank. Accessed March 19, 2020. http://documents.worldbank.org/curated/en/332881525873182837/The-Global-Findex-Database-2017-Measuring-Financial-Inclusion-and-the-Fintech-Revolution.

Di Maggio, Marco, and Vincent W. Yao. 2019. Fintech Borrowers: Lax-Screening or Cream-Skimming? *SSRN*. Accessed March 19, 2020. https://papers.ssrn.com/sol3/papers.cfm?abstract_id=3224957.

DiCaprio, Alisa, Ying Yao, and Rebecca Simms. 2017. Women and Trade: Gender's Impact on Trade Finance and Fintech. Asian Development Bank Institute. Working Paper 797.

Ding, Ding, Guan Chong, David Lee Kuo Chuen, and Tan Lee Cheng. 2018. From Ant Financial to Alibaba's Rural Taobao Strategy—How Fintech Is Transforming Social Inclusion. In *Handbook of Blockchain, Digital Finance, and Inclusion, Volume 1*, ed. K.C. David Lee and Robert Deng. Elsevier Inc.

Ding, Jie, Jinbo Huang, Yong Li, and Meichen Meng. 2019. Is There an Effective Reputation Mechanism in Peer-to-Peer Lending? Evidence from China. *Finance Research Letters* 30: 208–215.

Duvendack, Maren, Richard Palmer-Jone, James G. Copestake, Lee Hooper, Yoon Loke, and Nitya Rao. 2011. What Is the Evidence of the Impact of Microfinance on the Well-Being of Poor People? *Social Science Research Unit*. University of London.

Dyhrberg, Anne H. 2016. Hedging Capabilities of Bitcoin. Is It the Virtual Gold? *Finance Research Letters* 16: 139–144.

Economic Times. 2016. Unified Payments Interface Will Be Transformational as Aadhaar. *ET Commentary*.

Financial Inclusion Center. 2016. *Better and Brighter? Responsible RTO Alternatives*. London: Financial Inclusion Center.

Fiserv. 2019. Fiserv Survey: Digital Loan Applications Rise as Mobile Device Use Increases. *Close-up Media Inc*. Accessed March 19, 2020. https://newsroom.fiserv.com/news-releases/news-release-details/digital-loan-applications-rise-mobile-device-use-increases.

Flögel, Franz, and Marius Beckamp. 2020. Will FinTech Make Regional Banks Superfluous for Small Firm Finance? Observations from Soft Information-Based Lending in Germany. *Economic Notes* 48 (2): 1–20.

Foerster, Stephen, Juhani T. Linnainmaa, Brian T. Melzer, and Alessandro Previtero. 2017. Retail Financial Advice: Does one Size Fit All? *Journal of Finance* 72: 1441–1482.

Foley, Sean, Jonathan R. Karlsen, and Talis J. Putnins. 2019. Sex, Drugs and Bitcoin: How Much Illegal Activity Is Financed Through Cryptocurrencies? *Review of Financial Studies* 32: 1798–1853.

French, Shaun, Andrew Leyshon, and Nigel Thrift. 2009. A Very Geographical Crisis: The Making and Breaking of the 2007–2008 Financial Crisis. *Journal of Regions, Economy and Society* 2 (2): 287–302.

Fuster, Andreas, Matthew Plosser, Philipp Schnabl, and James Vickery. 2018. The Role of Technology in Mortgage Lending. NBER Working Paper #24500.

———. 2019. The Role of Technology in Mortgage Lending. *The Review of Financial Studies* 32 (5): 1854–1819.

Gabor, Daniela, and Sally Brooks. 2017. The Digital Revolution in Financial Inclusion: International Development in the FinTech Era. *New Political Economy* 22 (4): 423–436.

Goldfarb, Avid, Shane M. Greenstein, and Catherine E. Tucker. 2015. *Economic Analysis of the Digital Economy*, 257–276. University of Chicago Press.

Haddad, Christian, and Lars Hornuf. 2019. The Emergence of the Global Fintech Market: Economic and Technological Determinants. *Small Business Economics* 53 (1): 81–105.

Halmari, Ella, Eleanor Sharman, Henry Whorwood, Jake Ford, Tanya Nyamadzawo, Ester Simoes, Daniel Osei, and Thomas Sheils. 2017. The Deal: Equity investment in the UK 2017. *Beauhurst*, London.

Hastings, Justin S., Brigitte C. Madrian, and William L. Skimmyhorn. 2013. Financial Literacy, Financial Education, and Economic Outcomes. *Annual Review of Economics* 5 (1): 347–373.

Hayek, Friedrich A. 1976. *Denationalisation of Money: The Argument Refined*. Institute of Economic Affairs.

Higgins, Sean. 2019. Financial Technology Adoption. Post Doc Dissertation, University of California, Berkeley.

Hornuf, Lars, Klus F. Milan, Todor S. Lohwasser, and Armin Schwienbacher. 2020. How Do Banks Interact with Fintech Startups? Center for Economic Studies and Ifo Institute Working Paper Series No. 7170.

Howell, Sabrina, Marina Niessner, and David Yermack. 2019. Initial Coin Offerings: Financing Growth with Cryptocurrency Token Sales. *European Corporate Governance Institute Finance Working Paper* 564: 1–71.

Hu, Albert, Christine A. Parlour, and Uday Rajan. 2019. Cryptocurrencies: Stylized Facts on a New Investible Instrument. *Financial Management* 48: 1049–1068.

Iyer, Rajkamal, Asim I. Khwaja, Erzo Luttmer, and Kelly Shue. 2015. Screening Peers Softly: Inferring the Quality of Small Borrowers. *Management Science* 62 (6): 1554–1577.

Jagtiani, Julapa, and Catherine Lemieux. 2018. Do Fintech Lenders Penetrate Areas That Are Underserved by Traditional Banks? *Journal of Economics and Business* 100: 43–54.

———. 2019. The Roles of Alternative Data and Machine Learning in Fintech Lending: Evidence from the LendingClub Consumer Platform. *Financial Management* 48 (4): 1009–1029.

Jagtiani, Julapa, Lauren Lambie-Hanson, and Timothy Lambie-Hanson. 2019. FinTech Lending and Mortgage Credit Access. Federal Reserve Bank of Philadelphia Working Paper, 19–47

Jain, Abhishek, Shalu Agrawal, and Karthik Ganesan. 2018. Lessons from the World's Largest Subsidy Benefit Transfer Scheme. In *The Politics of Fossil Fuel Subsidies and their Reform*, ed. Jakob Skovgaard, 212–228. Cambridge: Cambridge University Press.

Jones, Emily, Ngaire Tui Woods, and Njuguna S. Ndung'u. 2016. Consolidating Africa's Mobile Banking Revolution. *Global Economic Governance Programme*. Accessed March 18, 2020. https://www.geg.ox.ac.uk/publication/consolidating-africas-mobile-banking-revolution.

Jünger, Moritz, and Mark Mietzner. 2019. Banking Goes Digital: The Adoption of FinTech Services by German Households. *Finance Research Letters*. Accessed March 19, 2020. https://doi.org/10.1016/j.frl.2019.08.008.

Karlan, Dean, Jake Kendall, Rebecca Mann, Rohini Pande, Tavneet Suri, and Jonathan Zinman. 2016. Research and Impacts of Digital Financial Services. NBER Working Paper #22633.

Kauflin, Jeff. 2019. The 11 Biggest Fintech Companies in America 2019. *Forbes*.

Lee, David K.C., and Gin Swee Teo. 2015. Emergence of FinTech and the LASIC Principles. *Journal of Financial Perspectives* 3 (3): 24–36.

Lin, William C., and Zhiguo He. 2017. Blockchain Disruption and Smart Contracts. *The Review of Financial Studies* 32 (5): 1754–1797.

Lin, Minfeng, Prabhala R. Nagpuranand, and Siva Viswanathan. 2013. Judging Borrowers by the Company They Keep: Friendship Networks and Information Asymmetry in Online Peer-to-Peer Lending. *Management Science* 59 (1): 17–35.

Lu, Lerong. 2017. Financial Technology and Challenger Banks in the UK: Gap Fillers or Real Challengers? *Journal of International Banking Law and Regulation* 32 (7): 273–282.

MarketWatch. 2019. At 50.2% CAGR, P2P Lending Market Size Raising to US$589.05 billion by 2015. *Marketwatch*. Accessed March 19, 2020. https://www.marketwatch.com/press-release/at-502-cagr-p2p-peer-to-peer-lending-market-size-raising-to-usd-58905-billion-by-2025-2019-10-17.

Mbiti, Isaac, and David N. Weil. 2011. Mobile Banking: The Impact of M-Pesa in Kenya. NBER Working Paper #17129.

Morse, Adair, and Karen Pence. 2020. Technological Innovation and Discrimination in Household Finance. NBER Working Paper #26739.

Morton, Fiona S., Florian Zettelmeyer, and Jorge Silva-Russo. 2003. Consumer Information and Discrimination: Does the Internet Affect the Pricing of New Cars to Women and Minorities? *Quantitative Marketing and Economics* 1 (1): 65–92.

Nakamoto, Satoshi. 2008. Bitcoin: A Peer-to-Peer Electronic Cash System. *Bitcoin*. Accessed March 18, 2020. http://bitcoin.org/bitcoin.pdf.

Palmer, Daniel. 2019. China's Central Bank Likely to Pilot Digital Currency in Cities of Shenzhen and Suzhou: Report. *Coindesk*. Accessed March 19, 2020. https://www.coindesk.com/chinas-central-bank-likely-to-pilot-digital-currency-in-cities-of-shenzhen-and-suzhou-report.

Parlour, Christine A., Uday Rajan, and Haoxiang Zhu. 2019. FinTech Disruption, Payment Data, and Bank Information. NBER Working Paper #22476.

Philippon, Thomas. 2015. Has the US Finance Industry Become Less Efficient? On the Theory and Measurement of Financial Intermediation. *The American Economic Review* 105 (4): 1408–1438.

Pizzala, Jeremy, and Ian Webster. 2015. FinTech: Are Banks Responding Appropriately? *Ernst and Young Viewpoint*.

Raskin, Max. 2013. U.S. Agencies to Say Bitcoins Offer Legitimate Benefits. *Bloomberg News*.

Raskin, Max, and David Yermack. 2016. Digital Currencies, Decentralized Ledgers, and the Future of Central Banking. NBER Working Paper #22238.

Raskin, Max, Fahad Saleh, and David Yermack. 2019. How Do Private Digital Currencies Affect Government Policy? NBER Working Paper #26219.

Roussou, Ioanna, Emmanouil Stiakakis, and Angelo Sifaleras. 2018. An Empirical Study on the Commercial Adoption of Digital Currencies. *Springer Nature* 17: 223–259.

Schueth, Samuel, and Alex Moler. 2017. The Effects of Demonetization on Financial Inclusion in India. *InterMedia*. Accessed March 18, 2020. https://www.centerforfinancialinclusion.org/indias-demonetization-one-year-later-what-was-the-impact-on-financial-inclusion.

Shevlin, Ron. 2019. How Much Do Banks Spend On Technology? *Forbes*.

Soederberg, Susanne. 2013. Universalising Financial Inclusion and the Securitisation of Development. *Third World Quarterly* 34 (4): 593–612.

Stulz, René M. 2019. FinTech, BigTech and the Future of Banks. *Journal of Applied Corporate Finance* 31: 86–97.

Tang, Huan. 2019. Peer-to-Peer Lenders versus Banks. *Review of Financial Studies* 32: 1900–1938.

The Economist. 2013. Why does Kenya Lead the World in Mobile Money?. Accessed March 18, 2020. https://www.economist.com/the-economist-explains/2015/03/02/why-does-kenya-lead-the-world-in-mobile-money.

The World Bank. 2008. *Finance for All? Policies and Pitfalls in Expanding Access*. Washington, DC: The World Bank.

———. 2013. *Global Financial Development Report: Financial Inclusion*. Washington DC: The World Bank.

The World Bank Group. 2015. *The Global Findex Database 2014*. Washington, DC: The World Bank.

———. 2016. *Migration and Remittances Factbook 2016*. Washington, DC: The World Bank.

Vallee, Boris, and Yao Zeng. 2019. Marketplace Lending: A New Banking Paradigm? *Review of Financial Studies* 32: 1939–1982.

Wang, Susan. 2014. Taobao Villages in Rural China Grow Tenfold in 2014. *Alizila*. Accessed March 18, 2020. https://www.alizila.com/report-taobao-villages-in-rural-china-grow-tenfold-in-2014.

Wang, Yao, Zdenek Drabek, and Zhengwei Wang. 2018. The Predicting Power of Soft Information on Defaults in the Chinese P2P Lending Market. Institute of Economic Studies Working Paper 20/2018. Charles University.

Wolfe, Brian, and Woongsun Yoo. 2017. Crowding Out Banks: Credit Substitution by Peer-to-Peer Lending. Federal Deposit Insurance Corporation.

World Economic Forum. 2015. *The Future of Financial Services 2015*. World Economic Forum.

Xiang, Tracey. 2014. Alibaba Launches Healthcare App for Prescription Purchases. *Technode*. Accessed March 18, 2020. https://technode.com/2014/12/04/alibaba-launches-healthcare-app-for-prescription-purchases/.

Yermack, David. 2018. FinTech in Sub-Saharan Africa: What Has Worked Well, and What Hasn't. NBER Working Paper #25007.

Zhu, Christina. 2019. Big Data as a Governance Mechanism. *Review of Financial Studies* 32: 2021–2061.

Index

S. Agarwal et al., *Household Finance*,
https://doi.org/10.1007/978-981-15-5526-8

The manufacturer's authorised representative in the EU is Springer Nature Customer Service Centre GmbH, Europaplatz 3, 69115 Heidelberg, Germany. If you have any concerns regarding our products, please contact ProductSafety@springernature.com

Printed and bound by CPI Group (UK) Ltd, Croydon, CR0 4YY
05/10/2026
02228121-0006